Transforming India

TRANSFORMING INDIA

Challenges to the World's Largest Democracy

SUMANTRA BOSE

Harvard University Press
Cambridge, Massachusetts, and London, England   2013

Library of Congress Cataloging-in-Publication Data

Bose, Sumantra, 1968–
  Transforming India : challenges to the world's largest democracy /
Sumantra Bose.
      pages cm.
  Includes bibliographical references and index.
  ISBN 978-0-674-05066-2 (alk. paper)
  1. Democracy—India.   2. India—Politics and government.   I. Title.
  JQ281.B67 2013
  320.954—dc23   2013007727

In memory of
Subhas Chandra Bose
and
Sisir Kumar Bose
who represented the best of what it means to be Indian
and
To the Soil and People of the Beloved Country

Contents

Transforming India

The Uniqueness of India's Democracy

I N 1959, the American social and political scientist Seymour Martin Lipset, soon to publish his magnum opus *Political Man: The Social Bases of Politics,* wrote: "The more well-to-do a nation, the greater the chances that it will sustain democracy."[1]

A century earlier, in 1861, the British political theorist and philosopher John Stuart Mill had written in his treatise *Considerations on Representative Government:* "Free institutions are next to impossible in a country made up of different nationalities. . . . It is in general a necessary condition for free institutions that the boundaries of government should coincide in the main with those of nationalities.[2]

If Lipset and Mill were right, this book would not exist, because there would be no such thing as India's democracy.

India is the world's second most populous country. According to the decennial national census, on March 1, 2011, the nation had a population of 1,210,193,422 (about 623 million males and 587 million females), 17 percent of the world's people and equal to the populations of the United States, Indonesia, Brazil, Pakistan, Bangladesh, and Japan combined. Of these 1.21 billion Indians, nearly half, close to 600 million people, lived in the five most populous states of the 28 states that comprise the Indian Union: Uttar Pradesh ("Northern Province"; UP) in the north (200 million), Maharashtra in the west (112 million), Bihar in the north (104 million), West Bengal in the east (91 million), and Andhra Pradesh in the south (85 million). Around 2020 India is likely to surpass China to become the planet's most populous country, and by 2030 India will have approximately 1.5 billion citizens. By 2050 the Republic of India is expected to have about 400 million more people than the People's Republic of China. Moreover, as China's population progressively ages over the next few decades, India's working-age population is expected to steadily rise, and by 2035 about 68 percent of Indians are expected to be in this category (15–64 years). A demographic dividend beckons India, but with a huge "if"—*if* the nation is able to properly educate and train its young people, ensure standards of public health that enable society to realize its productive potential, and generate the magnitude and array of employment opportunities that can make India the world's most populous developed country two decades from now. In late 2012 the U.S. National Intelligence Council, which is responsible for longer term analysis and forecasting, asserted: "in 2030, India could be the rising economic powerhouse that China is seen to be today."[3]

India is also—famously—a land of contrasts and contradictions. It has the world's third largest armed forces after China and the United States, is a nuclear-weapon state and the world's single largest arms importer, and in 2012 successfully tested an intercontinental ballistic missile. India has a wide-ranging and successful space program and in 2011 established an Indian Agency for Partnership in Development, loosely modeled on the U.S. Agency for International Development, to coordinate and monitor its growing portfolio of aid given to other countries. In mid-2011, 54 countries around the world were in receipt of Indian loans totaling $6.43 billion. In 2010–2011, India extended its single largest loan for development projects, worth $1 billion, to neighboring Bangladesh. Between 2001 and 2011 Indian aid to Afghanistan—in the form of outright grants to support various development, infrastructure, and social welfare projects—topped $2 billion. In June 2012, on the occasion of a G20 summit held in Mexico, India donated $10 billion to the crisis-ridden Eurozone's bailout fund. In mid-2011, just before India's economic growth slowed due to the combined effect of internal and global problems, the Asian Development Bank, headquartered in Manila, forecast that 70 percent of Indians could be "middle class" by 2025.[4]

At the same time, "a third of the planet's population who are below the World Bank's extreme poverty line live in India . . . [and] half of all children in the country are malnourished." In 1991, there were just 5 million landline telephones in all of India; in 2011, 840 million Indians used a mobile phone (and 930 million in 2012). Also in 2011, 47 percent of all Indians, nearly 600 million people, did not have a family toilet/bathroom. The same proportion, 47 percent, had access to clean drinking water in or very close to their dwelling, and the rest did not. Three out of eight Indian households (37 percent), overwhelmingly in rural India, did not have an electricity connection to their home. Of Indian families, 45 percent had a bicycle, and another 21 percent a motorbike or scooter. Although India is emerging as a key automobile manufacturing hub of Asia—15 million motor vehicles were produced in India in 2010–2011 by Indian and foreign manufacturers—just 5 percent of Indian families had a car in 2011.[5]

Confounding Lipset, during the three decades in which India built and consolidated its democracy—after emerging as a sovereign country in 1947 in an impoverished, virtually pauperized condition from nearly two centuries of colonialist occupation and systematic, rapacious exploitation of its people and resources—India's per capita growth rate averaged just 1.3 percent per annum from 1951 through 1979. A "green revolution" in India's agriculture in the late 1960s and early 1970s did, on paper, eliminate the chronic shortages of essential food-grains the nation suffered during the 1950s and 1960s, but the sharp rise in farming productivity was limited to a few zones of the vast country, and ensuring food security for all Indians remains an unmet goal four decades later.

The socioeconomic disparities in both rural and urban India continue to be extraordinarily stark six and a half decades after freedom from colonialism was achieved. In rural India, where over 70 percent of Indians live and at least 60 percent will live even in 2030, the extremes are represented by Pavitar Pal Singh Pangli, 54, a wealthy farmer who owns 80 acres of land in his village in the northern Punjab state's Ludhiana district, and Kamlabai, 61, a widow in the Vidarbha region of Maharashtra. Pangli, a prosperous wheat-grower, has benefited from multiple Union and state subsidy schemes for farmers and lives in a sprawling chalet-style residence that could easily belong in Switzerland. He has been able to send his two sons to Canada for higher education, at his own expense. In the 1970s Kamlabai's husband was the *sarpanch* (chief) of their village in Maharashtra's Wardha district and a well-to-do farmer who grew cotton on the family's 16-acre landholding. From the 1990s he had trouble getting a remunerative price for his cotton in changed national and global conditions and gradually sank into debt, first with banks and then, fatally, with private moneylenders operating in the region. Trapped by these usurers, he committed suicide in February 2009, aged 64—one of hundreds of farmers in Maharashtra's Vidarbha region who have in recent years taken that exit route from the stress and shame of indebtedness. The family's tragedy had just begun. In November 2009, his and Kamlabai's older son committed suicide, aged 38, and in November 2011 the younger son, aged 34, also killed himself. Kamlabai now lives with her grandson, aged five, her younger son's child, and suffers constant harassment from the loan sharks. She says: "We eat once a day. How can I repay loans?"[6]

In a shantytown in the Vasant Vihar neighborhood of the national capital, Delhi, Basant Kumar, who is 52, struggles to support a family of five—his wife and three children—on a monthly income of 5,000 rupees (less than $100). He runs a small shop in the slum township and works occasional construction jobs to supplement his income. The family lives in a one-room shack measuring 10 by 10 feet. They can afford only secondhand clothes and shoes, and that only once or twice a year. Not far away, in Noida, a satellite township of Delhi, Priya Batra, 39, lives in a spacious house with her husband and two-year-old son. She is head of marketing for a multinational firm, and her husband is a director at an insurance company. She earns 375,000 rupees a month, and she and her husband make close to the equivalent of $200,000 a year. She and her husband each have a chauffeur-driven car, and the chauffeurs are paid 10,000 rupees per month. Their toddler has a full-time nanny who is paid 4,000 rupees a month. On Saturdays the family heads to the nearby mall—malls have sprung up in Indian cities over the past decade to cater to the growing numbers with "disposable income"—and spend an average of 10,000 rupees every weekend on designer clothes, shoes, watches, and toys, eating at a restaurant, and watching a movie.[7]

Confounding Mill, India has been able to build a functioning democracy in a country composed of diverse nationalities. Certainly, a sense of an overarching Indian national identity was widespread at the time of independence—a legacy of three decades of nationalist mobilization to drive out the colonial power—and such an identity has, on the whole, become more deeply embedded in the six decades since then. But India is a land of multiple identities. The sense of being Indian coexists with, indeed is built on, very powerful communitarian identities. These have evolved over centuries and are based on complex permutations and combinations of ethnicity, language, religion, caste, and other characteristics. The most important forms of community are strongly territorialized. Thus most of India's major ethnolinguistic communities inhabit and are concentrated in particular regions of the country: Bengalis in a part of eastern India, Gujaratis in a part of western India, Tamils in a part of southern India, and so on.

The evolution of India since the 1950s as a moderately decentralized union of autonomous "states"—states formed primarily and broadly on the ethnolinguistic principle—allowed democratic space to these communitarian identities. This arrangement, which gives institutionalized expression to India's mosaic of diversity, has been generally successful in

Figure 1. Voters line up outside a polling station in Tamil Nadu to vote in India's fifteenth national Lok Sabha election (May 2009). AFP/GETTY IMAGES.

fostering a framework of complementary and mutually reinforcing identities, in which territorialized communitarian identities coexist with a commitment to Indian national identity and India's unity. This is the pillar on which India's democratic stability rests. The sheer scale of India's breathtaking and sometimes bewildering diversity is comparable to that of the entire European Union, which is a multinational, suprastate entity consisting of 28 sovereign nation-states from Scandinavia to the Balkans, the Iberian peninsula to the Baltic, and the British and Irish isles to the heart of eastern Europe. In India, a similar scale of diversity exists under a single sovereign polity divided into 28 states endowed with extensive powers of self-government. That this has been possible—albeit with some flaws and warts—is nothing short of a contemporary political marvel. The key factor in the success and resilience of India's formula of nationhood can be expressed by putting a twist on Mill—the internal, quasi-federal boundaries of government do coincide in the main with those of its constitutive "nationalities."

Reading This Book

In this book I tell the story of the extraordinary political odyssey of the world's most populous and diverse democracy. My narrative has two salient features. First, I emphasize how the trajectory of India's democracy has been shaped since 1947 not simply by elite politics and the decisions of leaders, as important as these have been, but by popular struggles, demands, and aspirations raised and waged from "below," by ordinary people. The strength and dynamism of India's democracy is largely due to the elixir of popular participation: a democracy is nothing without an engaged and involved demos. Second, while India has evolved over the past six decades as a very robust democracy, in some ways unique in the annals of the contemporary world given the pitfalls of poverty, inequality, and diversity, India's democracy is, simultaneously, still in the making or a "work in progress"—a moving, churning object rather than a substance that has achieved some sort of end state. That is precisely what makes the saga of India's democracy in the early twenty-first century so fascinating.

Nonetheless, the fundamental trajectory of India's democracy in the early twenty-first century is clear, and this book highlights that trajectory. Over six decades and 15 nationwide elections, since the first election of 1951–1952, India has moved gradually but inexorably from single-party dominance and a relatively centralized union and toward a multiparty democracy that reflects the nation's diversity of communities and a genuinely federal union that is built on the autonomy of its constituent parts, the states. The turning point was the ninth national election, in November 1989, which saw the eclipse of four decades of hegemony of the Congress party, the legatee of India's independence movement, and the sharp acceleration during the 1990s of the "regionalization" of the country's polity, that is, the emergence of a plethora of political parties representing particular communitarian identities and interests and each based in one state of the Indian Union.

Chapters 1 and 2 chart that transformation of India's democracy— Chapter 1 from independence to the watershed of November 1989, and Chapter 2 from that point to the present time. Chapter 3 tells the story of transformation from the perspective of a state: West Bengal. One of the first regionalist challenges to Congress's nationwide hegemony emerged in West Bengal in national and state elections of 1967. In 1977 this state-specific alternative, led by communists, came to power in West Bengal and proceeded to govern the state for the next 34 years, until 2011, winning a total of seven consecutive state elections during that time. This is the most durable political regime in the history of India's democracy. Chapter 3 shows how this extraordinary continuity and longevity came to be, as the combined effect of Bengali ethnolinguistic pride and the popular propoor stance adopted by the regionalist communists. Chapter

3 also shows how this edifice of hegemony came apart after more than three decades, the principal agent of change being an alternative regionalist party, specific to West Bengal, born in 1998 of a split in the state's Congress party.

Seymour Martin Lipset was right that in general a nation's level of socioeconomic development correlates strongly with its prospects of sustaining democracy. That insight can help explain one of the biggest contemporary problems of India's democracy—the appeal among a section of the nation's very poor (particularly Adivasis, India's indigenous inhabitants, who are about 8 percent of the nation's population) of a radical leftist ("Maoist") movement that rejects the legitimacy of the democratic system and is waging a rural insurgency of uneven and variable impact across a swathe of India's states and nearly a third of the country's 650 administrative districts. Chapter 4 explains this phenomenon with reference to the failings and shortcomings of India's democracy but also subjects the Maoists' alternative vision to close scrutiny and finds it unviable.

Chapter 5 focuses on what I call the "Achilles' heel" of India's democracy: the bitter alienation of a significant proportion of the people of the Indian state Jammu & Kashmir (J&K), especially in the region known as the Kashmir Valley, from Indian national identity and the Indian Union. I explain this alienation as the outcome of a policy of authoritarian intervention and control inflicted on the state, and particularly on the Kashmir Valley, by the "Center"—the Congress party governments in New Delhi—between 1953 and 1989. In India's evolution as a decentered, democratic federation of regional (state-based) polities in the early twenty-first century, I see a glimmer of possibility of amelioration of the perennial weak spot of India's democracy.

Chapters 4 and 5 suggest that India's transformation into a polity "of the people, by the people, for the people" is contingent on the substantive and honorable inclusion of the most estranged segments of the demos. The conclusion reflects on the future of India's democracy, focusing in particular on the challenges that lie ahead. In doing so, I make broad-brush comparisons with the dilemmas of the other ascendant Asian nation with a completely different political system and political culture: China.

The story of India's democracy is an epic of our times. It is worthy of study in its own right but is also vital to understanding the present and future of the world as the Euro-Atlantic declines and Asia recovers the global preeminence lost since the second half of the eighteenth century.

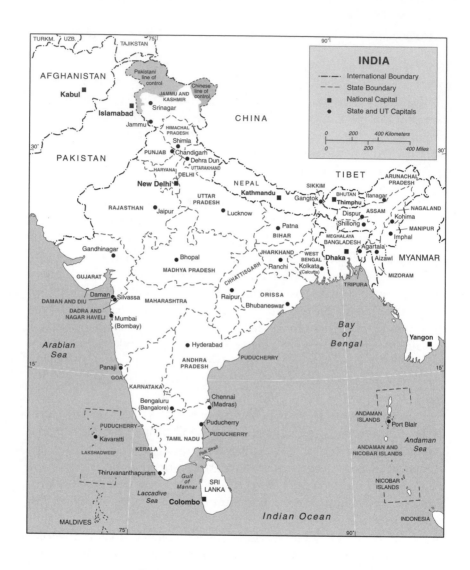

CHAPTER ONE

From Independence to 1989

I N NOVEMBER 1989, the world's attention was riveted on global transformations. That autumn, the one-party states of central and eastern Europe and the Balkans crumbled like dominoes. In November, the most dramatic development of all occurred. The Berlin Wall, which had stood for three decades as a symbol of the world's division between East and West, came down, signaling the imminent end of the post-1945 world order and the dawn of a new era in global history and international relations.

In India, the nation's attention was riveted on events within the country. In November 1989 India went to the polls for the ninth time since independence in 1947 to elect the national government. The (normally) five-yearly election to constitute the directly elected chamber of the national Parliament, the Lok Sabha, "House of the People," is the centerpiece of India's democratic process and the world's biggest exercise of democratic franchise.

The November 1989 election was a particularly tense and fraught affair. The ruling Congress party, founded in 1885 as the Indian National Congress, which led the mass struggle for freedom from colonial subjugation under Mohandas K. Gandhi's guidance from the early 1920s onward and had thoroughly dominated independent India's politics for over four decades, faced a spirited challenge from a rainbow spectrum of opposition parties. This spectrum included groups comprised of old and new defectors from Congress, "regional" parties based among ethnolinguistic communities in some of the Indian Union's (then) 25 states, communists, and right-wing Hindu nationalists. The communists and Hindu nationalists had formed a loose alliance with the "National Front"—an umbrella grouping of anti-Congress political formations based primarily in northern India and regional parties based primarily in the south of the country. The Congress leader and prime minister, Rajiv Gandhi, who had inherited both mantles five years earlier, aged just 40, through hereditary succession from his mother, Indira Gandhi (prime minister 1966–1977 and 1980–1984) and grandfather Jawaharlal Nehru (prime minister 1947–1964), faced a tough personal challenge from the National Front's leader, Vishwanath Pratap (V. P.) Singh, who had until 1987 been a close colleague. V. P. Singh had served during Indira Gandhi's second premiership as the chief minister (head of the elected government) of Uttar Pradesh (UP), India's most populous state and a vast sprawl across the Gangetic plain of northern India, from 1980 to 1982. He had then served in Rajiv Gandhi's cabinet as finance minister, and briefly as defense minister, between 1985 and 1987. Since his dismissal from the cabinet and resignation from Congress in mid-1987, V. P. Singh had emerged as the focal point for the rainbow spectrum of parties striving to undermine Congress's entrenched dominance of India's polity. The opposition claimed that Singh had been hounded out of the finance and defense ministries for seeking to investigate high-level corruption in the Congress party and Rajiv Gandhi's government.

The November 1989 election was the turning point in India's evolution as a democratic country. In the eighth Lok Sabha, elected in December 1984, Congress had held 415 of the 542 seats, or about 77 percent of the parliamentary "constituencies"—single-member electoral districts spread across the country where the candidate who wins the single largest share of the vote becomes the constituency's representative in Parliament through the plurality or "first-past-the-post" electoral principle. Five years later, the party's tally plummeted to just 197 of the 543 seats, about 36 percent of the total. The Congress share of the nationwide popular vote slumped from 48.1 percent in 1984 to 39.5 percent in 1989. While at first glance less than drastic, this fall of nearly nine percentage points in fact represented a severe erosion, a loss of nearly one-fifth of the party's vote base. This decline in popular support combined with a second factor—the coordinated though not totally unified challenge from the diverse spectrum of opposition parties, who tried to put up a common candidate against Congress in as many parliamentary constituencies as possible—to deal the grand old party of India a devastating political defeat.

The overall outcome was a "hung parliament"—a fractured verdict in which no party or preelection coalition wins an absolute majority (at least 50 percent plus one) of seats in the legislature—in which Congress was still the single largest party. The Janata Dal (People's Party), a federated entity of anti-Congress factions based primarily in northern India and fronted by V. P. Singh, won the second largest number of seats—142. The bulk of the Janata Dal's seats in Parliament came from two giant states in predominantly Hindi-speaking northern India, UP and Bihar, where the party won 54 of 85 and 31 of 54 seats, respectively. In UP, V. P. Singh's home state, the Congress seat tally collapsed from 83 of the 85 constituencies won in 1984 to just 15 in 1989, and in Bihar from 48 to just 4. The other big gainer was the Hindu nationalist Bharatiya Janata Party (Indian People's Party; BJP), India's established but hitherto marginal right-wing party, which increased its parliamentary representation from 2 to 86 seats, almost all of which were won in a swathe of states in northern and western India. On the other side of the political spectrum, a left-wing coalition led by India's largest parliamentary communist party, the Communist Party of India-Marxist (CPM), won in 53 constituencies, 38 of which were in the populous state of West Bengal in eastern India. Congress was routed in almost all the states of northern, eastern, and western India.[1] As many as 135 of its 197 seats in Parliament came from just five states: the populous western state of Maharashtra (of which Mumbai, previously Bombay, is the capital), and the states of Andhra Pradesh, Karnataka, Kerala, and Tamil Nadu in southern India. (And in Tamil Nadu, in India's deep south, Congress's success was due to its electoral alliance with one of the state's two main "regional" parties.)

Together, the Janata Dal, the BJP, and the communist-led bloc had a majority of seats in Parliament. In early December V. P. Singh assumed the prime ministership of India at the head of a Janata Dal/National Front minority government, propped up from its two flanks by "outside support" extended by the Hindu nationalists and the communists. His tenure as premier was to be short-lived—just 11 months, until November 1990—but that brief period was extraordinarily eventful and fraught with vast implications for India's political trajectory through the 1990s and beyond.

Congress had recovered from serious electoral setbacks on two previous occasions—in the fourth national election held in 1967 and the sixth national election in 1977—and re-asserted its hegemony in India's polity within a few years by winning decisive victories in the fifth national election (1971) and the seventh national election (1980). But the crisis of hegemony revealed by the debacle of late 1989 was to prove permanent. In midterm national elections held in mid-1991, the party won 232 of the 543 parliamentary constituencies—well short of an absolute majority in Parliament (272 seats) but an improvement on the 197 seats the party had managed to win a year and half earlier. This semblance of recovery was an illusion, however, and primarily due to a lesser degree of unity among the range of anti-Congress parties compared to 1989. In fact, the party's share of the nationwide vote declined further in 1991—from 39.5 percent to 36.5 percent. In UP, Congress won just five of the 85 parliamentary constituencies; in Bihar, just one of the 54 constituencies. Congress had virtually ceased to exist in the two northern states that together accounted for more than a fourth of India's Parliament.[2]

The ninth national election of November 1989 was the watershed in the evolution of the world's largest and most complex democracy, as the Congress era (1947–1989) yielded to the post-Congress era. Since 1996 India has been governed by unwieldy and polyglot coalition governments, in sharp contrast to the single-party Congress governments of the first four decades after independence. And in the two decades that have elapsed since the passing of Congress hegemony from India's politics, the "regionalization" of India's political landscape has deepened and intensified, as parties with a popular base in just one of the 28 states comprising the Indian Union—and particularly in the dozen or so most populous states— have proliferated and utterly changed the terms and parameters of the functioning of the world's most populous, most unruly, and most vibrant democracy.

Formation: The 1950s and 1960s

The paradox of the long Congress era in independent India's political history is that the party was never as dominant at the societal level, among the masses of India's people, as it was at the institutional level, where it wielded formidable levers of power and patronage. Throughout its four decades as the hegemon and pivot of Indian politics, the Congress party never succeeded in gaining an absolute majority of the national vote. It came closest to the 50 percent threshold in the eighth national election of December 1984 when, after the assassination of Indira Gandhi, party leader and prime minister, the party, led by her neophyte son Rajiv, polled 48.1 percent of the nationwide ballots riding an all-India "sympathy wave." In independent India's first national election, held between October 1951 and February 1952, Congress secured just 45 percent of the nationwide vote. In subsequent elections in 1957, 1962, 1967, 1971, 1977, and 1980, the party obtained 47.8 percent, 44.7 percent, 40.8 percent, 43.7 percent, 34.5 percent, and 42.7 percent, respectively. This record stands in contrast to that of a true "majority" party, South Africa's African National Congress. In the first postapartheid national election of

1994, the African National Congress won 63 percent of the nationwide vote and improved to 66 percent in 1999 and 70 percent in 2004, before declining slightly to 66 percent in 2009.

Congress's hegemonic power in India's polity was enabled and sustained by the "first past the post" electoral system operating across single-member parliamentary constituencies—the same system as that of India's former colonial ruler and fellow parliamentary democracy, Britain. The system rewards the party that wins the single largest share of the popular vote with a disproportionately high share of seats in the legislature. This system typically magnifies the plurality share of the popular vote secured by the frontrunner into a decisive and often commanding parliamentary majority. Thus in Indian democracy's founding election in 1951–1952, 55 percent of Indians who voted cast their ballots for non-Congress parties, but Congress won 364 of the 489 seats in the first national Parliament. In an election held under rules of proportional representation, based on party lists, the party would have been entitled to 220 of the 489 seats. The pattern recurred in all national elections until the watershed of 1989, with the exception of 1977, when the ruling party was resoundingly defeated by a hastily cobbled together opposition coalition in the wake of Indira Gandhi's overt attack on the nation's democratic edifice during her dictatorial "Emergency" regime of 1975–1976. In 1957 Congress got 371 of the 494 seats in the Lok Sabha, and in 1962 it bagged 361 of the 494. In 1967, when the party suffered—and survived—the first major jolt to its supremacy, it still won a reduced majority of 283 of the 520 seats in Parliament. In 1971 Congress rebounded with 342 of the 518 seats in Parliament. In 1980, as the victorious opposition coalition of 1977 disintegrated amid factional and personality feuds, necessitating a midterm election, the grand old party returned to power under Indira Gandhi's leadership, winning 353 of the 529 parliamentary constituencies. In 1984 her older son and successor, Rajiv Gandhi, won a victory whose scale surpassed those of his grandfather Jawaharlal Nehru, prime minister from independence in August 1947 until his death in May 1964, and his mother. In the mid-1980s, with Congress holding 415 of the 542 seats in Parliament's directly elected chamber, it did not seem that the end of the Congress era—and of dynastic rule—was at hand.

The four decades of Congress hegemony were not solely due to the electoral system. A second, powerful factor was at work—the fact that no other party existed, or arose, that could remotely rival the India-wide voter base and organizational presence that was Congress's inheritance from its leading role in the mass movement for freedom from colonialism between the early 1920s and 1947. Thus the majority non-Congress vote was splintered from the first election of 1951–1952 onward among a diverse spectrum of opposition parties and groupings, and Congress towered over its disparate assortment of Lilliputian rivals. This meant that Congress's dominance of India would not be undermined until the party's base was severely weakened in at least a critical mass of the dozen or so most populous states of the Indian Union. That would not happen until the late 1980s, when it would signal a great transformation in the nature of India's politics, a transformation that would unfold through the 1990s and continues to unfold in the early twenty-first century.

The fact of one-party dominance was a very mixed blessing for India. In a vast country inhabited by numerous ethnic and linguistic groups, religious communities and castes—a mosaic of diversity—it was obviously useful for the newly independent state and its nascent polity that a nationwide party with strong popular legitimacy existed to take on the many challenges of postcolonial state-building. The existence of the Congress party was in this sense a boon during the early years of independent India. As an Indian author has observed, "in the fifties and sixties [Western] reporting about India was full of metaphors of the region-of-uncertainty or area-of-darkness kind. There was a great deal of superior moaning about how awful, poor, divisive, filthy . . . India was. . . . Of course democracy simply did not have a chance in this illiterate and hungry land; at best it would be a farce and at worst a chaotic Babel that would encourage all the latent fissiparous forces, ensuring the . . . destruction of the country."[3]

That this gloom-and-doom prognosis proved incorrect is due in large part to the Congress party providing the glue that held a vast and diverse nation together. The contrast with the early years of Pakistan, the other state to emerge in the subcontinent in 1947, is instructive. There the Muslim League, the party that spearheaded the movement for Pakistan, proved to be weakly rooted in the regions of northwestern and eastern India that became Pakistan, and having achieved its objective of a sovereign Muslim state, the party lost its raison d'être and withered away within a few years of the formation of Pakistan. No other party or parties with a Pakistan-wide presence and purpose arose to fill the vacuum. The void provided the opportunity for an alliance of civilian bureaucrats and military officers based in West Pakistan (the post-1971 rump Pakistan) to increasingly dominate the country during the 1950s, with disastrous consequences for both democratic development and relations between the two wings of Pakistan (East Pakistan seceded in 1971 and became sovereign Bangladesh). Pakistan's first military coup in 1958 set the country firmly on the path of military-bureaucratic authoritarianism, which continues to shape the fate of the erstwhile West Pakistan more than a half century later. Thus "the Muslim League failed to fulfill the nation-welding role which, under different circumstances, the Chinese Communist Party provided from just this time onward in China, the Indian National Congress in India, and later the United Malay National Organization in Malaysia and the Tanganyika African National Union in Tanzania."[4]

India's constituent assembly finished its work by late 1949, and the Republic of India was proclaimed on January 26, 1950. During Nehru's long tenure in office, the country completed three national parliamentary elections within 15 years of independence, setting India firmly on the path of democratic development (by contrast, the constitution of Pakistan was not framed until 1956, and its first nationwide election was held in 1970, 23 years after the country came into existence). By the mid-1950s the crucial question of the political structure of the Indian state had been resolved, and the process of organizing India as a union of relatively autonomous ethnolinguistic states—the broad principle being that significant language groups should have their own states—was set in motion. (This process proceeded incrementally, and the drawing of the internal political map of India took until the early 1970s, although it was substantially complete by 1966. Prior to this, between 1947 and 1949 several hundred nominally independent feudal principalities known as "princely states" scattered across the country, a residue of the British practice of "indirect rule," were absorbed into India, in all but a few high-profile cases without conflict.) Also in the mid-1950s, an important "modernization" was enacted by Parliament with the reform of Hindu family law on inheritance, marriage, divorce, and adoption.

But if the Congress party of Nehru's India was a guarantor of stability and democratic development, it was also a force of profound social and political conservatism. The Nehru regime "was based on a coalition of urban and rural interests united behind an urban-oriented industrial strategy. Its senior partners were India's small but politically powerful administrative, managerial and professional urban middle classes and private-sector industrialists. . . . The junior partners were rural notables, mostly large landowners who survived intermediary abolition and blocked the implementation of land-ceiling legislation."[5] All of these privileged groups were largely comprised of Hindu upper castes.

The leaders of the "Congress system" sought to offset, and perhaps obscure, its bias toward traditional dominants and the social status quo with a vaguely socialist official rhetoric of state-led industrial development.[6] The state thus occupied the "commanding heights" of the economy, with a monopoly over much of heavy industry and other "strategic" sectors, while the rest of the manufacturing economy was subjected to, and some would say shackled by, a pervasive system of government regulation, which over the decades came to be known in India as the license-permit Raj (a snide reference to British imperial rule in India, which was referred to as the Raj). The license-permit system spawned vast patron-client networks linking politicians (usually from Congress), influential bureaucrats (the Indian Civil Service, known as the "steel frame" of the British Raj, was succeeded after independence by the Indian Administrative Service, an indigenized but otherwise unaltered successor), and private business interests, particularly a handful of big capitalists who formed protected monopolies or oligopolies in various manufacturing sectors. The penetration of foreign capital into the economy was strictly limited by state controls. After four decades of generating tepid growth at best and stagnation at worst, this economic regime came apart in crisis in 1991, and a reformed regime emphasizing deregulation and liberalization, including openness to foreign investment, was then instituted out of necessity.

In the predominantly Hindi-speaking states of northern India, where upper or "forward" castes (Brahmins, Rajputs, Bhumihars, Baniyas/Vaishyas, and Kayasths) comprised less than a fifth of the population, these castes made up 65 percent of Congress MPs elected to the Lok Sabha in 1952, 60 percent in 1957, 57 percent in 1962, and 52 percent in 1967. In UP, home to a sixth of all Indians, upper castes accounted for 59 percent of Congress MPs elected in 1952, and 55 percent in 1957 and 1962.

The most underrepresented groups among the Congress MPs were the intermediate or middle castes, who fall under the classification Other Backward Classes (OBC; i.e. they are neither forward castes nor "scheduled" castes, the "untouchables" of the caste hierarchy, who have special constitutional rights and protections in independent India). For example, Yadavs and Kurmis, two large OBC communities, each comprised just 1.6 percent of the Congress MPs elected from UP in 1962. (Jats, a less numerous but sizable middle-caste farming community concentrated in western UP, were also poorly represented.) The scheduled castes (SC), the lowest rungs of the caste hierarchy, were strongly represented among Congress MPs elected in the 1950s and 1960s from Hindi-speaking north India, including UP, albeit mostly from "reserved" constituencies earmarked for the SC only. Indeed, until the late 1980s the Congress voting base in UP as well as the huge neighboring state of Bihar consisted primarily of a curious combination: upper castes (especially Brahmins, the highest caste in ritual terms), SC, and Muslims (a sizable minority of about 15–16 percent in both states). Nonetheless, other statistics relating to the SC were not encouraging. In 1968 the SC were just 5 percent of the members of the Pradesh Congress Committee in UP (the council or board of the UP Congress)—or less than a fourth of the SC proportion of the population of UP—while upper castes accounted for a staggering 81 percent (and Brahmins alone were 33 percent).[7] As for the social advancement of the SC, "until 1980 no medical college in Uttar Pradesh," a state where Congress held hegemonic sway with few interruptions over four decades, "admitted a single scheduled-caste student."[8]

At the other end of the country, in Tamil Nadu in the deep south of India, culturally nearly a world apart from UP, the Congress party of the Nehru period was dominated by Tamil Brahmins, a privileged group, out of all proportion to their tiny percentage of the Tamil population. A predominantly middle-caste movement against the "Brahminical" domination of Tamil society and politics—a domination seen as derived from "Aryan" north Indian culture imposed on the racially distinct "Dravidian" south—emerged as early as the 1930s. In the 1967 election of the state legislature, the movement's postindependence incarnation, the political party known as the Dravida Munnetra Kazhagam (Dravidian Progress Federation) swept the Congress party out of power in Tamil Nadu, riding a wave of popular resentment among the intensely language-proud Tamils against a clumsy attempt in the mid-1960s by the Congress government in New Delhi to impose Hindi, the dominant language in northern India but the "mother tongue" of fewer than 40 percent of Indians, on the whole country. Congress not only has never been returned to power in the state capital Chennai (formerly Madras); it has been relegated ever since to a marginal position in Tamil Nadu's politics. The rise of "regionalism" in Tamil Nadu and the marginalization of Congress preceded the same developments across northern and eastern India by two to three decades.

In West Bengal, a journey of 900 miles from Delhi across the vast expanses of UP and Bihar to the state capital of Kolkata (formerly Calcutta), the Congress party and government were dominated throughout the Nehru period by the socially and politically most conservative elements of the preindependence Congress party in the province of Bengal, whose eastern two-thirds were hived off to form the eastern wing of Pakistan in 1947. These elements had constituted a small minority of the preindependence Congress party in Bengal, and they owed their ascendancy in post-1947 West Bengal simply to their loyalty to the central Congress leadership in New Delhi. In the West Bengal of the 1950s and

1960s the Congress party was disproportionately dominated by privileged and status quo–oriented groups, particularly large landlords and rich peasants.[9] The party lost power in the 1967 election to the state legislature to a motley alliance of communists, socialists, and Congress defectors and suffered a heavy defeat in a further midterm state election in 1969 by the same assortment of opposition parties. Although ideologically couched as a battle between "left" and "right," the rise of the opposition in West Bengal was equally a manifestation of a "regional"— and regionalist—challenge to the hegemon of Indian politics.

Antonio Gramsci, the Italian communist who wrote perceptively about political transitions and class dynamics in the context of post–World War I Italy, would almost certainly have characterized the Congress of the Nehru period as "revolutionaries of yesterday, today become reactionaries."[10]

The political conservatism of the Nehru regime appeared in exceptionally sharp relief when the crucial question of how India ought to be territorially structured and governed—as a centralized or a decentralized state— came up in the aftermath of independence. On this the commitment made by the preindependence Congress party, which had mobilized and led the nation on the long march to freedom, was quite unequivocal. Starting in 1916 the highest leadership of the Congress party consistently affirmed that free India would be a union, possibly even a federation, of autonomous territorial units formed on the basis of the major linguistic communities of the nation, who for the most part lived in distinct geographical regions (for example, Bengalis in a swathe of eastern India, Gujaratis in a zone of western India, Tamils in a large area of the far south, and so on). The commitment was repeated in 1920 and 1928, the decade during which the struggle for independence became a mass movement. In the late 1930s the top Congress leadership made specific commitments with regard to particular ethnolinguistic communities. In 1937–1938, for instance, they committed to the formation of states for three major ethno-linguistic groups in southern India—Andhra for speakers of Telugu, Karnataka for speakers of Kannada, and Kerala for speakers of Malayalam.

But after independence Nehru's government "dramatically reversed [this] position."[11] Instead Nehru, supported by his home (interior) minister, Vallabhbhai Patel, a Congress party leader from Gujarat known for his conservative views on most matters, started pushing for "a strong Center" to rule India, while the country would be divided into several "administrative zones"—largely following the model on which the British Raj had ruled India—rather than into substantively autonomous states formed on ethnolinguistic lines. This was of course a formula for top-down, centralized governance. In practice, it would perpetuate "the centralist straitjacket of the unitary colonial regime" rather than creating a layered and devolved structure of governance based on statutory and institutionalized division of powers between central and state governments. The political map of India would not be based on the ethnolinguistic identities and cultures that constitute the basis of most Indians' sense of being and provide the essential foundation for a broader sense of belonging and allegiance to an Indian nation—the reason that Congress adopted the unequivocal position it did during the freedom struggle.

Nehru sought to justify his alternative model on grounds of "security and stability" in the aftermath of the bloody partition and the formation of Pakistan. In fact, it was precisely the fear of being dominated as a religious minority in a post-British centralized state controlled by the Congress party—a secular organization but mostly led by and based among Hindus—that attracted huge numbers of the subcontinent's Muslims in the 1940s to the idea of Muslim self-determination and the Pakistan concept. Nehru's government appointed a commission "to re-examine the concept of linguistic states," which "dutifully reflected the new thinking of Nehru and Patel and recommended in the strongest terms that administrative convenience and not language" should be the basis of India's internal political framework, that "the British principle should stay" and the country should be divided into four administrative zones under a powerful central government.[12] If implemented, this meant that India would be a top-down, centralized polity rather than a decentralized polity built on the recognition of cultural diversity and acknowledgment of the fundamental identities of India's people.

The attempt to renege on one of the bedrock commitments of the independence movement was disrupted from an apparently unlikely quarter. In October 1952, Potti Sreeramalu, a devout middle-aged follower of Mahatma Gandhi, started a fast unto death with the demand that the Congress government of free India fulfill the promise to form a state in southern India's Telugu-speaking region, which then comprised the northern part of the "Madras Presidency," one of the administrative entities created by the British. Sreeramalu had dedicated his life to the freedom struggle and participated in such legendary events of that struggle as the Salt March of 1931 and the Quit India Movement of 1942. Nehru "issued a few appeals to Sreeramalu to end his fast, then ignored him." (C. Rajagopalachari, an extremely conservative Tamil Brahmin Congress party leader who then headed the government of Madras Presidency, did nothing.) In mid-December, Sreeramalu died in the city of Madras (now Chennai), aged 51, after 58 days on hunger strike, on the same day that Nehru presented the preamble to India's first five-year plan for economic development to Parliament in New Delhi.[13] Massive unrest and rioting erupted in the Telugu-speaking region. Within a few days the government of India caved in, and Nehru announced the formation of the Telugu-speaking state Andhra Pradesh ("pradesh" means "province"). Formed on October 1, 1953, the state was subsequently enlarged in 1956 with the addition of the Telangana region, a former "princely state," also Telugu-speaking but with a distinct historical personality. Hyderabad, located in the Telangana region and today one of India's six largest cities, became the capital. Most important, the Andhra events spurred the appointment by the government of India of the three-member States Reorganization Commission in late 1953, which after two years of work presented its report: a detailed blueprint for a union of autonomous ethnolinguistic states.

Six decades later, it is clear that this framework has facilitated democratic stability in India. Conflicts exist—between the "Center" and the states as well as between and within states—but such conflicts are a normal feature of federal-type systems and are to be expected in a social and political environment as complex as India's. More serious problems, in the form of violent antisystemic insurgencies, have arisen where this framework has not taken root and/or has been undermined from New Delhi—as in Kashmir, Punjab in the 1980s, and in the marginalized states of northeastern India, a region bordered by China, Bhutan, Myanmar, and Bangladesh.

A strong strain of state-centralism has persisted through the decades, however, despite India's structure as a democracy in which states enjoy statutory autonomy, directly elected state legislatures (known as legislative assemblies) have extensive powers to legislate—that is, make as well as implement public policy—in most areas of governance, and states have their own judicial systems and other institutional paraphernalia of autonomous functioning. The enduring practice of referring to the Union government in New Delhi as the "Center" can in itself be suggestive of a mentality that regards the rest of the country as some sort of "periphery." In comparison to fully fledged federal systems of countries such as the United States, Germany, Canada, or Switzerland, the Indian setup is weakly federal—perhaps best described as a semifederation or quasi federation—although it clearly goes further than the devolved but essentially unitary prototype of the United Kingdom after the establishment of autonomous governments in Scotland (and Wales) in the late 1990s, or Spain after decentralization to autonomous regions since the early 1980s. In India the Center retained the power to encroach on the jurisdiction and autonomy of states through a variety of constitutional mechanisms (including an extensive list of "concurrent" subjects of governance under joint jurisdiction, as well as the vesting of residual powers in the Center). The Center also retained the power to intervene directly in states, including the right to dismiss elected state governments and impose "president's rule" (in effect direct rule by the government in New Delhi, as the Indian presidency is a ceremonial post).

The latter right, codified as Article 356 of India's constitution, was supposed to be invoked only in the event of a breakdown of constitutional machinery or of law and order in a state but became a political tool of Congress governments in New Delhi to remove opposition state governments. The abuse of the power conferred by Article 356 became especially notorious in the 1980s during Indira Gandhi's second premiership, but the practice started in the Nehru period. In 1959 a communist-led government that had come to power in Kerala through democratic elections was dismissed in this manner. Even earlier, in 1953, Nehru and his government were complicit in the sordidly engineered removal from office of the charismatic premier of Jammu & Kashmir, Sheikh Abdullah, who had come to be viewed as unreliable in New Delhi. After Abdullah's dismissal and imprisonment, a strategy of coercive integration of Jammu & Kashmir into the Indian Union was put into motion, implemented through unrepresentative puppet governments in that state. This not only fatally undermined Jammu & Kashmir's autonomy within the Indian Union (enshrined as Article 370 of the Indian constitution) but utterly subverted democratic institutions and processes there.

Federalism, in the full sense of the term, consists of two pillars: "self-rule" for the constituent territorial units, and "shared rule" by representatives of those units at the political center.[14] In India the self-rule of the states has been circumscribed by the Center's powers of control and intervention, and mechanisms of shared rule are relatively underdeveloped in comparison to those of full-fledged federations. Shared rule is normally institutionalized in federal states through "robust bicameralism"—an upper chamber of the federal Parliament constituted as a house of the regions. India has such an upper chamber: the Rajya Sabha (Council of States), almost all of whose 250 members are indirectly elected by members of state legislatures. The Rajya Sabha is a less powerful institution than the U.S. Senate or Germany's Bundesrat and thus represents an example of less than robust bicameralism, while other joint Center-state bodies, such as the Inter-State Council established in 1990, are toothless and peripheral to the political process.

The centralist features of India's political system were established during the formative period of the Indian Union, coinciding with the Nehru years, and were relatively immune to challenge during the four decades of Congress party hegemony. In the post-Congress era, defined by the rise of "regional" parties and politicians based in particular states as the arbiters of India's politics, the top-down "strong Center perspective" is increasingly anachronistic, left behind by the transformation of India's democracy. The imperative in the changed circumstances, as an Indian author wrote in the mid-1990s, is the forging of "a strong *Union*, rather than a strong *Center*, with strong States as its constituents."[15]

Transition: The 1970s and 1980s

Nehru died in mid-1964, a sadly broken man after India's demoralizing defeat in a border war in late 1962 with the People's Republic of China, a country whose friendship he had cultivated during the first half of the 1950s. With his death the last of the titans of the independence movement passed from the scene—Mahatma Gandhi had been assassinated in early 1948, and Subhas Chandra Bose died in a plane crash in August 1945. In early 1966, as India reeled from an economic crisis in the aftermath of the 1965 war with Pakistan—initiated by Pakistan over disputed Kashmir—Nehru's only child, his daughter Indira Gandhi, became prime minister. A year later she faced the biggest challenge since independence to the Congress party's dominance of India, in national and state elections held in 1967.

The Congress party returned to power at the Center, but with a sharply reduced majority of 283 of the 520 seats in the Lok Sabha (down from 361 of the 494 parliamentary constituencies it won in 1962; the party's share of the nationwide popular vote fell from nearly 45 percent to under 41 percent). The real story of the 1967 polls lay, however, in the states—by now well established as the building blocks of India's polity—where sweeping winds of change severely rocked Congress's entrenched hegemony.

The party was defeated and ousted from power in Tamil Nadu, Kerala, Orissa, and rather embarrassingly the national capital, Delhi. In five other states—UP, Bihar, Rajasthan, Punjab, and West Bengal—Congress for the first time failed to win outright majorities and was reduced to being the largest minority party in the state legislatures. Opposition parties were subsequently able to form coalition governments in UP, West Bengal, and Punjab. The Congress share of the popular vote declined alarmingly, to well below the party's nationwide average, in UP and Bihar (33 percent and 35 percent, respectively) and fell in most other states, including Orissa (33 percent) and Punjab (37 percent).[16] The 1967 polls also saw attrition in the Congress organization, as prominent leaders in several states—including Chaudhary Charan Singh in UP, leader of an emerging class of well-off, intermediate-caste (Jat) farmers who were beginning to gain from rising productivity in agriculture in some locales of northern India (the "green revolution"), and such party veterans as Ajoy Mukherjee in West Bengal and Harekrishna Mahatab in Orissa—left Congress and floated alternative "regional" parties.[17]

For the post-Nehru Congress party, the challenge of recouping lost ground across the country presented a complex problem. The assortment of "regional" opposition parties challenging Congress in the states spanned a very heterogeneous spectrum. These included, for example, a party representing Tamil ethnolinguistic pride and middle-caste aspirations in Tamil Nadu; communist and socialist parties operating in the very different settings of West Bengal and Kerala; Hindu nationalists, socialists, and emerging intermediate-caste political formations in UP; socialists, Hindu nationalists, and communists in Bihar; and so on. The fragmented nature of the opposition and the absence of a coherent national alternative were in one sense a blessing for the Congress party, because these conditions precluded any threat in the short term to its power at the Center. But from the vantage point of New Delhi, it was equally clear that unless Congress could recover its eroded base in populous states across northern, southern, and eastern India, it would be only a matter of time before its hold over national power would be challenged. And Congress, as the only party with a nationwide base, needed to devise a strategy for recovery that would have nationwide resonance and appeal, cutting across regions. A strategy that worked in the north but not in the south or the east, or vice versa, would not suffice.

Indira Gandhi had acceded to the prime ministership of India in 1966 after the early death of Nehru's successor, Lal Bahadur Shastri, a respected Congress leader from UP, primarily because of her identity as Nehru's daughter. But her leadership of the Congress party was neither absolute nor secure. Both at the national level and in many states, Congress's organizational setup was in the grip of conservative, old-guard politicians, a so-called syndicate of entrenched but increasingly ineffective figures from the Nehru period. The consolidation of Indira Gandhi's authority and the renewal of the Congress party had one requisite in common: the removal or sidelining of this deadwood party officialdom.

In the second half of 1969 the impasse was resolved when the Congress party split. Large majorities of Congress's MPs and of the 700 or so members of the All-India Congress Committee, the party's plenary body, consisting of delegates from state units from across the country, sided with Indira Gandhi in her battle with the conservatives and the old guard were reduced to a rump faction. Simultaneously, her politics took a marked left-wing and populist turn as her government nationalized the country's banking sector and moved to abolish the "privy purses" of the several hundred feudal princely families who had been dispossessed of their fiefdoms in the late 1940s but were parasitic on the public exchequer, having been granted standing allowances by the state in return.

Indira Gandhi had been underestimated by many in India until 1969, because of both her gender and her relative lack of political stature. The bold initiative with which she tackled her inner-party opponents and asserted her leadership of the Congress party established her credentials as a canny and even ruthless politician. She followed up by devising a strategy to arrest the Congress party's decline in popular support and restore its faltering hegemony. That strategy was pithily expressed in the slogan "Garibi Hatao!" (Abolish Poverty!). A recharged Congress went to the people in national and state elections in early 1971 with this slogan, led by its relatively youthful leader (aged 53), who proved to be a charismatic and even mesmerizing campaigner with crowds across the nation. Indira Gandhi had found a campaign platform of nationwide resonance, with a slogan that appealed directly to the poverty-stricken majority of the country and particularly to key social groups within this majority such as the SC (the former "untouchables" of the caste hierarchy, known today as Dalits: The Downtrodden), scheduled tribes (ST: India's impoverished and marginalized tribal communities, known as the Adivasis (Original Inhabitants), and Muslims, the main religious minority of 11–12 percent of the national population, who also struggled with above-average levels of poverty and lack of opportunity.

   The Congress party led by Indira Gandhi stormed to power with a nearly two-thirds parliamentary majority, winning 342 of the 518 seats in the Lok Sabha (the rump Congress faction won in just 16 parliamentary constituencies, 11 of which were in Gujarat, where the conservatives retained a base). The party led by Indira Gandhi polled 43.7 percent of the nationwide popular vote, and the conservative faction got 10.4 percent. The combined total, 54.1 percent, was a massive increase on the 40.8 percent received by the united Congress party in 1967. While the rump faction's vote was a mix of traditional Congress voters and voters who had supported right-wing opposition parties in 1967, this was the only time in the history of independent India that the "Congress" label got a majority of the nationwide popular vote.

   As in 1967, the deeper meaning of the elections could only be discerned by looking at the states. Congress led by Indira Gandhi regained

Figure 2.   Prime Minister Indira Gandhi addresses a mass meeting in Delhi (1971). AFP/GETTY IMAGES.

power in all the states the united Congress had lost in 1967, except Tamil Nadu. (In West Bengal the Congress party headed by Indira Gandhi regained power in state elections held a year later, in 1972.) And in spite of the rump faction cutting into the Congress vote base in most states, quite significantly in some cases, the Congress led by Indira Gandhi polled a much higher share of the popular vote in many populous states than the united Congress had in 1967. The most dramatic case was UP, where Congress led by Indira Gandhi won 49 percent of the popular vote, compared to just 33 percent won by the united Congress in 1967. The corresponding figures were 40 percent in Bihar (35 percent in 1967) and 39 percent in Orissa (33 percent). In other states where Congress had held on in 1967, the share of the popular vote polled by Congress led by Indira Gandhi was similarly much higher than that received by the united party in 1967—for example 50 percent in Rajasthan (40 percent for the united Congress in 1967), 46 percent in Madhya Pradesh ("Central Province"; 41 percent), and a whopping 56 percent in Andhra Pradesh (47 percent).

Clearly "Garibi Hatao" had resonated throughout the length and breadth of the country and attracted large numbers of new voters to a party that had rebranded itself as a progressive force for social change, no longer the linchpin of a deeply unequal social status quo. While lineage had propelled Indira Gandhi to the prime ministership in 1966, she emerged in the early 1970s as a mass leader in her own right. This elegant and aristocratic woman of slight build, known for her personal shyness, was referred to as "Indira Amma" (Mother Indira) among women of poverty-stricken communities in Andhra Pradesh, while in West Bengal university students chanted this Bengali slogan in her honor, which can be rendered in English as: "Long live Indira Gandhi, the new sun of New Delhi, the new fortress of a new Asia!"

The peak of her prestige and power was in 1972 after she deftly handled the international crisis that erupted in March 1971 centered on East Pakistan, where a popular uprising for independence elicited a savage West Pakistani military crackdown that sent some 10 million Bengali refugees fleeing into India. Already fortified by her mandate at home, the prime minister took a strong stand on the atrocities and traveled overseas canvassing support for her position. As the crisis worsened, the Nixon administration in the United States backed Pakistan, which had been a U.S. strategic ally in the Cold War since the mid-1950s and in the summer of 1971 emerged as the conduit for the operation led by Henry Kissinger, the secretary of state, to reach a U.S. rapprochement with China. In response, Indira Gandhi's government concluded a treaty of friendship and cooperation in August 1971 with the Soviet Union, the common foe of the United States and China. In late 1971 she authorized the Indian armed forces to invade East Pakistan, and with the aid of Bengali guerrilla fighters and much of the local population, Bangladesh was liberated in a two-week war in December 1971. After this victory Indira Gandhi was hailed by Atal Behari Vajpayee, a Hindu nationalist opposition politician who would himself serve as prime minister from 1998 to 2004, as an incarnation of Durga, a notable goddess in the Hindu pantheon of deities.

Thereafter the Indira magic began to unravel, and she went the way many charismatic populists tend to, succumbing to autocratic temptations. In Indira Gandhi's case, the autocratic turn led in short order to resorting to open dictatorship. By 1974 the euphoria of 1971–1972 was wearing thin, and the high hopes aroused by the promise to abolish poverty were yielding to a growing sense of disillusionment, among the middle and laboring classes alike, with poor economic conditions and the lack of a purposive development agenda. First students rioted in urban centers of Gujarat, and then hundreds of thousands of railway workers—the vast Indian rail network built during British rule was then and substantially remains the vital form of transportation for people and goods across the country—went on a national strike. A prominent opposition figure and veteran of the independence movement, the septuagenarian socialist Jaya Prakash (J. P.) Narayan, emerged in 1974–1975 as the focal point of a large-scale protest movement in his home base, Bihar. The slogan he gave this movement, in whose vanguard were university students, was "Total Revolution" against social inequality and injustice. Indira Gandhi grew increasingly defensive and fearful, and she apparently suspected that the protests emerging in various parts of the country were part of a wider plot to topple her from power by spreading disorder. She was certainly aware that national and state elections were due in 1976 and that her own popularity was on the wane.

In June 1975, one day after the Congress party was ousted from power in Gujarat by an opposition coalition in fresh state elections, a high court judge in UP, where Indira's own parliamentary constituency was located, ruled in response to an opposition petition that she had misused official machinery during her election campaign in 1971, declared her election to the Lok Sabha null and void, and barred her from contesting elections for six years. This was one provocation too many for the beleaguered leader. Instead of taking the judicial route to challenge the dubious and draconian ruling, she and her advisers got the Congress loyalist who held the ceremonial presidency of India to invoke an article of the constitution and declare a nationwide "emergency" on grounds of internal disturbance.

The Emergency is remembered as a grim anomaly in the history of India's democracy. It lasted for 21 months and was formally lifted only in March 1977, although it was relaxed in January 1977. During this period India's framework of parliamentary democracy at the national level and in the states (the opposition-run governments in Tamil Nadu and Gujarat were summarily dismissed) was replaced by the rule of a motley cabal around Indira Gandhi and the younger of her two sons, Sanjay Gandhi—a young man in his late twenties—and constitutionally guaranteed civil liberties came under vicious assault.

Mass arrests targeted two groups in particular throughout the country: leaders and prominent activists of the diverse assortment of opposition parties, and members of the equally diverse and thriving free press. Tens of thousands of opposition leaders and activists and thousands of newspaper journalists and editors were picked up and cast into jail during the Emergency, most under a Maintenance of Internal Security Act, which was enacted by the Congress-dominated Parliament in New Delhi. A photograph of George Fernandes—a socialist opposition leader and trade unionist who helped organize the 1974 railway workers' strike—raising his manacled hands in defiance became an iconic image of the

Emergency. A small number of Congress politicians who dared to dissent were also imprisoned. The total number of arrests during the Emergency topped 100,000 persons, and the arrests' selective and targeted nature was indicative of a plan, which largely worked, to prevent the organizing of mass protests and to control public opinion by muzzling the press.

A climate of fear spread across the country. Harcharan Singh Longowal, a leader of the Akali Dal, a significant "regional" party with a large base among the ethnoreligious Sikh community in Punjab, succinctly expressed the implications for India's democracy: "The question before us is not whether Indira Gandhi should continue to be prime minister or not. The point is whether democracy in this country is to survive or not. The democratic structure stands on three pillars, namely a strong opposition, independent judiciary, and free press. The Emergency has destroyed all these essentials."[18]

The most infamous public statement of the Emergency period was uttered by a Congress politician from Assam who had been handpicked by Indira Gandhi to serve as the national president of the Congress party. He gained permanent infamy in India's political annals by declaring: "Indira is India and India is Indira." In fact, the driving force of the Emergency regime was not even Indira herself but her son Sanjay Gandhi. A warped cult of personality portrayed Sanjay, a young man of no discernible achievement but with a keen nose for the politics of intimidation and coercion, as a youth icon who represented the great hope for India's future, and senior Congress leaders, including chief ministers of states, literally prostrated themselves before him. The ostensible purpose of the Emergency was to foster an orderly and disciplined environment in which measures of socioeconomic development could be rapidly implemented. In reality, as a popular joke went, unlike in Mussolini's fascist Italy, even the trains did not run on time, and the "development" agenda spawned such grotesque schemes as a sterilization program for men (and less frequently women) in some states of northern India. This program was inspired by the discredited Malthusian conception of the dangers of population growth and apparently was a pet project of Sanjay Gandhi.

As it turned out, the one lasting legacy of the Emergency was the conversion of the Congress party—historically a "broad church" that led one of the great popular mobilizations of the first half of the twentieth century, the Indian independence movement—into a family firm controlled by Jawaharlal Nehru's direct descendants. The culture of servility and sycophancy toward the Nehru-Gandhi family and, in particular, the principle of hereditary succession to power that took root in Congress during the Emergency have proved enduring, even as memories of that dictatorial interregnum have largely faded from public consciousness.

In January 1977 Indira Gandhi decided to seek a fresh mandate from the people. (The national and state elections due in early 1976 had of course not been held.) She had apparently been advised by some in her coterie, including members of the career bureaucracy, that she stood a good chance of winning. The Emergency was relaxed, political prisoners were released, and India prepared to go to the polls once again. Indira Gandhi's gamble proved a miscalculation. In the national election of March 1977 Congress was decisively defeated and ousted from power. The ruling party won just 154 of the 542 parliamentary constituencies comprising the Lok Sabha, and its share of the nationwide popular vote slumped to 34.5 percent. The party was almost wiped out in a huge swathe of northern India. It won none of the 85 parliamentary constituencies in UP, none of the 54 in Bihar, and only one of the 40 in Madhya Pradesh—three populous states that together elected one-third of the Lok Sabha. The party won one of the 25 Lok Sabha seats from Rajasthan and none in the smaller northern states of Punjab, Haryana, and Himachal Pradesh. The party also fared disastrously in the eastern states of West Bengal and Orissa, where it won three of 42 and four of 20 parliamentary constituencies, respectively.

Congress was saved from annihilation, however, by its strong performance in southern India. In an early illustration of the emerging diversification of India's political landscape, as many as 92 of the 129 parliamentary constituencies in the four southern states of Andhra Pradesh, Tamil Nadu, Karnataka, and Kerala returned Congress candidates. In Andhra Pradesh, the most populous state of the south, Congress took 57 percent of the popular vote and 41 of the 42 parliamentary constituencies and made a similar sweep in Karnataka (whose capital, Bangalore, now known as Bengaluru, is India's information technology hub in the early twenty-first century), winning 26 of the 28 parliamentary constituencies and 57 percent of the popular vote. In Kerala the party bagged 11 of the 20 parliamentary constituencies and in Tamil Nadu 14 out of 39.

The contrast between north and south was due to a mix of factors. The authoritarian excesses of the Emergency had been relatively milder in the south. In Andhra Pradesh, Congress benefited from antipoverty and social welfare policies instituted in the 1970s by its state government, and equally so in Karnataka, where a reformist Congress government headed by a popular chief minister, Devaraj Urs, had been in power since 1972. These advantages combined with the relative weakness of opposition parties in these two states. Congress benefited in Kerala from its poll alliance with a communist faction and in Tamil Nadu from its poll alliance with one of the two major parties to have emerged from the regionalist Dravidian movement. (The unified party that had ousted Congress from power in Tamil Nadu in 1967 had split in the early 1970s, and the breakaway group, which allied with Congress in the March 1977 national election, had since gained great popularity under its leader, the former film actor M. G. Ramachandran.)

In western India, Congress's dominance was eroded, but the party performed better than in the north (or east), winning 20 of the 48 parliamentary constituencies in Maharashtra and 10 of the 26 Lok Sabha seats from Gujarat. The party gained 47 percent of the popular vote in both these states, a sign that the heterogeneous social base that had coalesced around the populist-progressive platform of the early 1970s was largely intact. In Gujarat, for example, Congress had in the 1970s built a rainbow social base known as KHAM—Kshatriya-Harijan-Adivasi-Muslim— bringing together the Kshatriyas, an upper-caste community, the Harijans, the deeply disadvantaged "untouchable" community, the Adivasis, the poor and marginalized tribals, and the Muslim minority of nearly 10 percent. This social base survived even the headwinds brought on by the Emergency.

But despite its southern comfort, Congress had suffered a complete rout in northern India, severe reverses in the east, and moderate reverses in the west.[19] Indira Gandhi suffered the personal humiliation of being defeated in her own parliamentary constituency in UP, and her son Sanjay lost badly in another UP constituency. The north was swept by the Janata Party (People's Party; not to be confused with the aforementioned Janata Dal of the late 1980s), a loosely knit alliance of socialist groups, the right-wing Hindu nationalist party, middle-peasant formations based among intermediate castes, Congress conservatives who had been sidelined by Indira Gandhi's ascendancy in 1969–1971 or had left the party even earlier to form a right-wing opposition, and Congress politicians who had quit the party in protest against the Emergency. This polyglot combination won an absolute majority in the Lok Sabha—295 of 542 seats. As many as 215 of these 295 MPs were elected from the states of northern India. Thus the Janata Party was a largely north Indian phenomenon, supplemented by Gujarat in the west, where Congress conservatives pushed aside by Indira Gandhi's rise had retained a base, and Orissa in the east, where Biju Patnaik, a charismatic regional figure and former Congress leader, joined the Janata Party. Morarji Desai, an octogenarian conservative from Gujarat who had been Indira Gandhi's main rival in the Congress leadership during the 1966–1969 period, became India's first non-Congress prime minister 30 years after independence.

India's first non-Congress (and de facto coalition) government proved to be an unhappy and unstable experience. In a little over two years the Janata Party disintegrated amidst factional feuding and ugly confrontations between overly ambitious and power-hungry leaders, the government lost its parliamentary majority and midterm elections had to be called. As the Janata Party unraveled, the doughty Indira Gandhi had been working to recover lost ground, traveling the length and breadth of the country to rally her loyalists. She gained considerable popular sympathy as a result of the Janata Party government's attempts to prosecute her for wrongdoing during the Emergency—public memory is notoriously short, and many Indians bought her stance that she was the victim of political vendetta. In 1978 she managed to reenter Parliament after handsomely winning a by-election from a constituency in Karnataka vacated for her by a loyalist.

In the midterm national election held in January 1980, she staged a stunning comeback. Her Congress (Indira), or Congress (I), party—so called to distinguish it from a rival faction consisting of left-leaning Congress politicians who had once been her staunch supporters but become disillusioned by her authoritarianism—won 353 of the 529 parliamentary constituencies that went to the polls, with 42.7 percent of the nationwide popular vote. The Congress (I)'s election campaign emphasized just one theme: the need for a stable national government. The party's slogan in the national election was "Elect a Government that works! Vote Congress (I)." This single-theme campaign focused public attention on the chaotic dysfunction of the Janata Party interlude—and it worked.

While Congress (I) won 353 constituencies and a two-thirds majority in Parliament, its competitors faced decimation. Two groupings built around the conservative and socialist wings of the disintegrated Janata Party coalition won just 31 and 41 parliamentary constituencies, respectively (with 19 percent and 9 percent of the popular vote), and the rival Congress faction won 13 constituencies and just over 5 percent of the nationwide vote. The single largest opposition contingent in the Parliament actually consisted of a communist-led bloc of 54 members. But this bloc, too, was no more than a "regional" lightweight compared to the nationwide Congress (I) juggernaut. Of the 36 parliamentary seats won by the largest communist party, the CPM, 28 were from West Bengal— where the CPM had captured power in state elections in June 1977 at the head of the alliance of communist and socialist parties known as the Left Front (LF)—and another six were constituencies in Kerala, which has had a strong communist presence since the 1950s. In order to showcase her pan-Indian appeal and reinforce her strength in southern India, Indira Gandhi ran from two parliamentary constituencies separated by 600 miles—one in UP and the other in Andhra Pradesh. She regained her UP constituency, Rae Bareli, where she had lost in 1977, with 58 percent of the vote. In Medak, the constituency she chose in the economically underdeveloped Telangana region of Andhra Pradesh, she won with 68 percent of the vote.[20]

All of this notwithstanding, the spectacular return of Indira Gandhi and the phoenix-like resurrection of the Congress party did not necessarily signal a lasting revival of Congress hegemony in India's politics. The victory of 1980 was not so much a ringing endorsement of Indira Gandhi and her party as the cumulative outcome of three factors—the failure of the Janata Party coalition to provide a responsible government to the country, the disunity of the opposition parties in the 1980 election, and the fact that Congress was still the party with the single largest base of support in almost all of the dozen most populous states of the country.

Of these dozen states, which together accounted for 470 of the 542 seats in the Lok Sabha, Congress in the national election of 1980 polled an absolute majority (more than 50 percent) of the popular vote in five states, Andhra Pradesh, Maharashtra, Karnataka, Gujarat, and Orissa, which translated into near-sweeps of the Lok Sabha seats from these states. In another five states—UP, Bihar, Madhya Pradesh, Rajasthan, and Kerala—Congress was the first-ranking party with the single largest share (plurality) of the popular vote, which in every case except Kerala translated into decisive majorities in Lok Sabha seats (including a near-sweep in Madhya Pradesh). As for the two other states, Congress won just over half the Lok Sabha seats from Tamil Nadu, thanks to its poll alliance with one of that state's two major "regional" parties. Only in West Bengal was the Congress party decisively outvoted—by the CPM-led Left Front, which won 51 percent to Congress's 37 percent of the popular vote and won 38 of the state's 42 Lok Sabha seats. This picture meant that if Congress dominance were to be undermined in a critical mass of the populous states *and* if the opposition parties were able to achieve a moderate degree of anti-Congress alliance-making in a future national election, the grand old party's hegemony would be under renewed threat.

Andhra Pradesh, the Telugu-speaking state of the Indian Union, was formed in dramatic circumstances in 1953—and enlarged with the addition of the Telangana region, including the city of Hyderabad in 1956—after Potti Sreeramalu fasted to death demanding its formation. It is southern India's most populous state, and almost a third (42) of the 129 members of the Lok Sabha from the four southern states are elected from Andhra Pradesh. Andhra or AP, as it is often called, is the fifth most populous state of the Indian Union after UP and Bihar, Maharashtra, and West Bengal.

Through the 1970s and into the early 1980s, Andhra Pradesh acquired a reputation as a bastion of Indira Gandhi's Congress party. Indira herself enjoyed vast popularity there, especially among women and the poor classes of society. In Congress's debacle in the national election of 1977, Andhra bucked the trend completely, and Congress won 41 of the 42 parliamentary constituencies there, with a thumping 57 percent of the popular vote. In the 1980 national election, as Indira's Congress (I) returned to power, the result was identical: Congress candidates won 41 of the 42 Lok Sabha seats allotted to Andhra Pradesh, and the party polled 56 percent of the popular vote there. This was clearly a state Indira could count on in sickness and in health. She herself won one of those seats in 1980, the Medak parliamentary constituency in the Telangana region, with 68 percent of the popular vote. As she had also been elected to Parliament from the Rae Bareli constituency in UP, she had to give up one of the two seats. She chose to retain Medak, in a gesture of gratitude to the people of Andhra Pradesh for standing by her through thick and thin.

In 1982 a popular actor in the Telugu cinema industry, Nandamuri Taraka Rama Rao—known as N. T. Rama Rao or simply NTR—floated a regional party in Andhra Pradesh. He called it the Telugu Desam Party (Telugu Homeland Party). Then nearly 60 years old, NTR had played starring roles in more than 300 Telugu-language movies over several decades and thus had ample name and face recognition with the people of the state. Moreover, in many of his hit movies he had played a variety of gods and deities from ancient Indian epics and Hindu mythology and developed a godlike image of his own among Andhra Pradesh's people.

His decision to diversify into politics was initially not taken too seriously. But he undertook a strenuous public relations campaign, traveling throughout the sprawling state in a van he called Chaitanya Ratham (Chariot of Awakening), attracting huge crowds wherever he went. His main plank was Telugu pride and self-respect: "Aarukotla andhrula atma gauravam" (Self-respect of 60 million Andhra people). Since Indira Gandhi's return to power in New Delhi in 1980, Andhra had been governed by four different Congress chief ministers in three years, as she repeatedly changed the incumbent of the post. Her behavior could be explained as just capricious or as an ongoing attempt to find the right man for the job but was almost certainly in part motivated by her fear of the emergence of strong leaders in important states who might in due course undermine her absolute, top-down control of the Congress party. This revolving-door practice reduced the Andhra Pradesh chief minister's post to a national laughingstock and caused chaos in the administration of the state and disaffection among its people, who viewed it as an affront. In this situation NTR, a son of the soil, appeared with his alternative regional party and an emotive appeal to offended Telugu sentiments. He also appropriated Congress's "social justice" platform and promised to implement a slew of antipoverty and welfare measures targeted at women and the poor if voted into power.

In state elections in January 1983, NTR crushed Congress in Andhra Pradesh. His Telugu Desam Party won 220 of the 294 single-member constituencies, a three-fourths majority in the state legislature. His party disproportionately featured Kammas, his own forward-caste community, comprising about 6 percent of the state's population. But his call for change evoked response from across Andhra Pradesh's society, particularly among the middle castes belonging to the OBC. The share of the popular vote won by Congress—a party dominated then as now in Andhra Pradesh by the "forward" caste Reddy community, about 6 percent of the state's population—slumped to just 33.5 percent, and Congress was reduced to 60 seats in the 294-member legislative assembly.

The emergence of the Telugu Desam Party in Andhra Pradesh as a regional party headed by a popular and charismatic figure from within the state was an early milestone in the regionalization of India's polity, which accelerated and deepened in the 1990s and increasingly dominates its democracy today. The Telugu Desam Party itself was no flash-in-the-pan phenomenon; NTR subsequently won another, midterm state election in March 1985 and governed the state as chief minister until December 1989. He regained power in December 1994, and from September 1995 the new Telugu Desam Party leader, his son-in-law N. Chandrababu Naidu, governed the state as chief minister until 2004, winning another state election on the way.

The debacle in Andhra Pradesh must have come as a very rude shock to Indira Gandhi. And the rise of a powerful regional challenge in Andhra was not an isolated event. Karnataka also went to the polls to elect its government in January 1983. Karnataka—a state largely populated by speakers of the Kannada language—was regarded, like Andhra Pradesh, as a virtually impregnable Congress stronghold. In the 1977 national election Congress won 26 of Karnataka's 28 parliamentary constituencies with 57 percent of the popular vote, and in 1980 the resurgent party won 27 of the 28 Lok Sabha seats allotted to Karnataka and 56 percent of the popular vote. It was from a parliamentary constituency, Chikmagalur, in this loyal state that Indira Gandhi reentered Parliament in 1978 after winning a by-election with a huge margin.

In January 1983 this Congress fortress crumbled, and a regional version of the disintegrated Janata Party emerged as the single largest party in the state legislature by winning 95 of the 224 constituencies, while Congress was relegated to second position with 82 members in the legislative assembly and a drastically diminished share—40 percent—of the popular vote. The Karnataka-specific reincarnation of Congress's vanquished national rival was subsequently able to gain a working majority in the assembly and form a government in Bangalore with support from eighteen Hindu nationalist and six communist legislators. (And it won a majority in the Karnataka assembly on its own in a midterm state election in March 1985 and continued to govern the state until 1989.)

The timing of the defeats in Andhra Pradesh and Karnataka was ominous for Indira Gandhi. They came just under two years before the next national election was due to be held in December 1984. In India, assuming that Parliament lasts its full five-year term, the political countdown—involving strategizing, positioning, and preparation—to the next national election typically begins about two years before the due date. The ouster of Congress from power in its two southern strongholds was sure to recharge the morale of opposition parties across the country and renew efforts at anti-Congress coalition-building, and it did.

Indira Gandhi was surely aware that in northern India Congress's position was not secure, despite the seeming revival of its fortunes in 1980. In both UP and Bihar, her party had won only a slender plurality, 36 percent, of the popular vote in the national election of January 1980. Congress had won the bulk of the parliamentary constituencies in the two giant northern states—51 of 85 in UP and 30 of 54 in Bihar—thanks to a divided opposition vote. The popular vote obtained by the two competing wings of the splintered Janata Party totaled 52 percent in UP and 40 percent in Bihar (adding in the votes won by the anti-Indira Congress faction and a communist party, 54 percent in Bihar had voted for opposition parties). This meant that if a substantial degree of consolidation of the opposition vote were to occur in UP and Bihar, the tables would be turned and Congress would face a rout even if it managed to hold on to its vote base, and if that base declined even modestly Congress would be looking at catastrophe.

The ruling party's prospects were also unpromising in some other populous states—in West Bengal, for example, the communist-led Left Front had won a second five-year term in state elections in May 1982, and Congress could not realistically hope to win more than a handful of the state's 42 parliamentary constituencies in the next national election. In Tamil Nadu the Congress base was too limited for the party to stand on its own legs, and it was dependent on its alliance with one of the two large regional parties in the state—the ruling party, led by M. G. Ramachandran (MGR), another movie actor turned successful regional politician—to gain a sizable chunk of the state's 39 seats in the Lok Sabha.

Indira Gandhi also had reason to feel vulnerable for other reasons. In June 1980, a few months after her triumphal return to power at the Center, her son Sanjay was killed when a small two-seater plane he was flying for recreation crashed in Delhi. Like her, he had regained his parliamentary seat from UP but was keeping a much lower profile than during the Emergency. For Indira this was not just the loss of a dearly loved son but of her closest political adviser and confidant. After Sanjay's death she inducted her other son—the apolitical Rajiv, a professional airline pilot—into politics as general secretary of the Congress party, apparently against the wishes of Rajiv's Italian wife, Sonia. By 1983 it was clear that Rajiv Gandhi was being groomed to eventually succeed his mother as Congress leader and prospective prime minister, but he was not a political animal in the way his younger brother had been and was settling slowly into his new role.

Indira Gandhi's regional woes worsened in February 1983. Since 1979 Assam—by far the largest of seven states in India's volatile northeast, a multiethnic frontier region bordered by Myanmar, China, Bhutan, and Bangladesh, and prone to chronic ethnic violence and insurgency—had been in the throes of a student-led protest movement. This movement, based among the state's ethnic Assamese, the largest segment of the state's population, was driven by their worry that large-scale illegal immigration into Assam over many years, mainly by Bengali-speaking Muslims from Bangladesh, was irrevocably altering the state's demography and undermining the language, the culture, and above all the political primacy of ethnic Assamese in their homeland. It had been impossible to hold elections in 12 of Assam's 14 parliamentary constituencies in January 1980 because of the unrest; one of the agitators' main demands was that the electoral rolls should first be purged of illegal settlers. The movement had strong chauvinist as well as secessionist overtones. (It spawned an armed organization, the United Liberation Front of Assam, which in the late 1980s launched an insurgency for a sovereign Assam.)

Nonetheless, the protesters' concerns had merit, and the movement also reflected deep-seated grievances among ethnic Assamese over the Center's perceived exploitation of Assam's oil reserves and the domination of its tea industry by businessmen from outside the state.[21]

As the protests continued unabated, Indira Gandhi chose confrontation over compromise and in early 1983 tried to force through a state election in a very troubled atmosphere. This provoked a boycott call from the protest movement and led to large-scale ethnic killings. In one of the worst carnages in independent India's history, 2,200 people, mostly Bengali-speaking Muslims, were massacred by mobs in a single incident. The Congress party won the dubious election, but Indira's policy aggravated the situation in Assam and turned the problem into a national crisis. It also added to a rising chorus of criticism of the prime minister across the country.

As 1983 progressed, the front pages of Indian newspapers were increasingly dominated by a rapidly developing crisis in another part of the country, geographically close to the center of power in New Delhi. This was Punjab, home today to about 28 million people, which was formed in 1966 as a Sikh-majority state but with a very large Hindu minority. The Sikhs of Punjab, adherents of a religion founded around 1500 A.D. that draws on but is distinct from both Hinduism and Islam, comprise about 60 percent of the state's population and are mostly agriculturists living in rural areas, while the Hindus, about 37 percent, are largely urbanites and traditionally concentrated in shopkeeping and trading. The urban professional classes come from both communities. (Sikhs can be found in most parts of India and comprise about 2 percent of India's population.)

In the early 1980s the Akali Dal (Believers' Party), the regional party of Punjab with a large base among intermediate-caste Jat Sikh farmers, launched a campaign of rallies and marches directed at the Congress-ruled Center with a charter of Sikh demands on political, economic, and religious issues. The campaign, which gathered momentum from 1982, was in large measure simply a strategy to mobilize Sikhs against the Akali Dal's archrival in the state's electoral politics: Congress, which was in power. Congress's support base in Punjab included most of the state's Hindus and a sizable proportion of its Sikhs—both relatively prosperous Jat Sikhs and the poorer Mazhabi Sikhs of "lower" caste origins—and the Akali Dal was the main opposition party. Its prospects of countering Congress's dominance in the state thus rested on a consolidation of Sikhs around an emotive campaign.

The government in New Delhi needed to handle the Akali Dal campaign for Sikh rights very carefully. Despite Sikhs' small proportion of the national population, they were (and are) a high-profile community throughout India, much respected for their hardworking ethos, their contributions to society in various domains, and their role in the 1947–1948, 1965, and 1971 wars with Pakistan, as well as the 1962 border war with China. Sikh officers and soldiers have constituted a significant part of the Indian Army since independence, and a sizable fraction of them are originally from the areas of the historical Punjab region that became part of (West) Pakistan in 1947, which they left during the bloodbath of the subcontinent's partition into India and Pakistan. The Sikhs developed a martial tradition from the late seventeenth century, when leaders of the faith faced violent persecution by the emperors of the Mughal dynasty who dominated the northern subcontinent from Delhi. Shaped by the experience of being a minority group wedged between far more numerous Hindus and Muslims, the complex historical inheritance of Sikhism includes powerful religious institutions and a puritanical strain.

Indira Gandhi took a hard-line stance toward the agitation. She made no concessions on its demands, and the Congress government of Punjab resorted to heavy-handed police action involving mass arrests of protesters. In November 1982 Delhi hosted a major sports event, the Asian Games—the equivalent of an Asian Olympics. Many Sikhs traveling from Punjab to Delhi to attend the Games through the Hindu-majority state of Haryana were subjected to intrusive searches and insulting treatment by police in Haryana and Delhi. As tensions worsened in Punjab, a Sikh extremist fringe increasingly assumed center stage in the Akali Dal's agitation. The leader of this fringe was the firebrand fundamentalist preacher Jarnail Singh Bhindranwale. A striking-looking and intensely charismatic young man in his midthirties, Bhindranwale had been little known even within Punjab. Now he emerged as the focal point for a radical wing of the agitation comprised of Sikh students and youth. In contrast to the generally moderate and civil tone of the mainstream Akali Dal leadership, Bhindranwale adopted a strident posture, drawing on the most puritanical aspects of Sikhism and on the Sikhs' historical memory of conflict with the power in Delhi.

As his flock grew, talk emerged of a sovereign Sikh state to be called "Khalistan," with borders approximating those of the Sikh kingdom that had existed in northwestern India at the height of Sikh power in the early nineteenth century. (That kingdom encompassed large areas of what became West Pakistan in 1947, in addition to large areas of post-1947 India, and its capital was Lahore, a city in Pakistan's Punjab province near the border with India.) Since the late 1970s Bhindranwale's small group of followers had been involved in lethal violence against heterodox Sikh sects and were also the prime suspects in murders of prominent Hindus in Punjab in the early 1980s. A somewhat sinister figure with a cult guru–like personality, he was according to some accounts patronized in those years by Congress politicians in Punjab, who saw him as a tool to divide the Akali Dal support base. After the Akali Dal agitation gathered momentum he was also patronized by senior Akali Dal leaders.

Bhindranwale turned out to be a Frankenstein's monster. He took up residence in Sikhism's holiest shrine, the Golden Temple complex in the city of Amritsar, and during 1983 and the first few months of 1984 converted the complex into an armed camp bristling with hundreds of men brandishing automatic rifles, light and medium machine guns, and even rocket launchers. In April 1983 a senior officer of the Punjab police, a Sikh, was shot dead by Bhindranwale's men as he was coming out of the Golden Temple complex after praying there. Since such large quantities of lethal weaponry could not have been procured in India, the source was probably in Pakistan. The bulk of the historical Punjab region became part of Pakistan in 1947, and Amritsar is close to the international border dividing Indian Punjab and Pakistan's Punjab province. The then ruler of Pakistan was the military dictator Zia-ul Haq, whose family roots were in eastern (Indian) Punjab. The Pakistani military had been nursing a bitter humiliation since East Pakistan had broken away with Indian support to become Bangladesh in late 1971, and the appearance of a secessionist tendency among Sikhs in India's Punjab—whose border with Pakistan saw large-scale hostilities during the wars of 1965 and 1971—presented a payback opportunity too tempting to be missed. By 1983–1984 the Pakistani military's Directorate for Inter-Services Intelligence was quite proficient in the art of crossborder assistance to insurgents in neighboring states, due to its central role in the U.S.-backed mujahideen war in Soviet-occupied Afghanistan.

As Punjab descended into anarchy and deadly attacks on the state's Hindus by militants of the Sikh zealot fringe became more frequent and indiscriminate, Jammu & Kashmir (J&K) to its north held elections to constitute the J&K state legislature and government. Jammu & Kashmir has a uniquely important and sensitive status in India's politics. J&K contains most of the territory and nearly three-fourths of the population of the preindependence princely state of the same name, whose rightful ownership has been disputed between India and Pakistan since 1947. The dispute over Kashmir has provided the principal focal point for

India-Pakistan enmity ever since, and triggered the wars of 1947–1948 and 1965. Since 1975 J&K's government had been run by its established regional party, the Jammu & Kashmir National Conference (JKNC). The JKNC's cooperation had been crucial to India's success in securing most of the disputed territory in 1947–1948. However, the party's leader, Sheikh Mohammad Abdullah, had soon come to be regarded as unreliable by Nehru's government and had been removed from office and imprisoned in 1953. The state had then been governed by a series of client politicians, installed through blatantly fraudulent state elections, who were happy to connive in New Delhi's policy of eroding the state's autonomous status and powers within the Indian Union.

In 1975 Abdullah, weakened by age and more than two decades of nearly continuous incarceration, was reinstalled as chief minister of J&K by Indira Gandhi in exchange for forsaking any ideas of "self-determination." The JKNC won a majority in J&K's legislature in subsequent state elections in 1977, primarily on the strength of its mass base in the overwhelmingly Muslim Kashmir Valley, one of the state's two populous regions. (The other populous region, Jammu, is multireligious but has an overall Hindu majority; J&K as a whole is two-thirds Muslim.) In September 1982 Abdullah—popularly known as the Sher-e-Kashmir (Lion of Kashmir)—died after passing on the mantle of leadership to his son Farooq Abdullah. Farooq led the JKNC into the state election battle of mid-1983 (unlike other states, J&K holds elections to constitute its government every six years rather than five).

Prior to this election Farooq Abdullah started to align himself and his party with opposition parties who had begun efforts to forge a nationwide anti-Congress alliance in the countdown to the national election due in late 1984, spurred by Congress's electoral debacles in Andhra Pradesh and Karnataka, the disastrous handling of the Assam agitation, and the mounting crisis in Punjab. This move seems to have deeply angered Indira Gandhi, for Farooq was breaking a tacit understanding his father had reached with her that in return for holding office in J&K the JKNC would not be party to any challenges to Congress's primacy in national politics. Indeed, in the national elections of 1977 and 1980, Congress and the JKNC had fielded candidates as allies in J&K. Indira Gandhi campaigned energetically in the 1983 state election, appealing directly to the Hindu voters of the Jammu region—among whom a current of resentment at the perceived dominance of the Kashmir Valley's Muslims in J&K's politics and government has existed since the late 1940s—with a strong message of national unity and national integration.

The strategy worked. While the JKNC again won a majority in the J&K legislature with a near-sweep of the Kashmir Valley, Congress won three-fourths of the seats in the legislature allotted to the Jammu region. Indira Gandhi's strategy of stoking polarization between J&K's Muslims and Hindus had struck a responsive chord among Jammu's Hindu electorate. In particular, the "[Hindu nationalist] BJP, with a traditional base of support in the Jammu area, lost every seat it contested" because of a "shift of Hindu BJP supporters to Congress." The pattern was repeated in elections held around the same time to the city government of Delhi, where Hindu nationalists have had a strong base since independence— mostly among Hindu partition refugees from West Pakistan and their descendants—and where there is a large Sikh population. Congress won decisively in Delhi, as "RSS cadres maintained a neutral stance . . . more *swayamsevaks* [volunteers] were clearly voting Congress."[22] The BJP was at this time led by the moderate Atal Behari Vajpayee, who had served as India's foreign minister during the Janata Party period of 1977–1979 and would go on to become the nation's prime minister at the head of a BJP-led coalition government in New Delhi from 1998 to 2004. The RSS is the Rashtriya Swayamsevak Sangh ("National Volunteer Organization"), the core of the *sangh-parivar* ("family of organizations") comprising the Hindu nationalist movement. Vajpayee had tried to moderate the BJP's strident Hindu nationalist stance. Clearly, many among the movement's traditional supporters, and other Hindus, were more attracted to Indira Gandhi's appeal to anti-Sikh and anti-Muslim sentiments.

As 1983 yielded to 1984, it became clearer that Indira Gandhi had used the J&K and Delhi elections as laboratories to hone a strategy that had the potential to command countrywide resonance in the national election due in late 1984 and thus ensure her reelection to power. Such a strategy was needed because her electoral defeat after the Emergency revealed that recourse to overtly authoritarian means to maintain power was not a viable option. The message now was that Congress was the guarantor not just of a stable national government (the slogan of 1980) but much more—that the ruling party led by Indira Gandhi was the defender of India's national unity and territorial integrity against a host of separatist and secessionist elements raising their heads in Punjab, Assam, and Kashmir. In the case of Kashmir, this portrayal of the JKNC party and government was patently unfair: this regional party accepted that J&K is a part of India, and Farooq Abdullah's attempts to coordinate with opposition parties elsewhere in the country was a manifestation of this commitment. The tarring of the Punjab and Assam agitations with the accusation of secessionism was also dubious, not least because her own policies had aggravated those problems.

Indira Gandhi had in the past proved her ingenuity in crafting a campaign theme with nationwide resonance: the Garibi Hatao ("Abolish Poverty") line of 1969–1971, targeted at India's poverty-stricken majority, that had led to a declining Congress's powerful resurgence in the 1971 national election. Now, in typically audacious style, she was experimenting with an altogether different and even more ambitious form of majoritarian populism, which appealed with increasing directness to the country's nominal Hindu majority of 80 percent—sometimes called a "census majority" because fault lines of region, ethnicity, language, and caste make the 80 percent of Indians census-classified as "Hindu" a very heterogeneous and fragmented bloc—to consolidate behind Congress against the alleged secessionist threats to the nation from an assortment of religious and ethnic minorities. It is not clear whether this strategy would have worked if Indira had lived until the national election of late 1984. At any rate, throughout 1984 dire warnings of the "antinational elements" besieging the nation with assistance from the "foreign hand"—a reference to Pakistan but possibly extending to China and the United States—were broadcast every day by state-controlled radio and television. The Union government had a national monopoly of radio and television broadcasting rights at this time.

In mid-1984, with the national election just months away, Indira Gandhi sharply escalated her strategy in both Punjab and J&K. In early June she sent units of the Indian Army to clear the Golden Temple complex in Amritsar of armed Sikh radicals. The command of the military action, codenamed "Operation Bluestar," was put in the hands of a Sikh officer, but its timing coincided with a major Sikh holy occasion, when the complex is thronged by pilgrims. Operation Bluestar turned into a bloody affair over two nights as Jarnail Singh Bhindranwale's heavily armed and fanatical followers fought back fiercely. When the fighting ended, historic buildings in the Golden Temple complex had sustained severe damage, although the central shrine escaped relatively unscathed. Bhindranwale and many of his diehards were killed in the battle, as were 83 Indian military personnel. The Sikh fatalities were officially 492—mostly militants but also some pilgrims—but may have actually been two to three times higher. A crisis of confidence in the Indian nation and the Indian Union gripped much of the Sikh community after Operation Bluestar, which many devout Sikhs saw as an act of desecration of their holiest site.

In the same month a plan hatched in New Delhi saw the fall from power of Farooq Abdullah's government in J&K, elected just one year earlier for a six-year term. Since winning election Farooq had enraged Indira Gandhi further by his leading role in conclaves convened by the non-Congress chief ministers of Andhra Pradesh, Karnataka, West Bengal, and J&K with the goal of fostering opposition alliance-making in the run-up to the national election due in late 1984. One-fourth of the JKNC's legislators broke away and formed a new government, with the support of the sizable Congress caucus in the legislature. The new government was headed by Farooq Abdullah's brother-in-law, G. M. Shah, who had nursed ambitions of inheriting Sheikh Mohammad Abdullah's mantle. All of the 12 defecting legislators were made ministers in the new J&K government. According to Farooq Abdullah, the plan was "hatched in 1 Safdarjang Road, New Delhi," the prime minister's residence, and "directed by Mrs. Gandhi."[23] This is a plausible claim. The executor of the plan in Srinagar—J&K's summer capital and the main city in the Kashmir Valley—was the state's governor, a man appointed by New Delhi just three months earlier after the previous governor reportedly refused to collude in conspiracies against a democratically elected state government.

The governors of Indian states are essentially figureheads, but with some constitutional powers to intervene in political matters. These powers were abused by Jagmohan, the handpicked governor of J&K—a man who had earned Indira Gandhi's trust as an administrator in Delhi during the Emergency a decade earlier—in dismissing Farooq Abdullah and installing the Congress-supported government. Jagmohan denied Farooq the constitutionally guaranteed right to try and prove his majority on the floor of the legislature and disregarded Farooq's appeal for fresh elections. For 72 of the first 90 days of the new government the Kashmir Valley was under curfew orders to prevent protests. The curfew was enforced by contingents of the Central Reserve Police Force (CRPF), paramilitary police under the authority of the Union home (interior) ministry, who were flown into Srinagar the night before the very thinly veiled coup d'état against democracy.

The case of J&K was not an isolated one. Two months later in August 1984, exactly the same strategy was deployed to dismiss NTR's government in Andhra Pradesh, which had been elected on a landslide with a three-fourths majority in the state legislature a year and a half earlier to a five-year term in office. A Center-appointed governor in the state capital, Hyderabad, was the executor of the plan. A groundswell of protest ensued in this southern state, as well as a nationwide outcry. Removal of

NTR proved unsustainable when the principal renegade, NTR's erstwhile finance minister, proved unable to muster anything remotely resembling a majority in the state legislature, and NTR was restored to office after a month of crisis. The episode revealed that Indira Gandhi's intolerance of democratic regional parties extended to all parts of the country. It is likely that a similar fate would have befallen the opposition government of Karnataka if the Andhra Pradesh coup had been successful.

As the American political scientist Paul Brass wrote, "relentless centralization and ruthless, unprincipled intervention by the Center in state politics have been the primary cause of the troubles in Punjab and elsewhere in India." He correctly detected "a major structural problem in the Indian system that requires a broader political solution. That problem arises from centralizing drives in a society where the predominant long-term tendencies are toward pluralism, regionalism, and decentralization."[24] The problem had existed in New Delhi since the premiership of Nehru in the 1950s—when Sheikh Abdullah was removed from office in Kashmir and an elected communist-led government was dismissed in Kerala, at the other end of the country—but attained its apogee during the last decade of Congress hegemony in India's politics, the 1980s.

On the morning of October 31, 1984, Indira Gandhi was riddled with bullets in the garden of her house in New Delhi by two Sikh members of her bodyguard detail who were motivated by a desire to take revenge for the storming of the Golden Temple complex she had ordered in June. Over the next three days about 3,000 Sikhs were murdered by mobs across northern India in retaliation. More than two-thirds of the dead were killed in Delhi, where Sikhs living in lower-middle and working-class neighborhoods were targeted by mobs instigated and led by well-known Congress politicians of the city.

Indira's son Rajiv Gandhi was sworn in as prime minister immediately after his mother's assassination, and in late December he led the Congress party to its biggest ever victory in a national election. The gruesome end of a frail 66-year-old woman who had dominated India's politics for nearly two decades deeply shocked and unnerved Indians throughout the country, and her only surviving child benefited from a nationwide "sympathy wave." In her gruesome death Indira Gandhi gave life to the "national unity and integrity" theme she had been working on for nearly two years as a political strategy for retaining power, and it was realized to an extent she could not have achieved had she lived. Congress won 415 of the 542 constituencies across the country, or 77 percent of the seats in the Lok Sabha, with 48.1 percent of the nationwide popular vote, the party's highest ever.

The only states that defied the trend were Andhra Pradesh, Assam, Punjab, J&K, and West Bengal. In Andhra Pradesh, NTR's Telugu Desam Party won massively, and just 6 of the 42 parliamentary constituencies elected Congress candidates. In Assam, the Asom Gana Parishad (Assam People's Forum), a new regional party born of the protest movement, won 7 of the 14 constituencies, while Congress got 4. In Punjab, the Akali Dal won in 7 of the 13 constituencies, and Congress prevailed in 6. In J&K, all three constituencies in the Kashmir Valley elected JKNC candidates with huge margins, while Congress won the state's other three parliamentary seats (two in the Jammu region and one in Ladakh). In West Bengal, the communist-led Left Front won 26 of the 42 constituencies and Congress got 16. Even in West Bengal, the opposition citadel was shaken as Congress quadrupled its tally of four in the 1980 national election and won 48 percent of the popular vote, its highest percentage in the state since 1957.

Elsewhere the sweep was unstoppable. In UP, Congress won 83 of the 85 constituencies, with 51 percent of the popular vote; in Bihar, 48 of 54 constituencies, with 52 percent of the vote; in Madhya Pradesh, all of the 40 constituencies with 57 percent of the vote; in Rajasthan, all of the 25 constituencies, with 53 percent of the vote; in Gujarat, 24 of the 26 constituencies, with 53 percent of the vote; in Maharashtra, 43 of the 48 constituencies, with 51 percent of the vote; in Karnataka, 24 of the 28 constituencies, with 52 percent of the vote; in Orissa, 20 of the 21 constituencies, with 58 percent of the vote. In all of these populous states in northern, western, southern, and eastern India, significant opposition parties were simply steamrolled by the Congress juggernaut. It was a result that Indira Gandhi, for all her skills and charisma, could not have dreamed of achieving in her lifetime.

Rajiv Gandhi, despite being politically inexperienced and untested—or perhaps because of it—began his five-year term as prime minister in January 1985 with a great deal of goodwill across the country. He was not only a bereaved son but a warm and personable character—unlike his mother, who in spite of her crowd-pulling charisma had an aloof personality, and his deceased younger brother Sanjay of Emergency infamy, who was known to be a thuggish individual. The fact that Rajiv was an initially reluctant politician who had chosen to stay away from the limelight until the early 1980s, preferring to lead a simple family life with his Italian wife, Sonia, and their two children, also played in his favor. He was a fresh face seemingly untainted by the Machiavellian reputations of his mother and brother. Aged just 40 when he became prime minister, he also had appeal with the younger generations.

Rajiv Gandhi did make some constructive moves. In 1985 he reached out to the student leaders of the Assam agitation and to a section of the Akali Dal leadership in Punjab. In doing so he replaced his mother's strategy of confrontation and escalation with a policy of negotiation and accommodation. "Accords" were reached in both cases. In Assam the accord between the Rajiv government and the student leaders dampened down the conflict and had the salutary effect of bringing the Asom Gana Parishad, the regional party born of the protest movement, into the democratic process—the party won state elections following the accord and formed a new government in Assam. But this co-optation was a limited palliative to this multiethnic northeastern state's complex troubles. Assam continued to be highly disturbed—it remains unsettled to this day—and by the end of the decade the United Liberation Front of Assam, the insurgent group spawned by the 1979–1985 agitation, launched an armed struggle to liberate Assam from Indian "colonialism" that peaked in the early 1990s and reappeared in the late 1990s.

The Punjab accord, which embodied some concessions by the Union government to Akali Dal demands, proved an outright failure. It was a case of too little, too late. The conflict between the Center and antigovernment Sikhs was beyond palliatives in the wake of Operation Bluestar and the killings after Indira Gandhi's assassination of several thousand innocent Sikhs in Delhi and elsewhere. Harcharan Singh Longowal, the moderate Akali Dal leader who signed the agreement with Rajiv's government, was murdered by Sikh radicals within weeks. Through the second half the 1980s Punjab was engulfed by a brutal war between armed Sikh militant groups and government forces, which included many Sikhs serving in the Punjab police. Deadly shootouts, terrorist bombings, summary executions of militant suspects, and torture were daily events in Punjab until 1992, when the militant groups were more or less eradicated.

In 1986 the Rajiv government also reached a pact with the Mizo National Front, an organization that had since the 1960s been waging an insurgency against Indian forces in an area on India's northeastern border. The Mizos are a small community of hill people. The Mizo homeland was recognized as a full state of the Indian Union, with all the institutions and powers thereof, as part of the deal, and the Mizo National Front won power in the first state elections. The Mizo accord was the only instance in which New Delhi's strategy of pacification through conciliation rather than repression proved a lasting success.

In late 1986 Rajiv Gandhi attempted to assuage simmering anger in J&K by effecting a patch-up with Farooq Abdullah, who was restored to the chief ministership of J&K pending fresh state elections in March 1987. This move backfired spectacularly. Farooq's willingness to be reinstated by New Delhi and its ruling party as arbitrarily as when they had dismissed him proved very unpopular in the Kashmir Valley, whose people had been subjected to the Center's manipulative whims ever since Sheikh Abdullah's dismissal in 1953. To make matters worse, Farooq's JKNC party and Congress fielded candidates in the new state election as allies. Public opinion in the Kashmir Valley was hostile to this alliance, and Farooq was seen as having sold out regional pride and self-respect in return for his restoration to office. A broad range of opposition groups in the Kashmir Valley came together as the Muslim United Front to fight the JKNC-Congress alliance in the state polls. The polls were egregiously rigged in the Kashmir Valley—in keeping with the tradition of fraudulent elections in J&K since the 1950s—to ensure a huge victory for the JKNC-Congress alliance and a near wipeout of the Muslim United Front. Large numbers of young Kashmiri Muslims had participated enthusiastically in the Muslim United Front election campaign, and many of these young men were then arrested, jailed, and in some cases tortured. The JKNC forfeited its remaining vestiges of credibility, and a spiral of radicalization gripped the Kashmir Valley. Angry young men went across the Line of Control to Pakistan-administered Kashmir in 1988–1989 and returned with weapons and training provided by the Pakistani military and its Directorate for Inter-Services Intelligence, which were only too happy to refocus on Kashmir—Pakistan's sacred national cause since 1947—as the Soviets withdrew from Afghanistan. By the second half of 1989 the Kashmir Valley was in ferment, and a popular uprising and armed insurgency against Indian rule erupted in early 1990.

Rajiv Gandhi's gravest and costliest political mistake was to continue the flirtation with Hindu majoritarianism—Hindu "communalism" in the Indian lexicon, denoting a bigoted mindset toward minorities in general and Muslims in particular—which his mother had strategically appealed to during her "national unity and integrity" campaigns of 1983–1984.

In October 1984, shortly before Indira Gandhi's assassination, the Vishwa Hindu Parishad (World Hindu Forum; VHP), the religious affairs wing of the Hindu nationalist sangh-parivar, launched a campaign focused on a disused sixteenth-century mosque in the small town of Ayodhya, an important Hindu pilgrimage center in eastern UP. In ancient Indian mythology Ayodhya is regarded as the birthplace of Lord Ram, a deity revered by devout Hindus, and the VHP claimed that the mosque, constructed in 1527 on the orders of Babar, the founder of the Mughal imperial dynasty that dominated most of India from Delhi through the sixteenth and seventeenth centuries, had been built on the precise site of Lord Ram's birth. This was a historically doubtful claim but carried much emotive resonance in northern India, and the VHP's call to "liberate" Ramjanambhoomi, the ancient birthplace of Ram, from its usurpation by the Babri Masjid (the "invader" Babar's mosque) was a political exercise in combative majoritarian communalism. Uttar Pradesh, where Ayodhya is situated, is India's most populous state and home to nearly a sixth of all Indians, and about 18 percent of the state's population is Muslim.

In 1985, after Rajiv Gandhi came to power, the VHP renewed its demand that a grand temple dedicated to Lord Ram be built on the site mostly occupied by the Babri Mosque. In February 1986 a judge at the district court with jurisdiction over Ayodhya issued an opinion, in response to a VHP lawsuit, that a Ram temple had existed at the site prior to the construction of the mosque. This provided some ballast to the Ramjanambhoomi agitation, and a triumphal gathering of Hindu monks and VHP activists congregated at the site to celebrate and pray before idols of Ram and his consort Sita. The Congress government of UP was an active player in the unfolding events. As an Indian journalist who witnessed the opening of the compound to the far-right activists wrote, "the [Congress] UP government . . . deliberately stepped into the controversy and took sides. The [Congress] chief minister [of UP] visited Ayodhya a few days before the [court] judgment and met VHP members. . . . On 1 February . . . a crowd of VHP supporters collected at the site. . . . This was seen as an indication by persons living there that they had advance knowledge of the [judicial] verdict. . . . A Doordarshan [state-controlled television] team too was present at the site, as if the [Union] government wished to publicize the entire event. The "victory" celebrations were filmed and broadcast on the national network [the all-India news channel, the only one at the time due to the Center's broadcasting monopoly] the same evening."[25]

This development sparked protests from Muslim community organizations across the country and particularly in northern India. They objected on the grounds that since India is a self-declared "secular state" committed to treating all religions equally and impartially, the claims articulated on behalf of one religious community should not be officially favored in a dispute. Muslim protests against the clearly emerging official slant toward Hindu communalists in the Ayodhya dispute could not be ignored by New Delhi. At the time Muslims, one-eighth of the nationwide population, comprised at least 10 percent of the electorate in nearly two-fifths of India's parliamentary constituencies (207 of 542) and over 20 percent in 81 constituencies.[26]

Indeed, the Rajiv Gandhi government soon made "a desperate bid to regain the Muslim constituency."[27] The way it attempted to placate Muslim opinion conformed to the pattern of behavior of Congress governments since independence, which preferred to neglect "the difficult business of [Muslims'] economic needs"—Muslims have levels of urban and rural poverty above the national average—and instead "concentrate on the protection of identity and religious rights."[28]

In the late 1970s Shah Bano, an elderly Muslim woman from Indore, a city in Madhya Pradesh state in north-central India, approached the courts to seek alimony from her husband, who had left her by simply saying the word *talaq* (divorce) three times, as he was allowed to do, because Muslims in India are allowed to follow the sharia (Islamic religious code) in personal and family matters. In 1986 the case ended up in India's highest judicial body, the Supreme Court in Delhi. The court invoked a code of criminal procedure enacted in 1973 that applies to members of all religious communities and ordered the former husband to pay regular maintenance to Shah Bano. The ruling was in effect based on the premise that in a secular state, in the event of a dispute the nation's laws should override the sharia in personal and family matters. The ruling led to an outcry from Muslim community organizations—led and controlled by males of a traditionalist disposition—that the constitutionally guaranteed freedom of Muslims to practice their religious code in personal and family matters was being infringed. At this point the Rajiv Gandhi government intervened in the controversy. Rajiv used his party's massive majority in Parliament to enact the "Muslim Women (Protection of Rights on Divorce) Act," which, far from providing succor to Muslim women abandoned by their husbands under the sharia, effectively nullified the Supreme Court's judgment and affirmed the Muslim traditionalists' position.

The government's action caused a national uproar. Liberal opinion was horrified, and women's rights groups were outraged. Progressive Muslims were also angered—a young, male Muslim MP elected to the Lok Sabha from UP on a Congress ticket resigned from the party in protest.

The postindependence Indian version of a secular state is distinctive in that it is not based on a formal "wall of separation" between church and state as in the Western model. The Indian model of state-secularism is defined by three key elements: (1) no state religion; (2) equal respect by the state toward all religions; and (3) extensive powers of state intervention in religious matters (a characteristic also found in another non-Western "secular state," Kemalist Turkey, where the model has been called the "control model" of state-secularism).[29] Thus Article 25 of the Indian Constitution guarantees the "right to freely profess, practice and propagate religion" but gives the government the right to "regulate and restrict" religious practices in the interests of "providing for social welfare and reform."[30] This power had been used since the 1950s to reform Hindu personal and family law on marriage, divorce, inheritance, and adoption, with the purpose of advancing the rights of women, and to undermine casteist practices, including untouchability, in the administration of Hindu shrines and temples.

The government's intervention in the Shah Bano case seemed to undermine women's rights and social reform, and that too in contravention of the judgment given by the country's highest court. This provided a powerful political cause and argument to the Hindu nationalists, who have criticized the Indian model as "pseudo-secular" since its inception for denying what they believe is the country's Hindu essence. They argued that while Congress governments had actively intervened to reform Hindu religious practices in the name of progress, the government's intervention in the Shah Bano affair showed that it was "appeasing" orthodoxy and dogmatism in the case of Muslims and thereby violating the tenet of equal treatment of all faiths. The Hindu nationalist critics further pointed out that one of the directive principles of the Indian Constitution enjoined the guardians of the secular state to strive toward the enactment of a Uniform Civil Code, which was to supersede religiously based codes of personal behavior and that Congress governments had done nothing about this for four decades. Despite its politically motivated nature, the Hindu nationalist argument about the "pseudo-secular" state and its double standard of Muslim "appeasement" found wide resonance.

In fact, the Rajiv government's roles in the Ayodhya and Shah Bano controversies amounted to pandering to—appeasing—the most obscurantist agendas being presented in the name of Hindu and Muslim rights. The main effect was to embolden Hindu nationalists and to increase the appeal of their politics, and the stage was set for a sharp escalation of Hindu-Muslim tensions. The government's conduct also exposed the hollowness of the modernist, forward-looking face the youthful prime minister had initially tried to project to the nation with catchy rhetoric about moving India toward the twenty-first century.

From mid-1987, the halfway point of his five-year term, the Rajiv Gandhi government became more and more unpopular. In April 1987 the first media reports surfaced that huge bribes ("kickbacks") had been paid by

Bofors, a Swedish arms manufacturing firm, to high-level figures in the Indian government to gain a contract to supply more than 400 155mm. artillery guns for the Indian army. The full facts of the Bofors affair remain murky and have not been conclusively established even today, but one of the alleged middlemen was Ottavio Quattrochhi, an Italian businessman who was known to be a personal friend of Rajiv and Sonia Gandhi. The Bofors scandal dogged Rajiv Gandhi until the end of his premiership in November 1989 and his death by assassination in May 1991. (The quality of the purchase is not in doubt—the Bofors howitzers performed admirably in the border war with Pakistan in a remote high-altitude zone of J&K in 1999 and are still in use by the Indian army.)

In July 1987 the ejection from Rajiv's cabinet of Vishwanath Pratap Singh, the defense minister (and former finance minister)—apparently because of his zeal while holding both posts in investigating corruption involving big business and high-level politicians—and his resignation from the Congress party provided the disparate opposition parties across India with a prominent rallying point. The impact of the V. P. Singh factor was greatest in his home state, UP, and in neighboring Bihar. As the opposition campaign led by V. P. Singh and centered on the corruption issue acquired momentum across the nation, Rajiv Gandhi became ever more beleaguered and defensive. His personal reputation was damaged by opposition slogans such as "Gali gali mein shor hai, Rajiv Gandhi chor hai" (The word in every lane and alley is, Rajiv Gandhi is a thief) and "Mr. Clean, Mr. Clean, gandhi kyun hai tope machine?" (Mr. Clean, Mr. Clean, why does the [Bofors] cannon stink?).

The prime minister's woes were compounded by a poorly judged attempt he made to end the ethnic civil war raging in neighboring Sri Lanka—the island state located off India's southeastern coastline—by sending a large Indian military force there. The Indian expeditionary force became embroiled from October 1987 in bitter fighting with ethnic Tamil guerrillas, and the disastrous involvement cost the lives of 1,155 Indian military personnel before the withdrawal of the force in March 1990. In May 1991 the militant Sri Lankan Tamil group that had fought the Indians exacted a macabre revenge when a woman member of the group detonated a bomb strapped to her body while greeting Rajiv at an election rally near Madras (Chennai), the capital of Tamil Nadu, during the midterm national election campaign of 1991. Rajiv was killed instantly, along with 14 other persons. A successful visit by the prime minister to China in late 1988 that laid the foundation for the normalization of Sino-Indian relations—disrupted ever since the Sino-Indian border war of late 1962—could not compensate for the government's litany of woes.

The crisis-ridden government resorted to crude propaganda to shore up its fading popularity. The main instrument was Doordarshan (Long-Distance Vision), the state-controlled station that held a monopoly on television broadcasting rights. By the late 1980s television was widely watched in cities and towns and had penetrated parts of rural India, so this was a powerful medium. Ever since Rajiv Gandhi—a photogenic person—had come to power, the sole state-controlled broadcaster had been lionizing his leadership and policies in excruciatingly groveling style. There was no question of discussion and analysis of his leadership and policies. Instead, Doordarshan promoted a cult of dynasty that fused Rajiv's purported virtues as a leader with a nauseatingly sycophantic narrative of his lineage. The political history of India since the 1920s was reduced in this account to the contributions of his great-grandfather Motilal Nehru (a Congress leader in northern India), his grandfather Jawaharlal Nehru, and his mother, Indira Gandhi. This propaganda went into overdrive as the government went into free fall in 1988–1989.

The harping on Rajiv's inspirational, indispensable leadership and the hereditary legitimacy of his rule looked and sounded like the output of the propaganda machine of a sultanistic autocracy. A popular joke referred to Doordarshan as "Doordharshan" (Long-Distance Rape). In August 1988, with the national election a little over a year away, the Rajiv Gandhi government launched an assault on the independent—and increasingly critical—print media by introducing an "antidefamation" bill in Parliament. The legislation was duly passed by the huge Congress majority in the Lok Sabha but subsequently dropped by the government, after prominent newspaper editors and journalists marched to Parliament in protest and a nationwide outcry ensued against the attempt to introduce Emergency-style censorship.

The basic problem bedeviling the dynastic scion's failing reign was a top-down, centralist political style and strategy at variance and in conflict with the diversity and pluralism of India's sociopolitical landscape. During his last two years in office, in search of a political plank that could turn around his fortunes and provide ballast to Congress in the national election due in late 1989, Rajiv Gandhi did try to craft a nationwide political agenda focused on people's empowerment and economic development at the grassroots level. The slogan was "Panchayati Raj" (Rule of Panchayats), a promise to establish *panchayat* structures—village-level organs of governance—across India's 600,000-plus villages as locally rooted motors of a nationwide framework of bottom-up socioeconomic development.

The trailblazers in establishing *panchayat* government had been two opposition-governed states, West Bengal and Karnataka. A year after coming to power in West Bengal, the communist-led Left Front had implemented, in 1978, *panchayat* legislation passed by the state's previous Congress government five years earlier. Elections in which political parties put up candidates were held to constitute a three-tiered *panchayat* system: *gram panchayats* (a council for a cluster of villages), *panchayat samitis* (a body at "block" or subdistrict level, the most important layer of the system), and *zilla parishads* or district councils. After the Janata Party formed the government in Karnataka in 1983, the state's new chief minister, Ramakrishna Hegde, had initiated a similar process. Its architect was Abdul Nazir Sab, who held the panchayat affairs portfolio in the state cabinet. Sab's blueprint for *panchayat* governance was implemented in Karnataka from 1985 because the president of India, a Sikh Congress politician from Punjab, picked for the largely ceremonial post because of his loyalty to Indira Gandhi, delayed granting his constitutionally required formal consent to the proposal for two years.

The West Bengal and Karnataka experiments proved popular and reasonably effective in fostering a sense of democratic participation in rural development. The *panchayat* arrangements were an equally useful tool for political parties for deepening their bases in the countryside. This was critically important to electoral prospects because in India, a predominantly agrarian country, the outcomes of both national and state elections are determined by rural voters. In West Bengal the implementation of the *panchayat* system was part of the strategy of the CPM, the dominant party of the Left Front, to achieve "a comprehensive [political] penetration of the countryside."[31] In the south, Karnataka's decentralized model was soon emulated by NTR's Telugu Desam Party government in neighboring Andhra Pradesh. NTR's government established 1,100 directly elected bodies called *mandals* at the subdistrict level across the state and aggressively promoted the participation of women, middle castes, Dalits, and Adivasis in these bodies. By contrast to these initiatives of regional parties in Karnataka, Andhra Pradesh, and West Bengal, "the Congress party had done very little for [the establishment and development of] *panchayats* in the states it controlled."[32]

When Rajiv Gandhi initiated his grand plan of nationwide Panchayati Raj beginning in late 1987, the way he went about it showed that it was part of a strategy of centralization of power in New Delhi, designed to bypass and marginalize the states and their polities. He first convened a series of workshops of district magistrates—the professional bureaucrats drawn from the Indian Administrative Service in charge of the routine administration of the country's 600 or so districts. He then called a conference of the chief secretaries of states—the chief secretary is the top bureaucrat in each state's administrative machinery—in New Delhi in July 1988. This was followed between January and April 1989 by Panchayati Raj conferences organized by the Rajiv Gandhi government in Delhi, Calcutta and Bangalore (the latter two cities being the capitals of the opposition strongholds of West Bengal and Karnataka). After the opposition government of Karnataka protested against the top-down, centrally sponsored nature of the event it was dismissed from office and Karnataka was brought under the direct rule of New Delhi. In May 1989, with the national election due in six months, the Rajiv government introduced legislation to establish Panchayati Raj across the country in the Lok Sabha.

This modus operandi

> generated grave doubts about the true intent of the Central Government. First, the [elected] State governments had been bypassed. Second, the Center had chosen to deal directly with the bureaucracy in the States, district officers and chief secretaries. Third, unprecedentedly high amounts [of funds] had been set aside for centrally sponsored schemes concerning State subjects [of governance] and arrangements made for the direct dispatch of funds to the districts and direct submission of implementation reports to the Center [New Delhi]. The Jawahar Rozgar Yojana [a nationwide employment-generation scheme named after Nehru] was one such scheme. Fourth, it seemed the Center was making use of IAS [Indian Administrative Service] officers in the States, over whom it had ultimate control, to push through its [agenda].[33]

The opposition parties across the length and breadth of the country smelled a rat and unanimously argued that the states' authority and autonomy—the basis of India's quasi-federal polity—should not be undermined in this way through central imposition. The legislation was passed in the Lok Sabha, where Congress held a three-fourths majority, but was blocked by opposition parties in Parliament's upper chamber, the Rajya Sabha (Council of States), whose members are elected by state legislatures. As the legislation involved amending India's Constitution, it needed to pass by concurrent two-thirds majorities in both chambers of Parliament, and Congress did not have a two-thirds majority in the Rajya Sabha.

With the Panchayati Raj plan stymied, the ruling party's self-described "high command"—meaning Rajiv Gandhi and his closest advisers, most of them "buddies" who had met Rajiv during his years at an elite boarding school in northern India or during his failed attempt to gain a degree at Cambridge University in the 1960s—scrambled to find an alternative strategy of nationwide resonance for the Lok Sabha election due in November 1989.

As the national election approached the Hindu communalists stepped up their agitation centered on the Babri Mosque. This rabid campaign, led by the VHP and the Bajrang Dal, a specially mobilized youth group, acquired major momentum across northern India from September 1989. Tens of thousands of people traveled to the Ayodhya site from villages and towns throughout northern India and lesser numbers from other parts of the country, carrying bricks for the proposed Ram temple. As the temple-construction movement intensified, violence against Muslims erupted in many places in northern India. The worst single outbreak was in Bhagalpur, a district in the eastern part of Bihar. Over 1,000 Muslims, mainly from a poor community of weavers, were massacred in Bhagalpur, dozens of Muslim villages were razed, and numerous local mosques and Sufi shrines were vandalized and destroyed.

Instead of confronting the lawlessness fomented by the Ramjanambhoomi movement and protecting the Muslims being attacked across northern India, Rajiv Gandhi decided to try to piggyback on the movement's momentum in a desperate bid to retain power. He kicked off the Congress party's national election campaign at Ayodhya, where he delivered a speech promising to establish *ram rajya* (the kingdom of Ram, depicted as a utopia in ancient mythology) if reelected to office. Two weeks before the election, the Congress-run Union and UP governments permitted the VHP to conduct a *shilanyas* (foundation-stone-laying ceremony) for the Ram temple at the disputed site. The Congress party then claimed that "the interests of the majority and minority communities had been successfully harmonized," and the home (interior) minister in Rajiv's cabinet is said to have suggested to the VHP that "the prime minister be allowed to lay the foundation stone."[34]

In December 1984 Congress's "national unity and integrity" campaign had paid off richly. The BJP, the political party of the Hindu nationalist movement, had been reduced to just two seats in the Lok Sabha as Congress appropriated its traditional planks of muscular Indian (read Hindu-majoritarian) nationalism and a strong central state. A large chunk of the relatively small but committed Hindu nationalist voting base in the cities and towns of northern India—comprised of "small industrialists and businessmen, traders and the lower ranks of the professions and the civil service . . . the salaried lower-middle class and shopkeepers"—had deserted to Congress.[35] Nanaji Deshmukh, a stalwart of RSS, the core organization of the Hindu nationalist movement, had publicly endorsed Rajiv Gandhi.

In November 1989 the outcome in northern India was strikingly different. The hard-line Hindu vote mobilized around the Ayodhya issue went overwhelmingly to BJP and the greater part of the moderate Hindu vote to the Janata Dal, the federated party created from secular anti-Congress groups and fronted by V. P. Singh. The Muslims in the northern states, most of whom had traditionally voted Congress, were alienated by Rajiv Gandhi's political opportunism, and many voted for the Janata Dal. Congress was heavily defeated in the states of northern India, western India (except Maharashtra), and eastern India (in West Bengal by the communist-led Left Front and in Orissa by the Janata Dal, led in the state by Biju Patnaik, a veteran regionalist politician).

The Congress tally in the Lok Sabha, comprised of 543 single-member parliamentary constituencies, collapsed spectacularly from 415 to 197 seats. V. P. Singh became the new prime minister of India, as the Janata Dal's 142-strong parliamentary contingent gained a working majority, due to outside support extended from the right by the BJP (86 MPs) and from the left by the communist-led bloc (53 MPs).

India's democracy had crossed a Rubicon.

CHAPTER TWO

The Transformation since 1990

THE FIRST four years of the post-Congress era in Indian politics were extraordinarily turbulent, indeed convulsive. The tumult of 1990–1993 was like the instability of post–World War I Italy as described by Antonio Gramsci: it was as if "all the conflicts . . . all the contradictions . . . inherent in the country's social structure" had come to "the surface with explosive force."[1]

Within days of taking office in early December 1989, the V. P. Singh government was plunged into the deepening crisis in Kashmir. Members of the Jammu and Kashmir Liberation Front, a militant proindependence group that had emerged in the Kashmir Valley in 1988–1989, kidnapped a daughter of Mufti Mohammad Sayeed, a Valley politician who had formerly been with the Congress party but had joined V. P. Singh and been appointed India's home (interior) minister in the new Union cabinet. The daughter, a trainee doctor in her twenties, was taken by the militants from a street in Srinagar, the Valley's capital city. The Jammu and Kashmir Liberation Front demanded the release from jail of five young men belonging to the group. They were released days later, amid celebrations by residents in the center of Srinagar, and the hostage was freed. The kidnap drama was a prelude to the outbreak of an uprising against Indian rule in the Kashmir Valley, which had been festering with discontent since the fraudulent J&K election of spring 1987. In January 1990, Jammu and Kashmir Liberation Front insurgents stepped up hit-and-run attacks, and huge demonstrations calling for *azaadi* (freedom) from India broke out in Srinagar and other Valley towns.

The government in New Delhi sent in paramilitary troops, who opened fire on these protests, killing hundreds. Thereafter the insurgency spread like wildfire, as thousands of young men enlisted in militant proindependence and pro-Pakistan groups. The Kashmir Valley descended into a maelstrom of violence as the insurgents' campaign met with a ferocious response by the Indian security forces. The brutal war intensified over the next few years, and the situation did not improve until 1996, when the security forces gained the upper hand over a weakening and divided insurgency.

While the unprecedented crisis in Kashmir dominated headlines in India and abroad, the United Liberation Front of Assam, a radical offshoot of the 1979–1985 Assam agitation, launched an insurgency in Assam, the largest state in India's restive northeastern border region. The United Liberation Front of Assam's slogan called for an independent Assam free of India's "colonial" domination. In 1990 and 1991 the Indian army had to undertake major counterinsurgency operations in Assam to contain the insurgents, who enjoyed significant popular support there. Meanwhile the brutal violence in Punjab, pitting the state's police and central paramilitary forces against armed Sikh militant groups, continued unabated. This conflict did not wind down until 1993, when the militants were more or less eradicated by the counterinsurgency campaign.

Although the revolts involving ethnic and ethnoreligious communities in three states on India's international borders presented serious security and political dilemmas, they did not impinge directly on the lives of the vast majority of Indians. That changed dramatically during the second half of 1990, when a festering cauldron of caste and religious tensions came to the boiling point and shook India's politics as never before since independence.

The Caste Cauldron

In August 1990 V. P. Singh announced that his government planned to implement the principal recommendation of the Backward Classes Commission, which had been set up in late 1978 by India's first non-Congress government. This five-member commission, popularly known as the Mandal Commission after the name of its chair, B. P. Mandal, a politician from Bihar, was tasked by the Janata Party government then in power in New Delhi to identify the socially and economically "backward" sectors of India's population and recommend policies for their advancement. The commission submitted its report in late 1980, by which time Indira Gandhi had returned to power. Its principal recommendation was that 27 percent of all levels of jobs in the Union government and places in institutions of higher education supported by that government be reserved for the "Other Backward Classes" (OBC): the vast and heterogeneous layer of middle castes between the forward or upper castes and the scheduled castes.

The commission argued this was fair because of the strong correlation between caste and class status in India and while the scheduled castes (SC; Dalits) had enjoyed a constitutionally mandated 15 percent of reserved places in public-sector employment and higher education since independence, no similar provision had been made for the OBC population. The commission claimed that 43.7 percent of India's population consisted of OBC Hindus and another 8.4 percent were OBC minorities (Muslim, Sikh, Christian), a grand total of 52.1 percent. This figure was criticized as methodologically dubious, calculated simply by subtracting from 100 the percentages of upper-caste Hindus (17.6 percent) claimed in an incomplete 1931 census conducted under the British—the last census to record caste identities—and the percentages of SC, scheduled tribes (ST; Adivasis), and non-Hindu religious groups, mainly Muslims, recorded by the 1971 national census (15 percent, 7.5 percent, and 16.2 percent, respectively). Moreover, it was said, "the OBC category is constitutionally and sociologically ambiguous" because of its vast diversity, "an amorphous category that includes both extremely deprived and [relatively] affluent groups." (One consequence of the V. P. Singh government's decision to implement the commission's recommendation was that Jats, a relatively prosperous farming community found in several northern states, decided to drop their claim to upper-caste (Kshatriya) status and agitate for OBC recognition in the 1990s.)[2]

Since the SC and ST, the most disadvantaged groups, were already entitled to 15 percent and 7.5 percent quotas in state employment and higher education (as well as to a similar proportion, variable across states, of constituencies reserved for them in the Lok Sabha), the implementation of the Mandal recommendation would increase the overall reserved proportion in state employment and higher education to 49.5 percent (27 percent OBC, 15 percent SC, and 7.5 percent ST).

V. P. Singh's decision to resurrect the Mandal report from the cold storage to which it had been consigned for a decade by the Indira and Rajiv governments was a profoundly political act. While Singh was himself from an upper-caste Rajput family who owned a landed estate in Uttar Pradesh, the social base of the Janata Dal—a federated party of anti-Congress factions based in the northern states that had coalesced around him—consisted disproportionately of OBC groups. In 1990 the new Janata Dal chief ministers of the two largest northern states, UP and Bihar, were both from the Yadav community, a numerous and politically assertive OBC caste. The rise of Mulayam Singh Yadav in UP and Laloo

Prasad Yadav in Bihar represented a fundamental shift in the politics of the two giant northern states that had been in the making for over two decades. The shift involved the weakening of the political dominance of upper castes and the growing political clout of intermediate caste groups included in the OBC category. The passing of Congress's hegemony in India's politics unleashed the full force of the change. In UP and Bihar, the Congress party remained disproportionately dominated by upper castes (particularly Brahmins) from independence through the late 1980s and relied on a voting base comprised of forward castes, scheduled castes, and Muslims. The OBC communities in these two states were severely underrepresented in the Congress organization and vote base and gravitated to anti-Congress political formations from the 1960s.

B. P. Mandal was himself a member of the Yadav caste and had been a Congress politician in Bihar from the early 1950s until the mid-1960s, after which he defected to a regional socialist opposition party. Four of the five members of the commission he chaired in 1979–1980 were OBC, himself included. In UP, Mulayam Yadav (born 1939) had been an activist in the same regional socialist current of northern India since the 1960s. Laloo Yadav (born 1948) joined politics as a student leader at the university in Patna, Bihar's capital city, in the early 1970s and come of age during the student-led movement against Indira Gandhi in the mid-1970s. V. P. Singh's Mandal Commission turn in 1990 was motivated by the fact that the anti-Congress social forces in UP and Bihar were rooted in a core base among OBC groups, particularly Yadavs; he sought to give national recognition to their aspiration to "social justice" (meaning upward mobility). He announced the decision in both chambers of Parliament on 7 August 1990 and highlighted it in his formal address to the nation on India's Independence Day, August 15.

From one angle, the implementation of the Mandal recommendation did not mean very much. In a country where millions seek to enter the workforce every year, the number of jobs—including clerical and menial ones—available in the Union government's administrative and bureaucratic apparatus was relatively paltry, and declining. The total number of such openings fell from 226,781 in 1985 to 204,288 in 1988. If OBC applicants had been given 27 percent of the jobs in 1988 just 55,158 persons would have benefited. However, in the India of 1990 job prospects were very different from today. The economy had been tightly controlled by the state for four decades; the private sector had been kept in check through a web of regulatory curbs imposed by the state, and foreign economic investment or activity was barely allowed. The breakdown of this system, put in place during the early years of the Nehru period, that would come amid economic crisis just a year later, and the beginning of the liberalization, deregulation, and opening up of the Indian economy from July 1991, was not yet anticipated. In a situation where the job-generating capacity of the domestic private sector was relatively limited and foreign capital nearly barred, the state employment pool was an obvious choice for job-seekers and came with the assurance of a long-term livelihood.

Moreover, OBC communities' resentment of upper-caste dominance of state employment was well founded in fact. According to the Mandal Commission, OBC caste members made up 13 percent of the "Central Services" (all grades) in 1980, as opposed to 19 percent for the SC and ST put together, some SC and ST having benefited from the long-standing job reservation policy for those of Dalit and Adivasi backgrounds (albeit mostly concentrated in low-level positions). The Mandal Commission claimed that 90 percent of Class I posts (the highest of the four grades) were held in 1980 by upper castes and only 5 percent by OBC castes.

In UP, where upper castes comprise about 20 percent of the population (and Brahmins 9 percent) the higher echelons of the bureaucracy were overwhelmingly dominated by upper castes. In 1984 upper castes held 94 percent of the principal secretary and secretary positions, the top tier, and Brahmins alone held 56 percent; 87 percent of the heads of administrative departments were from upper-caste groups. Positions in the upper ranks of the bureaucracy were coveted partly for their prestige but also because they represented lucrative opportunities for bribe-taking and other corrupt practices. In 1985, 79 percent of UP's district magistrates were upper-caste persons, including 41 percent Brahmins and 25 percent Kayasths. The district magistrate, or "collector," is the head of the district's administrative machinery, and the position has been important since the British era, when the district magistrate was the local face and representative throughout India of the centralized colonial state. The district magistrates of that era were members of the elite Indian Civil Service, which was renamed the Indian Administrative Service after independence but retained its character as well as its attraction for clever and ambitious youth. In 1984, 95 percent of the managing directors of "public sector undertakings"—large firms owned and operated by the Union government in industrial and mining sectors—located in UP were from the upper castes.[3] Not surprisingly, Uttar Pradesh emerged as a principal battleground of the Mandal Commission controversy at the beginning of the 1990s.

The V. P. Singh government's Mandal Commission announcement sparked a spate of protests among upper-caste students and youth belonging to middle- and lower-middle-income families in cities and towns across

Figure 3. A student protester against the Mandal Commission's proposal for affirmative action for "backward classes" in public-sector jobs sets himself on fire in Delhi (September 1990). AFP/GETTY IMAGES.

northern India. In September a student of Brahmin background at Delhi University set himself on fire after a nine-day hunger strike. He survived with serious burns but inspired 151 others, mostly university students, to set themselves alight in subsequent weeks. The first successful suicide—a symbolic act of sacrifice for a higher cause, known as "self-immolation"— happened within a few days of the first attempt and was committed by a young man of Rajput background. In all, 63 individuals, mostly young people, burned themselves to death. The anti–Mandal Commission agitation affected cities and towns in most parts of India, but the really intense agitation was confined to the north. Of the 58 people killed by police in the stormy autumn of 1990, 51 were in northern states. Uttar Pradesh and Bihar led the death toll, with 16 and 12 killed, respectively.[4] The ruling Janata Dal organized pro–Mandal Commission rallies in Delhi, UP, and Bihar that were addressed by top party leaders, including V. P. Singh and Sharad Yadav.

The Mandal Commission conflagration was a lesson in how emotive and polarized disputes over affirmative action can become. Both sides invoked the same argument: equality of opportunity. An American scholar of northern India's politics has written that "as a result of [a] complex of changes . . . that undermined . . . the forward castes, the demand for reservations in educational institutions and government posts by the backward classes was a signal for all-out struggle. . . . What is at issue is the age-old privileged position of the upper castes on all fronts: social status, economic strength, educational advantages, high-prestige occupations, and political power."[5] Some of the anti–Mandal Commission students and youth argued that theirs was not a defense of age-old privilege but of the equality of opportunity guaranteed to all citizens by the democratic republic, and they pointed out that many upper-caste families have modest means or even live in poverty. The pro–Mandal Commission camp countered that equality of opportunity was not possible without affirmative action, given entrenched inequities amounting to structural discrimination.

The confrontation spotlighted the deep fissures festering in the caste-ridden social structure of northern India, which democratic politics had finally brought to a head. In northern states like UP and Bihar, the political leadership and socioeconomic advantages of upper castes had not been decisively eroded until 1989–1990, primarily because of their hold on the Congress party in these states. In UP and Bihar, Congress governments held power continuously for over four decades after independence, except for relatively brief periods in the late 1960s and late 1970s. The situation was different in southern states like Tamil Nadu, where Tamil regionalists won power in 1967 on a platform of ethnolinguistic pride and implemented education and job reservations to benefit their core intermediate-caste base through the 1970s and 1980s, or Andhra Pradesh, where the rise to power in 1983 of NTR's regional party, the Telugu Desam, was rooted in a similar mix of ethnolinguistic pride and intermediate-caste support.

The visceral nature of the Mandal conflict was due to the fact that it was about not just access to material opportunities but deep-seated issues of status and respect in a hierarchically stratified society. The events of 1990 signaled the "Mandalization" of politics in northern India, particularly UP and Bihar; the term denotes the primacy of caste identities in politics and of caste-based education and job quotas becoming a permanent feature of political strategies.

Rajiv Gandhi, the leader of the opposition in the Lok Sabha, condemned the Mandal scheme as divisive and accused his bête noire, V. P. Singh, of bringing "the country to the edge of caste war."[6] But Congress had been placed on the defensive by the powerful rhetoric of "social justice" and did not undertake any political campaign against the Mandal Commission, as that would have completely alienated vast numbers of OBC voters in the north and quite possibly other parts of the country. The floundering response of Congress, a party in decline, stood in contrast to the dynamic strategy devised by a party on the ascendant in Indian politics, the Hindu nationalist Bharatiya Janata Party.

The Growth and Decline of Hindu Nationalism

While Congress nursed the shock of its November 1989 defeat, the BJP had been greatly encouraged, and its ambitions whetted, by its performance in the same national election, when it had increased its presence in the 543-member Lok Sabha from 2 to 86 members. Yet 52 of these 86 were elected from just three states (Madhya Pradesh and Rajasthan in the north and Gujarat in the west), and the BJP remained a relatively marginal force in the politics of the two largest northern states, UP and Bihar. The BJP was also weak in the rest of the country, with almost no base in southern and eastern India.

India's Hindu nationalist political party was formed in 1951, just before the country's first national election. The initiative came primarily from leaders of the Rashtriya Swayamsevak Sangh ("National Volunteer Organization"; RSS), founded in 1925. From its early years the RSS fixated on differences and conflicts between Hindus and Muslims and the threat its leaders perceived from Muslims to the security of Hindus and the territorial integrity of India, and the RSS largely abstained from the Congress-led struggle against colonial rule. The RSS was active in the Partition violence of 1947, particularly in northern India, and helped Hindu refugees from West Pakistan. Supporters of the RSS were implicated in the murder of Mahatma Gandhi in January 1948, and the organization was briefly banned. Gandhi's assassin, Nathuram Godse, was a militant Hindu activist who viewed the Mahatma's preaching of religious tolerance and amity during the Partition violence as an intolerable affront to Hindus. Godse belonged to the Chitpavan Brahmin community, a Brahmin subcaste, found in the western state of Maharashtra, that has produced many top RSS leaders since the inception of the group. From its early years the RSS cultivated a militia-like character. The sight of RSS cadres—all men, as the RSS is an all-male organization, although it has an affiliated women's wing for relatives of RSS members—dressed in khaki shorts drilling in military-style formation while brandishing sticks and waving saffron-colored flags is common in many Indian cities and towns.

The political party born of the womb of the RSS was known as the Bharatiya Jan Sangh (Indian People's Organization) until 1980, when its name was slightly changed to Bharatiya Janata Party.[7] Its ideology is based on the political concept of Hindutva, which can be translated as "being Hindu." Hindutva is often mistakenly regarded as a form of atavistic religious fundamentalism. It is in fact a very modern political formulation of Indian nationalism that developed from the 1920s alongside and in opposition to the secular and inclusive nationalist creed of the freedom movement led by the Indian National Congress.

The first proponent of this alternative ideology of Indian nationhood was Vinayak Damodar Savarkar (born 1883), a native of Maharashtra who began his political life as an anticolonial revolutionary and was jailed by the British before being pardoned and released in 1921 after signing a statement renouncing antiimperialist activity. In his seminal book, *Hindu Rashtra Darshan* (A vision of the Hindu state), Savarkar, who was atheist, wrote: "The concept of 'Hindutva' is more comprehensive than 'Hinduism.' It is to draw pointed attention to this distinction that I coined the word . . . Hinduism concerns the religious systems of the Hindus, their theology and dogma. But this is precisely a matter that [we] leave entirely to individual or group conscience and faith. . . . 'Hindutva' refers not only to the religious aspect but comprehends [the Hindu nation's] cultural, linguistic, social and political aspects as well." Savarkar argued that "common affinities—cultural, religious, historical, linguistic and racial—[have] through countless centuries of association and assimilation molded us into a homogenous and organic Nation and . . . induced a will to lead a corporate and common National Life. The Hindus are an organic National Being." Thus the "Hindustan of tomorrow must be . . . a unitarian nation from Kashmir to Rameshwaram [on India's southern tip], from Sind to Assam," and should be a "centralized state."[8] Savarkar was clear that while most non-Hindu religious communities could be assimilated into this ideal of a Hindu nation and state, the subcontinent's Muslims could not. He believed that their roots and major holy sites lay not in India but in the Middle East and they were like a foreign organism in the organic national body that he exalted.

The Hindutva ideology fits the Indian scholar Ashis Nandy's category of "religion as ideology," which he distinguishes from "religion as faith." While the latter is "definitionally non-monolithic and operationally plural," the former denotes "religion as a sub-national, national or cross-national identifier of populations contesting for . . . political or socioeconomic interests"; it is an "ideological principle useful for political mobilization," to "homogenize co-believers into proper political formations."[9]

Savarkar's vision was built on and elaborated by Madhav Sadashiv Golwalkar, another Maharashtrian, who served as the RSS *sarsanghchalak* (supreme director) from 1940 until his death in 1973. Golwalkar is revered as *shri guruji* (master-teacher) by the postindependence generations of Bharatiya Jan Sangh and BJP leaders, almost all of whom had their political socialization in the RSS. In his magnum opus, *Bunch of Thoughts,* Golwalkar wrote: "the most important step will be to bury for good all talk of a federal structure . . . [and] to sweep away the existence of all autonomous and semi-autonomous states within Bharat [India] and proclaim 'One Country, One State, One Legislature, One Executive' with no trace of fragmentational [*sic*], regional, sectarian, linguistic or other types of pride being given scope for playing havoc with our integrated harmony. . . . Let the Constitution be redrafted, so as to establish this Unitary form of Government."[10] It is not surprising that the RSS and the Bharatiya Jan Sangh strongly supported Nehru's attempt in the early 1950s to prevent the reorganization of India as a union of autonomous ethnolinguistic states; his preference for a powerful central state ruling over administrative zones was very much to their taste. The Hindu nationalists were also avid supporters of the efforts in the 1950s and 1960s of Congress politicians and factions based in northern India to foist Hindi on India as the sole national and official language, although Hindi and its dialects is the mother tongue of at most 40 percent of Indians, almost all of whom live in northern India.

On the caste system and its oppressions and inequities, Golwalkar wrote that while in the twentieth century "the caste system has degenerated beyond all recognition," it has "in fact served as a great bond of social cohesion for thousands of years of our glorious national life."[11] The dismissal of internal cleavages was all-encompassing. Savarkar declared that "the interests of both capital and labor will be subordinated to the interests of the Nation as a whole" and that the "same principle" would apply to landlord and peasant-tiller in the agrarian economy.[12] An RSS publication of the late 1980s spoke of how the labor wing of the Hindu nationalist *sangh-parivar* ("family of organizations") "rejects the theory of class conflict" as well as the "idea of collective bargaining by workers" and instead of encouraging a "separatist labor consciousness" works on the basis of the concept of "the industrial family" in which "the capitalist, the laborer and the managerial staff" coexist in integrated harmony. The farmers' wing is said to operate on the same premise, thereby "eliminating class conflict and other socially self-destructive propaganda," and the student wing too is supposed to foster "integrated harmony" in colleges and universities.[13]

The grand ideological vision of Hindu nationalism—the Indian ana-logue of the fascist movements of interwar Europe—contrasted most unfavorably with the marginality of this brand of politics in postinde-pendence India's democracy. Until late 1989 the high point of the Hindu nationalist Bharatiya Jan Sangh's electoral performance was in the na-tional election of 1967, when it gained 9.4 percent of the nationwide vote and won 35 of the 520 constituencies comprising the Lok Sabha. The advance was spatially limited to northern India—all of these 35 con-stituencies were located there (12 in UP, 10 in Madhya Pradesh, 6 in Delhi, 3 in Rajasthan, and 1 each in Bihar, Punjab, Haryana, and Chan-digarh, the shared capital city of Punjab and Haryana). While the Bharatiya Jan Sangh contested 251 constituencies across the country, 80 percent of its nationwide vote came from northern India. Moreover, even this base was socially limited. The Bharatiya Jan Sangh wins were over-whelmingly in urban constituencies, and its core vote in them came from a class of petty shopkeepers and traders known colloquially as *baniyas*.[14] A decade later Bharatiya Jan Sangh was one constituent of the Janata Party, the opposition coalition that won a parliamentary majority in the post-Emergency national election of 1977 and whose government im-ploded in personal and factional feuds in 1979, enabling Indira Gandhi's return to power. In the December 1984 national election, the BJP (name slightly changed from Bharatiya Jan Sangh) did very poorly. It contested 229 of the 543 Lok Sabha constituencies and won in just 2; its share of the nationwide vote was 7.4 percent.

In short, the organic, monolithic "Hindu nation" encompassing 80 percent of India's people on which the Bharatiya Jan Sangh/BJP premised its politics appeared to exist "to a large extent within the party's imagi-nation."[15] The BJP did well as part of the coordinated opposition chal-lenge to Congress in November 1989, but the spatial and social limits of its base remained; 62 of the 86 BJP MPs were elected from just four states in northern and western India (Madhya Pradesh, Rajasthan, Guja-rat, and Maharashtra; another four seats were won in Delhi) and dispro-portionately from urban or partly urban constituencies. The party re-mained a marginal force in the giant northern states of UP and Bihar and very weak throughout southern and eastern India.

Nonetheless, the Bharatiya Jan Sangh/BJP had always fancied itself the national alternative to Congress, and that ambition was whetted by its results in the national election of November 1989, its best performance by far since independence. Eager to break out and expand the BJP base across the nation in the wake of Congress's decline by propagating the message of "Hindu unity," the legatees of the ideological tradition of

Savarkar and Golwalkar were placed in a terrible bind by the eruption of the Mandal Commission furor. This conflict, by pitting Hindu caste groups against each other, threatened to end any prospect of uniting Hindus around the ideology of Hindutva. The RSS was especially horrified, as it had always opposed caste-based reservation policies. But coming out openly against the Mandal Commission was not an option—that would antagonize huge numbers of Hindus, particularly the OBC communities.

The Hindu nationalist camp rapidly devised a counter-strategy. From 1984 to 1989, the Ram *mandir* (temple) agitation had been spearheaded by the VHP, the *sangh-parivar*'s organization dealing with religious matters, with the help of the Bajrang Dal (Monkey Brigade; named after the monkey-god Hanuman, Ram's acolyte), a lumpen youth group specially raised for the Ayodhya campaign. Now the BJP stepped to the forefront. On September 25, 1990, Lal Krishna (L. K.) Advani, one of the party's two top leaders, got on a minibus decorated to resemble a *rath* (ancient chariot) and set out for Ayodhya from Somnath, a place in the western state of Gujarat. Somnath is the site of a famous Hindu temple that was repeatedly vandalized or destroyed by marauding Muslim conquerors between the eighth and eighteenth centuries. The temple was repeatedly rebuilt by Hindu rulers, and the ruins underwent a politically controversial restoration—initiated by Nehru's home (interior) minister Vallabhbhai Patel, a conservative Congress leader from Gujarat—shortly after independence.

From Somnath, Advani's bus-chariot traversed through the heartland states of northern India for a month, to raise Hindu consciousness and foster Hindu unity in the cause of "liberating" Ramjanambhoomi (the birthplace of Ram) and building a grand temple dedicated to Ram on the Ayodhya site, mostly occupied since 1527 by the Babri Mosque. The *rath yatra* (journey by chariot) evoked an enthusiastic response en route, and emotionally charged crowds gathered as it passed. The chariot excursion also triggered serious communal violence between Hindus and Muslims in several states. On October 23, a week away from his destination, Advani was arrested by police while riding through Bihar, on the orders of the state's Janata Dal chief minister, Laloo Yadav, himself a major symbol of the political rise of OBC communities in northern India. A week later thousands of militant Hindu activists attempted to storm the Babri Mosque in Ayodhya. The Janata Dal chief minister of UP, Mulayam Yadav, another prominent OBC politician, ordered the state police to open fire to disperse the mob, and several dozen were killed (the precise number is disputed). He was referred to for many years afterward as "Mullah Mulayam" by Hindu nationalists in UP.

Within days the BJP withdrew its support from the Janata Dal–led government in New Delhi, and V. P. Singh resigned, having lost his working majority in Parliament. Chandra Shekhar, a onetime left-wing Congress leader turned opposition politician from eastern UP who was resentful of V. P. Singh's meteoric rise to the top job, subsequently formed a rickety government consisting of a dissident bloc of Janata Dal MPs, which was propped up by opportunistic outside support from Rajiv Gandhi's 197 Congress MPs. It was clear that this was no more than a stopgap arrangement and that a midterm national election was imminent. Within months the Congress party withdrew its support, and a conflict-racked India went to the polls in several phases between May 20 and June 15, 1991.

The supplanting—at least superficially—of explosive caste tensions by communal violence directed at the Muslim minority had had a recent precedent. In Gujarat in 1985, after the state's Congress government had tried to sharply increase the quota in its higher education institutions and administrative apparatus reserved for OBC castes, violent upper-caste protests against the move had initially targeted public buildings and transport but quickly turned into deadly attacks on the state's Muslim minority, especially in Ahmedabad, the state's largest city.[16] This episode was crucial in the BJP's rise to become a significant party—with a solid backbone of upper-caste support—in Gujarat in the second half of the 1980s and its subsequent rise to power in Gujarat in the mid-1990s.

In their strident anti-Muslim campaign centered on the Ayodhya issue, the Hindu nationalists had an additional weapon. This was the rapidly worsening situation in Jammu & Kashmir, where an uprising and insurgency against Indian authority had broken out in the overwhelmingly Muslim Kashmir Valley in early 1990. The Hindu nationalists constantly played on this as an additional example of Muslim perfidy—that Kashmiri Muslims were attempting to secede from India, to inflict a "second partition"—and that, too, in collusion with Pakistan. The Hindu nationalists particularly focused on the exodus of the bulk of the Kashmir Valley's tiny Hindu minority (Kashmiri Pandits) from there during the first few months of the uprising. The *sangh-parivar*'s emphasis on Kashmir and the Pandit issue touched a chord in India's urban middle classes.

The lengths to which the Hindu nationalists were prepared to go to demonize Muslims in pursuing power in the early 1990s reflected the pathological hatred "Guruji" Golwalkar expressed in a book he published in the late 1930s, early in his life and political career (and before the emergence of the demand for Pakistan in 1940): "the non-Hindu people of Hindustan [India] must either adopt Hindu culture and language [*sic*], must learn and respect and hold in reverence the Hindu religion, must entertain no idea but glorification of the Hindu race [*sic*] and culture. . . . In a word they must cease to be foreigners . . . or [they] may stay in the country, wholly subordinated to the Hindu nation, claiming nothing, deserving no privileges, far less any preferential treatment—not even citizens' rights."[17] Muslims were by far the largest "non-Hindu people" of India, comprising over a quarter of the population. Golwalkar, the top RSS leader from 1940 to 1973, admired the "race spirit" of Nazi Germany, but he is also on record decrying "Christian" atrocities on Jews through Europe's history and later voiced strong support for the Jewish state born in 1948 in the predominantly Muslim Arab Middle East.

The BJP increased its representation in the Lok Sabha to 120 seats (from 86) in the mid-1991 national election. The party achieved a big breakthrough in Uttar Pradesh, the home state of the Ayodhya agitation, where it won 51 of the 85 constituencies.[18] However, the popular vote in UP was not a Hindutva landslide—the BJP won just under 33 percent of the ballots. The party benefited, as Congress had in the past, from the "first-past-the-post" electoral system in single-member constituencies and from the division of the non-BJP vote among two Janata Dal factions (21 percent and 11 percent, respectively, together almost equal to the BJP vote) and Congress (18 percent). Nonetheless, there had been a major surge in BJP support in UP. The main source of this surge was a large-scale defection of upper-caste voters—the social groups threatened and enraged by the Mandal Commission issue—from Congress to the BJP. Congress's vote in UP fell precipitously, from 32 percent in late 1989 to 18 percent in mid-1991.

In simultaneous state elections in UP, the BJP won a majority in the state legislature, with a similar plurality of the popular vote, and Kalyan Singh, a BJP leader from an OBC caste (Lodh) was made the chief minister. In the nationwide context, BJP actually lost ground in seats compared to 1989—it won 34 more seats in the Lok Sabha (120 as opposed to 86), but the gains were concentrated in UP, where the party won 51 constituencies, as opposed to 8 in 1989.

But by other criteria the BJP advance was striking, even spectacular. The party had contested 468 of the 543 Lok Sabha constituencies—more than double the number it had contested in 1989 or 1984—and won 20.1 percent of the nationwide vote. The decision to put up candidates across the length and breadth of the country was indicative of the BJP's ambition to emerge as a truly national party that could rival and then displace the weakening Congress. In other words, the Hindu nationalists believed the time had finally come for their emergence as the new pivot and hegemon of India's politics and that a BJP-ruled India was within reach. This ambition was encouraged not just by the big breakthrough in UP, India's most populous state, but by huge increases in the BJP vote in states outside northern India.

In 1989 the BJP had polled 1.7 percent of the popular vote in West Bengal and 2.6 percent in Karnataka. In 1991 the party got 11.7 percent in West Bengal, a sevenfold increase, and 28.8 percent in Karnataka, an elevenfold increase. To be sure, the party contested many more constituencies in these two states than before—it fielded candidates in all of West Bengal's 42 constituencies and Karnataka's 28—and state-specific factors at work in both West Bengal and Karnataka partly explain the BJP's surge. Yet the Ramjanambhoomi campaign and BJP's aggressive posturing as India's true nationalist party also had a major impact. For the first time, the party of Hindutva gained a significant vote share in major states outside northern India. The votes did not translate into many seats in Parliament—the BJP won none of West Bengal's 42 constituencies and only four of Karnataka's 28—but it seemed that the Hindu nationalists were at last breaking out of the geographic and social confines of their northern bases. The fruits of the national-unitarian message with strong Hindu majoritarian overtones, sown by Indira Gandhi a decade earlier and indulged by her son's government, were being reaped by the BJP.

Unsurprisingly, and egged on by RSS mentors, the BJP kept promoting its openly Hindu communalist variant of that message. In January 1992 the party's national president, Murli Manohar Joshi, a Brahmin from UP, undertook his own *yatra*—to Kashmir to raise the national flag in the center of Srinagar, the capital of the Kashmir Valley, on India's Republic Day (January 26, the date the republic was declared in 1950). At the time, Srinagar was a war zone and teemed with Kashmiri Muslim insurgents seeking secession from India, so this was a high-voltage demonstration of the BJP's muscular nationalist credentials.

The incendiary apogee of Hindutva mobilization occurred toward the end of 1992. On December 6, 1992, a huge mob of Hindutva activists stormed the Babri Mosque in Ayodhya and demolished it in a frenzied attack lasting several hours, as UP state police and troopers of Union paramilitary forces assigned to guard the disputed site looked on.[19] Advani, Joshi, and other senior BJP leaders were present in the town—the notable absentee was the party's moderate figure, Atal Behari Vajpayee, who had kept aloof from the Ayodhya campaign—and watched the demolition with thrilled expressions on their faces. Communal violence erupted in cities and towns across India in the aftermath, and several thousand people were killed, mostly Muslims. The worst single outbreak

Figure 4.   Hindu nationalist militants attack the Babri Mosque in Ayodhya in Uttar Pradesh (December 1992). AFP/GETTY IMAGES.

occurred in Bombay (Mumbai), India's leading center of commerce, in January 1993. There members of the Shiv Sena, a thuggish far-right regional party allied to the BJP, went on a rampage against the city's Muslims in collusion with elements of the police force. Muslim elements of the Mumbai underworld with links to the Pakistani military's Directorate for Inter-Services Intelligence retaliated two months later by exploding a string of car bombs at prominent public places in the city, killing 257 people.

For a few months it seemed that India was teetering on the brink of anarchy. After the demolition of the mosque the Congress government, precariously in power in New Delhi, acted to dismiss the BJP state governments in UP, Madhya Pradesh, Rajasthan, and Himachal Pradesh (a small northern state), and these states were placed under temporary central rule pending fresh state elections.

Congress had managed to regain power at the Center in June 1991, but only just. It won 232 of the 543 seats in the Lok Sabha, 40 short of a parliamentary majority. The tally was better than the 197 constituencies the party won in November 1989, but Congress's share of the nationwide vote slipped further, from 39.5 percent to 36.5 percent. The party would have fared worse had it not benefited from a sympathy factor—ranging from mild to moderate across states—after the grisly assassination of Rajiv Gandhi on May 21, 1991. Most of the country went to the polls in several phases after this date, and the election was completed on June 15, 1991. That the horrific scenes of Rajiv's mutilated body lying in pools of blood at the assassination site near the city of Madras (now Chennai), broadcast nationwide on television and splashed on newspaper front pages, did not trigger a nationwide tidal wave of sympathy and lead to a Congress landslide, as happened in December 1984 after Indira Gandhi's assassination, revealed both the waning appeal of the Nehru-Gandhi dynasty and the tectonic churning that had taken place in India's politics between 1989 and 1991.

As the single largest party in a "hung" Parliament, Congress formed a minority government, and P. V. Narasimha Rao, a veteran Congress politician from Andhra Pradesh who had served in Indira Gandhi's 1980–1984 cabinet as foreign minister and briefly as home (interior) minister, emerged from semiretirement to become prime minister. He was India's first prime minister from the south—specifically the Telangana region of Andhra Pradesh—and only the second Congress prime minister since independence who was not from the Nehru-Gandhi family. (The other, Lal Bahadur Shastri, from UP, served briefly from June 1964 until his death in January 1966; so India was ruled by Nehru, his daughter, and her son for 38 of the 42 years, 1947–1989, of Congress's hegemonic era in India's democracy.)

Narasimha Rao was a shrewd and seasoned politician whose decades of political and administrative experience at the state (Andhra) and national levels stood in contrast to the callowness of Rajiv Gandhi, whose promise as an Indian Camelot was exposed as hollow within a few years. But in the twilight of his five-decade political career, it was beyond Narasimha Rao's ability to stem the unfolding transformation of India's democracy in the post-Congress era. His minority government lasted for five years, primarily because none across India's political spectrum wanted another midterm national election—except perhaps the BJP—and it was not possible for the BJP, with its 120 MPs in the 543-member Lok Sabha, to topple Rao's government without the support of nearly all the other non-Congress parties represented in Parliament.

Immediately on assuming office, Narasimha Rao's government was confronted with an economic crisis whose gravity was unprecedented in independent India. The economic system dominated and regulated by the state, established in the early years of the Nehru period, was on the verge of collapse after four decades. The chief symptom was, in the succinct summary of a retired officer of the Indian Administrative Service,

> A severe balance of payments crisis. Although precipitated by two years of political instability (1989–1991) and the [first] Gulf War (1990–1991) the crisis was the cumulative result of economic management in the 1980s. Indeed its underlying causes extended to policies pursued over a much longer period. During the 1980s fiscal and balance of payments deficits had grown to unsustainable levels due to a variety of factors, domestic and external, beginning with the second oil price increase of 1979. When the crisis erupted in the first half of 1991 inflation was running high, the external solvency of India was at rock-bottom, investor confidence had ebbed away and fiscal deficits were accelerating out of control.[20]

On July 24, 1991, Narasimha Rao initiated a process of far-reaching reform of India's long moribund and now collapsing economy. His chief point man was Manmohan Singh, an economist and technocrat of Sikh background whom he appointed finance minister after his first choice, I. G. Patel, a former governor of India's central bank who had just returned to India after serving from 1984 to 1990 as the director of the London School of Economics and Political Science, declined the role and chose instead to retire to Gujarat, his home state. The reforms

> comprised a three-part strategy. To pull back the external account from the red, the first was a set of emergency measures which included a strong dose of devaluation [of the rupee] and resort to the IMF and the World Bank [for bailout loans to avert an imminent sovereign default]. The second was a macro-economic stabilization program addressed to curtailing demand through fiscal, monetary and exchange-rate policies. The third, running concurrently with the second, consisted of comprehensive policy reforms over a wide front: policies relating to international trade and industrial investment, domestic and foreign; fiscal, monetary and exchange-rate policies; adjustments to administered prices; tax reforms; financial sector reforms; restructuring of public sector enterprises; labor market policies, including the institution of safety nets; and protection of outlays on basic social services in order to cushion the impact of adjustment on the poor.[21]

The first and second parts of the program were successfully completed during Narasimha Rao's term in office (1991–1996). The third part, marked by incremental and halting progress, remains unfinished business two decades later.

Two decades have passed since the peak of the Mandal Commission conflict, the demolition of the Babri Mosque, and the launch of India's economic reforms. During these two decades the defining feature of India's democracy in the early twenty-first century—the regionalization of the nation's political landscape—has spread and deepened. For nearly five decades before 1996, India was governed by single-party governments at the Center. For all but two and half years in the late 1970s these governments were those of the Congress party. Even that sole exception was a single-party government with a clear parliamentary majority, although in an informal sense the Janata Party government of 1977–1979 might be regarded as India's first episode of coalition government, because the Janata Party was an agglomeration of anti-Congress parties based mostly in northern India.

Since 1996 India has seen nothing but coalition governments of polyglot composition in New Delhi. The long era of single-party rule effectively ended in November 1989, and by the mid-1990s it became clear that the process of pluralization of India's politics was an accelerating and irreversible fact. It is extremely unlikely that the world's largest democracy will again be governed by one dominant party at any time in the foreseeable future. Instead, the rainbow coalitions that have become the norm in New Delhi will endure in shifting permutations and combinations, and the future of India's democracy will be defined by regionalization and regionalism.

In a sense this can be regarded as a natural state of affairs—if India's social landscape is dizzyingly complex and heterogeneous, why should its polity be any different? The legitimacy to govern the nation that the Congress party inherited from its stewardship of the struggle for political freedom and sovereignty finally petered out in the late 1980s. The BJP's attempt to supplant Congress as India's dominant party and construct a new formula for hegemonic rule around Hindu majoritarianism hit the ceiling of possibility with a sharp and bruising bump by the second half of the 1990s, for the simple reason that no stable, politically mobilizable majority based solely on that formula exists in India or indeed in any state of India.

The transformation of India's democracy in the post-Congress era can be seen instead as a uniquely Indian and contemporary variant of the concept of the "democratic revolution" that the French thinker Alexis de Tocqueville coined in his 1830s classic, *Democracy in America,* after his travels in the United States. In this two-volume work, described accurately by Thomas Blom Hansen, a scholar of contemporary India, as "a parable of modern mass politics," Tocqueville argued that the democratic revolution signaled the end of "the possibility of power ever [again] being legitimate, as in a pre-modern age, [by] successfully presenting itself as a divinely sanctioned [or] self-evident general interest embodying the unity of society and defining its boundaries." Tocqueville described the democratic revolution as "a process," replacing "earlier . . . certainties," and one "through which all the founding elements of pre-modern societies—the divine legitimacy of power, the naturalness of hierarchy, the fatalism of the masses—gradually came to be questioned and undermined by the new revolutionary creed of democracy, the belief in freedom and equality."[22]

Congress resisted coming to terms with the new realities of Indian politics for nearly 15 years after its historic displacement from hegemony in November 1989. In 2004, after losing three consecutive national elections and being shut out of the corridors of power in New Delhi for eight years, Congress finally accepted that making electoral alliances with regional parties representing a variety of social groups and spatially defined communities across the nation was unavoidable. But the top leadership of the ex-hegemon live in nostalgia for the pre-1989 era, and their accommodation of the regionalized and plural character of contemporary India's political landscape is fundamentally grudging and reluctant. This mindset reflects a continuing attachment to an obsolete and unviable model of centralized rule and top-down governance. Ironically, it was the BJP—the standard-bearer of the ideology of a monolithic Indian nation organically united by Hindutva—who proved much quicker to recognize and adapt to the centrifugal dynamics of India's politics in the post-1989 era.

The BJP's journey from illusion to reality started in November 1993, when elections were held to constitute new governments in Uttar Pradesh, Madhya Pradesh, Rajasthan, and Himachal Pradesh, all in northern India. The BJP governments of these states had been dismissed and the states brought under temporary central rule after the demolition of the Babri Mosque in December 1992. The BJP had won two-thirds majorities in the legislative assemblies of Madhya Pradesh and Himachal Pradesh in 1990 and a simple majority in that of UP in 1991. In Rajasthan the party had since 1990 been the dominant partner in a coalition government with the Janata Dal, and the coalition had a two-thirds majority in the state legislature. Uttar Pradesh and Madhya Pradesh were large states with 85 and 40 seats in the Lok Sabha, Rajasthan was a middle-sized state with 25 seats, and Himachal Pradesh was a small state with four seats in Parliament. Since the autumn of 1990 the Hindutva movement's Ayodhya campaign had had a major impact in all these states, and the BJP was expected to additionally profit in the November 1993 elections from the fact that its elected governments in these states had been dismissed by the action of the Center's Congress government after the demolition of the mosque.

When the results came in, the BJP's expectations were confounded. The party was decisively defeated by Congress in Madhya Pradesh, as well as in Himachal Pradesh. In UP, the key battleground, the BJP lost its majority in the legislature, and although it emerged as the single largest party in a hung (fractured) assembly, it was kept out of power by an alliance of two powerful regional parties—the Samajwadi Party (Socialist Party; SP) and the Bahujan Samaj Party (Party of the Social Majority; BSP)—whose coalition government was supported by small blocs of Janata Dal and Congress legislators.

The SP was led by Mulayam Singh Yadav, the OBC politician who, as UP's Janata Dal chief minister in October 1990, had ordered the state police to fire on the Hindutva activists attempting to storm the site of the Babri Mosque. In October 1992 he launched the SP as a distinct political party in UP, and it acquired mass support from his own OBC community (Yadavs) and from the 18 percent Muslim component of the state's electorate. The BSP was formed in 1984 to provide an autonomous political voice to the scheduled castes (erstwhile "untouchables," now known as Dalits or "the oppressed"), a segment that in UP and most other states consistently voted for Congress until the 1980s. In the 1990s the BSP gained mass support among the 21–22 percent Dalit electorate of UP. The founder of the BSP was the veteran Dalit activist Kanshi Ram, and the party's initial supporters came from among Dalits who had benefited from jobs reserved for the SC in state employment. The driving force of the BSP's rise among the Dalit masses of rural UP—most of whom are landless laborers—was Mayawati, a young woman born in 1956 into the *chamar* subcaste of the Dalit community, who was personally recruited into Dalit politics in the late 1970s by Kanshi Ram. The daughter of an illiterate mother and a father who worked as a clerk in the Union government's posts and telegraphs service, Mayawati gave up her dream of becoming an officer of the elite (and Brahmin-dominated) Indian Administrative Service to follow Kanshi Ram into Dalit and BSP politics. Although BSP was originally conceived as a national party geared to Dalit assertion and empowerment across India, it succeeded in developing a mass base only in UP, thanks in large part to the charisma and commitment of Mayawati, who is known as Behenji (respected sister) to her supporters.[23]

The Hindu nationalists were also unable to win an outright majority in the legislature of Rajasthan, where—as in Madhya Pradesh—the BJP had developed a strong social base and organizational presence even before the Ayodhya campaign. Congress put up a strong fight in Rajasthan, and the Hindu nationalist victory was by points rather than knockout;

the BJP fell marginally short of a majority in Rajasthan and was able to form a state government that lasted its full five-year term. The only election in November 1993 that the BJP won decisively was to a new legislative body established for urban Delhi and its immediate hinterland.

The lesson was clear: the Hindutva card's appeal was both limited and transient and could not guarantee BJP success even in northern India. In Maharashtra, the populous state in western India that accounts for 48 seats in the Lok Sabha, the BJP came to power after state elections in February 1995 but as a junior partner of the regional Shiv Sena party, a nativist, "son-of-the-soil" party with a base among the state's Marathi-speaking lower-middle and working classes. This was an important advance for BJP because Maharashtra had been a Congress stronghold since independence, but the BJP's success was qualified by its second-fiddle status to a maverick regional party and rendered tenuous by the fact that the BJP–Shiv Sena alliance won just 29 percent of the statewide vote, fell marginally short of a majority in the Maharashtra legislature, and was compelled to form a government with support from legislators elected as independent (no party affiliation) candidates.

Of the two nonnorthern states where BJP had made impressive gains in the popular vote in the midterm national election of mid-1991, Karnataka in the south and West Bengal in the east, the party was able to hold on to a sizable base in Karnataka but was not able to win power in the state until 2008 (when it narrowly emerged in first place in a three-cornered contest with Congress and the Janata Dal-Secular, a regional party). In West Bengal the BJP regressed back into marginality. In Uttar Pradesh, BJP remained the single largest party through the 1990s, but its primacy was relative, based on a one-third share of the popular vote. Even this relative primacy waned in the late 1990s; in the autumn 1999 national midterm election, the BJP's vote in UP slipped by a few percentage points, and the party was able to win only in only 29 of the state's 85 constituencies, compared to 57 in the midterm national election of early 1998. Thereafter the decline continued, and in the new century the BJP was decisively relegated to third place in the state behind the two regional parties, Mulayam Yadav's SP and Mayawati's BSP.

The complexity and fluidity of politics in India's major states put paid to the ambition the BJP harbored during the first half of the 1990s of emerging as the new hegemon of India's politics.

The outcome of the national election of April–May 1996 confirmed the trends of Congress decline and BJP stagnation. Congress contested 529 of the 543 constituencies and won in just 140, a drastic fall from the 232 it had won in 1991. The party's share of the nationwide popular vote crashed by nearly eight percentage points, from 36.5 percent in 1991 to 28.8 percent. In as many as 127 constituencies, Congress candidates obtained under one-tenth of the polled votes.

The BJP fielded candidates in 471 constituencies, the highest number it has ever contested in any Lok Sabha election till today. It won in 161 constituencies, up from 120 in 1991. But the fact that the party had negligible support in vast swathes of the country was revealed by the fact that BJP candidates garnered less than one-tenth of the vote in a staggering 180 constituencies. The nationwide BJP vote was 20.3 percent. This was about the same as in 1991, albeit beefed up slightly by seat-sharing alliances that BJP struck with regional parties in two populous states: the Samata Party (Equality Party), a faction of the Janata Dal, in Bihar, and Shiv Sena in Maharashtra. (In addition, BJP allied with a breakaway Congress group in the small northern state of Haryana.) By contrast, Congress's only state-level seat-sharing alliance—the long-standing tie-up with the Anna Dravida Munnetra Kazhagam (Anna's Dravidian Progress Party; ADMK), the ruling party in Tamil Nadu since 1977—came a cropper. Most of the Congress party in Tamil Nadu revolted against the alliance with the ADMK, whose government in the state had become very unpopular, and formed a breakaway regionalist Congress party that ran in the election in alliance with the Dravida Munnetra Kazhagam, the state's main opposition party and the ADMK's regional rival. This alliance swept the polls in Tamil Nadu.

The 1996 results were significant for two reasons. First, the only two parties that could plausibly claim to have something resembling a nationwide profile and base—Congress and to a lesser extent the BJP—together polled under half, 49 percent, of the nationwide popular vote. Thus over half the electorate voted for parties that were either explicitly or effectively regional. (An example of the latter was the largest communist party, the CPM, with a base limited to West Bengal, Kerala, and Tripura, a tiny state in northeastern India.) In short, the regionalization of Indian politics was deepening. Second, the BJP, as the single largest party in a hung Parliament, was given the first chance by the president of India to try and form a government. The BJP government, headed by the moderate politician Atal Behari Vajpayee, resigned after 13 days in office because there was no way it could muster the 272 MPs required for a parliamentary majority. (The party had 161 MPs and its three allied parties in Maharashtra, Bihar, and Haryana another 24.) From this time, the BJP gradually toned down its Hindutva-heavy politics and moved toward a strategy of forging alliances with regional parties, based on a pragmatic recognition of its own limits and the deepening regionalization of India's political landscape.

Regionalization

In 1996–1997 India's national government consisted of an unstable post-election coalition cobbled together from the spectrum of non-BJP, non-Congress parties represented in Parliament. This coalition, the United Front, was far short of a parliamentary majority and depended on outside support extended by Congress. The United Front produced two prime ministers in 18 months: H. D. Deve Gowda, a Janata Dal politician from Karnataka, and Inder Kumar Gujral, a onetime Congress politician from northern India who later joined the Janata Dal. The United Front period lasted until December 1997, when Congress withdrew its support, and a midterm national election was held in February 1998.

The BJP contested the election with an expanded network of regional allies, and this yielded dividends for the party. The BJP contested significantly fewer constituencies than in 1996 (388, down from 471) but won in 182 (up from 161), one-third of the seats in the Lok Sabha. The BJP's share of the nationwide vote increased to 25.6 percent, due mostly to votes transferred to the party's candidates from the support bases of allied regional parties. The party polled less than one-sixth of the votes in just 57 of the 388 constituencies it contested. The BJP's network of regional allies now included, in addition to its 1996 allies in Maharashtra, Bihar, and Haryana, the ADMK in Tamil Nadu, the Biju Janata Dal in Orissa (a regional incarnation of the splintered Janata Dal of 1989–1990), the Sikh-based Akali Dal in Punjab, and the Trinamool Congress (Grassroots Congress), a new regional party formed in West Bengal by a dissident Congress faction there. The BJP and its assortment of allies held 254 of the Lok Sabha's 543 seats, and Vajpayee was able to form a coalition government that commanded a working parliamentary majority of 280-plus, with outside support from several other regional parties.

Congress, which contested the election with virtually no allies, did very poorly. The party won in 141 constituencies, the same as in 1996, but its share of the nationwide vote dropped another three percentage points, to 25.8 percent from 28.8 percent in 1996. And Congress won less than one-sixth of the polled votes in nearly one-third, 153, of the 477 constituencies it contested.

The BJP-led coalition that assumed office in March 1998 was formalized in May 1998 as the National Democratic Alliance (NDA). As almost all the regional constituents of the NDA opposed the Hindutva ideology, the BJP had to agree to shelve the three key demands that had driven the politics of Hindu nationalism for nearly a decade: the construction of a temple dedicated to Ram on the site of the demolished mosque in

Ayodhya; the enactment of an uniform civil code for all citizens of the country regardless of religion (to supersede Muslims' right to invoke the sharia in personal and family matters); and the abrogation of Article 370 of the Indian Constitution, which since 1949 codified Muslim-majority Jammu & Kashmir's autonomy within the Indian Union.

In April 1999 the NDA government lost a vote of confidence by just one vote on the floor of the Lok Sabha after the withdrawal from the co-alition of one constituent, the ADMK of Tamil Nadu. In yet another midterm national election held in September 1999, the formalized pre-election coalition represented by the NDA proved a decisive advantage for the BJP and its regional allies.

In the post-Congress era of India's politics, the national political arena is no more than an aggregation of many very different state-level politi-cal arenas, and the outcome of a national election is the sum total of of-ten hard-to-predict outcomes in various states, where elections are usu-ally closely fought and dominated by state-specific factors. In 1977 and 1989 the states of northern India voted for the opposition, and the states of southern India for Congress, but in the past two decades neither north nor south has shown any such uniform pattern, as the polity has frac-tured and diversified along state fault lines in both north and south. Yet in a national election the issue of a stable government at the Center does figure as a concern of the electorate. This was particularly true in the autumn of 1999, when India faced its second midterm election in two years. The NDA, which went to the people with an agreed common mini-mum program shorn of the Hindutva items and led by the most respected politician in the nation, Atal Behari Vajpayee, prevailed.

The BJP contested significantly fewer constituencies than in 1998 (339, down from 388), and the other 200-odd constituencies were contested by 13 regional parties from across the length and breadth of the country who ran under the NDA umbrella. The BJP won exactly the same num-ber of constituencies as a year and a half earlier (182, a third of the Lok Sabha's 543 seats), with 23.7 percent of the nationwide vote. The re-gional NDA parties won in another 88 constituencies and together polled another 13.3 percent of the nationwide vote, taking the NDA vote to just over 37 percent. The combined seat tally, 270, carried the NDA to within a whisker of the 272 Lok Sabha seats required for a parliamentary ma-jority, and Vajpayee formed a coalition government with stable outside support extended by Andhra Pradesh's Telugu Desam Party, which had 29 MPs in the new Lok Sabha.

This was India's first coalition government that lasted its full five-year term, until 2004. India's fragmented polity had finally adjusted to the inevitability of rule by coalition at the Center, with all its stresses and strains. The most successful regional NDA parties in the autumn 1999 national election were the Janata Dal-United of Bihar, which was essentially the renamed Samata Party, the Shiv Sena of Maharashtra, the Dravida Munnetra Kazhagam of Tamil Nadu, the Biju Janata Dal of Orissa, and the Trinamool Congress of West Bengal. The NDA also included the Akali Dal of Punjab, the National Conference of Jammu & Kashmir and the Asom Gana Parishad of Assam, parties rooted in communities which had been stigmatized as secessionist by Indira Gandhi's government in the first half of the 1980s. It was a remarkable rainbow coalition covering all parts of the country and diverse social groups and ethno-linguistic communities. None of the regional NDA parties except the Shiv Sena shared the BJP's Hindu nationalist ideology. Indeed, the cohabitation of the Hindu communalist BJP and avowedly secular parties like the Janata Dal-United of Bihar and the Trinamool Congress of West Bengal was altogether counterintuitive, and the cohabitation of the national-unitarist BJP and autonomist parties like the Akali Dal of Punjab and the Asom Gana Parishad of Assam even more so.

Congress, whose leadership had been taken over in early 1998 by Rajiv Gandhi's Italian-born widow, Sonia, contested 453 of the 543 constituencies. It won in just 114 constituencies, Congress's worst ever Lok Sabha seat tally, although the party's share of the nationwide vote improved slightly to 28.3 percent.

The decline of the grand old party was driven by two main factors, both of which illustrate the transforming nature of India's politics since the last decade of the twentieth century. The first was the exit of popular regional leaders from Congress. In late 1997 Mamata Banerjee, a young woman who had risen in the 1990s to become by far the most popular leader of Congress in West Bengal, ruled since 1977 by the communist-led Left Front, was expelled from the Congress party by its "high command" in New Delhi for insubordination. She then launched the Trinamool Congress, and in February 1998 she entered into a seat-sharing alliance in West Bengal with the BJP, a marginal party in West Bengal but a major party in the national context. The bulk of grassroots Congress activists in West Bengal joined the Trinamool Congress, and in the 1998 and 1999 Lok Sabha elections the fledgling party gained the bulk of the very large Congress vote base in the populous eastern state, reducing Congress there to a decimated rump.

In May 1999 Sharad Pawar, a veteran Congress leader of Maharashtra, was expelled from the party after he questioned the right of the foreign-born Sonia Gandhi to lead Congress. He and his supporters then launched the Nationalist Congress Party as a significant regional party in Maharashtra. Unlike Trinamool, the Nationalist Congress Party did not join the NDA; the BJP already had an established regional ally in Maharashtra in the Shiv Sena. But the Nationalist Congress Party cut deeply into Congress's vote base in Maharashtra, India's second most populous state, and severely damaged Congress there in the autumn 1999 national election. The total vote share of Congress and the Nationalist Congress Party, 52 percent (30 percent the former, 22 percent the latter), was much greater than that of the BJP-Shiv Sena alliance (38 percent). But because of the vertical split, the latter won 28 of Maharashtra's 48 constituencies.

The developments in West Bengal and Maharashtra in the late 1990s sharply underscored the incapacity of the centralized Congress party to accommodate powerful regional leaders with mass bases in their own states. This character defect was—and is—a severe handicap to the party's ability to adjust to India's regionalized polity of the late twentieth and early twenty-first centuries.

The second factor is the peeling off from the Congress vote base of social groups whom the party had taken for granted for decades. Nowhere has this been more dramatic than in Uttar Pradesh.

In the February 1998 national election, Congress polled 6 percent of the vote in UP. (It had polled 51 percent in UP in its nationwide landslide of December 1984 and 32 percent even in November 1989, when it lost across northern India.) A decade later things had not improved. In the UP state election of May 2007, Congress got 8.6 percent of the popular vote and won just 22 of the 403 legislative assembly constituencies, despite an energetic campaign by the party's national heir apparent, Rajiv and Sonia Gandhi's son Rahul Gandhi. In 2007 the BSP, the Dalit-based party led by Mayawati, won a simple majority in UP's legislature (206 of the 403 seats, majority threshold 202) on the basis of a slender plurality of under 31 percent of the popular vote (thanks to the "first-past-the-post" electoral system in single-member constituencies that magnifies slender pluralities of the popular vote into legislative majorities). Mulayam Yadav's SP, which ruled the state from 2003 to 2007, emerged as the largest opposition, with 26 percent of the vote and 97 seats (the BJP finished third, with 19 percent of the vote and 51 seats). Thus the two regional parties of UP, BSP and SP, won the votes of 57 percent of the state's electorate and three-fourths of the seats in its legislature.

For four decades, from the early 1950s through the late 1980s, the Congress vote base in UP was comprised mainly of upper castes, Muslims, and the scheduled castes (Dalits). The upper castes (especially

Brahmins but also Rajputs, Kayasths, and Khatris, altogether about 20 percent of the population) had good reason to support Congress, as they dominated the party's organizational apparatus in UP and saw the party as the source and guarantor of their superior socioeconomic status. The Muslims (17–18 percent of the population) saw Congress's secularist commitment as some guarantee of their security and rights. The socially downtrodden and impoverished Dalits (21–22 percent) were politically largely passive and voted for the ruling party, which adopted a stance of benevolent paternalism toward them and whose policy of reservations for SCs in government jobs and education benefited the upper stratum of the community.

After the Mandal Commission affair erupted in 1990, the anxious and beleaguered upper castes abandoned Congress for the BJP, whose promotion of an overarching Hindu unity held out the promise of papering over the deep fractures of caste conflict. The Muslims were alienated by the Rajiv Gandhi government's complicity in the Hindu nationalists' Ayodhya campaign between 1986 and 1989 and enraged by the Narasimha Rao government's failure to protect the Babri Mosque in December 1992. Most of the community switched allegiance to Mulayam Yadav's SP, formed in the autumn of 1992, which they saw as the best available protector of their security and rights (as the UP chief minister in the autumn of 1990, Mulayam Yadav had authorized police firing to disperse the first attempt by Hindutva zealots to storm the Ayodhya mosque and earned the sobriquet "Mullah Mulayam" in Hindu nationalist circles). In the 1990s the Dalit population of UP shifted more or less en masse to the BSP, a party formed specifically (in the mid-1980s) to advance Dalit rights and empowerment. Neither the Dalits nor the Muslims had much to be grateful to Congress for; after four decades of voting for the party, the bulk of these communities remained poor and deprived. Moreover, Dalits continued to be subjected to everyday humiliations, and Muslims were subjected to serious communal violence in UP during the 1980s, when Congress reigned supreme both nationally and in the state.

The OBC communities had since the 1960s largely supported opposition parties in UP. Once the upper castes, Muslims, and Dalits switched allegiance in droves—to the BJP, SP, and BSP, respectively—Congress nearly ceased to exist in UP. Congress's fate in UP is a contemporary example of how Antonio Gramsci described Italy in the throes of systemic upheaval in the 1920s: "at a certain point in their historical lives, social groups become detached from their traditional parties. The traditional parties in that particular organizational form are no longer recognized [by these groups] as their expression."[24]

The collapse of Congress in UP revealed that the party's "centrist," "catchall" politics had become obsolete in a context of social change and political transition. It was not until the national election of May 2009 that a section of UP's Muslims and upper castes voted again for Congress. Congress won 21 of the 80 constituencies in UP in the Lok Sabha election of May 2009. Its share of the popular vote in the state, 18 percent, was about the same as the BJP's and less than the BSP's 27 percent and the SP's 23 percent. But the expectation that this partial recovery heralded the resurgence of India's grand old party in the country's most populous state proved unfounded.

In Uttar Pradesh's 2012 state election, Rahul Gandhi fronted a high-voltage campaign to build on the advance of 2009 and reestablish Congress as a significant party in UP. The campaign failed spectacularly. The BSP government elected in 2007 was voted out of power in a backlash against its reputation for corruption and Mayawati's arrogant style of leadership. The BSP's popular vote declined to 26 percent (from nearly 31 percent in 2007), and the party won in only 80 of the 403 constituencies making up the state legislature. The big gainer was the SP, whose government had been voted out in 2007; it returned to power in UP with a simple majority of 224 of the 403 seats in the legislature on the basis of a slender plurality, 29 percent, of the popular vote (up from 26 percent in 2007). The outcome was almost identical to the 2007 state election, except that the SP and the BSP switched places, with the SP emerging as the front-runner and the BSP slipping to second place—a close second, as the SP was in 2007, in the popular vote, though not in the number of seats in the new state legislature (due to the "first-past-the-post" electoral system). The two major regional parties of UP, SP and BSP, won three-fourths of the seats in the state legislature, exactly the same as in 2007. The BJP finished a distant third, with 15 percent of the statewide popular vote and 47 seats (marginally down from 51 in 2007).

Congress trailed far behind, winning in only 28 of the 403 constituencies, marginally up from 22 seats in 2007. It improved its share of the popular vote in UP relative to 2007—15 percent as opposed to under 9 percent in 2007. But part of this increase was due to Congress's alliance with a small UP-based regional party, and overall the outcome was a disaster for Congress and a bitter disappointment for its lead campaigner, Rahul Gandhi. It became clear in 2012 that Congress is very far from rebuilding a mass base in UP. The BJP's "also-ran" status was confirmed as well, a far cry from the 1990s, when the Hindu nationalists, galvanized by the Ayodhya agitation, had emerged as the state's single largest party. The continuing primacy of regional parties in UP, which accounts for 15 percent of the seats in the national Parliament (80 of 543), and Rahul Gandhi's failed battle to reverse the tide is a telling example of the transformed nature of India's politics in the post-Congress era.

A similar dynamic of Congress collapse unfolded in the neighboring state of Bihar in the 1990s and deepened in the first decade of the new century. In the most recent state election in Bihar, held December 2010, Congress won four of the 243 legislative assembly constituencies and came second in just another eight, despite a high-profile campaign by Rahul Gandhi. The party polled a pathetic 8.4 percent of the popular vote. The Janata Dal-United, a regional party founded on a core base of some (non-Yadav) OBC castes in the 1990s but recently diversified to include Dalit and Muslim support, won a five-sixths majority in the Bihar legislature in an alliance with its junior partner, BJP, which has support among the state's upper castes.

Congress compounded its predicament with an ostrich-like denial of the unfolding transformation of India's democracy. In September 1998, as the NDA settled into its first term, the Congress leadership gathered for a retreat at Pachmarhi, a hill resort in the north-central state of Madhya Pradesh. After discussions chaired by its new leader, Sonia Gandhi, the party adopted a policy statement it called the "Pachmarhi declaration." It "affirm[ed] that the Party considers the present difficulties in forming one-party governments a transient phase in the evolution of our polity, pledg[ed] to restore the Party to its primacy in national affairs, [and] decid[ed] that coalitions will be considered only when absolutely necessary and that too on the basis of agreed programs which will not weaken the Party." Sonia Gandhi's speech proclaimed: "let us not allow political parties to divide us, to inflame religious passions, to ignite caste tensions, and to fan regional sentiments. A divided India cannot survive. A fractured India cannot prosper."[25]

Congress did have one practical problem in making alliances with regional parties: many of those that joined or associated with the NDA faced Congress as principal rival in their respective states, such as the Telugu Desam Party in Andhra Pradesh, the Biju Janata Dal in Orissa, the Akali Dal in Punjab, and the Asom Gana Parishad in Assam. Their natural incentive was therefore to ally with the BJP against Congress. But the manner—at once imperious and absurd—in which Congress dismissed the regionalization of India's polity and the contempt it showed toward regional parties in general simply deepened its isolation and fortified the BJP's coalition-based alternative.

It took Congress until 2004 to modify this position in practice, though not in principle. In the national election of April–May 2004 the NDA was widely expected to be returned to power. In the first years of the twenty-first century the Indian economy began to grow rapidly—the result of the reforms undertaken since the early 1990s—after five languid decades. The Union government undertook ambitious infrastructural projects such as the building of a new national highway system. A mood of optimism was discernible among the growing middle class in the cities. The NDA went to the polls with the slogan "India Shining," coined by BJP strategists. The nearly universal expectation of a comfortable NDA victory was confounded when both the BJP and most of the regional NDA parties lost ground. The BJP won in 138 constituencies (down from 182 in 1999); the downturn included heavy losses in Uttar Pradesh. The regional NDA parties won in only 43 constituencies (down from 88 in 1999), and the NDA as a whole got 181 seats, just one-third of the Lok Sabha. The BJP's pan-Indian reelection strategy for the NDA, built on "India Shining" and Prime Minister Vajpayee's respected image, had run aground on the complex patterns and dynamics of politics in various states, and the net outcome was that the NDA had failed to renew its mandate.

There was no winner in the election. The outcome was another "hung" (fractured) Parliament, in which Congress emerged as the single largest party, albeit with just 145 seats, slightly higher than the BJP tally. The count of 145 represented a modest increase on the 114 constituencies the party won in 1999 and was about the same as its tally of 140 and 141 seats, respectively, in the 1996 and 1998 national elections. This was far from a resurgence, and in fact Congress's nationwide vote fell slightly, from 28.3 percent in 1999 to 26.5 percent in 2004. (In 2004 the party contested 417 constituencies, slightly fewer than the 453 it contested in 1999.) The NDA had, however, failed to renew its mandate, and Congress was able to cobble together a minority government with 70 MPs belonging to non-NDA regional parties.

This postelection alliance, with a strength of 215 in the 543-member Lok Sabha, was named the United Progressive Alliance (UPA) and was able to gain a working parliamentary majority thanks to outside support extended by the communist-led bloc, which elected 59 MPs (the majority from West Bengal). Several other regional parties, notably the SP and the BSP, both of which did well in UP, also assented to the UPA taking power. Manmohan Singh, the soft-spoken technocrat who had entered political life as Narasimha Rao's prime minister in 1991, became the new prime minister.

The composition of the 2004–2009 Lok Sabha reflected the regionalization of India's political landscape. The only two parties with a nationwide orientation and a vote base in numerous states, Congress and BJP, together held just over half of the seats in Parliament—283 of 543. The other 260 seats were held by a wide range of explicitly or effectively regional parties.

Congress belatedly realized the indispensability of coalition-building to gaining power at the Center, as the BJP had years earlier. Congress entered the April–May 2009 national election at the head of a preelection (rather than postelection) UPA coalition, just as the BJP had entered the September 1999 national election at the head of a formalized preelection coalition with regional allies. The promise of continuity and stability and the decent reputation of Prime Minister Manmohan Singh worked well for Congress, just as the NDA's similar promise and Vajpayee's image had brought success to the BJP in 1999. Congress won in 206 constituencies— its best performance in two decades—and its regional allies won another 56, making a total of 262, just short of the 272 needed for a parliamentary majority.

Manmohan Singh then formed what was called the UPA II government, with West Bengal's Trinamool Congress, Tamil Nadu's Dravida Munnetra Kazhagam, and Maharashtra's Nationalist Congress Party as the main regional partners in the government and outside support from several other regional parties, including the SP and the BSP. The communists, the outside prop of the "UPA I" government (2004–2009), were left in the cold, having withdrawn support from the government in a huff in July 2008 when Manmohan Singh concluded an agreement on civil nuclear cooperation between India and the United States. Allergic to the United States, the communists withdrew support in protest against the alleged capitulation to imperialism, but UPA I survived the remaining eight months of its term. In the 2009 national election the communists suffered severe reverses, especially in their bastion of West Bengal at the hands of Mamata Banerjee's Trinamool Congress. The communist-led bloc was reduced from 59 MPs elected in 2004 to 24 in 2009, and its dominant party, the CPM, was reduced from 43 to 16 MPs. The Congress-communist estrangement made it possible for the Trinamool Congress to leave the NDA and join the UPA. The move made sense because in West Bengal, a state where over one-quarter of the electorate is Muslim, the link to the BJP was a liability for Trinamool.

Despite the surge in seats, Congress's share of the nationwide vote remained stagnant at 28.5 percent (the party contested 440 of the 543 constituencies, slightly more than in 2004). The UPA's victory was by points rather than knockout, and its main reasons were slippage of support for BJP and disarray in the opposition NDA coalition. The BJP obtained 18.8

percent of the nationwide vote and won in 116 constituencies (down from 138 in 2004). The party got less than one-sixth of the polled votes in as many as 170 of the 433 constituencies it contested, a stark reminder of the Hindu nationalists' weak to nonexistent base in much of India. The BJP's decline between 2004 and 2009 mirrored Congress's decline from 141 to 114 seats in Parliament between the national elections of February 1998 and September 1999. The BJP was adversely affected by preelection departures from the NDA; West Bengal's Trinamool Congress switched to the UPA coalition, and Orissa's Biju Janata Dal, the ruling party in that eastern state, took a late decision to run more or less independently rather than in alliance with BJP. The BJP's remaining regional allies got 43 seats between them, making an NDA total of 159, still substantial but over a hundred fewer than the UPA's tally of 262 in the Lok Sabha. The BJP (and NDA) lacked a credible leader to project as the prime ministerial alternative to Manmohan Singh, the aged and ailing Vajpayee having retired from politics after the shock defeat of 2004. Led astray in 2004 by the elitist and boastful "India Shining" slogan, the opposition coalition and its leading party were also unable in 2009 to come up with an effective counter-strategy to the populist Congress/UPA plank of "inclusive growth"—meaning a poor-friendly policy emphasis, reflected mainly in a nationwide scheme to generate part-year employment for the rural poor undertaken by the UPA I government.

The Regionalized Present and Future of India's Democracy

As India approaches its sixteenth national election in April–May 2014, it is clear that the regionalization of Indian politics is far from the "transient phase" Congress declared it to be in September 1998. The goal the party's leadership declared at that time of regaining "primacy in national affairs," and which it reiterated almost verbatim in a resolution adopted in 2010, has turned out to be a chimera and is very likely to remain so. The ambition that the BJP had two decades ago of supplanting Congress as India's hegemonic party has also been exposed as fantasy, thwarted by the sheer plurality of India's society and political landscape. The demand for the Ram temple in Ayodhya that propelled the Hindu nationalist ascendancy of the early 1990s became a peripheral issue by the late 1990s and has been relegated to near irrelevance since then. In the twenty-first century the once incendiary issue has had next to no resonance in the politics of even Uttar Pradesh, its home state.

In India's decentered polity of the early twenty-first century, the key arbiters of the nation's present and future are its most influential regional politicians: the political entrepreneurs of the post-Congress era who have a mass base in one of the dozen or so most populous states of the Indian Union and especially the most populous half-dozen states. (UP, Maharashtra, West Bengal, Andhra Pradesh, Bihar, and Tamil Nadu account for well over half the nation's parliamentary constituencies—291 of the 543 seats in the Lok Sabha. Madhya Pradesh, Karnataka, Gujarat, Rajasthan, Orissa, and Kerala account for another 149.)

The democratic stability of the Indian Union is fundamentally strong. The organization of the country as a union of autonomous states provided a framework for fostering national unity on the basis of recognition of the ethnolinguistic and sociocultural diversity of the nation. Conflicts between the Center and territorially based communities developed and assumed a chronic form where this structure of democratic quasi federalism did not take root—as in Kashmir and the region on India's northeastern frontier. The establishment of the states in post-1947 India was a gradual and incremental process, but by the early 1970s the internal contours of the Union had been largely formed. In the four decades that have passed since then, more territorially based communities have launched campaigns to achieve the status of states—in itself indicative of the centrality of states as the constitutive elements of the Indian polity. Statehood confers powerful symbolic recognition as well as extensive institutional powers.

A number of these demands have been met. In November 2000 three new states were created at the initiative of the NDA government in New Delhi—Jharkhand, comprising the districts of southern Bihar; Uttarakhand, comprised of the mountainous northwestern tip of Uttar Pradesh; and Chhattisgarh, comprising the eastern and southeastern districts of Madhya Pradesh. The legislatures of Bihar, UP, and Madhya Pradesh assented. Jharkhand was created in democratic accommodation of a popular agitation among the Adivasis of southern Bihar for statehood that had existed since independence and gathered momentum since the 1970s (although only a quarter of the population of the contemporary state of Jharkhand, a mineral-rich area that has attracted migrants for decades, belong to the ST). The birth of Uttarakhand was similarly in response to a popular agitation in the 1990s for recognition of the distinct sociocultural character of the northwestern tip of UP, whose hill people felt marginalized as part of this giant state. Chhattisgarh was not formed due to a popular agitation, but one-third of the state's population consists of Adivasis, the most marginalized and impoverished of India's medley of communities. The state, a long, finger-shaped sliver of territory, is unique in that it has borders with states of northern, eastern, southern, and western

India. There is a proposal to carve four states out of UP, ostensibly to improve the quality of administration through smaller units while also recognizing the historical character of its subregions.

None of the new states was formed on the grounds of a distinct language-based culture—the principle that guided the establishment of states during the formative phase of the Indian Union in the 1950s and 1960s. Jharkhand and Chhattisgarh are essentially multilingual states, albeit with a preponderance of Hindi in urban centers, while in Uttara-khand Hindi dominates in towns and mountain dialects in rural areas. If UP is divided, Hindi and dialects of Hindi will be the language of the vast majority in all four zones.

A popular movement for statehood that has reemerged in recent years in Telangana, the northern part of Andhra Pradesh, is similarly not pre-mised on language; Telangana is Telugu-speaking like the other two sub-regions of the state, coastal Andhra and Rayalaseema. Rather, the state-hood movement invokes the distinct historical character of Telangana, which was incorporated into Andhra Pradesh in 1956, and a long record of agitation for Telangana's recognition as a full-fledged state of the In-dian Union, including a student-led uprising in 1969. The main sticking point in Telangana's formation is the future of the city of Hyderabad, Andhra Pradesh's capital and a center of the construction and informa-tion technology industries, which is located in the heart of Telangana.[26] Another demand for statehood status that escalated in the mid-1980s among the Nepali-speaking Gorkha people who inhabit the Darjeeling hills in the northern tip of West Bengal was assuaged in 1988 by the es-tablishment of an autonomous entity within West Bengal. The movement for separation from West Bengal and the establishment of the state of Gorkhaland was driven by a feeling of marginalization, as the Gorkhas are a tiny minority in the populous Bengali-speaking state they are part of. The demand for Gorkhaland reemerged in 2008 and continues to simmer, while the political spectrum of West Bengal is united against con-ceding a separate state.

The evolution of India since the 1950s as a union of states, overriding the initial centralist preferences of Nehru's government, and the continuous allure of statehood for territorially based communities over the half cen-tury since then means that the states have always been the key arenas of India's democracy. Yet during the four decades the Congress colossus dominated India, the relationship between the Center and the states was a distinctly lopsided one. The same party ruled at the Center and in the vast majority of the states. Although the constitutional architecture of

India embodies a hybrid of unitary and federalist features, ultimately power was concentrated in New Delhi and the apex leadership of the nationwide hegemonic party. The relationship became even more lopsided in the 1970s and 1980s due to the conversion of the Congress party into a family fiefdom and the personalized centralism of Indira and Rajiv Gandhi.

The overweening Congress-ruled Center was always intolerant of strong regional parties. Sheikh Abdullah was removed from power in Jammu & Kashmir in 1953 because he was a charismatic and popular leader who headed a strong regional party and could not be easily bent to New Delhi's will. The dismissal, orchestrated from New Delhi, of Kerala's communist-led state government in 1959 is another case in point. In the 1980s the Congress-held Center's antidemocratic and antifederal interventions in states were both brazen and desperate, exemplified by the harassment of N. T. Rama Rao's government in Andhra Pradesh and the removal of Farooq Abdullah's government in J&K.

The Congress centralists' fear of regional parties was well founded, however. Despite the absence of a national opposition party, Congress's hegemony was rocked in the 1967 national election by the rise of regional opposition parties in various states. In 1989 it was the coalescing of a spectrum of regional opposition parties that ended Congress's hegemony in India's politics.

In the post-Congress era the effective balance of power between the Center and the states has shifted decisively toward the states. For two decades it has been inconceivable that any government at the Center can deploy centralist provisions of the Indian constitution like Article 356 to get rid of elected state governments for partisan political purposes. The reason for the seismic shift in the effective balance of power is fundamental: regional parties either dominate or figure as significant players in the politics of the large majority of India's states, including the half dozen most populous states, and the chieftains of regional parties determine who governs at a Center much diminished in power—Congress or BJP—and how.

Regionalist power at the Center can have a very dark side. In 2008 the minister of telecommunications in the UPA I government, a Dalit politician belonging to the Dravida Munnetra Kazhagam of Tamil Nadu, allotted 122 licenses for second-generation (2G) bandwidth to a number of private telecom companies in a manner that can only be described as scandalously corrupt. When the matter came to light a year later, the "2G scam" became a national scandal that paralyzed Parliament during 2010 and touched off a citizens' protest movement against high-level corruption that peaked in 2011. It is likely that Prime Minister Manmohan

Singh failed to act in good time against the errant minister because he belonged to an allied regional party whose support was important to the Congress-led minority government. The ex-minister was subsequently arrested and sent to prison, as were the key bureaucrats and businessmen involved in the affair, and Dravida Munnetra Kazhagam, the ruling party in Tamil Nadu since 2006, suffered a crushing defeat in state elections in May 2011. In February 2012 India's Supreme Court canceled all the 122 licenses and ordered the process redone in a transparent manner. The court noted that its intervention had been necessitated by an exceptionally outrageous breach of "the public interest."[27]

Yet egregious episodes such as the 2G scandal will not undermine the transformation of India's politics in favor of regionalists and regionalism. The regionalization of the nation's political landscape is deeply rooted in structural and historical causes, and the contemporary impact of that regionalization goes beyond the rise of regional parties. It extends to the creeping regionalization of one of the only two parties with a substantively "national" orientation, the BJP.

India's best known BJP politician of the (relatively) younger generation is Narendra Modi (born 1950), who has been the chief minister of Gujarat since late 2001. Modi is controversial in India and abroad because it was under his watch that India's only major outbreak of religious violence, since the Ayodhya-fueled riots of 1992–1993, occurred in Gujarat in 2002. In the spring of 2002 at least 1,000 men, women, and children of Gujarat's 9 percent Muslim minority were killed in pogrom-like attacks by mobs led by Hindu nationalist activists. These killings happened after a train carrying Hindu nationalist supporters who were returning to Gujarat from a trip to Ayodhya was attacked and set alight while passing through Godhra, a small town in Gujarat with a substantial Muslim population, allegedly by some local Muslims. Fifty-nine people burned to death in the incident, including women and children. Although tainted by the 2002 Gujarat atrocities against defenseless Muslims, Modi has flourished in the decade that has passed since then by positioning himself very effectively as the champion of Gujarat's regional identity and economic development. His landslide victory in state elections in December 2002 can be attributed to ugly majoritarian chauvinism, but not his reelection to office five years later in December 2007. In Gujarat's state election of December 2012 he won a third consecutive landslide, decisively defeating Congress (and simultaneously routing a challenge from a disgruntled Hindu nationalist faction). The BJP won in 115 of the 182 single-member constituencies comprising the state legislature (as opposed to 117 in

2007 and 127 in 2002), with 48 percent of the statewide popular vote, a decisive margin over Congress's 40 percent (which translated into 61 seats).

Narendra Modi's success owes little if anything to the BJP's insipid and floundering national leadership or to the RSS, whose top brass he has coldly ignored in recent years, although he cut his political teeth in his youth as an RSS *pracharak* (volunteer preacher of Hindutva values), like most ranking BJP politicians. His enduring popularity in Gujarat is due to the image he has cultivated as an advocate of Gujarati *asmita* (pride rooted in ethnolinguistic identity) and the reputation he has built as a hardworking, uncorrupt, and efficient leader of the state's administration and socioeconomic development strategy. As an Indian commentator wrote after his resounding reelection as Gujarat's chief minister in December 2012: "Modi's appeal to his electorate is framed in strictly regional [state-specific] terms. He tells voters that he represents the pride and hopes of millions of [fellow] Gujaratis. . . . As Congress has no leaders of stature in the state, it is easy to portray it as a party of servile pygmies who take orders from Delhi."[28]

Modi's Gujarat-specific formula is the most striking but not the only example of the regionalist evolution of the BJP. In the few other states where the party of Hindu nationalism is on a strong footing—such as Madhya Pradesh and Chhattisgarh—it has popular regional leaders who have standing on their home turf and are seen as credible representatives of their states' aspirations to competent administration and socioeconomic development.

Of the two parties with a national orientation, the BJP is better placed to adapt to a regionalized polity, as it has traditions of collective leadership and internal democracy. For Congress, the hollowed-out colossus of Indian politics, the dilemma posed by regionalization is truly colossal. The best guarantee for survival and relevance in the twenty-first century would have been for Congress to reinvent itself as a federal nationwide party, with autonomous state units headed by popular leaders and mechanisms of collective decision-making by those leaders at the national level.

But this was never more than a theoretical proposition. Congress operated as a top-down, centralized party controlled by members of a single nuclear family throughout the 1970s and 1980s. When the party faced crisis in the late 1990s it turned for leadership to the apolitical Sonia Gandhi, Indira's daughter-in-law and Rajiv's widow, and she was able to pull the party together by providing a focal point of unity. The principle of hereditary succession to power returned, along with the reassertion of family control, and her son Rahul Gandhi, who entered politics in 2004, has been spoken of ever since then by Congress officials not just as the party's supreme leader in the making but as the nation's prime minister in waiting. Yet the spectacular failure of his efforts to revive the emaciated Congress in Uttar Pradesh in 2007 and 2012 and Bihar in 2010 shows that parachute missions from New Delhi are no substitute for strong organizations and leaders rooted in the soil of states. (In Gujarat in late 2012, fitful campaigning by Sonia and Rahul Gandhi on behalf of Congress was simply steamrolled by Narendra Modi's charismatic and well-strategized regionalist juggernaut.) Condescending paternalism from above is outdated and ineffective in the early twenty-first century, when the average Indian voter has developed the consciousness of being a citizen and not a subject.

Although she inherited power primarily as her father's daughter, Indira Gandhi subsequently became a mass leader with nationwide appeal. Her relatively uncharismatic grandson Rahul has no such prospect in the very different political era of the early twenty-first century, in which India's politics has been transformed by the breakdown of the Congress hegemony and the rise of popular regional leaders across India. The era in which a "dynasty" could dominate India from New Delhi is well and truly in the past.

To be sure, Rahul Gandhi is not the only dynast on the contemporary Indian political scene. The dynastic bug afflicts many regional parties. In Uttar Pradesh's SP, the 40-year-old son of the aging Mulayam Yadav has partly taken over his father's mantle. The son, Akhilesh Yadav, became UP's chief minister in March 2012. In Tamil Nadu's Dravida Munnetra Kazhagam, two sons of M. Karunanidhi, the aged party leader, compete for the succession. Both sons, M. K. Stalin and M. K. Azhagiri, are in their early sixties. In Punjab's Akali Dal, Sukhbir Singh Badal, the middle-aged son of the party leader, Prakash Singh Badal, who is the chief minister of Punjab, is poised to be his aging father's successor. In Maharashtra's Nationalist Congress Party, Supriya Sule and Ajit Pawar, the daughter and the nephew of Sharad Pawar, the party's aging leader, both hold leadership roles. Also in Maharashtra, the Shiv Sena's founder, the aged demagogue Bal Thackeray, handed the leadership reins to one of his sons, Uddhav Thackeray, well before his death in November 2012. Orissa's Naveen Patnaik, now in his third consecutive chief ministerial term, is a son of the famous regional leader Biju Patnaik. Omar Abdullah, J&K's chief minister, is the grandson of Sheikh Abdullah and son of Farooq Abdullah. In Andhra Pradesh a rising regional party, the YSR Congress, born of a bitter split in the state's Congress party, is led by Jagan Mohan Reddy, the son of the deceased Andhra Pradesh Congress leader, Y. S.

Rajasekhara Reddy, after whom the party is named. (He was the Congress chief minister of Andhra Pradesh from 2004 until his death in a helicopter accident in 2009.) So there is nothing unique in Rahul Gandhi being projected as the successor to the mantle of Congress leadership held by his mother—who has been in poor health since 2011—and earlier by his father, grandmother, and great-grandfather, all prime ministers who led India for 38 years between them.

But there is something unique, and unviable, about the scale of the ambition. The regional dynasts are focused on their respective states. Rahul Gandhi has been portrayed by Congress officials as India's national leader in the making, in the same way his father was three decades ago. In the event, Rajiv Gandhi proved grossly unequal to the great challenges of leading India responsibly and effectively when he inherited the prime ministership after his mother's sudden death. In the second decade of the twenty-first century, with Congress's dominance of India well in the past and the nation's polity defined by regionalization, the very idea of one nationwide leader is obsolete. This applies as much to successful regional (state-based) politicians like Gujarat's Narendra Modi, who is wrongly seen by some Hindutva supporters as India's next national leader, as to Rahul Gandhi. Certainly, any claim to leading the nation that is based principally on dynastic lineage is utterly unsustainable today. Modi at least is a self-made leader from an ordinary Indian family of Gujarati OBC origins who has risen to prominence through a mix of talent, luck, hard work, and political skullduggery.

Several high-profile and assertive women leaders are in the front rank of the regional politicians of the new India. All are self-made to varying degrees. Mayawati (born 1956), sometimes referred to as the "Dalit queen" of Uttar Pradesh, was mentored by the BSP founder Kanshi Ram but otherwise owes her political career to her own skills and resilience. J. Jayalalitha (born 1948) of Tamil Nadu was similarly mentored in politics by M. G. Ramachandran, the founder of the ADMK and a very popular chief minister of Tamil Nadu from 1977 until his death a decade later, whom she met in the 1960s when both were actors in the thriving Tamil cinema industry. She took over the ADMK after her mentor's death and is known as Amma (Mother) and Puratchi Thalaivi (Great Leader) among her mass base. Mamata Banerjee (born c. 1955) of West Bengal, the leader of the Trinamool Congress, is of humble social origins and emerged as a mass leader in West Bengal in the 1990s through her own efforts. She is simply Didi (Older Sister) to her followers in West Bengal. All three women are seasoned political veterans, having been active in politics for three and a half decades. They know that their importance stems from the devolution of politics and power in the post-Congress era and are stoutly resistant to any perceived impositions or bullying from New Delhi.

Thus in October 2011 Mayawati wrote a strongly worded letter to Prime Minister Manmohan Singh after she received a letter from his minister of rural development, a Congress politician, that asked for her "concurrence for a CBI probe" (an investigation by the Central Bureau of Investigation, the government of India's premier investigative agency) into allegations of embezzlement in UP of funds of the Mahatma Gandhi National Rural Employment Guarantee Scheme (MNREGS), the Union government's flagship nationwide welfare program for the poor launched in 2006. The letter also warned her that the Union government had the right to stop disbursements from this fund to her state. The UP chief minister retorted that "he [the Union minister] seems to think that Central grants for sponsored programs are discretion he bestows on States." She advised the minister to learn about "Center-State fiscal arrangements provided in the Constitution" and realize that funds disbursed to states under programs like the MNREGS are not "largesse bestowed by the Center" but revenue-sharing under the quasi-federal system. Mayawati could respond in this way because while she enjoys a mass base in UP, a state of over 200 million people, both the prime minister and his rural development minister are unelected politicians who hold membership in Parliament's upper chamber and belong to a party that is a shadow of its once dominant self.[29]

Jayalalitha, the chief minister of Tamil Nadu, at the other end of the country from Uttar Pradesh, did not bother to attend a meeting convened in New Delhi in October 2011 of the National Development Council, a Center-States forum established during the Nehru period. But she sent a speech that was read into the record at the conference by a representative. The speech read: "I am not sure the Government of India recognizes the States as partners, let alone equal partners, and respects their viewpoints. These meetings are at best ritualistic and are exercises in futility. There are attempts by the Center to weaken the States with too much interference, thereby reducing them to glorified municipal corporations. The Center is continuously proving that it is out of sync with ground realities." Jayalalitha particularly complained that the disbursement of funds under the Congress-led Union government's 13 nationwide development, welfare, and infrastructure-improvement programs—almost all of which are named after various members of the Nehru-Gandhi family— view the state governments as mere implementers and also curtail their

ability to deploy funds received from the Center according to locally determined priorities. In essence, like Mayawati, she accused the Congress-
led government in New Delhi of the top-down, condescending, politically motivated approach to grassroots development and empowerment
that had characterized Rajiv Gandhi's Panchayati Raj plan of 1988–
1989. She signed off with an excoriation of a common nationwide law
against communal violence proposed by New Delhi as "fascist" and "a
blatant attempt" to encroach on state jurisdiction. In the pre-1990 era of
Congress hegemony, it would have been unthinkable for a non-Congress
chief minister to present this sort of speech at such a conference in New
Delhi.[30] An implicit subtext of Jayalalitha's speech was that Congress is a
minor party in Tamil Nadu, in a state polity that is dominated by her
ADMK and its rival Dravida Munnetra Kazhagam and populated by
smaller regional parties.

Unlike Jayalalitha's ADMK and Mayawati's BSP, Mamata Banerjee's
Trinamool Congress entered the post–May 2009 UPA II government in
New Delhi as a regional ally of Congress and indeed as the ruling coalition's second largest party in the Lok Sabha, with 19 MPs elected from
West Bengal. In May 2011 she stormed to power in West Bengal, ending
the 34-year dominance of the state, since 1977, by the communist-led
Left Front. The Trinamool Congress won a nearly two-thirds majority in
the state legislature, and Banerjee's government commanded a three-
fourths majority with its junior ally in the state, the Congress party, of
which Banerjee was a leader until 1997. After coming to power in West
Bengal, Banerjee's behavior was determined by her knowledge that Congress was dependent on her support at the Center and is a weak, almost
marginal party in West Bengal.

Thus she vetoed the Center's plan to set up a nuclear plant with Russian
collaboration in a coastal rural area south of the state capital, Kolkata, citing local residents' concerns over loss of farmland and environmental
risks. This was a snub to Prime Minister Manmohan Singh, whose main
achievement in office has been the 2008 agreement with the United
States on nuclear cooperation for civil purposes, which opened the way
for India to collaborate with the United States and other nations such as
Russia and France on developing nuclear energy facilities.[31] Then she
opposed and effectively vetoed Singh's plan to conclude a treaty on
sharing the waters of the Teesta, a regional river, with the neighboring
state of Bangladesh, on the grounds that West Bengal's interests had not
been sufficiently taken into account. In late 2011 she was a leading voice
in successful protests against the Congress-led Union government's
plans to allow foreign multibrand retailers like WalMart and Tesco to

open stores in 53 Indian cities with populations over 1 million, citing the risks to the small "Mom and Pop" stores in India's urban centers. Also in late 2011, her party intervened strongly in the parliamentary debate over proposed legislation to institute a national Lokpal (Ombudsman). The demand for such a body to tackle corruption among politicians and bureaucrats had been popularized by an urban-based civil society movement against high-level corruption during 2011. The Trinamool Congress argued that the establishment of state-level ombudsman bodies should be left to state governments and not be imposed from the Center.

Mamata Banerjee's behavior was that of a confident, successful regionalist, secure in her mass following in her own state and fully aware of the regionalized nature of India's polity. Comparing India's body politic to a human body, she said: "blood needs to circulate freely throughout the body. Blood cannot be bottled up just in the heart. If power is concentrated in Delhi democracy will be endangered." She added: "I don't wish to abolish the Center. But the protection of States' rights is essential to a healthy relationship between the Center and the States." West Bengal's largest Bengali-language newspaper reported that Mamata's stance on Center-state relations was supported by many other non-Congress chief ministers, including Nitish Kumar of Bihar, Naveen Patnaik of Orissa, Jayalalitha of Tamil Nadu, Narendra Modi of Gujarat, and Mayawati of UP, as well as N. Chandrababu Naidu, former chief minister of Andhra Pradesh and leader of the Telugu Desam Party, founded by his father-in-law, N. T. Rama Rao. The newspaper claimed that even the Congress chief ministers of Maharashtra (where Congress governs in coalition with the Nationalist Congress Party, the breakaway Congress faction) and Rajasthan agreed with Mamata's position.[32]

In September 2012 Banerjee withdrew her party from the post-2009 "UPA II" coalition government in New Delhi after Congress, the leading constituent of that government, announced that it would go ahead with the proposal to allow big foreign companies—such as WalMart, Carrefour, and Tesco—to operate in the multibrand retail sector (in effect, set up supermarkets in Indian cities). Banerjee denounced the policy as against the public and national interest. The majority of India's state governments also announced that they would exercise their right to not implement the policy in their states (in March 2013 Tamil Nadu's Dravida Munnetra Kazhagam, the third largest constituent of the "UPA II" government formed in 2009, also left the ruling coalition, citing a different reason). After quitting the Congress-led Union government, Banerjee floated the ambitious idea of a "federal front"—effectively an alliance of regional parties based in various states—to govern the country after the 2014 national elections.[33]

That idea faces numerous obstacles to being realized in practice, but it is incontrovertible that the spectrum of regional parties and politicians constitutes the new pivot of India's decentered democracy in the early twenty-first century. This can be regarded as a natural evolution, with the diversity of the political landscape mirroring the vast heterogeneity of Indian society. The two ideological variants of encompassing, expansive politics represented by Congress and the BJP have shared a common trait—denial that diversity is the essence of Indian society and therefore naturally the lifeblood of its polity. Their ideological frameworks could not recognize, let alone accommodate this diversity and plurality.

Hence Sonia Gandhi's declaration in September 1998: "let us not allow political parties to divide us, to inflame religious passions, to ignite caste tensions, and to fan regional sentiments. A divided India cannot survive. A fractured India cannot prosper." This statement put the political assertion of disadvantaged and even oppressed castes and the democratic expression of ethnolinguistic identities and interests in the same category as the pseudoreligious politics of the Hindutva movement and condemned them all literally in the same breath. It was also the invocation of a stale unitarist ideology whose hegemony in Indian politics had ended a decade earlier. For its part the RSS, the fount of the Hindu nationalist movement, had warned against the proliferation of divisions and fractures as early as 1988: "the Sangh has viewed the problem of various centrifugal forces raising their heads with slogans of various types of separate identities and interests as being due to the drying up of the unifying life-sap of society. The best solution to these internal stresses and strains lies in strengthening and nurturing the Hindu ethos, out of which all the various sects and creeds, languages and dialects, customs and traditions, doctrines and theories have emerged."[34]

While Congress had no substantive solution at all to the problem it identified, the Hindu nationalists' solution proved to be a chimera once it left its ideological cocoon and encountered the deep, choppy waters of mass democratic politics. First the would-be hegemon and then the former hegemon of India's polity had to adjust to the world of Indian politics as it really exists—divided and fractured—as the wishful world of their ideological visions came up against the realities of India's democracy in the contemporary era.

Regionalization has deepened the representative character of India's democracy and given a degree of voice and space to myriad communities across the nation. The devolution of Indian democracy through regionalization has aided increasing awareness of rights and the value of political participation among ordinary people, including historically disadvantaged and even oppressed groups who have mobilized to better their condition and demand a say in decision-making and a share of political power. Political institutions and processes have become more relevant than before to the lives of many Indians in the post-Congress era of regionalization. If India's democracy is so vibrant today, it is in large measure because of this. It is of course also more unruly and messy than ever before and frequently resembles brawling. That too is a sign of a vigorous, constantly evolving democracy rather than one based on sterile notions of "stability."

But as two Indian authors wrote in 2004, in a book aptly subtitled "Divided We Stand," the range of "regional or caste-based parties" with a presence in one state of the Indian Union would, like Congress and the BJP, "take their support base for granted at their own peril."[35] These regional parties and politicians cannot rely on appeals to primordial identities—and enmities—as an indefinite source of legitimacy or electoral dividend. As India's democracy continues to evolve in the early twenty-first century, their prospects depend increasingly on their ability to provide (relatively) uncorrupt and responsive governance in their respective states and to meet their electorates' aspirations to socioeconomic advancement and development.

The evolution of politics over the last two decades in the northern state of Bihar is a case in point. For 15 years, 1990–2005, Bihar had a government headed by a charismatic regional politician, Laloo Prasad Yadav. He became chief minister of Bihar after state elections in March 1990 as a leader of the Janata Dal, the federated party of anti-Congress factions based predominantly in Uttar Pradesh and Bihar that decisively defeated Congress in the two giant northern states in the national election of November 1989. (Of the 139 constituencies in UP and Bihar—comprising over a quarter of the Lok Sabha—the Janata Dal won in 85 and Congress in just 19 constituencies, 15 in UP and 4 in Bihar.)

In the early 1990s Laloo was a mascot of the rising clamor for "social justice"—meaning equality and opportunity for socioeconomic advancement—among the subaltern castes and classes of Bihar, where economic and political power had been nearly monopolized since independence by landed castes who dominated the Congress party and its governments in the state. Born into a family of cattle-herders and poor farmers in 1948, Laloo spoke in a rustic idiom that fitted this counter-hegemonic image and appealed to the rural poor. It mattered to him not a bit that his rustic demeanor and style made him a figure of fun among affluent urban Indians. He had solid political credentials; he had been a leader in opposition student politics at the university in Patna, Bihar's capital, in the first half of the 1970s and had been imprisoned during the Emergency of 1975–1977.

Once he was in power, Laloo's promise of social change translated primarily into a policy of patronage of his own caste group, the Yadavs, a numerous OBC community both in Bihar and UP, who had been prominently represented since the 1960s in "socialist" opposition parties in the two Congress-dominated states. During his first term in office (1990–1995) the Yadavs gained significantly in political clout through their dominance of the new ruling party of Bihar and in employment opportunities, due to implementation of reservations for OBC castes in the state's administrative machinery. But members of the much broader spectrum of OBC castes—many of whom were more disadvantaged than the Yadavs—did not.[36] The other social group whose loyalty Laloo cultivated were Bihar's Muslims, nearly a sixth of the state's population. Having mostly voted for Congress since independence, Bihar's Muslims were bitterly alienated from their traditional party by traumatic events such as the massacres of Muslims in the eastern Bihar district of Bhagalpur in late 1989—which occurred during the last months of Congress hegemony in Bihar's and India's politics—and by the Congress national government's role in pandering to the Hindu communalist campaign centered on Ayodhya, which is located in the eastern part of neighboring UP, adjacent to Bihar. In October 1990 it was Laloo Yadav who, as Bihar's chief minister, ordered the state police to arrest the BJP leader L. K. Advani while he was traveling through Bihar on his march across northern India to Ayodhya. The fears of Bihar's Muslims were aggravated by the toxic communal climate in northern India during 1990–1993, and they were outraged like Muslims elsewhere in India, particularly northern India, by the Congress national government's failure to protect the Babri Mosque from demolition by Hindutva gangs in December 1992. Bihar's Muslims turned to Laloo Yadav as a reliable protector of their safety from communal attack, and he reciprocated by recruiting Muslims in significant numbers into his party apparatus, including prominent positions.

This Muslim-Yadav (M-Y) electoral base saw Laloo through to consecutive victories in state elections in 1995 and 2000. During these second and third terms, Bihar's "Laloo Raj" became a byword throughout India for corruption, lawlessness, and chaos. After being personally indicted in a corruption scandal, Laloo was forced to formally relinquish the chief ministership of Bihar in 1997. But he continued to rule the state through a "proxy" chief minister he managed to get appointed to the post—his apolitical and barely literate wife, Rabri Devi, who had married him when she was 14 and borne him seven daughters and two sons. The "Laloo-Rabri Raj" of Bihar became synonymous with corrupt and dysfunctional administration, criminal gangs who roamed at will due to nearly nonexistent law enforcement and in many cases protection from the ruling party, the lack of any program of socioeconomic development, and the deterioration and near collapse of already poor infrastructure in roads, electricity, health, and education. When Laloo came to power in 1990 Bihar was one of India's most underdeveloped and poverty-stricken states, especially notorious for caste oppression and violence. Over his 15 years in power it became a national laughingstock as India's foremost backwater state.

The challenge that finally unseated Laloo was led by a rival regionalist politician of very similar background and trajectory. Nitish Kumar was born in 1951 into a family of the Kurmi caste, an OBC community. Like Laloo he was a socialist student leader at Patna University in the 1970s and participated in the major opposition agitation of 1974–1975 in Bihar that had been one of the reasons for Indira Gandhi's resort to the Emergency. Active in opposition politics in Bihar during the 1980s, he was a prominent leader of the Janata Dal campaign that ousted Congress from power in Bihar (and neighboring UP) in 1989–1990 and brought OBC communities to political center stage in both states. In contrast to Laloo Yadav's flamboyant style, Nitish Kumar was known for his sober personality. In 1994 he broke with Laloo and became a leader of a new regional party, the Samata Party (Equality Party), which aligned with the BJP from the mid-1990s and became an important constituent of the BJP-led National Democratic Alliance in 1998. In 2003 the Samata Party absorbed a smaller anti–Laloo Janata Dal faction in Bihar and was renamed the Janata Dal-United.

In the spring of 2005, state elections in Bihar produced an indecisive verdict, and a new state government could not be formed. Laloo's ruling Rashtriya Janata Dal (National People's Party) lost much ground, and while the opposition alliance comprised of the Janata Dal-United as senior partner and the BJP as junior partner won the single largest bloc of seats in the legislature, it was short of a majority. In fresh elections in late 2005 this alliance won a decisive legislative majority of 143 in the 243-member Bihar assembly (Janata Dal-United won in 88 constituencies and BJP in another 55). Laloo's party, which had joined the Congress-led United Progressive Alliance at the Center and fought the election in

Bihar with Congress as junior partner, was reduced to 54 seats (Congress got another 9). Laloo Yadav had boasted: "jab tak samose mein rahega aloo, raj karega Bihar mein laloo" (as long as potatoes fill samosas—a snack almost always made with potato filling—Laloo will rule in Bihar).

The late 2005 vote in Bihar was more a vote against Laloo—whose reign had become known as the "jungle Raj" in Bihar and nationally— than a vote in favor of his opponents. Nitish Kumar himself recalled in late 2012: "I was given my first term in power because people wanted change, desperately." There was little if any expectation that the new government could or would do much to change Bihar's abysmal plight. But after taking over as chief minister, Nitish Kumar confounded those low to nonexistent expectations. (Until Jharkhand was formed as a separate state from southern Bihar in November 2000, Bihar was the Indian Union's second most populous state after UP but even in its downsized version had a population of 104 million as of 2011.)

Nitish Kumar's government embarked on a well-conceived recovery and rejuvenation strategy that it pursued with vigor. Nitish first sent the criminal gangs who had had the run of the state during Laloo's later years in power packing by enforcing a no-nonsense, zero-tolerance approach to law and order. This in itself earned him much gratitude from Bihar's citizens. He then initiated an extensive road-building program across Bihar; apart from drastically improving very poor connectivity in the sprawling and overwhelmingly rural state, this generated local employment. He next focused on elementary and secondary education, with a special emphasis on getting girls to attend and stay in school. His Mukhyamantri Balika Cycle Yojana (Chief Minister's Cycle Scheme for Girls) entitled all girls enrolled in high school to a free bicycle or a grant to buy one. Within a couple of years a new sight became common in Bihar's rural landscape—midteen girls cycling confidently between home and school, often along newly built roads, without fear of becoming victims of violent crime. The rates of female enrollment in and graduation from high school rose exponentially, powered by the "girls on cycles." One of the prime manifestations of Bihar's backwardness malaise had been huge school dropout rates among girls and the poor status of women in society more generally.

Nitish Kumar's government then initiated a scheme that entitled every girl in Bihar attending elementary and middle school to a grant to buy school uniforms, books, and classroom supplies. A tenth-grade girl student of a rural high school said in August 2010: "no previous government ever thought about girls and women in this way. We will prevail upon the villagers to prefer such leaders."[37] In 2006 the government raised the proportion of positions in elected village and urban councils reserved for women to 50 percent in Bihar from the nationally mandatory minimum of 33 percent. Nitish's government also took measures to rebuild the nearly broken primary health-care system in rural Bihar and to improve the state's electricity supply. The recovery of India's basketcase state began to make news not just across the country but abroad.

As state elections approached in late 2010 Nitish Kumar wrote on his blog that "the caste factor will be relegated to the backseat for the first time [in Bihar's electoral history] . . . this time the people will rise above caste considerations to vote for development-centric policies." He observed that "this trend was already discernible in the parliamentary elections last year [2009] when the NDA won 32 of the 40 Lok Sabha seats in Bihar," even though the BJP-led opposition alliance fared poorly in the nationwide context. He expressed optimism that young people casting their vote for the first time would favor his reelection, as his government had worked for the benefit of all the state's people without regard to caste and religion. (India's voting age was lowered from 21 to 18 in the late 1980s.) And he placed particular faith in the support of Bihar's women: "In earlier polls women did not have any separate identity as voters and would generally vote as their male relatives asked them to." This was in the process of changing, he predicted.[38]

In December 2010 the Janata Dal-United/BJP alliance won in 206 of the 243 single-member constituencies comprising Bihar's legislature—a five-sixths majority rarely achieved in India's electoral history. (The Janata Dal-United won 115 seats in the new Bihar assembly and the BJP another 91 seats; the BJP, whose support is largely limited to upper castes, benefited statewide from Nitish's popularity.) A slightly greater proportion of women than men voters exercised the right to vote, and 34 women—the highest number ever—were elected to the legislature.

Laloo Yadav had allied in this election with a smaller regional party led by a Dalit politician, clearly in the hope of adding a substantial Dalit vote to his Muslim-Yadav base. Laloo's party won in just 22 constituencies and his junior ally in another 3. Congress decided to run candidates in all the 243 constituencies with the objective of reasserting its presence in Bihar. This was part of Rahul Gandhi's strategy of resurrecting Congress from the grassroots in Bihar and UP. Congress was nearly wiped out; it won in four constituencies and came second in just another eight. Its vote share statewide was pitiful: 8.4 percent, marginally greater than the 6.1 percent it had polled across the 51 constituencies it had contested as Laloo's junior ally in late 2005. In late 2012 Nitish Kumar recalled that Bihar's people "were surprised that governments could work. That was the basis of the second mandate in [late] 2010."

Nitish Kumar's call to Bihar's people to transcend caste allegiances and fault lines and vote on the basis of performance and for continued development actually achieved only limited success. In fact, the Janata Dal-United/BJP combine's share of the popular vote increased marginally from 36 percent in late 2005 to 39 percent in late 2010, and it was the "first-past-the-post" electoral system in single-member constituencies that delivered the huge legislative majority. The opposition alliance led by Laloo Yadav polled nearly 26 percent of the vote. And they were not the only ones engaged in caste-based tactics—Nitish himself targeted the votes of exceptionally deprived castes among both OBC castes and Dalits.

Yet Nitish Kumar's attempt to move the discourse of politics in northern India away from caste identities to performance and competence was both audacious and significant. The Mandal Commission controversy died down from 1993 after India's Supreme Court upheld the constitutionality of OBC reservations in higher education and government jobs, albeit with a caveat that the "creamy layer" of OBC castes—those with parents already employed in upper-level administrative positions and those whose families owned substantial landholdings—should be excluded from affirmative action. The upper castes resigned themselves to this outcome, and through the 1990s and beyond, the deregulation and liberalization of the Indian economy opened up sought-after job opportunities in the private sector, which meant that state employment was no longer as coveted or especially lucrative. But the enduring legacy of the Mandal Commission fracas of the early 1990s was the "Mandalization" of politics in northern India, particularly in Uttar Pradesh and Bihar. This meant above all the growth of caste-based political parties.

There is nothing intrinsically wrong or illegitimate about caste-based politics. The problem has been the proclivity of caste-based parties to become breeding pools of corruption and criminality once in government. The degeneration of Laloo Yadav was the most extreme example but not the only one. His caste-kinsman in UP, Mulayam Yadav, proved equally unable to break out of the politics of patronizing his core Yadav base, which was supplemented by the vast numbers among UP's 18 percent Muslim minority, who turned to him as protector in the 1990s, having lost faith in Congress and fearful of the BJP. Mulayam Yadav's last tenure as UP chief minister (2003–2007) became notorious for its Mafia-like character—as a "goonda [thug] Raj" run by his party's local bosses. The BSP's Mayawati, who replaced him in 2007, won a slender majority in UP's legislature on the basis of a slim plurality (under 31 percent) of the popular vote, gained by cultivating the support of poorer Brahmins and some Muslims, which was added on to her mass support among the state's Dalit electorate of 21–22 percent. But while the single-party government led by a Dalit woman in UP was a historic development, her government too was dogged by rampant corruption, and—perhaps most important—she proved unable to move beyond her perch as the "Dalit queen" to embrace a broader social constituency and agenda.

Nitish Kumar's project to move beyond caste mobilizations and polarizations, and his promise to "make Bihar a developed state . . . [as] that will help all of us," has its limits.[39] Bihar has virtually no manufacturing industry, and its former mineral wealth now lies in Jharkhand. Bihar is an overwhelmingly agrarian state where landholding patterns are extremely biased toward upper and upper-intermediate castes, and three-fourths of the very poor are landless—mostly Dalits but also the most deprived OBC castes and Muslims. But land reform and the redistribution of farmland to the landless is a no-go area for his government. That would upset not just his junior coalition partner, the BJP, which has its core base in Bihar in upper-caste support, but trigger a backlash from upper castes in general, as well as the landowning OBC segments. Yet his effort to make the legitimacy of regionalist politics contingent on delivering good governance for his state and all its citizens still marks him out as a regional leader with a difference.[40] Kumar acknowledged in late 2012 that "expectations are high, very high, because after a long time people have seen a government that works." His strategic priorities during his second term are to substantially improve productivity and marketing of produce in Bihar's agriculture—76 percent of the population farms for a livelihood—and to provide an electricity connection to every home in the state by August 15, 2015 (India's Independence Day).[41] In addition, his government is undertaking various programs designed to reinforce his image of a champion of women's empowerment. One of these programs aims to ensure that at least one-third of those recruited to the state police are women; another aims to ensure that women are 50 percent of post-holding officials in local cooperative associations across Bihar.

There are definite indications that the cleverest and most dynamic of India's regional leaders have realized the formula for successful regionalism in the early twenty-first century. In September 2011 the most successful of the BJP's regional politicians, Chief Minister Narendra Modi of Gujarat, whom Nitish Kumar does not like, undertook a three-day fast—publicized as "a prayer for togetherness"—in Gujarat's largest city, Ahmedabad. (He followed up with token fasts held in towns across the western state.) On this occasion his government took out full-page ad-vertisements in newspapers across India displaying an open letter from Modi:

> today I begin my three-day fast. . . . It aims at unity, harmony and brother-hood among all. . . . The Indian history is a witness that casteism and com-munalism have never done any good to society. This is also my own firm conviction. Gujarat has understood this and having overcome these evils has adopted the path of Inclusive Development. We are committed to work for a developed Gujarat for a developed India. . . . I am grateful to all those who pointed out my genuine mistakes during the last ten years. . . . As chief minister, the pain of each and every citizen [of Gujarat] is my own pain. . . . The six crore [60 million] people of Gujarat are working together. . . . Everyone has inculcated the state's ethos of "Development of all with Coop-eration of all."[42]

This remarkable letter was in large part a politician's attempt at an im-age makeover, aimed at living down the taint of the communal violence directed at Gujarat's Muslim minority in 2002, during Narendra Modi's first year as chief minister. But it was also a charter of "can do" regionalism in the changing, aspiration-driven India of the early twenty-first century.

At the other end of the country, in eastern India, Chief Minister Ma-mata Banerjee of West Bengal—an avowedly secular politician and for-mer Congress leader—also understands that her prospects of gaining a second five-year term in office in 2016 depend on her government's abil-ity to deliver decent governance and socioeconomic development to the people of her state.

Most of contemporary India's challenges are best addressed through good governance and effective development policies at the level of the states, the building blocks of India's polity. This includes extreme poverty and marginalization, which has bred support for the radical "Maoist" movement against India's democracy in several states, including parts of Chhattisgarh, Jharkhand, Bihar, Orissa, and Andhra Pradesh as well as pockets of UP, West Bengal, and Maharashtra. Such top-down schemes conceived in New Delhi as a nationwide food security legislation pro-posed by the Congress party, which promises to supply subsidized staple foods to nearly two-thirds of all Indians, are in part motivated by an agenda of undermining the inexorable regionalization of India's polity. The scheme may represent a dubious approach to eliminating the hunger and malnutrition that are part of the lives of several hundred million citi-zens, and it definitely represents an obsolete and dying paradigm of cen-tralized decision-making and control of implementation. Thus, said the *Hindustan Times* in late 2011,

the National Food Security Bill looks unwieldy to even its staunchest supporters such as development economists Jean Dreze and Abhijit Sen....
"It's a bad bill, frankly, from the point of view of implementation," says
Sen.... No such legislation should bother with the exact details of the de-
livery mechanism, which are best left to the States. Dreze considers such
excessive central control as a "serious flaw." [Moreover] the splurge is not a
one-off. By giving citizens a continual legal right to food, the [Union] government ties itself into a perpetual financial knot.... For Congress chief
Sonia Gandhi, not having the food bill is not an option.... [She says] "We
must take it to the people and make it a central part of our political campaign" [for the 2014 national election].... Sen's verdict: While a Food Security Act is very much needed, this one is certain to fail.[43]

Another top-down scheme rolled out by the Congress party's government in New Delhi during 2013, providing for direct cash payments
from the Center to rural laborers, students, and senior citizens in administrative districts across India, is equally unlikely to stem, let alone reverse, the devolutionary dynamic of India's democracy.

Coalition governments in New Delhi are a certainty for the foreseeable
future, but that is only the most obvious manifestation of the transformation of India's democracy. The bottom-up federalization of India's
politics in the post-Congress era—an evolution rooted in the nation's diversity and driven by the will of its people—means that the lives of the
vast majority of Indians will be shaped by the dominant feature of India's
decentered democracy in the early twenty-first century: regionalization
and regionalism(s). It is apt that India's diversity, unparalleled in the
world, defines the nature of its democracy.

INDIA

West Bengal

WEST BENGAL

N

Map Not to Scale

SIKKIM

BHUTAN

DARJEELING

NEPAL

JALPAIGURI

COOCHBEHAR

NORTH
DINAJPUR

ASSAM

BIHAR

SOUTH
DINAJPUR

MALDA

BANGLADESH

JHARKHAND

MURSHIDABAD

BIRBHUM

BARDHAMAN

NADIA

PURULIA

BANKURA

Singur

HOOGHLY

NORTH 24
PARGANAS

WEST
MEDINIPUR

HOWRAH

JHARKHAND

Medinipur

KOLKATA

Jhargram

Nandigram

SOUTH 24
PARGANAS

EAST
MEDINIPUR

ORISSA

Bay of
Bengal

CHAPTER THREE

Democracy in West Bengal

JUST BEFORE dawn on a chilly winter morning in December 2006, a girl in her midteens stepped out of her modest home in a village located about 25 miles from the city of Kolkata (formerly Calcutta), the capital of the eastern state of West Bengal. It is very likely that she went out to answer the call of nature, as like several hundred million poor people in rural India, her family had no toilet of their own nor access to shared toilets.

Just after daybreak villagers spotted a small fire burning in a shallow pit a few hundred yards from the girl's home. When they rushed to investigate they found the girl lying in the pit, her body on fire. By the time the flames were doused she was largely charred. Grisly photographs of the semicharred, contorted corpse were published on the front pages of newspapers across West Bengal the next day.

The horrible death of Tapasi Malik, the daughter of a poor peasant family who was 16 or 17 years old, was neither suicide nor an "ordinary" crime. In the last three to four months of her life Tapasi had emerged as a well-known political campaigner in the area. She was an enthusiastic volunteer for the Krishi Jomi Rakhha Committee (Save Farmland Committee), established in a cluster of local villages to campaign against the state government's decision to acquire 1,000 acres of farmland cultivated by the villagers for one of India's highest-profile manufacturing projects. Under the plan, the automobile-making arm of the Tata Group—a huge conglomerate of businesses established in India for a century that enjoys a respectable reputation in India and abroad— would set up a factory on the acquired land to build a small, economically priced car branded as the Tata "Nano." The Tata Group envisioned that the Nano would bring car ownership within the reach of the millions of nonaffluent Indian households who use two-wheelers—motorbikes and scooters. Tata Group also envisioned that the Nano plant at Singur—the agricultural area close to Kolkata where Tapasi lived—would generate a range of jobs for locals and dramatically increase the area's prosperity. They picked Singur, situated in proximity to one of India's largest metropolises, because the area is close to interstate highway routes to other parts of India. The government of West Bengal, keen to attract large-scale investment to a state that was once an industrial powerhouse of India but has been steadily denuded of its strength in manufacturing since the 1970s, welcomed the Nano project with open arms.

A large section of the local farming population was not similarly enthused. They did not wish to part with their land and were not convinced either by the modest level of monetary compensation offered by the state government or the prospect of jobs and greater prosperity. In the second half of 2006 a movement to resist the takeover of land emerged among Singur's farming population, who are predominantly peasant-proprietors cultivating small plots in the fertile agricultural zone but also include some *bhagchashis* or *bargadars* (landless or land-poor peasants who work on land owned by others for a share of the crop produced) and *khetmajurs* (landless laborers who work on others' land for a wage). Tapasi Malik, whose father earned food for the family as a sharecropper and sold fish as a side activity, was drawn to this movement and became one of its most enthusiastic foot soldiers. She became known locally as not simply a participant but an organizer of protest rallies and marches.

By the time Tapasi died on that winter morning in December 2006, Singur was on the boil, and the agitation was making headlines in West Bengal and across India. The government of West Bengal resorted to police action against the Singur protesters as soon as the agitation escalated in September 2006 and proceeded to block off the lands earmarked for the car factory and its ancillary facilities with a boundary wall and fencing. The government of West Bengal, an alliance of communist and socialist parties dominated by India's largest parliamentary communist party, the Communist Party of India (Marxist) (CPM), felt secure in facing down the protesters. A few months earlier, in May 2006, this alliance, the Left Front (LF), had won its seventh consecutive state election since 1977 in West Bengal and held a massive majority in the state legislature—233 of the 294 single-member constituencies making up the state's legislative assembly had elected LF candidates, and the CPM alone had won in 176 constituencies. The longevity of the CPM-led government of West Bengal was (and is) unrivaled in the annals of India's democracy. In seven consecutive state elections in 1977, 1982, 1987, 1991, 1996, 2001, and 2006, the LF never won fewer than two-thirds of West Bengal's 294 electoral constituencies, and on all but one occasion (2001) the alliance's dominant party, the CPM, won well over half of those 294 seats in the state legislature.

In May 2006 the Left Front stormed back to power for its seventh consecutive term with the campaign slogan "Krishi amader bhitti, shilpo amader bhobishyot" (Agriculture is our foundation and industry our future). Shortly afterward the Tata Group announced that its small-car plant would be sited in West Bengal. This was a coup for the state's CPM-led government, and it was determined to not allow pesky protesters to obstruct the showpiece project. The government accordingly treated the local protests in Singur as a nuisance and the protesters as miscreants. The protesters were met by police wielding truncheons and firing tear-gas shells, and large numbers were arrested, including numerous women. One woman was carrying her two-year-old daughter at a protest, and the infant went to jail with the mother. The protesters alleged that the police crackdown was accompanied by a campaign of intimidation conducted by local cadres of the CPM. When Mamata Banerjee—the state's top opposition leader and one of India's most prominent politicians—attempted to visit Singur in solidarity with the protesters, she was intercepted by police and forced back to Kolkata. In early December Banerjee went on hunger strike in the city center of Kolkata to protest the repression in Singur. Tapasi's death happened halfway through Banerjee's nearly monthlong protest fast.

Tapasi Malik's death proved to be the catalyst of a chain of events such that four and a half years later, in state elections in May 2011, independent India's most resilient political regime—the entrenched hegemony over three and a half decades of the CPM in West Bengal—toppled. The statewide outcry that ensued after her death compelled the CPM-led state government to reluctantly agree to an inquiry conducted by the Central Bureau of Investigation, India's equivalent of the FBI. The Bureau determined that Tapasi had been attacked, raped, and then strangled, after which her body had been set on fire. The Bureau indicted and arrested two men for involvement in the planning and perpetration of the crime: one the zonal secretary of the CPM in Singur (the area's top party organizer) and the other a local supporter of the ruling party.

This chapter is a study of political contestation, continuity, and change in West Bengal, India's fourth most populous state (in 2011, the state had over 91 million people and an electorate of 56 million). It shows how the aspirations of nonprivileged rural classes combined with a sense of (predominantly urban-based) regional pride rooted in Bengali ethnolinguistic identity to bring the CPM to power in West Bengal. And it shows how the disillusionment of much of the subaltern classes of rural society with the CPM led to regime change in West Bengal after 34 years and brought the world's most durable democratically elected communist regime to an end. The driving force and beneficiary of that change was a regional party specific to West Bengal: the Trinamool (Grassroots) Congress formed by Mamata Banerjee in 1998 after her expulsion from the Congress party. The rise of the Trinamool Congress in West Bengal since the late 1990s signaled the complete regionalization of the state's politics, because the CPM's lengthy primacy in West Bengal was also an essentially regional (or state-specific) phenomenon. Regionalization has, of course, been the defining feature of India's democratic evolution through the 1990s and into the first and second decades of the twenty-first century. The story of regime continuity and change in West Bengal is also rife with insights into why India's democracy is so robust; it is powered by struggles from below and the participation of the nonelite masses of society.

West Bengal was created as a state of the Indian Union by the 1947 partition of the subcontinent into India and Pakistan. Two sprawling and populous provinces of the subcontinent were divided in 1947: Punjab in the northwest and Bengal in the east. In 1947 Bengal's population was approximately 54 percent Muslim and 43 percent Hindu. The partition created a Muslim-majority "East Bengal," which took in 63 percent of Bengal's territory and became the eastern wing of Pakistan (and the sovereign state of Bangladesh in 1971). A Hindu-majority "West Bengal" was carved out of the other 37 percent of the land of Bengal, with its capital at Calcutta, located in the southern part of the newly created state. Calcutta (now Kolkata) was then and remains by far the largest city in the eastern part of the subcontinent and was the capital of British-ruled India until 1911, when the capital shifted to Delhi in the north.[1]

The partition into West Bengal (India) and East Bengal (Pakistan) did not eliminate religious heterogeneity in either part. Of West Bengal's 21 million people in 1947, just over one-quarter—5.3 million—were Muslims. Muslims constitute about the same proportion of West Bengal's population today. Across the new border, about 11 million of the 39 million people of East Bengal were Hindus, some 28 percent of the population. This proportion has declined steadily over the past six decades, and Hindus are today about 10 percent of the population of Bangladesh.

As in the rest of India, West Bengal's politics was dominated by the Congress party, and the state was ruled by Congress governments from independence until Congress's nationwide hegemony was shaken in the national and state elections of 1967. But through the 1950s and 1960s a strong communist opposition developed in West Bengal, due to a number of historical and contemporary factors.

The undivided province of Bengal had been a stronghold of the nationalist movement for emancipation from colonial rule throughout the first half of the twentieth century. The nationalist movement failed to elicit significant participation from the province's Muslim majority, the vast bulk of whom were impoverished peasants, and Bengali Muslims were attracted to the idea of Pakistan in the 1940s. This failure notwithstanding, Bengal was known and even renowned throughout India as a bastion of resistance to the colonial power. From its formative period in the first decade of the twentieth century, the anticolonial nationalism that developed in Bengal had a militant streak. In 1908 an 18-year-old youth, Khudiram Bose, a native of the Medinipur district south-west of Calcutta, was hanged by the colonial government after he and another teenaged revolutionary attempted to assassinate a British official and killed two British women by mistake. Khudiram famously went to the gallows unfazed and smiling and shouted "Bande Mataram" (Hail Motherland) as he was executed. Khudiram's martyrdom had a lasting effect in Bengal. In subsequent decades a sizable element of Bengali Hindu youth—including some women—took up arms against the British Raj. The peak of this campaign of revolutionary violence occurred between 1930 and 1934, when a spate of assassinations and bombings shook colonial power in Bengal, the province the British had used as the base for their conquest of the subcontinent in the late eighteenth and early nineteenth centuries.

During the last two decades of the independence movement in the 1930s and 1940s, Bengal produced one of the top three leaders of the freedom struggle alongside Gandhi and Nehru—Subhas Chandra Bose, revered as Netaji (The Leader) by hundreds of millions in India and other countries of South Asia even today, long after the sun set on the British Raj in the subcontinent. Subhas Bose was a left-wing nationalist who combined unbending resistance to British imperialism with progressive ideas about the social emancipation of women and the poor and a staunchly secular vision of the equal role of Hindus and Muslims in liberating the subcontinent and building a free Indian nation-state.[2]

Communism as Regionalism, Regionalism as Communism

The Communist Party of India (CPI)—from which the CPM was born through a split in 1964—could not claim legitimacy from the freedom struggle, and not simply because it was a bit-player. During World War II the CPI adopted a policy of active collaboration with the British Raj against nationalist patriots after Nazi Germany attacked the Soviet Union. To the Indian communists, the defense of the Soviet Union took precedence over India's struggle for freedom, and the colonial power, Great Britain, ceased to be an enemy and became an ally worthy of support from June 1941 onward. The CPI actively opposed the nationwide mass movement calling on the British to "quit India" that was launched by Mahatma Gandhi in August 1942, and CPI members assisted British police and intelligence operations against the nationalists struggling for independence under the broad Congress banner. After 1947 the communists compounded the taint of wartime collaboration by ridiculing independence as a sham. The party went through a radical phase from 1948 to 1950, egged on by the Stalin regime in Moscow, and agitated for revolution. Communist students marched in Calcutta shouting "Yeh azaadi jhuta hai" (This freedom is a lie). The revolutionary strategy proved unviable, given the communists' puny presence across the nation (in stark contrast to China in the late 1940s, where the communists, having emerged as the bearers of the mantle of Chinese nationalism, completed a revolutionary seizure of state power). The most notable episode of the Indian communists' radical phase was a communist-led peasant movement in the late 1940s in southern India's Telangana region, which would become part of the state of Andhra Pradesh in 1956. Thereafter the CPI realized that the path of revolution represented a dead end and decided to partake of India's "bourgeois" democracy.

The communists established themselves as a presence in West Bengal's politics from the first state election of 1952, when the CPI obtained nearly 11 percent of the statewide popular vote and the CPI's candidates won in 28 of the 238 single-member constituencies comprising the Vidhan Sabha (state legislature). Thereafter the communist presence in West Bengal registered a steady upward graph. In the state election of 1957 the CPI obtained almost 18 percent of the statewide vote and elected 46 legislators to the 252-member legislature. In the state election of 1962 the CPI obtained 25 percent of the statewide vote, and 50 communists took seats in the 252-strong West Bengal legislature.[3]

The communists had made an initial attempt to build a rural base in prepartition Bengal in 1946 and early 1947, when the CPI's peasant wing led an agitation for sharecropper rights in several districts of the undivided province. This agitation is known as the Tebhaga (One-Thirds) movement because it demanded that sharecroppers should retain two-thirds of the crop produced by their labor and the landowner should not get more than a third. But the emergence of the communists as the principal political opposition in West Bengal in the 1950s and 1960s was rooted in postindependence and postpartition circumstances.

The national census of 1951 recorded a massive influx into West Bengal of Hindu refugees from the Pakistani province of East Bengal. By 1951 the recorded number of refugees from the east was 2.1 million people (the actual number may have been higher). The refugees came in two main waves, the first just after partition and the second in 1950. By May 1948 at least 1.1 million Hindus moved to West Bengal from the east, and this first wave consisted overwhelmingly of *bhadralok* (literally "gentlemen," meaning highly educated urban professional classes) and well-off landed Hindus of rural background. This uprooted mass of highly literate and prosperous people were confronted with the challenge of rebuilding their lives from scratch, and many, perhaps most, were plunged into hardship and even penury. Deeply embittered by the trauma of displacement and the marginality and poverty they experienced in West Bengal, this population provided the core base for the communists' steady rise in West Bengal over the next two decades. The refugees harbored deep feelings of injustice and betrayal, and their sense of grievance targeted Congress, as Congress's national leadership, headed by Nehru, had agreed to the partition of Bengal (and India), and the Congress governments of West Bengal of the early postindependence period showed indifference toward the problems of the dispossessed from the east. In northern India the same strong anti-Congress sentiment among Hindu refugees from West Pakistan motivated many to join the Hindu nationalist RSS, which undertook relief efforts among them—for example, the RSS developed a loyal following among Hindu refugees from Pakistani Punjab who settled in and around Delhi. In West Bengal the refugees gravitated to a different brand of anti-Congress politics, represented by the communists. The highest concentrations of refugees could be found in Calcutta's suburbs, in a huge adjoining district called the "24 Parganas" (a name derived from historical administrative classifications) and in the district of Nadia, just north of the 24 Parganas. The refugee-dominant areas showed high levels of communist support in elections in the 1950s and 1960s, produced numerous leading communist cadres, and continued to be bastions of CPM strength during the three decades of LF rule in West Bengal that began in 1977.

In early 1950 intense communal violence targeted at Hindus erupted in East Bengal, and about 1 million more refugees arrived in West Bengal from the east. Unlike the first wave of 1947–1948 these refugees were largely poor, lower-caste peasants and other nonlandowning rural folk and faced even worse prospects in displacement. The national census of 1961 found that over 3 million people in West Bengal were of refugee origin. More refugees came in 1964, fleeing another outbreak of communal violence in East Pakistan. Of the 10 million people who fled to West Bengal and other Indian states from East Pakistan in 1971 during the Pakistani army's onslaught against the Bangladesh independence uprising, about 70 percent were Hindus, and many did not return to liberated Bangladesh. By 1973 the total population of refugee origin in West Bengal was over 6 million, nearly a seventh of the state's people, and a quarter of the state's urban and semiurban population was of refugee origin.[4] This refugee society constituted a bedrock of communist support.

The other factor that facilitated the gradual communist ascendancy in West Bengal was equally regionally specific. For two decades, from independence until the late 1960s, the Congress party in West Bengal was run by a cabal of conservative politicians who had represented a small minority in the preindependence Bengal Congress. In the preindependence period Congress in Bengal was overwhelmingly dominated by followers of Subhas Chandra Bose. In 1938 Bose became Congress's national president. The holder of this prestigious position usually changed every year, and when Bose decided to put himself forward for a second term the following year, this time against Mahatma Gandhi's wishes, he faced off against a candidate put up, with Gandhi's support, by Congress's conservative wing. The electorate consisted of the nearly 3,000 delegates elected to the All-India Congress Committee by the Congress party organizations in various provinces. Bose comfortably won the election, by 1,580 votes to 1,375 for his rival. He won a majority of delegates from various provinces, including the United Provinces (postindependence UP) and (undivided) Punjab in the north, Assam in the northeast, and Tamil Nadu, Karnataka, and Kerala in the south. But his biggest and ultimately decisive margin came from his home province, Bengal. Of the 538 All-India Congress Committee members from Bengal who voted in the election, 469 supported Bose and 69 his conservative-backed rival (who was from Andhra Pradesh, in the south). After independence it was elements of the latter, minority faction of the Bengal Congress who controlled the Congress party in West Bengal. (Subhas Bose died in August 1945, and his older brother Sarat Bose, also a prominent Bengal Congress leader of the preindependence era, died in February 1950.) These elements represented social and political conservatism and owed their dominance of Congress in West Bengal to their allegiance to the national Congress leadership headed by Nehru.

With Congress in West Bengal having abdicated its socially progressive and left-wing tradition, the field was open for opposition parties to articulate their versions of this tradition. In 1953 communist supporters set buses and trams on fire in Calcutta to protest an increase in public transport fares. By 1959 they were able to launch a more serious agitation—a *khadyo andolan* (food movement) to highlight the problem of food insecurity in rural West Bengal. This was an especially sensitive issue because as recently as 1943–1944, during the final years of colonial rule, rural Bengal had been ravaged by a famine that may have killed as many as 3–4 million people of the undivided province's population of 60 million.[5] In 1959 large numbers of rural poor descended on the city center of Calcutta to demand reliable access to food and were met with harsh police action. A second agitation on the same theme occurred in 1966. By then the communists had emerged as the principal voices of social change and subaltern politics in West Bengal.

The rise of the communists in West Bengal was one of the earliest examples of the growth of a regionally rooted opposition to the Congress hegemony in India's politics. The only other state where the communists developed a popular base during the first two decades of India's democracy was several thousand miles away in the southern state of Kerala. There a communist-led government came to power in state elections in 1957, only to be deposed in 1959 by action from Congress-ruled New Delhi. (Even today, the CPM has a mass base only in West Bengal, Kerala, and the tiny state of Tripura in northeastern India, bordering Bangladesh.) In historical retrospect, West Bengal was a trailblazer in the emergence of regional (state-specific) political forces and in the process of regionalization that has defined and transformed India's polity since the end of the era of Congress's nationwide hegemony in 1989.

But it was far from smooth sailing for the regional variant of oppositional communism on the ascendant in West Bengal. In 1964 the CPI split in two. The split was precipitated by the post-Stalin Soviet leadership's bid to cultivate friendly relations with India—in effect with its Congress government—in the global context of deepening Cold War with the United States and emerging estrangement between the Soviet Union and Mao Zedong's China. Nehru had pursued a foreign policy of "nonalignment" with either superpower, and in late 1962 Sino-Indian relations collapsed when a border dispute between the two countries escalated to a brief but bitter military conflict in which India was severely defeated. The leadership in Moscow, headed until 1964 by Nikita Khrushchev, put pressure on the CPI to adopt a nonconfrontational stance toward the Congress party and government in India. A large segment of the CPI was unhappy with the prospect of becoming Congress's "B-Team" and broke away to form the CPM in

1964. The breakaway faction claimed to be the authentic Marxist party of India.

The 1967 national and state elections proved to be a watershed in West Bengal. The outcome confirmed the terminal decline of the conservative Congress regime that had wielded power in the state since 1947. The results also confirmed the emergence of the breakaway CPM as the principal standard-bearer of anti-Congress politics in West Bengal.

In the February 1967 state election, Congress for the first time failed to win an outright majority in West Bengal's legislature. It was still the single largest party, with 127 of the 280 seats—down from 157 of 252 in 1962—but the outcome signaled the end of the party's hegemony in West Bengal and the beginning of a period of ferment and instability. Congress faced serious setbacks in 1967 in states across northern and eastern India; in West Bengal, Congress's share of the popular vote fell from 47.3 percent in 1962 to 41.1 percent in 1967. As in other states, such as UP in the north and Orissa in the east, Congress was damaged in West Bengal by the exit of prominent regional leaders. Like Charan Singh in UP and Harekrishna Mahatab in Orissa, two senior leaders of the West Bengal Congress, Ajoy Mukherjee and Jahangir Kabir, quit the party prior to the election and floated a regional party called the Bangla (Bengal) Congress. This rebel regionalist Congress did well in the election, but the single largest non-Congress group in the new legislature was the CPM, which won in 43 constituencies. The two communist parties, the CPM and the CPI, respectively polled 18.1 percent and 6.5 percent of the popular vote. The total communist vote was about the same as the 25 percent polled by the united CPI in 1962, but the fact that the CPM won three-fourths of the communist votes in 1967 firmly established it as the favored vehicle of the communist support base in West Bengal.

Like the national election to constitute the Lok Sabha in New Delhi, elections to constitute the legislatures of India's states are supposed to be held every five years. The February 1967 election in West Bengal was followed by three more state elections within the next five years—in February 1969, March 1971, and March 1972. The late 1960s and early 1970s were a period of extraordinary turmoil in West Bengal.

After the February 1967 state election, the Congress rebel Ajoy Mukherjee became West Bengal's first non-Congress chief minister at the head of a so-called United Front government, a shaky postelection alliance of the communist parties, several smaller socialist parties, and his Bangla Congress. This coalition government did not command a majority in the fractured state legislature and collapsed in November 1967, after which West Bengal was brought under direct central rule for a year, pending fresh state elections. That state election in February 1969 was much more decisive in its outcome. The Congress polled the same proportion of the popular vote (41.3 percent) as in 1967 (41.1 percent) but could win in only 55 of the 280 single-member constituencies making up the state legislature—fewer than half of the 127 it had won in 1967. This was because the communist and socialist parties and the Bangla Congress formed a preelection alliance and Congress was faced with a single anti-Congress candidate put up by this alliance in the vast majority of constituencies. The alliance won a decisive majority in the state legislature due to the consolidation of the anti-Congress popular vote, and the Bangla Congress's Ajoy Mukherjee became chief minister again, heading what came to be known as the second United Front government. The biggest gainer in the 1969 state election was the CPM, which emerged as the single largest party in the new legislature with 80 members. As the dominant constituent of the second United Front government, the CPM secured two key cabinet portfolios: home (interior), which meant jurisdiction over the police, and land affairs. As in 1967, the veteran communist politician Jyoti Basu—who would go on to become India's longest-serving chief minister (1977–2000) at the head of West Bengal's post-1977 "Left Front" regime—became the home minister, and Harekrishna Konar, a top leader of the CPM's peasant wing, took charge of the land ministry.

The second United Front government lasted just over a year before West Bengal was again brought under direct central rule in March 1970. The main reason was the outbreak of unprecedented levels of political violence in the state in 1969–1970, caused by a deadly schism in the ranks of the CPM. Since its formation in 1964 the CPM had contained a sizable element that was inspired by the revolutionary model of Mao's China and wished to emulate it in India. This Maoist element of the CPM was enthused by the "Great Proletarian Cultural Revolution" which began in China in 1966 (and whose anarchy brought Chinese society to the brink of implosion by the end of the decade). In 1967 the Maoists in the CPM found a point of reference for their vision of peasant-led revolution in a local uprising of Santals—an Adivasi (tribal) community who live in parts of West Bengal and Jharkhand—organized and led by pro-Maoist CPM activists in an area of West Bengal's northernmost district, Darjeeling. The militant agitation took hold between March and May 1967—immediately after the first United Front government assumed power in Calcutta with the CPM as its single largest constituent—in three rural police station areas in the foothills of the Himalayas in the Darjeeling district: Naxalbari, Phansidewa, and Kharibari. From then on the uprising became known as the "Naxalbari" movement, and the Maoist tendency of the CPM as "Naxalites."

The unrest in the Naxalbari area peaked in late May 1967 when a police officer was killed by Santals armed with traditional weapons (bows and arrows) and the local police shot nine Santals dead, of whom six were women and two children. The unrest involved "incidents of un-authorized occupation of lands, looting of paddy belonging to big land-lords and assaults by Santals and other tribals," according to an official statement of the government of West Bengal.[6] The Naxalbari agitation presented a dilemma for the first United Front government and particu-larly for the CPM—a party committed to propoor land reforms but also to parliamentary democracy—because it revealed that a section of the CPM was increasingly attracted to the path of armed insurrection. The Naxalbari unrest remained a localized affair and fizzled out by August 1967 after three months of concerted police action ordered by the United Front government (whose home minister, in charge of the state police, was the CPM politician Jyoti Basu). But the episode deepened the rift between the CPM's moderates and the militant Maoist elements and pro-vided a romantic point of reference for the Maoist group's vision of a Chinese-style revolution in India.

The propaganda organs of the People's Republic of China fed this thinking. Sino-Indian relations had collapsed completely after the border war of late 1962, and normal diplomatic ties did not exist. On June 28, 1967, Radio Peking announced:

> "a phase of peasants' armed struggle led by the revolutionaries of the Indian Communist Party has begun in the countryside of the Darjeeling district of West Bengal state in India. This is the front paw of the revolutionary armed struggle launched by the Indian people under the guidance of Mao Ze-dong's teachings." This radio broadcast was followed a week later by an edi-torial in China's *People's Daily:* "a peal of spring thunder has crashed over India. Revolutionary peasants in the Darjeeling area have risen in rebellion. Under the leadership of a revolutionary group of the Indian Communist Party, a red area of rural revolutionary armed struggle has been established. This is a development of tremendous significance.... The revolutionary group of the Indian Communist Party has done the absolutely correct thing and done it well."[7]

Shortly after the second United Front government came to power in West Bengal in February 1969 with the CPM as its dominant constituent, the Maoists launched their own political party, the Communist Party of India (Marxist-Leninist) (CPI[ML]). The decision to establish the party was fi-nalized on Lenin's birthday, April 22, and announced at a public meeting held in the city center of Calcutta on May Day 1969. The CPI(ML) rejected parliamentary democracy entirely and asserted that the "semifeudal, semicolonial" conditions of Indian society could only be changed by armed revolution waged on the Chinese model, through a protracted people's war whereby liberated "red" zones would first be created in rural areas and then the cities would be encircled, culminating in a revolutionary seizure of state power. The main ideologue of this grand revolutionary agenda was the middle-aged Charu Mazumdar, formerly a district-level organizer of the CPM in the Darjeeling district of West Bengal. Most of the other top leaders of the CPI(ML) were, like Mazumdar, middle-ranking functionaries of the CPM in West Bengal and men of the social class known as the *bhadralok* (highly educated urban intelligentsia).

The actual impact of this grand vision of an India-wide revolution was pitifully limited. In West Bengal, where the Naxalites' strength was concentrated, the Maoist revolutionaries were able to launch significant rural insurgencies in parts of only two districts: Medinipur in the southwest and Birbhum in the west. The Medinipur insurgency peaked in late 1969 and petered out by mid-1970, partly because of the police response but mainly due to the movement's weak organization and strategic incoherence. The Birbhum insurgency commenced early in 1971 and met a similar fate by late 1971. The only other places in rural India where the Maoists launched serious campaigns were in a few districts of the coastal and Telangana regions of Andhra Pradesh (notably the coastal Andhra district of Srikakulam, where their activities peaked during 1969) and in pockets of Bihar. As in West Bengal, these campaigns attempted to mobilize impoverished tribal communities (Andhra Pradesh) or other very poor social groups of lowly caste status (Bihar) but were mostly led by highly educated, upper-caste urban activists.

The Naxalite insurrection, however, caused significant disruption in Calcutta and some of West Bengal's towns. This was because a sizable cohort of college and university students—almost all of nonproletarian background, ranging from the sons of affluent families to those belonging to the lower middle class—responded with enthusiasm to the revolutionary call and in particular to Charu Mazumdar's instruction to implement *khatam* (liquidation) of enemies of the revolution. From 1969 to 1971 this juvenile brigade engaged in an orgy of violence in and around Calcutta, where Naxalites established a presence in several suburbs, and some other urban centers in the state. Wall graffiti proclaiming "Naxalbari lal salaam!" (Red salute to Naxalbari!) appeared in various parts of Calcutta, and colleges and universities resounded to cries of "Chiner chairman amader chairman!" (Chairman Mao of China is our chairman!).

Statues of Bengal's cultural and political icons were routinely defaced and vandalized by Naxalite youths, causing revulsion among most middle-class Bengalis. The hurling of homemade bombs, shooting and stabbing murders of policemen directing traffic, and above all a murderous war between cadres of the CPM and the Naxalites that left hundreds dead on both sides spread fear across urban West Bengal.

It was in this climate of insecurity bordering on anarchy that the second United Front government was replaced in March 1970 by direct rule from New Delhi. The police in Calcutta and elsewhere in West Bengal, the prime target of Naxalite attacks, then began systematic and frequently brutal operations against the Naxalites. Summary executions of captured Naxalites—from middle-aged leaders to young men in their late teens and twenties—became commonplace. Many of the thousands of arrested Naxalites, including some women, were subjected to brutal torture in police detention, and there were several large-scale killings of Naxalite prisoners held in West Bengal's jails in the early 1970s. By 1971 India's first Maoist insurrection was largely suppressed by the counteroffensive launched by the police, who were supported by contingents of the Union government's paramilitary forces and, in rare instances, by detachments of the Indian army.

The radical spark of Naxalbari failed to ignite a prairie fire of revolution in West Bengal, let alone across India. But the radical critique of India's democracy that was born in West Bengal in the late 1960s lived on, and in the 1980s and 1990s found a renewed following in other states of India. The third generation of the Maoist revolutionary movement, active across a large swathe of India, poses the most significant internal challenge to the authority of the Indian state in the early twenty-first century.

By March 1971 the Naxalite rampage had been contained, and another state election was held in an attempt to restore democratic government to West Bengal. This election threw up a fractured verdict, but there were signs that a bipolar polity was emerging, dominated by Congress and the CPM, replacing the fractiousness of the years since 1967.

The March 1971 state election in West Bengal coincided with the national parliamentary election that gave Indira Gandhi a decisive nationwide mandate and cemented her leadership of Congress and the country. As in the rest of India, Congress in West Bengal had split in late 1969 into pro-Indira and old-guard factions. Indira Gandhi's sweeping victory in the nationwide context was not replicated in West Bengal, where the CPM won in 20 of the 40 parliamentary constituencies and smaller left-wing parties took another 6. But the Congress faction loyal to

Indira—referred to in West Bengal at the time as the *naba* (new) Congress—secured the vast bulk of the Congress vote base in the state, as it did across the nation. Indira's Congress won in 13 of West Bengal's 40 constituencies, and the old-guard faction won none.

In the simultaneous state election, the *naba* Congress won in 105 of the 280 constituencies making up the West Bengal legislature, with 29.3 percent of the popular vote; the old-guard faction won in just two constituencies and gained 5.6 percent of the total vote. With this election the dinosaur-like conservatives who had run the Congress party in West Bengal since independence and dominated state politics until 1967 faded into oblivion. Yet the total vote polled by the two Congress factions, 35 percent, was significantly lower than the 41 percent polled by the united Congress in the state elections of 1967 and 1969. This was in contrast to other states, including UP, Bihar, Madhya Pradesh, Rajasthan, Orissa, and Andhra Pradesh, where Congress led by Indira Gandhi won significantly higher shares of the popular vote in 1971—riding the "Garibi Hatao" (Abolish Poverty) plank—than the united Congress party had in 1967. The reason the *naba* Congress won as many as 105 of the 280 seats in the West Bengal legislature was that the anti-Congress United Front of 1969 had disintegrated and the non-Congress vote was split, unlike in 1969, between the erstwhile front's constituents: the two communist parties, several small socialist parties, and the Bangla Congress. But even so, the single largest party in the West Bengal legislature elected in March 1971 was the CPM, which contested 241 of the 280 constituencies (and 38 of the 40 constituencies in the parallel Lok Sabha election) on its own. The CPM candidates won in 114 constituencies, and CPM polled the single largest share, 33 percent, of the statewide popular vote.

The real significance of the March 1971 elections in West Bengal was the arrival of the CPM as the regional (state-specific) alternative to Congress. The CPM's breakthrough was enabled by a strategy of agrarian mobilization conducted since 1967 and particularly during 1969–1970 through the CPM's wing dedicated to organizing peasants on a mass scale, the Krishak Sabha (Peasant Front). This campaign produced "dramatic changes in peasant political outlook and support" in West Bengal and saw "voters in areas the size of full districts turn away from the previously dominant political party, Congress, towards . . . the CPM."[8] This was crucial to the evolution of state politics because West Bengal, like the rest of the country, is predominantly rural, and peasant voters are the ultimate arbiters of India's democracy. The strategy of peasant mobilization that led to the CPM's March 1971 breakthrough provided the model for the agrarian-based strategy that would make the CPM the hegemonic party in rural West Bengal after 1977 and keep West Bengal's CPM-dominated LF government in power for nearly three and a half decades, 1977–2011.

The CPM strategy in rural West Bengal during 1967–1971 was to mobilize the largest possible number of peasants in a broadly based movement targeted against the biggest landowners in the countryside. These big landlords, known as *jotedars,* were men who owned much more land than the then legally permitted limit of 25 acres per individual. In most cases they owned several hundred acres, often holding it *benami* (under false names) to circumvent the law, and in many cases they were "absentee" landlords who did not actually live in the village but in a nearby provincial town or even in Calcutta. The *jotedars* were relatively few in number—in the early 1960s, just 0.7 percent of rural households in West Bengal owned more than 20 acres of land (and those households owned only 6.6 percent of the total cultivated land in the state).[9] The *jotedars* were typically local leaders or known supporters of Congress, the ruling party in West Bengal for the two decades up to 1967. Shortly after the demise in late 1967 of the state's first non-Congress government— the shaky United Front postelection coalition of which the CPM was the single largest element—the CPM initiated a drive to expand the membership of the Krishak Sabha in West Bengal. The drive proceeded through 1968 and 1969, and by late 1969 nearly a million peasants in West Bengal (939,000) were enrolled in the CPM's peasant organization. After the second United Front government came to power in West Bengal in early 1969, this time as a preelection alliance with the CPM as the dominant element, the CPM launched its anti-*jotedar* campaign in the countryside.

A typical anti-*jotedar* incident involved several thousand people (sometimes as many as 10,000–12,000, according to contemporary newspaper accounts) marching on a *jotedar*'s lands, some brandishing crude weapons such as sticks, spears, bows and arrows, and a variety of sharp implements used for everyday purposes in homes and fields. In some cases the land held in excess of the legal limit was seized outright and distributed among peasants, and in other instances the *jotedars* were not formally but effectively dispossessed, with former sharecroppers taking control of almost all of a *jotedar*'s land as his "tenants." Harekrishna Konar, the CPM leader who was the land minister in the first and second United Front governments, famously told his peasant supporters: "Jomi kaerae lae" (Just seize the land). The anti-*jotedar* campaign on the ground was enabled by the CPM's control of vital organs of state power, notably the home (interior) and land affairs ministries in the second United Front government. This gave the party jurisdiction over the police and bureaucracy, and control of the administrative and developmental apparatus in rural areas. This meant that the local police would not come to the succor of the jotedars under attack and that local officials in charge of administration and development would fall in line with the new "policy."

The CPM leadership was categorical that its class war in West Bengal's countryside must be targeted at the *jotedars* (big landlords) alone and that the movement should make every effort to involve all other sections of the rural population, including relatively well-off peasants owning middle-sized landholdings and even wealthier peasants with substantial land. The fiery Harekrishna Konar was clear that "the middle peasants must be made a close ally, otherwise our strength will sag." Thus "middle and [even] rich peasants were not targeted. On the contrary, efforts were made to get them to join the movement in order to keep the anti-CPM forces to a minimum. . . . Because of this the issue of [landless] day-laborers' wages seems to have been toned down."[10] Nearly a third of West Bengal's 5.5 million rural households in the early 1970s were landless and dependent for survival on wage labor on landowning peasants' fields.

The self-limited nature of the CPM's campaign was in part due to the composition of the peasant support base the communists had gradually built up in West Bengal through the 1950s and 1960s. The core of this base, including key organizers at the village level, consisted of people belonging to the "middle peasant" category rather than the poorest sections of rural society, belonging to low-caste groups and tribal communities. Thus the local leaders of the movement "were often from among college-educated, fairly well-off individuals of clean [ritually high] caste." School-teacher sons of prosperous peasants who had gained higher education in nearby provincial towns or in Calcutta were especially prominent among the organizers. Benoy Choudhury, then the top organizer of the Krishak Sabha in the Bardhaman district (a center of the anti-*jotedar* movement) and later the land minister for nearly two decades in post-1977 LF governments, was candid on this point: "these middle peasants, they're educated, they're vocal, so they would sometimes lead, due to certain traditions. They enjoyed more clout with the local people, who were mostly illiterate."[11] Indeed both Benoy Choudhury (born 1910) and Harekrishna Konar (born 1915), who was also from Bardhaman, represented a certain tradition and trajectory of Bengali middle-class radicalism. Both were well-educated men who cut their teeth in militant anticolonial nationalist activities before being converted to communism in the late 1930s.

The limited, anti-*jotedar* focus of the CPM's peasant mobilization meant that its tangible results were also limited. In the Bardhaman district, a large sprawl across the south-central part of West Bengal, only about 30,000 acres of land were taken over during 1969–1971 and distributed among a maximum of 30,000 peasant families, an average of an acre per family (according to later estimates by the movement's leaders in the district). At most, 6 percent of rural households in the district received a small amount of land as a result of the campaign (a landholding of 2.5 acres being the minimum necessary to sustain a family of five). There were simply not many *jotedars* to target with displays of "people's power"—the entire Bardhaman district had seven or eight "major" *jotedars* (very big landlords), and the pool of "minor" *jotedars* was a few hundred.

Yet the CPM's strategy of broadly based, "cast the net wide" peasant mobilization targeted at the thin top stratum of the landed elite proved very effective in expanding the party's influence and maximizing its electoral support in rural West Bengal. Until 1967, according to a CPM peasant organizer in the Bardhaman district, "we had only a few pockets of strength here and there." By 1971 the CPM "had in some respects become the new government of the countryside, the dominant political force [in the district]." In the state election of February 1967 the CPM got 35 percent of the votes in the central and eastern parts of the Bardhaman district—the agricultural zone of the district, the western part is an industrial and mining belt—while Congress got 47 percent. In the February 1969 state election the CPM vote rose to 42 percent, slightly higher than Congress's 39 percent. In the March 1971 state election the CPM got 53 percent of the votes, nearly double Congress's 27 percent. The Bardhaman district was an area where the CPM was strong and its ascendancy particularly striking, but the trend there reflected a shift of political power across much of the state's countryside from the formerly dominant party, Congress, to an emerging dominant party, the CPM. In March 1971 the CPM became the single largest party in West Bengal both in the share of the popular vote it secured (33 percent) and the number of constituencies that elected CPM candidates to the 280-seat state legislature (114). In the context of "village society the Marxist movement was new and old at the same time. It was new in mobilizing the masses and particularly the low castes in a broad movement, and old in the sense that it largely behaved and was perceived as a patron, only more just and more potent than the older patrons."[12]

The 34-year rule of the CPM-led Left Front in West Bengal from 1977 was based on the same image of a "just" hegemon and a similar strategy that combined grassroots organizing with the use of state power. And throughout that period, until political change came to West Bengal in 2011, the Bardhaman district was famed as the CPM's *lal durgo* (red citadel).

The CPM's advance in West Bengal was derailed within a year. A stable state government could not be formed because of the "hung" (fractured) legislature elected in March 1971 in which no party secured a majority, and no postelection alliance with a working legislative majority (50 percent plus 1, i.e. 141 of the 280 seats) materialized either. In June 1971 West Bengal was put back under direct central rule pending fresh state elections.

By then the troubled state was reeling from the impact of the dire political and humanitarian crisis unfolding in East Pakistan, just across the border that had severed Bengal in two in 1947. In late March 1971, the (West) Pakistani military began a massive crackdown on Bengali nationalists in East Pakistan, an overwhelmingly Bengali and predominantly Muslim province. The Bengali nationalist movement, led by Bengali Muslims who had unsuccessfully sought autonomy for their homeland within Pakistan and cultural and economic equality with the western wing of the country for nearly two decades, responded by declaring independence and the formation of sovereign Bangladesh. As the Pakistani military crackdown spread and became an indiscriminate terror campaign, huge numbers of Bengalis, Hindus and Muslims, began to flee across the border to India. In a few months about 10 million people—one out of seven of East Pakistan's population—arrived in India as refugees. The large majority crossed the border into West Bengal. (The rest went to states in northeastern India that also border Bangladesh.) West Bengal had to cope with this overwhelming influx, and it became the frontline state in the subcontinental crisis of 1971.

The crisis was resolved in December 1971 when Bangladesh was liberated in a two-week operation by the Indian armed forces with the support of Bangladeshi resistance militias. When in March 1972 West Bengal went to the polls for the fourth time in five years to elect its state government, the outcome was a stunning victory for the Congress party.

Congress won in 216 of the 280 constituencies, with 49 percent of the statewide popular vote. Its junior ally, the CPI, the rump of the party from which the CPM had split in 1964, won in another 35 constituencies. (The CPI, Moscow-centric as always, teamed up with Congress after Indira Gandhi's government concluded a treaty of friendship and cooperation—effectively a strategic alliance—with the Soviet Union in August 1971.) The CPM won in just 14 constituencies and claimed that the election was blatantly rigged. The election was indeed marred by large-scale fraud. It was held under "president's rule"—direct central rule, in effect the rule of the Congress government in New Delhi. Moreover, since the Congress split of 1969, the majority faction led by Indira

Gandhi had attracted youth and student supporters in West Bengal. These young men were drawn to Indira's charisma and her populist, propoor stance. The freshly minted activists of the Indira-led party's youth and student wings in West Bengal engaged in strong-arm tactics on a wide scale on polling day.

But the dramatic victory of Indira Gandhi's Congress in West Bengal was not solely due to intimidation and fraud. In fact, the proportion of the statewide popular vote the CPM obtained in the March 1972 state election (28 percent) did not represent a drastic decline from a year earlier (33 percent), and the drop was in part because the CPM contested fewer constituencies in March 1972 (208) than in March 1971 (241), as it relinquished some constituencies to candidates put up by small allied left-wing parties. Since April 1971 Indira Gandhi had gained immense popularity in West Bengal because of her championing of the Bangladesh cause. The March 1972 state election in West Bengal happened just three months after the liberation of Bangladesh, an outcome for which Indira Gandhi was responsible more than anyone else. The CPM's prospects were also damaged by the reputation for violence that left-wing politics had acquired in the state because of the Naxalite terror and the bloody clashes between the CPM and its breakaway Maoist faction in many locales of West Bengal during 1969–1971. Siddhartha Shankar Ray—a prominent Calcutta lawyer and a grandson of Chittaranjan (C. R.) Das, a renowned leader of the anticolonial struggle in Bengal during the second and third decades of the twentieth century—had emerged during 1971 as Indira Gandhi's point man in West Bengal. He became the chief minister of the state in March 1972.

The 1972–1977 Congress government in West Bengal proved disappointing, if not dysfunctional. It became notorious for widespread hooliganism perpetrated by the ruling party's youth and student wings, and was terminally damaged by the dictatorial Emergency regime Indira Gandhi imposed on the country in 1975–1976. When state elections were held in June 1977, the LF—an alliance of state-based leftist parties led and dominated by the CPM—stormed to power. The LF won in 230 of the 294 single-member constituencies comprising the West Bengal legislature, and the CPM alone won in 178 constituencies.

The outcome of the June 1977 state election revealed that the base of peasant support the CPM had built in the West Bengal countryside in the late 1960s and early 1970s was largely intact. But the CPM victory was fundamentally the result of a backlash against the dysfunctional governance and authoritarianism Congress had inflicted on the state and the nation. In 1977 few if any would have predicted that the CPM-led LF would become the most durable political regime in the annals of India's democracy: that it would win another six state elections (1982, 1987, 1991, 1996, 2001, and 2006) and govern West Bengal for an uninterrupted 34 years until 2011. The CPM has a mass base in only one other populous state of India, Kerala. The CPM has never come close there to the protracted hegemony it achieved in West Bengal. Over the three-decade period from 1980 to 2011, CPM-led left-of-center governments alternated in power in Kerala with right-of-center Congress-led governments. For a total of 16 years during this time CPM-led coalition governments ruled Kerala, and Congress-led coalition governments held office for an almost equal duration.

A Hegemonic Regime

The foundations of the CPM's 34-year supremacy in West Bengal were laid during the Left Front's first term in office (1977–1982). The CPM strategy was focused entirely on the countryside and had two prongs: the establishment of *panchayats* (organs of rural self-government) elected through competition between political parties, and a program of official registration of sharecroppers (*bhagchashis* or *bargadars,* typically land-poor or landless peasants who farm land owned by others for a share of the crop) designed to protect them from arbitrary evictions and increase their share of the produce.

In the summer of 1978, a year after the CPM-led government came to power in West Bengal, elections were held throughout the state's vast countryside to constitute a three-tiered pyramidal system of *panchayat* government. The base tier consisted of *gram panchayats,* a council covering a cluster of villages, the intermediate tier of *panchayat samitis,* a body covering a substantial part (block) of a district such as Bardhaman or Medinipur or Nadia or the 24-Parganas, and the top tier of *zilla parishads* (a council for the district). Of the three tiers the intermediate one is the most important, because the block is the unit through which most socioeconomic development and welfare programs are administered in rural India. In 2013 there were 3,351 *gram panchayats* and 333 *panchayat samitis* across West Bengal's 19 districts and 60,426 elected positions across the three tiers of the *panchayat* system (of which one-third have been reserved for women since 1993, a proportion that rose to 50 percent beginning in 2013).

The legislation to establish the *panchayat* system in West Bengal had been passed by the state's Congress government in 1973, but it was the CPM-led government that implemented it in 1978 and reaped its political dividends. In the first *panchayat* elections of 1978, candidates running on CPM tickets won 67 percent of the seats at the *gram panchayat* level, 74 percent at the *panchayat samiti* level, and 87 percent at the district level. The Congress had been routed across rural (and urban) West Bengal in national and state elections just a year earlier and was in no position to compete effectively in the *panchayat* polls. In addition, the party had split at the national level following the post-Emergency Lok Sabha debacle of March 1977, and Congress (I)(*I* for Indira), which would return to national power in January 1980 and simultaneously emerge as the main opposition to the LF in West Bengal, was still at a nascent phase. In the second *panchayat* elections of 1983, Congress put up a fight in some parts of rural West Bengal, and LF and CPM dominance was slightly diminished but not significantly eroded. The dominance of the *panchayat* structures by the LF—meaning in most districts and locales the CPM—would not be undermined for three decades, until West Bengal's seventh *panchayat* elections in 2008. In the fifth *panchayat* elections of 1998, the newborn Trinamool Congress, formed as a regional alternative to the CPM by the charismatic and popular Mamata Banerjee after her split from Congress, mounted a spirited challenge but did not make more than a dent in the CPM's dominance of rural West Bengal. In the sixth *panchayat* elections of 2003, the CPM recovered its limited losses of 1998. It was not until a groundswell of opposition to the CPM's domination emerged in agrarian society in 2007–2008 that the CPM's supremacy in rural West Bengal was ended.

The CPM's triumph in the first *panchayat* election of 1978 marked the beginning of its protracted hegemony in West Bengal. The heavy losses the CPM suffered exactly 30 years later in the *panchayat* elections of 2008 signaled the beginning of the end of the most durable political regime seen in any Indian state since the nation's independence.

From the beginnings in 1977–1978, the CPM's adoption of the *panchayat* system as the mechanism of local empowerment and grassroots development in rural West Bengal was driven by an instrumental purpose—to implant a vast network of party control and patronage in an institutionalized form across the countryside of West Bengal. Atul Kohli, an Indian-American scholar who between 1979 and 1983 studied the CPM-led dispensation of West Bengal, accurately characterized it as more than just another state "government": an emerging political "regime" with distinctive characteristics. His sympathetic account of the regime's reformist agenda was categorical on this point: "since coming to power, the CPM has sought to consolidate its rural power base further. Central to this task are the new politicized *panchayats* . . . aimed at a purposive penetration of the countryside. The purpose is to bring lower and lower-middle rural classes within the influence of the party. It is hoped that [thereby] . . . the party position will be strengthened." He found this motive understandable: "The CPM is after all a political party and not a charitable organization."[13]

He also conducted a random sample survey of the social origins and profiles of *gram panchayat* seat-holders elected on CPM tickets in two districts, Bardhaman and Medinipur. While the sample was too restricted and its size too small to draw definite statewide conclusions, the findings were suggestive of broader patterns. Only 7 percent of those surveyed said they were full, card-carrying members of the CPM; the vast majority were persons who did not hold full party membership but had a history of involvement with the CPM's mass organizations, particularly the Krishak Sabha (58 percent had participated in such activities for at least two years and another 22 percent for over five years). A majority of those surveyed (60 percent) were farmers owning at least some land, just 8 percent were landless wage laborers, and the other 32 percent were engaged in nonfarming occupations, mostly rural schoolteaching. (This last group were predominantly sons of prosperous farmers who had been able to provide their offspring with some higher education.) The large majority of those surveyed (69 percent) were of "middle peasant" origins, with family landholdings of 2–5 acres, and another 19 percent were of upper-middle peasant background, with landholdings of 6–10 acres. Of the 60 percent of the sample who were landowning farmers, five-sixths employed the landless as waged labor.

To the extent that this data is suggestive of broader patterns, it is clear that the CPM members of the base tier of the *panchayat* system consisted disproportionately of the relatively better-off "middle" segments of the agrarian population. About one-third of the rural households in West Bengal—some 2.2 million households in the mid-1980s—were landless, and this rural proletariat was thinly represented among the CPM *gram panchayat* members. Another 20 percent of rural households owned land of one acre or less and comprised a poor peasantry. The rural strategy of the CPM in the late 1960s and early 1970s had aimed to maximize electoral support by emphasizing broadly based, "cast the net wide" mobilization and treated only the small pool of *jotedars* in the West Bengal countryside—big landlords who were frequently absentee owners—as "class enemies." In 1976 the CPM central committee elevated this strategy to an operational doctrine in a formal resolution: "the unity of the [landless] agricultural laborers [and] poor, middle and rich peasantry, based on agricultural laborers and poor peasants, is sharply emphasized."[14]

The *panchayat* system was the institutional conduit through which the CPM entrenched party control over West Bengal's countryside. From the late 1970s, the two lower tiers of the system administered and supervised matters of great importance in rural life, such as the provision of credit and farming inputs to peasants owning small landholdings and the implementation of local development programs like road-building intended to benefit the landless and the land poor, who would be given a combination of cash and food-grains in return for their work. Kohli wrote:

> during my visits to the panchayats it became clear that the major local governmental decisions were made in continuous informal and formal consultation with the local party representatives. . . . In conjunction with local party cadres, the panchayats decide the projects to be undertaken, choose who will be employed, and administer the funds. . . . As public resources come to be controlled by a new local elite, new patterns of patronage are developing. . . . Many of the landless working on the FWP [food-for-work] projects noted in interviews that they were grateful for the role of the panchayat pradhan [head of the elected gram panchayat council] as a benefactor. . . . Those who gain employment from FWP projects tend to be CPM sympathizers or as a result of the gained opportunities become CPM supporters.[15]

Kohli saw this situation in a broadly positive light: as delivering limited benefits to poor people under the watchful eye of a disciplined party guided by a reformist agenda.

A less positive interpretation would have emphasized the emergence of a reconfigured hierarchy of power, control, and patron-client relations in the West Bengal countryside and the blurring of the distinction between party and state. In 1978 the CPM had about 33,000 full party members in West Bengal, a minuscule number in a population of over 50 million. The *panchayat* system provided the conduit for the CPM to spread its tentacles wide and deep in rural West Bengal and establish the edifice of a "Big Brother" party-state. The CPM played to its comparative advantage—the main opposition, Congress, had no agrarian strategy and no functioning peasant wing in the state. By contrast the membership of the Krishak Sabha, the CPM's peasant organization in the state, increased from 1,284,892 in February 1978 to 3,860,992 in 1981 and 7,037,456 by 1987.[16]

The second prong of the CPM's post-1977 agrarian strategy focused on the rights of sharecroppers—*bhagchashis* or *bargadars* in Bengali—peasants who till land owned by another as tenant farmers and pay the owner "rent" in the form of an agreed share of the crop produced. Share-cropping is virtually the only type of land tenancy found in rural West

Bengal, and in the early 1980s the number of *bargadars* in the state was estimated to be about 3 million.[17] The typical *bargadar* is usually, though not invariably, a poor peasant who owns too little land of his own to feed his family through the year and therefore takes out a *barga,* or share-cropping tenancy. (Some better-off peasants also take out *bargas* to supplement income, and at the other end of the scale, some *bargadars* own no land at all.) The extent of land poverty in rural West Bengal explains the prevalence of the practice of *barga.* According to figures compiled in 1972, nearly one-third of all rural households in the state were landless and largely dependent on daily wage labor during the seeding and harvesting seasons in others' fields, which would yield employment for one-third of the year at most. Another one-fifth of rural families owned an acre or less, and yet another one-fifth owned between 1 and 2.5 acres. The 40 percent of land-poor households with ownership of 2.5 or fewer acres owned about a quarter of all cultivated land. The 13–16 percent of middle peasant households with plots of 2.5–5 acres owned 26–29 percent of the land; the 7–9 percent of upper-middle peasant households with plots of 5–10 acres owned 28–31 percent of the land; and the 2 percent of rich peasant households with plots of 10–20 acres owned 12 percent of the land.[18]

In September 1977, three months after coming to power, the LF government passed legislation to strengthen security of tenure for sharecroppers by transferring the onus of proof in disputes from the sharecropping tenant to the owner of the land. This bolstered existing legislation on sharecropper rights, including security of tenure provisions and the legal entitlement of sharecroppers to 75 percent of the produce. Then, in mid-1978, the CPM-led government launched a statewide program of official registration of sharecroppers, which emphasized to sharecroppers the importance of being registered with the government in order to enjoy legal protections and benefits. The program, known as Operation Barga, attracted much attention in India and abroad and impressed many scholars and practitioners in Western countries as an example of progressive reform. Operation Barga was the brainchild of Benoy Choudhury, the experienced leader of the CPM's peasant mobilization in the Bardhaman district a decade earlier, who had taken over as West Bengal's land minister in June 1977. (His predecessor as land minister in the United Front governments of 1967 and 1969–1970, Harekrishna Konar, died in 1974.) By the time Operation Barga went into effect, Choudhury was the top leader of the Krishak Sabha. His ministry supervised the program, and the registration work was done by local-level employees of the "old" bureaucratic machinery in the countryside (not the *panchayats,* which were just coming into existence) acting under the instructions of the professional bureaucrats running the districts' administration. But local CPM party cadres and Krishak Sabha members were in the frontline of the grassroots implementation of Operation Barga.

Operation Barga was largely completed by 1982. By early that year 1,125,826 *bargadars* were recorded, and in November 1982 the figure was almost 1.2 million. By September 1985, by which time the program had run its course, there were 1,329,087 registered sharecroppers in West Bengal.[19] Despite the CPM's grassroots organizational presence in most parts of West Bengal and the resolve of the state government to implement its showpiece program, Operation Barga achieved only partial penetration of the countryside, as the number of *bargadars* was probably around double the number registered by 1985. But the identification and registration of 1.2 million sharecroppers in a four-year period between 1978 and 1982, climbing to over 1.3 million by 1985, was still a formidable endeavor. Most important, Operation Barga enabled the CPM to consolidate its grassroots presence in areas of party strength in the state and expand it in areas of relative weakness.

It is difficult to form a precise picture of the actual benefits of registration to sharecroppers, given Operation Barga's vast scale and the many variations in the agrarian sector across West Bengal. One random sample survey in the second half of 1983 of 300 registered sharecropper households across three of the state's most populous districts—24-Parganas, Medinipur, and Bardhaman (100 families in each district)—did suggest tangible gains. Of the households surveyed, half (49 percent) reported that in addition to the land held under sharecropping tenancy they owned an acre or less of land, 14 percent said they owned more than an acre, and 37 percent said they owned no land at all. In short, the vast majority of the households were either poor peasant families owning very small plots or landless families. Two-thirds of the 300 families held sharecropping tenancies over plots of less than an acre, 25 percent over plots of one to two acres, and 9 percent over plots of two to five acres. The vast majority of the surveyed households (87 percent) reported that before registration they had shared the crop fifty-fifty with the owner of the land, and 66 percent said that after registration they were receiving three-fourths of the produce (the legal entitlement); the proportion still sharing on a fifty-fifty basis had fallen from 87 percent to 32 percent.[20]

Regardless of the tangible benefits, the lasting significance of Operation Barga was the appearance of the *lal* (red) party's government in the role of patron and benefactor of much of the rural populace. This pro-poor image and the enhanced grassroots penetration and presence gained through Operation Barga would make the CPM the hegemonic party of rural West Bengal for a quarter century after Operation Barga came to an end, the party's primacy in the countryside continually reinforced through its domination of the *panchayat* system.

In the first state election in which the CPM-led LF sought a renewed mandate from the people, in May 1982, the vote was exactly even in the 22 constituencies in inner Kolkata: the LF won in 11 and Congress in 11. Two prominent CPM leaders—Ashok Mitra, the cerebral finance minister in the 1977–1982 government, and Buddhadev Bhattacharya, who would serve as the state's chief minister from November 2000 to May 2011—lost in urban Kolkata constituencies to Congress candidates. But outside the capital's urban core, the CPM-led alliance left the Congress opposition very far behind. Congress won in 53 of the 294 constituencies comprising the state legislature, and the LF won in 228 constituencies, of which the CPM alone won in 174 constituencies. The LF had gained a second five-year term in power with a three-fourths legislative majority, as in 1977. The 1977 victory had been above all due to public rejection of Congress, but the 1982 triumph was powered by a majority in rural West Bengal who wished to reelect the self-styled *garibaer sarkar* (government of the poor) to govern them.

The CPM's rural base was augmented by a sizable section of the urban middle-class electorate of West Bengal. The appeal of the CPM for this electorate was the CPM's identity as the major regional party of the Indian Union's Bengali-speaking state. In this perspective, the CPM represented a plucky challenger, homegrown in the soil of West Bengal, to Congress, the nationwide hegemonic party. After Congress, led by Indira Gandhi, returned to power in New Delhi in January 1980, the CPM-led LF government of West Bengal—one of very few non-Congress state governments in the country—was viewed by its urban middle-class supporters as not just a force for progressive social change in the state but a bastion of regional resistance to an overweening Congress-ruled Center. The CPM's support among the urban electorate was particularly strong among the several million middle- and lower-middle-class voters of "refugee" origins—the people who had arrived in West Bengal from the severed east after the 1947 partition. These families of *udbastu* (uprooted) origin typically harbored strong antipathy toward Congress, and Kolkata's suburbs, where they predominated, were CPM strongholds; there and elsewhere, the *udbastu* population was a reliable source of cadres and electoral support for the CPM.

The CPM-led LF government played up this image of being a West Bengal–based David struggling valiantly against the all-India Goliath represented by Congress. Through the 1980s CPM leaders in West Bengal emphasized that the LF government faced discrimination and hostility from a Leviathan-like Center controlled by Congress in New Delhi. This thinly veiled appeal to Bengali ethnolinguistic identity and regional pride had significant resonance among educated Bengalis throughout the state. The appeal was buttressed by the preponderance of *bhadralok* (gentlemen)—highly educated men of upper caste and urban background— among the upper echelons of the CPM leadership at the state and district levels in West Bengal. The preeminent public face of the CPM in West Bengal through the 1980s and 1990s was Jyoti Basu (born 1914), the state's chief minister from June 1977 until his retirement in November 2000. Basu, a communist politician since the mid-1940s, is the longest serving chief minister of any state in the history of India's democracy. He was of quintessential *bhadralok* background: born into an upper-middle-class family of Kolkata with roots in eastern Bengal, he was converted to communism while studying law in London in the late 1930s.

In state elections in March 1987, the LF sought its third consecutive term from the people of West Bengal. Rajiv Gandhi, the youthful prime minister of India, flew in from Delhi and conducted an energetic campaign for Congress in West Bengal. At the time he was still a popular figure in the country, especially among urban middle-class Indians—his slide into unpopularity started in mid-1987. When the votes were counted, the LF had won a four-fifths majority in the West Bengal legislature, winning 243 of the 294 constituencies in the state. The CPM alone elected 187 members to the new legislature. Congress won in just 40 constituencies, down from 53 in 1982. The outcome of state elections in May 1991 was a near-repeat of 1987: the LF won 245 of the 294 seats in the West Bengal legislature, of which the CPM alone won 188, and just 43 constituencies elected Congress candidates. The potent mix of "propoor" and regionalist politics had prevailed yet again.

The election of the fourth consecutive LF government in 1991, for a five-year term until 1996, took the duration of continuous CPM rule in West Bengal to nearly two decades since 1977. The Left Front was (and is) a "CPM-plus" alliance built on the statewide vote base and organizational apparatus of the CPM. The other three LF parties of any size (the Forward Bloc, the Revolutionary Socialist Party, and the CPI, the last of which belatedly joined the LF in 1979) have no more than pockets of strength in the state. Since the LF's formation the CPM has always run candidates in nearly three-fourths of West Bengal's 42 parliamentary constituencies in national elections and nearly three-fourths of the 294 legislative assembly constituencies in state elections, leaving the remainder to its junior allies. The rule of the LF in West Bengal essentially meant the supremacy of the CPM.

By the early 1990s the seemingly rock-solid dominance of the CPM in West Bengal stood out as one of the very few constant features of India's fluid and rapidly changing political landscape. This hegemony—quite remarkable and anomalous in the nationwide context—presented a genuine puzzle. The CPM regime of West Bengal had not undertaken any major policy initiatives since its first term in power (1977–1982), when it established the *panchayat* system and implemented Operation Barga. (And indeed it would not do so, until the botched industrialization initiative launched by the seventh LF government in 2006–2007!) Yet an increasingly moribund regime with a mediocre record of governance seemed unassailable in power.

A sharply critical study of the governance record of West Bengal's post-1977 CPM regime published in 1993 argued: "the Left Front has been able to achieve gratuitous victories due to the bitter factionalism of the State's Congress opposition, which has long been held in even greater disrepute than the Left Front. When faced with the two alternatives many voters still feel the Left Front to be the better [for] government. Thus . . . the Left Front [has] continued in power by default, from lack of a credible alternative."[21] The longevity of the CPM regime was indeed in part due to the absence of a credible alternative, but the weaknesses of the Congress opposition in West Bengal went far beyond factionalism.

The highly efficient organizational apparatus of the CPM in West Bengal gave it a decisive advantage over Congress at election time. This apparatus had a pyramidal structure, with a vast network of statewide "local committees" making up the base tier, supervised by "zonal committees" at the subdistrict level, and topped by district committees. The structure was very similar to the three-tiered *panchayat* system instituted in 1978 that would be the pillar of CPM supremacy in rural West Bengal for the next three decades. The CPM's well-oiled organizational machine in West Bengal was built under the leadership of Promode Dasgupta (born 1910), a dour apparatchik of (typically) upper-caste and eastern Bengal origin who headed the party organization in the state until his death during a visit to Beijing in November 1982.

By comparison the Congress party in West Bengal resembled a disorganized rabble, utterly unable to compete with the CPM's meticulous election management at the booth (polling station) level in *panchayat*, state, and national elections. The CPM's machine acquired a reputation for "rigging" elections in West Bengal through a variety of methods. These included deletion of the names of likely opposition voters during updating of electoral rolls (a process conducted by members of a CPM-affiliated "coordination committee" of state government employees), impersonation of genuine voters to cast "false" votes on election day, and outright intimidation of opposition activists and voters to prevent the casting of anti-CPM ballots. The claims of systematic fraud were sometimes exaggerated but contained a significant element of truth. As CPM hegemony became a long-term fact of life in West Bengal, the party's influence over the police and bureaucracy who were involved in administering and supervising elections grew in strength. It was not until the state election of 2006—won handsomely by the LF—that India's increasingly competent and activist Election Commission, an independent national body, was able to ensure a fully free and fair election in West Bengal through stringent security and monitoring measures.

Congress retained a formidable mass base in West Bengal. In the state elections of 1982, 1987, and 1991 the party polled 40 percent, 42 percent and 35 percent, respectively, of the popular vote. (The drop in 1991 was due to a dramatic but transient surge of the BJP vote, which rose from 0.5 percent in 1987 to 11 percent in 1991 before falling back to 6 percent in 1996.) Even as the CPM regime became more and more entrenched, the Congress opposition stayed alive and competitive, and its vote came from all social classes, belying the LF's claim to represent all of the state's *mehanati manush* (working people). The resilience of a mass opposition base in India's "red" state, the sharp polarization of the electorate between communist and opposition supporters, and very high levels of politicization in the population (reflected in turnouts in national and especially state elections that are among the highest in India, typically 80–85 percent or even higher during the past two decades) imparted an intensely adversarial and combative character to the state's politics. This bred a culture of political violence through the decades of LF rule—including frequent murders of individuals and sporadic small-scale massacres—perpetrated by both camps but especially the ruling CPM.

The LF remained well ahead in the popular vote, however, polling 51 percent in 1982 and 1987 and 48 percent in 1991. Through the 1980s and into the 1990s, Congress in West Bengal did not have a widely popular leader in the state it could project as an alternative to Jyoti Basu, the veteran CPM chief minister. Such a homegrown opposition leader was sorely needed, given the essentially regional (state-specific) character of the CPM party and regime. In state elections in May 1996 the LF resoundingly won a fifth consecutive term with a two-thirds legislative majority: LF candidates won in 202 of the 294 constituencies, and the CPM alone won in 157 constituencies. Congress won in 82 constituencies, but its share of the statewide popular vote, 39.5 percent, was nearly ten points behind the LF's 49 percent. It was clear that continuity would prevail over change in the state unless the two essential planks of the CPM regime's popularity—the agrarian base and the regionalist appeal—were undermined.

In the simultaneous national election of May 1996, Congress was severely defeated and ousted from power at the Center, and the party's drift and disarray deepened. In West Bengal it became clearer than ever that if Congress had proven unable to successfully challenge the CPM regime through the 1980s—when Congress was still the dominant nationwide party and ran single-party governments in New Delhi with huge parliamentary majorities—it was far less likely to be able to mount such a challenge in a condition of steep decline in the second half of the 1990s. Yet half of West Bengal's population had voted against the LF in elections since 1977, and Congress had consistently got about 40 percent of the statewide popular vote over the two decades since the CPM-led regime's rise to power. This opposition mass base found a tough and determined representative from 1998 in a new regional party, the Trinamool Congress, founded and led by Congress's most popular leader in West Bengal, Mamata Banerjee.

A Regionalist Challenger

Mamata Banerjee was born around 1955 into a family of modest means living in a run-down neighborhood of Kolkata. This lower-middle-class family, formally of the Brahmin caste, was pushed into poverty by her father's early death when Banerjee was in her midteens. A large family, consisting of the widowed mother and six brothers and two sisters, they faced a struggle for survival. Banerjee persevered with her studies in adversity, and between the mid-1970s and early 1980s she earned bachelor's and master's degrees from Calcutta University, a law diploma, and a qualification to be a schoolteacher.

But Banerjee's real passion lay in politics. Born into a staunchly pro-Congress family, she began her political life in the mid-1970s as an activist of Congress's student wing in West Bengal. By the early 1980s, with the LF firmly in power, she was a regular speaker at Congress public meetings in Kolkata. In the 1982 state elections she conducted an energetic door-to-door campaign for Sisir Bose, the legendary Subhas Chandra Bose's nephew and a leading pediatrician, who stood for Congress in a predominantly middle-class south Kolkata constituency and was elected to the West Bengal legislature.

Mamata Banerjee's big break in politics came in late 1984, when she was selected to stand as the Congress candidate in one of West Bengal's 42 parliamentary constituencies in the December 1984 national election. This was the Jadavpur constituency, a vast sprawl across Kolkata's southern suburbs and a swathe of adjoining rural areas. Although she was an obscure party worker, Banerjee was asked to run because better known leaders were reluctant to stand in Jadavpur, which was considered an impregnable CPM bastion. The constituency was represented in Parliament by Somnath Chatterjee, a lawyer and prominent CPM leader who would later serve as the Lok Sabha's speaker from 2004 to 2009. Banerjee became a household name in West Bengal when she narrowly defeated Chatterjee and took the red fortress of Jadavpur. The sensational "upset" was powered by the nationwide sympathy wave for Congress in the December 1984 national election after the assassination of Indira Gandhi. The wave reached West Bengal, and the Congress vote in the state jumped from 36.5 percent in the January 1980 national election to 48.2 percent in December 1984 (and fell back to 41.4 percent in the November 1989 national election). Sixteen of the 42 Lok Sabha constituencies elected Congress candidates in 1984, as opposed to four in both 1980 and 1989. But although she was a beneficiary of the surge generated by Indira's murder, Mamata Banerjee deserved some independent credit for winning a constituency as difficult as Jadavpur. She undertook a tireless grassroots campaign, walking across the constituency on foot to speak directly to voters and encourage party workers. Many party workers—and voters—were impressed by the energy and determination of this slightly built woman of humble social origins.

Banerjee narrowly lost her bid for reelection to Parliament from Jadavpur to a CPM candidate in November 1989, but her ascent to iconic status in the state's opposition politics began months later in August 1990. On August 16, 1990, she was leading a small, peaceful procession of party workers in a middle-class residential area of south Kolkata close to her home in support of a one-day *bandh* (general strike) called by Congress in West Bengal. The procession was attacked by CPM cadres wielding iron rods—frequently used in political street fighting in West Bengal—and other crude weapons. Banerjee later wrote: "I saw Lalu Alam [the man who led the assault] and a couple of others carrying iron rods and firearms approaching. . . . The first thing Lalu Alam did, was to hit me on the head with an iron rod. I was drenched in my own blood but somehow did not feel the pain. My assailants were wearing police [style] helmets. . . . [Then] there was a second blow to my head . . . the second hit came pretty close to the brain. . . . Almost in slow motion I saw the

Figure 5. The Trinamool Congress leader Mamata Banerjee addresses a rally in Kolkata (July 2003). AFP/GETTY IMAGES.

third rod descending and in a split-second reflex I covered my head with my arms. The rod hit [one of] my arms and shattered the ulna [the long forearm bone] but if it had hit the skull I would have died. I still recall quite vividly that at that precise moment I did not feel any pain. . . . [Then I] blacked out."[22]

The savage beating elevated Mamata Banerjee to heroine status among Congress supporters in West Bengal and made her the focal point for the party's activists across the state. The attack revealed that the CPM viewed her as the principal threat to their supremacy in West Bengal. It is unlikely that the murderous attack on a prominent opposition politician in the heart of Kolkata was the work of a rogue group of ruling party cadres, as at the time of the incident the CPM was known for its strict organizational discipline, which frayed gradually over the next two decades. The CPM was particularly rattled by Banerjee's proficiency in street agitation and protest, tactics the communists had used extensively during their slow but steady rise in West Bengal during the 1950s and 1960s. When Banerjee mobilized hundreds of thousands in an opposition rally in Kolkata in November 1992, the CPM was quick to respond with an even larger rally held at the same venue four days later.

The next landmark in Banerjee's political career occurred on July 21, 1993. The youth wing of Congress in West Bengal, which she led, organized an *abhijaan* (march) on the red-brick colonial-era building in central Kolkata that houses the administrative headquarters of the state government. As a journalist who covered the day's events recalled 17 years later, "usually these 'marches' are symbolic and political activists walk to a certain point where they are prevented [intercepted] by police [cordons] and then 'court' arrest [are loaded into buses and vans and taken away to be released within a few hours]."[23] This march, however, turned violent, and pitched battles ensued between tens of thousands of protesters and a heavily outnumbered police force. The police fired tear-gas shells to disperse the huge crowds, and this aggravated the situation. The police then fired live ammunition in several locations in central Kolkata, killing 13 protesters. Since July 21, 1994, the first anniversary of the deadly clash, Mamata Banerjee has held an annual rally in central Kolkata to commemorate the 13 young men killed on July 21, 1993. Since the formation of the Trinamool Congress on January 1, 1998, the July 21 rally has been the biggest day in the annual calendar of the party.

By the time of the 1996 national and state elections Mamata Banerjee had developed a huge loyal following among Congress activists in West Bengal and emerged as the lodestar of opposition politics in the state. After she was elected to the Lok Sabha from the urban Kolkata South constituency in the national election of May 1991 as one of just five Congress MPs victorious from West Bengal, she was appointed a junior minister in Congress's Union government, headed by P. V. Narasimha Rao, but she quit her ministerial job in 1993 to focus on state politics. In West Bengal Banerjee was increasingly drawn into conflict with the "official" faction of the state's Congress party, which was led by a dull (and male) apparatchik whose political career had begun in the early 1960s. Most of the established Congress politicians in the state, men who had emerged in the late 1960s and early 1970s, did not like Banerjee's meteoric rise and her growing popularity, particularly among young party workers and supporters. The conflict escalated during the process of selecting party candidates for the state and national elections of 1996, when Banerjee felt that her loyalists did not receive a fair share. The relationship between Banerjee and the official faction continued to deteriorate, and in August 1997 she announced the formation of "a separate Trinamool [grassroots] platform within the Congress fold" at a rally of her supporters in Kolkata.[24] This marked a point of no return, and in December 1997 she was expelled from Congress by the party's national leadership for dissidence and insubordination. The formation of the Trinamool Congress as a separate party was then announced at an emotionally charged rally held in Kolkata on December 29, 1997, attended by about 100,000 Congress activists from across West Bengal. Banerjee was one of nine Congress MPs elected to the Lok Sabha from West Bengal in 1996. Of the other eight MPs, two—Ajit Panja and Krishna Bose—joined the Trinamool Congress.

The Trinamool Congress emerged in spectacular fashion as West Bengal's second largest party after the CPM and as the state's principal opposition in the midterm national election of February 1998. The newborn party contested 28 of West Bengal's 42 constituencies and won in 7 of them, and polled over 9 million votes across the state. Congress contested all 42 constituencies and won in just one. The bulk of Congress's mass base in West Bengal had gone over to its regional splinter. In the autumn 1999 national midterm election the Trinamool Congress consolidated its mass base. Its candidates won in eight constituencies in West Bengal, and the party maintained its share of the statewide popular vote.

The Trinamool Congress's emergence in West Bengal in the late 1990s was one of the most important examples of the predominant trend in India's politics, regionalization, in the wake of the end of the long era of Congress's nationwide hegemony at the end of the 1980s and the BJP's failed attempt to emerge as the new nationwide hegemonic party during the first half of the 1990s. The Trinamool Congress's success in West Bengal was due to several mutually reinforcing factors. Mamata Banerjee's reputation as the sole militant voice of opposition to the state's CPM regime brought her mass support from the huge anti-CPM element of West Bengal's polarized electorate. Moreover, she was a self-made, homegrown leader, a daughter of the soil of West Bengal with a girl-next-door image. There was simply no question of Sonia Gandhi, Congress's national leader since the beginning of 1998, being able to compete with Mamata Banerjee's appeal to the anti-CPM part of West Bengal's population. Banerjee's nonelite social background meant that the poor—who comprised the bulk of West Bengal's Congress-voting electorate—could readily identify with her. And the Trinamool Congress's identity as an underdog regional challenger to the CPM regime played well with some sections of the middle- and lower-middle-class electorate.

In the 1996 national election Banerjee persuaded Krishna Bose, a college professor and writer, to run as the Congress candidate in Banerjee's old constituency, Jadavpur. Bose won Jadavpur back for Congress and became the only woman Congress MP from West Bengal apart from Banerjee herself, defeating the incumbent CPM MP, a woman who had narrowly defeated Banerjee in November 1989 and been reelected in 1991. Bose's win was narrow; she garnered just 13,038 more votes than her CPM rival (499,254 to 486,216). But she trailed by 24,377 votes in the Jadavpur legislative assembly segment of the constituency, one of seven constituencies of the West Bengal legislature making up the constituency. This legislative assembly segment of the eponymous parliamentary constituency was an urban area dominated by middle- and lower-middle-class voters of *udbastu* origin—postpartition refugee families from eastern Bengal, most of them resolutely anti-Congress and steadfastly loyal to the CPM. Bose stood as a Trinamool Congress candidate in the 1998 national election and resoundingly won re-election to Parliament from the constituency—a mix of urban, semiurban, and rural areas—polling 78,201 more votes than her CPM rival, a sixfold increase on her thin margin of victory in 1996. In the Jadavpur legislative assembly segment of the constituency, where she had trailed by 24,377 votes in 1996, she led by 15,556 votes. The huge swing was an unmistakable sign that *udbastu* voters who had voted against Bose when she stood as a Congress candidate were prepared to vote for her when she stood as the candidate of a regional party that had broken away from Congress. This erosion of the long-reliable *udbastu* base, a mainstay of the communists in the state since the 1950s, was particularly frightening for the CPM because the Jadavpur assembly segment was represented in the West Bengal legislature by the prominent CPM leader Buddhadev Bhattacharya, the man poised to succeed the ageing Jyoti Basu as the chief minister of West Bengal (which he did in November 2000). In the autumn 1999 national election Bose comfortably held the Jadavpur constituency for the Trinamool Congress, despite a determined CPM campaign to regain it, getting 66,765 more votes than her CPM rival. In the Jadavpur assembly segment, where the state's ruling party concentrated its efforts, she led by 6,136 votes.

But despite the Trinamool Congress's spectacular start and her own charisma, Mamata Banerjee's struggle to topple West Bengal's entrenched CPM regime turned out to be an uphill battle. This was primarily because the CPM's agrarian base remained solid and resilient to the Trinamool challenge. In addition to the loyal agrarian base, fortified by its continuing domination of the *panchayat* system, the CPM enjoyed a decisive organizational advantage over its rival. The CPM's well-oiled organizational apparatus, a proven election-winning machine, was far superior to the comparatively ramshackle organizational capabilities of the Trinamool Congress, a legacy from the Congress tradition of organizational ineptitude in West Bengal.

As the May 2001 state elections in West Bengal approached, India was rife with speculation that the end was nigh for the 24-year CPM regime and that the Trinamool Congress would storm to power in Kolkata. But the outcome of the election belied this expectation.

The Trinamool Congress had forged an alliance with the Hindu nationalist BJP in the 1998 and 1999 national elections and became an important constituent in the BJP-led NDA coalition governments formed in New Delhi in March 1998 and subsequently in October 1999. The Trinamool-BJP alliance was a relationship of mutual convenience born of circumstance. The Trinamool Congress's strong commitment to unity and amity between Hindus and Muslims in West Bengal was at odds with the BJP's Hindutva ideology. The Trinamool electoral symbol—two flowers on a bed of grass, personally designed by Mamata Banerjee—was derived from this secularist commitment. It was inspired by a line from a poem by the famous twentieth-century Bengali political poet and songwriter Kazi Nazrul Islam: "Ek brintay dui kusum, Hindu-Mussalman" (One stem [i.e. the Bengali people] from which two buds blossom, Hindu and Muslim). As a party born in the late 1990s as a regional splinter of Congress and faced with a formidable opponent in the CPM party and government, the Trinamool Congress sought an anchor in the emerging NDA coalition, led by the BJP but comprised almost entirely of regional (and mostly secularist) parties. The BJP was more than happy to welcome the Trinamool Congress—a party born of a rupture in Congress, the

BJP's principal rival, in one of India's most populous states—into the NDA fold. This fit into the BJP strategy of building a nationwide network of allied regional parties based in various states. In addition, as a fringe party in West Bengal's politics, the BJP was happy to tag along as the Trinamool Congress's junior ally in the state, and thanks to this alliance the BJP elected one MP from West Bengal in 1998 and two in 1999, something it could not have achieved on its own.

Yet the Trinamool-BJP relationship was fundamentally uneasy, primarily because over a quarter of West Bengal's electorate consists of Muslims, and large-scale support from Muslims was essential to the Trinamool Congress's objective of winning power in the state. The relationship with the BJP did not seem to trouble the large numbers of Muslim activists in Congress who switched to and worked for the Trinamool Congress from its formation, or the pro-Congress Muslim voters who voted in large numbers for the Trinamool Congress in the 1998 and 1999 national elections, particularly in the state's southern districts around Kolkata, where the new party was strong. But Banerjee was aware that some Muslims who might otherwise support the Trinamool Congress would not do so as long as it stayed aligned with the BJP. In March 2001, two months before the May 2001 state election widely anticipated to produce a change of regime in West Bengal after 24 years, she suddenly broke off the alliance with the BJP and concluded an alliance with Congress for the West Bengal polls. (She had earlier distanced herself from the BJP by resigning as the NDA Union government's minister of railways in September 2000.) Congress, a decimated rump in the state after the emergence of Trinamool and out of power in New Delhi, agreed to contest the May 2001 state elections as a junior ally of the Trinamool Congress. The last-minute alliance did not work.

The Left Front was elected to govern West Bengal for the sixth consecutive time, winning a two-thirds majority in the state legislature: 196 of the 294 constituencies. The Trinamool Congress contested in 226 constituencies and won in only 60. The Congress, which put up candidates in 60 constituencies, won in 26. The outcome was nearly identical to the 1996 state election, when the LF won 202 of the 294 seats in West Bengal's legislature and the united Congress got 82 seats. The LF maintained its share of the statewide popular vote—48 percent, as opposed to 49 percent in 1996. And the combined vote of the Trinamool Congress–Congress alliance—39 percent, with 31 percent for Trinamool and 8 percent for Congress—was the same as the 39.5 percent obtained by the united Congress in 1996. The only silver lining for opposition politics in the state was that for the first time since the LF had come to power in West Bengal in

1977, the CPM failed to obtain an outright legislative majority (or more than half the 294 seats) of its own; it won in 143 constituencies, down from 157 in 1996. The BJP, which ran candidates in 266 of the 294 constituencies after being dumped by the Trinamool Congress, managed to prove its marginality in West Bengal's politics by polling 5 percent of the statewide popular vote and failing to win a single constituency.

The failure of 2001 set off five years of decline in the Trinamool Congress's fortunes. It remained the second largest party after the CPM in a thoroughly regionalized West Bengal polity but suffered successive electoral defeats between 2003 and 2006. In the five-year elections to *panchayat* bodies held in 2003 the Trinamool Congress did poorly, and the CPM regained the limited ground it had lost in rural West Bengal in the face of Trinamool ascendancy in the mid-1998 *panchayat* polls. The 2003 *panchayat* elections proved a bellwether of the direction of political winds in the state. In the May 2004 national election, in which the ruling NDA suffered a shock defeat despite widespread predictions that it would be reelected, the Trinamool Congress fared disastrously in West Bengal. It won in only one of the state's 42 constituencies, Kolkata South, where Mamata Banerjee was reelected but with a drastically reduced margin of victory compared to 1999. From nine members of Parliament in the outgoing Lok Sabha, the Trinamool Congress was reduced to just one. The debacle was mainly the result of drift and demoralization in the Trinamool ranks after the successive setbacks of 2001 and 2003. The Trinamool Congress was also badly damaged by the fallout among West Bengal's Muslim electorate from the anti-Muslim violence in BJP-ruled Gujarat in 2002. This violence—the first major episode of communal killings since the BJP-led coalition had come to power in New Delhi in 1998—deeply frightened Muslims across India. In West Bengal the CPM campaigned among urban and rural Muslim communities in the run-up to the May 2004 national election with video recordings of the Gujarat violence, reminding Muslims of the Trinamool Congress's relationship with the BJP. This campaign had an impact, and a sizable chunk of the Trinamool Congress's Muslim support base either did not vote at all or voted for the CPM in 2004.

By the time of the 2006 state elections in West Bengal, held in April–May, the Trinamool Congress was utterly in the doldrums, and the CPM was not only dominant in the state but influential at the Center as the provider of the "outside support" necessary for the working parliamentary majority of the Congress-led UPA minority government. The LF stormed to power for the seventh consecutive time, winning in 233 of the 294 constituencies, with 50 percent of the statewide popular vote, and CPM candidates won in

176 of those constituencies. The Trinamool Congress contested in 257 constituencies and won in only 30. Congress put up candidates in 262 constituencies and won in 21 constituencies, but these wins were concentrated in a few districts where the party retained a base, and the large majority of Congress candidates (176) lost their security deposits. That is, they forfeited the small amount of money required as a deposit from all candidates who stand for election because they polled less than one-sixth of the popular vote in their constituencies. The Trinamool Congress remained the principal opposition party of West Bengal, with 27 percent of the statewide popular vote, and the total vote for the opposition parties came to 44 percent: 27 percent for Trinamool, 15 percent for Congress, and 2 percent for BJP, not far behind the LF's 50 percent. But the magnitude of the LF's victory was undeniable. The 2006 state election in West Bengal was largely free of allegations of intimidation and fraud for the first time in the post-1977 period because India's national Election Commission was able to implement strict security and monitoring measures. The turnout was high as usual; 82 percent of registered voters exercised their franchise.

In mid-2006 the most resilient political regime in India's democracy looked unassailable in West Bengal and its hegemony entrenched for the foreseeable future.

The Winds of Change

That was not to be. In a dramatic turnaround, the CPM's supremacy came unhinged after three decades from 2008 onward. Just as the 1978 *panchayat* elections signaled the consolidation of CPM dominance of rural West Bengal, the unraveling of that grassroots dominance was signaled by the *panchayat* elections of May 2008. In those elections, held exactly two years after the LF's sweeping victory in the 2006 state election, the CPM suffered heavy losses in a number of West Bengal's districts, particularly in the base and middle tiers (*gram panchayat*s and *panchayat samitis*) of the three-tiered *panchayat* system. This was an unmistakable sign of erosion of the agrarian base, which had formed the bedrock of CPM power in the state for three decades. The main gainer was the Trinamool Congress. The CPM leadership "initially reacted with disbelief," and "a leader of its peasant organization explained the [reverses in] the 2008 *panchayat* election as 'a grave and momentary mistake the people have committed.' "[25]

In fact, the *panchayat* polls were the beginning of a series of electoral defeats for the CPM regime. A year later, in the May 2009 national election, the LF was able to win in just 15 of West Bengal's 42 constituencies, down from 35 in 2004. This was by far its weakest performance in a national election since coming to power in the state in 1977. (The previous weakest was in the December 1984 national election, when Congress surged temporarily in West Bengal during the nationwide sympathy wave following Indira Gandhi's assassination, but even then the LF won in 26 of the 42 constituencies.) The Trinamool Congress emerged as West Bengal's most popular party in the 2009 national election, winning in 19 of the 42 parliamentary constituencies. Then in May 2010 the LF lost badly in elections to municipal governments in cities and towns across West Bengal. The worst debacle was in the capital, Kolkata, where the LF not only lost power but was routed by the Trinamool Congress, which won a two-thirds majority in the Kolkata Municipal Corporation, the city assembly.

The denouement arrived in the state election of May 2011, when the most resilient political regime in the history of India's democracy and the world's most durable elected communist government came to an end. The LF was reduced from 233 to 61 seats in the West Bengal legislature and the CPM from 176 to 39 seats. The Trinamool Congress won in 185 of the 294 constituencies and secured a commanding legislative majority. Congress ran as its regional splinter's junior alliance partner and won in another 42 constituencies, giving the alliance 227 seats, a three-fourths majority, in the new state legislature. The composition of the new legislature was almost identical to the one elected in 2006 but with the ruling and opposition parties' strengths reversed. The change in the statewide popular vote was not as dramatic but nonetheless decisive. The LF got 41 percent, about the same level as Congress's support in West Bengal through the 1980s and 1990s, and the Trinamool Congress–Congress alliance 49 percent, about the same proportion that had propelled the LF to seven successive victories in state elections between 1977 and 2006.

The CPM-led regime that looked unassailable in 2006 was reduced to lame-duck status from 2008, hit by progressively worsening electoral defeats. In May 2011 the regime's bête noire, Mamata Banerjee, realized her lifelong goal of driving the CPM from power in West Bengal and took over as the first woman chief minister of the state. After three decades of continuity, truly exceptional in the annals of India's democracy, the winds of change in West Bengal acquired a seemingly unstoppable momentum from 2008 onward.

When the seventh consecutive LF government assumed office in 2006, nobody could have imagined the dramatic upheaval that would unfold in the state during its tenure. That upheaval was driven by the decline of the agrarian support base that the CPM built in rural West Bengal between

1967 and 1971 with its campaigns against big landlords and consolidated in the late 1970s and the first half of the 1980s with its campaign for sharecroppers' rights (Operation Barga). The seemingly sudden slippage of the CPM's long-solid agrarian base was catalyzed by peasant resistance to the seventh LF government's attempt to acquire farmland for the purpose of building industrial hubs funded by Indian and foreign private capital in two rural areas of the state. One was Singur, near Kolkata, where India's giant Tata Group wished to build its automobile factory. The other was Nandigram, about 75 miles southwest of Kolkata, where the CPM-led state government had plans to site a petrochemical complex to be built by the Salim Group, a large Indonesian business conglomerate.

By early 2007 Singur was on the boil after police action against the protesters, Mamata Banerjee's solidarity hunger strike in Kolkata, and the gruesome death of Tapasi Malik, the teenaged activist. Then unrest flared in Nandigram as locals learned of the state government's plans to acquire at least 10,000 acres of farmland for the Salim Group's petrochemical project. In late December 2006 a notice announcing the acquisition was issued by the Haldia Development Authority, a state government agency in the East Medinipur district, where Nandigram is located. This was apparently done on the instructions of the Authority's chair, a man known to be the district's CPM strongman and who was the area's MP. The locals responded by forming the Bhoomi Uchhed Pratirodh Committee (Committee to Resist Eviction from Farmland) in January 2007 and dug up roads leading into Nandigram to keep the state police and officials out. In March 2007 a large police force attempted to enter Nandigram and was confronted by crowds of angry villagers, some of whom threw stones and bricks at the advancing police. The police fired, killing 14 villagers, before retreating. The protesters alleged that CPM cadres accompanying the police force also attacked the villagers and committed arson, looting, and sexual violence against women. After this incident 1,500–2,000 people belonging to pro-CPM families were forced out of Nandigram's cluster of villages amid violent reprisals and took shelter in an adjacent area dominated by the CPM, and the Committee to Resist Eviction took control of the Nandigram zone. The Committee's leadership consisted in part of local Trinamool Congress activists but also local CPM activists who joined the protest movement.

The second chapter of the Nandigram saga unfolded in November 2007, when the CPM launched an armed operation to retake the rebel zone. Hundreds of party cadres entered the zone from several directions on columns of motorbikes, firing guns as they advanced. Several state police detachments stationed at friction points separating the rebel zone

Figure 6.   Villagers in West Bengal gather to protest against the takeover of their farmland for an automobile plant in Singur, Hooghly district (July 2006). INDIA TODAY GROUP/GETTY IMAGES.

from adjoining CPM-dominated territory disappeared just before the operation commenced. The Committee to Resist Eviction tried to mobilize processions of villagers to confront the advancing columns, but these took casualties from gunfire and were quickly dispersed. Within a few days the CPM's red flag with its hammer-and-sickle symbol embossed in the center fluttered in the roads and villages of the rebel zone. The secretary (organizational head) of the West Bengal CPM, a party veteran in his seventies who also held the position of LF chairman, hailed the operation as "sunrise" over Nandigram after eight dark months.

It turned out to be a pyrrhic victory. The ostensible purpose of the operation, to return the displaced CPM families to their homes, simply could not be realized in the face of the overwhelming hostility to the ruling party and regime that now gripped the Nandigram area. The use of party goon squads to recapture the rebel zone and allegations of atrocities against the local population during and after the operation sparked a statewide outcry and made headline news across India. The CPM, continuously in power since 1977 and intoxicated by its huge victory in the state election of May 2006, had underestimated the resolve of the people of Nandigram. The Nandigram area lies in a part of West Bengal that has a distinguished history of political struggle. After Mahatma Gandhi declared the nationwide "Quit India" movement against the British in August 1942, the eastern part of the Medinipur district— where Nandigram is situated—rose in insurrection against the colonial power. An extensive "liberated zone" was established by the nationalist freedom fighters, led by local Congress activists, and lasted until 1944, despite severe police and military repression. In the West Bengal *panchayat* elections of May 2008, the villages of Nandigram voted overwhelmingly for the Trinamool Congress, and the larger district where the area is situated—East Medinipur, created by the administrative bifurcation of the sprawling historic Medinipur district into "East Medinipur" and "West Medinipur"—was one of two West Bengal districts where the CPM was decisively defeated by the Trinamool Congress at all three levels of the *panchayat* system. In the Hooghly district, closer to Kolkata, where Singur is located, the CPM won an overall victory in the 2008 *panchayat* elections but was massively defeated in the Singur area by the Trinamool Congress.

The drive to industrialize West Bengal in the new century through big-ticket investments by Indian and foreign private capital was the first major policy initiative of the CPM regime for over two decades, since the wrapping up of Operation Barga in the mid-1980s. The end of Operation Barga had marked the end of the CPM's agenda of agrarian reform. Although at that time "as much as 2–2.5 million acres of . . . *benami* land" (land registered under false names) were held in excess of the legal maximum of 15 acres for a family of five in the West Bengal countryside, any initiative to recover and redistribute such lands to the landless and land-poor peasantry was deemed legally too complicated and politically too risky by the LF.[26] Nor was there any significant LF initiative to improve the wages of the rural proletariat—the landless agricultural laborers *(khetmajurs)* who comprised a third of all rural households in the state. Any such program would have clashed with the interests of the landowning "middle" peasantry who formed the backbone of CPM support in rural West Bengal and who commonly employed the landless as hired workers. Instead the CPM was content to rest on its laurels. The agrarian base it had built with its campaigns against the biggest landlords in the 1967–1971 phase had been expanded and consolidated by the sharecropper rights program undertaken by the first LF government from 1978 onward. The domination of the *panchayat* system provided the CPM with the institutional mechanism to entrench its supremacy in the countryside, and the party's organizational infrastructure in rural West Bengal made sure that the agrarian base delivered the CPM's spectacular run of electoral victories through the 1980s and 1990s and into the first decade of the twenty-first century.

Focused on the agrarian strategy and satisfied with its electoral dividends, the CPM regime utterly neglected West Bengal's industrial sector for nearly three decades. West Bengal, one of India's most industrialized states in the 1950s and 1960s, was progressively denuded of its industrial capacity from the late 1960s onward. The onset of political instability in the late 1960s marked the beginning of capital flight as private Indian businesses faced a volatile and uncertain environment. In the post-1977 period, more and more of the state's "public sector undertakings"—large firms owned and operated by the Union or state governments or both—became chronically "sick." (That is, they continued to exist because they were not formally closed down but became financially unviable, suffering crippling losses year after year.) By the 1990s West Bengal's industrial landscape was a desolation, dominated by closed factories and sick public enterprises.

Some elements in the upper echelons of the CPM regime started to think about a strategy of industrial rejuvenation beginning in the mid-1990s, but nothing much happened until the seventh LF government came to power in May 2006 with the slogan "Krishi amader bhitti, shilpo amader bhobishyot" (Agriculture is our foundation and industry our future). Buddhadev Bhattacharya, the state's chief minister since November 2000, and Nirupam Sen, the industries minister and an important CPM leader from the Bardhaman district, then set in motion a plan of reindustrialization premised on attracting Indian and foreign private capital to invest in large projects based in West Bengal. Both Bhattacharya (born 1944) and Sen belonged to a relatively younger generation of CPM leaders, and they recognized the limitations of the agrarian focus and the need to rectify the dire situation of the industrial sector. The Indian economy had for the first time registered growth impressive by world standards in the first years of the new century, driven largely by growth in the liberalized nonstate industrial sector. West Bengal risked "missing the bus" in a new era of industrial activity in which the country's states competed with each other to attract investments of Indian and foreign private capital.

The decision of the Tata Group to situate its small-car plant in West Bengal was a huge coup for the CPM-led state government elected in May 2006, for it signaled that the new-found friendliness of the state government toward private capital had attracted a top Indian corporate entity. That the Tata Group's "Nano" car would be produced at the factory in Singur, 25 miles from Kolkata, meant that West Bengal had secured a very prestigious project; this would surely induce other top-drawer industrial capitalists, Indian and foreign, to consider West Bengal. The state government's willingness to grant Indonesia's Salim Group a "special economic zone" to set up a petrochemical complex in Nandigram was more dubious. The Tata Group is regarded as reputable in India and abroad. The founder of the Salim Group—Sudono Salim (born 1916), an Indonesian of Chinese extraction—built his business empire as a crony of Suharto, the dictatorial ruler of Indonesia from 1967 to 1998, who came to power in the wake of mass killings of hundreds of thousands of suspected members and supporters of the Communist Party of Indonesia in 1965–1966.

The primary attraction of West Bengal as an investment destination for big business lay in the remarkable stability of its political regime. This was, after all, the only state of the Indian Union that had elected the same party/alliance to power for seven consecutive times over three decades, and after the crushing defeat of the opposition in the 2006 state election the LF's hegemony looked unassailable. The apparently rock-solid edifice of CPM dominance wobbled badly in 2007 and cracked wide open beginning in 2008.

The CPM regime's response to the peasant protests against dispossession from land in Singur and Nandigram had a common feature: the quick and almost reflexive resort to force rather than restraint and dialogue. The victims of the coercion-intensive approach were the very kind of people whom the CPM-led alliance had claimed to be representative of for three decades: poor rural folk struggling to eke out a living. Tapasi Malik of Singur belonged to this category, as did those killed in Nandigram. The people at the receiving end of the violence of the state police and ruling party thugs were also typically of "low" caste background or—in the case of Nandigram, an area with a heavily mixed population of Hindus and Muslims—members of West Bengal's 25 percent–plus Muslim minority. In January 2009 a by-election took place to the seat in the state legislature allotted to Nandigram when the legislator elected in 2006 (from the CPI, a minor LF constituent) resigned after being indicted on corruption charges unrelated to the land conflict. Mamata Banerjee nominated Firoza Bibi, a middle-aged, apolitical Muslim woman whose son Imad-ul Islam was among the 14 shot dead in March 2007, to stand as the Trinamool Congress candidate. The *shahidaer ma* (martyr's mother) defeated her LF rival by a huge margin.

The identification in public perception of the CPM regime with violence against the poor deepened in November 2008, when Bhattacharya, the chief minister, was targeted in an improvised explosive device attack by the radical Communist Party of India (Maoist), which is waging an insurgency in a swathe of India's states. The attack happened in the West Medinipur district just after Bhattacharya had started in a convoy of vehicles toward Kolkata after the laying of the foundation stone for another megaindustrialization project, a steel and power plant to be built by a company of the Jindal Group, a major India-wide private corporate specialized in steel production. The chief minister escaped unscathed, as did the owner of the Jindal firm and the Union government's junior minister for steel, who were accompanying him. After the attack, which occurred in Salboni, about 125 miles from Kolkata, close to the site of the proposed plant, the state police launched a widespread crackdown in the district to ferret out Maoists. The crackdown was clumsily conducted and led to brutalities against Adivasi (tribal) and other socioeconomically deprived communities. This in turn sparked a local uprising backed by the Maoists that became known across India as the "Lalgarh movement" after Lalgarh, a tiny township at the epicenter of the uprising's rural heartland. The situation escalated through 2009 and 2010, and parts of the West Medinipur district were gripped by a cycle of brutal violence pitting Maoist militants against the state police, special counterinsurgency forces sent by the Union government, and heavily armed CPM militia. The armed CPM cadres set up camps in villages across the affected area in 2010. In January 2011, four months before the state election that would oust the Left Front from power in West Bengal, cadres in one such camp opened fire on the villagers after an altercation, killing nine villagers, including several women. The timing of the incident was propitious for the Trinamool Congress opposition, which campaigned strongly about the terror unleashed by CPM *harmads*—"bandits," a term coined by Mamata Banerjee—in the Maoist-active areas of the state.

The CPM regime had been implicated in episodes of egregious violence against poor people long before Singur, Nandigram, or Lalgarh. A notorious episode occurred as early as 1979 at Marichjhapi, a small island in the Sunderbans (Beautiful Forest), the mangrove forest south of Kolkata that is famous as the original habitat of the royal Bengal tiger. In 1978, after the LF came to power, a group of about 20,000 people who had come to West

Bengal from East Pakistan as refugees after communal violence in 1950 and 1964 had established a settlement on this remote, uninhabited island. Under a 1960s resettlement program they had been packed off to the Dandakaranya region of Madhya Pradesh. (Dandakaranya is now mostly in the southern part of the state of Chhattisgarh, carved out of Madhya Pradesh in 2000, and is a stronghold of the Maoist insurgency.)

They were "in the main from the lowest castes . . . people who had been at the bottom of the pile in East Bengal and been thrown entirely on the mercy of government" after displacement. The Dandakaranya resettlement area was "a barren waste of scrub and forest . . . in a low plateau where the soil was arid and infertile and where previously there had been no settled population at all. Its inhabitants were nomads, mainly Gond forest peoples." In the words of a woman refugee sent to Dandakaranya: "we were completely unaccustomed to hills and forests. The water was so bad, there were too many mosquitoes and malaria, diarrhea and other killer diseases. Above all it was not Bengal and locals did not know our language."

When a new government led by a regional party with a strong pro-poor and pro-refugee reputation came to power in West Bengal in mid-1977, the Dandakaranya people worked up the courage to make their return to West Bengal. But they were not banking on handouts from that government. With their own labor and resources they built on Marichjhapi "a burgeoning village with a school, a health center, well laid-out roads, a bakery and tube-wells [to draw water]." They named the settlement Netaji Nagar (Netaji Town), in honor of the legendary Bengali and Indian anticolonial nationalist Subhas Chandra Bose, who is popularly known in the subcontinent as Netaji (Leader).

The recently elected CPM regime refused to tolerate the "illegal" settlement, on the grounds that it intruded on a tiger reserve and disturbed the Sunderbans' ecological balance. What followed was "the mother of all Nandigrams." The state police blockaded the island in January 1979, and after five days several thousand desperate residents attempted to break the blockade in a flotilla of handmade boats; some were armed with bows and arrows and other crude weapons. Nitai Mondal was then a young CPM activist in Kumirmari, the mainland village opposite Marichjhapi, who had joined the CPM while studying at university in Kolkata in the early 1970s. In 2011, as the secretary (head) of the CPM local committee for the area, he recalled the carnage that ensued once the breakout boats reached Kumirmari: "the police started raining bullets as soon as the refugees landed in our village. I like everybody else fled as I could see people falling to bullets—injured or dead—everywhere." The estimates of the number killed range from 50 to 1,000. The refugee hunt continued for another three days, and in May 1979 the state police landed in Marichjhapi and forced the remaining 10,000 residents off the island. The settlement was then razed. The survivors of Marichjhapi dispersed to villages across the impoverished Sunderbans belt.[27]

In April 2011, on the eve of the end of the 34-year CPM-led regime of West Bengal, Nitai Mondal, the local CPM leader, was asked how the state government got away with the Marichjhapi atrocity. He replied: "it was 1979, the Left Front was in its prime and there was no opposition [in the State]."[28]

Three decades later the situation was entirely different. The regime established in 1977 was in a state of advanced decay, and there was an opposition in the state, spearheaded by an alternative regional party, Trinamool Congress, and its charismatic leader, Mamata Banerjee, who for two decades had been driven by a single-minded commitment to oust the CPM regime from power.

Conflicts between the state and the people over land acquisition for industrial and infrastructural projects are a recurrent issue in contemporary India. Since 2006 there have been deadly clashes in Orissa, neighboring West Bengal, between police and locals protesting the acquisition of their land by the state government, which is run by a regional party, the Biju Janata Dal, for large-scale steel and mining projects funded by Indian and foreign big business. In 2011 there were violent confrontations in Uttar Pradesh between police and villagers unhappy with the compensation for land acquired by the state government (then run by a regional party, the BSP, replaced in 2012 by another regional party, the SP) for highway construction and industrial zones. There are also ongoing standoffs between the Union government and local communities in Tamil Nadu and Maharashtra over the proposed sites of nuclear power plants. But only in West Bengal did the land issue precipitate a statewide upheaval and the toppling from power of an entrenched regime.

This was partly due to the skill of Mamata Banerjee, a populist agitator par excellence, in turning the localized sparks of Singur and Nandigram into the vanguard of a blazing statewide movement for *paribartan* (change of regime). The Trinamool Congress undertook a sustained campaign of agitation and protest on the Singur, Nandigram, and Lalgarh issues, emphasizing the oppressive, violent actions of the CPM regime toward the poor and downtrodden. The message was powerful; it appropriated the LF's propoor rhetoric and turned the CPM regime's propoor image on its head. The defense of smallholding peasants' right to their land was particularly effective in undermining the CPM's agrarian base because struggles and programs to advance peasant rights had been the mainstay of communist politics in West Bengal for six decades: the Tebhaga movement at the time of India's independence, the antilandlord campaigns of the late 1960s and early 1970s, Operation Barga from the late 1970s through the mid-1980s. In 2009 Banerjee coined a pithy slogan to express her politics and its priorities: "Ma, Mati, Manush" (Mother, Land, People). The slogan, laden with idiomatic and cultural meaning, resonated in rural West Bengal. In October 2008 the Tata Group pulled the plug on its Singur plant, citing the impossible situation due to relentless agitation, and relocated its small-car factory to the much more big-business-friendly state of Gujarat, governed by the BJP's Narendra Modi, like Banerjee a charismatic and popular regional politician. The Salim Group's Nandigram project was effectively canceled.

Yet Singur, Nandigram, and Lalgarh simply catalyzed a rising current of deep disenchantment in West Bengal with Indian democracy's most resilient political regime. In the second half of 2010, monsoon rains were much below normal in West Bengal. In the vast agricultural zone of Bardhaman district, known as the state's "rice bowl" and a CPM bastion for four decades, a rash of suicides due to crop failure occurred among landless sharecroppers and poor peasants with very small plots who were unable to repay loans taken at exorbitant interest rates from local moneylenders to buy seeds, pesticides, and fertilizers. The crop failed because the regime in power for 33 years had not built any irrigation facilities to cope with the vagaries of the weather. The names of some of the distressed peasants who killed themselves—Gosain Patra, Jitu Bagdi, Sheikh Yunus—reveal their low-caste or Muslim identities.[29] In 2006 the CPM won in 24 of the 26 state legislature constituencies in the Bardhaman district; in 2011 it won in only 9 of 25.

Closer to Kolkata, West Bengal's traditional industrial belt ringing the capital in the North 24-Parganas and Hooghly districts presented a picture of desolation in the run-up to the 2011 state election. This landscape of closed factories—some shut since the 1980s—had become a rust belt in the true sense. Jute mills, factories making paper, tires, steel rods and wires, were all shut, and thousands of people were out of work. Unsurprisingly, "rage [was] evident among people," and "the industrial belts of North 24-Parganas and Hooghly [were] abuzz with a one-point agenda of change at any cost." An observer predicted that "after tasting disaster in the 2009 Lok Sabha [national] polls, the CPM may well witness a catastrophe here [in 2011]." This was precisely what happened. As an unemployed factory worker eking out a living as a daily wage laborer put it: "the Left has ruined us." A CPM labor union organizer admitted: "our major mistake was to take people for granted."[30]

Other notable instances of taking people for granted came back to haunt the LF in the 2011 state election. In 2005 the Union government constituted a committee to inquire into "the social, economic and educational status of the Muslim community of India." The committee, popularly known as the Sachar Committee after the last name of its chairman, submitted its report in November 2006. The report found that India's 13.4 percent Muslim population (as of the 2001 national census) suffered significant inequity and disadvantage, nationwide and in all states, in socioeconomic status, educational achievement, and employment opportunities in the public sector. The findings about West Bengal's 25.2 percent Muslim population (as of 2001)—the third highest of any state after J&K and Assam—aroused much interest across India. The report claimed that while 12 percent of the urban population and 25 percent of the rural population in West Bengal lived in extreme poverty in 2005, 27 percent of the state's urban Muslims and 33 percent of the state's rural Muslims lived in extreme poverty. Moreover, Muslims were pitifully underrepresented, worse than in many other states, in state government employment in West Bengal, holding just 4.7 percent of higher-level jobs and 1.8 percent of lower-level jobs (and only 8 percent of all posts in the state police).[31] It appeared that after three continuous decades in power, the CPM-led regime with its secularist and propoor credentials had done very little for the advancement of West Bengal's Muslims, about half of whom had consistently voted for the LF since 1977.

The final unraveling of the 34-year hegemonic regime of West Bengal was driven by a backlash against the strong-arm methods the ruling party had routinely used for at least two decades to maintain its supremacy in the countryside. One morning in February 2010, Debirani Ghosh opened the door of her home in Kamdebpur village, in the Hooghly district, to find a piece of white cloth fluttering from the bamboo pole in her courtyard. When the family went to bed the previous night the Trinamool Congress flag—the saffron-white-green tricolor with the party's two-flowers-on-grass symbol in the center—had been aloft on that pole. The white cloth that had replaced it during the night was a *thaan,* the white borderless sari traditionally worn by Hindu widows as a mark of mourning for deceased husbands. This "was a warning people in rural [West] Bengal understood quite clearly." Prior to *panchayat,* state and national elections in West Bengal over the preceding two decades, it was common for a *thaan* to be anonymously deposited on the doorstep of opposition activists. In the words of a police officer, "one *thaan* can keep thousands under control in villages. . . . It is the fear [the *thaan* induces]." The Ghoshes, sharecroppers who had benefited from Operation Barga, had been staunch CPM supporters for three decades until Debirani's husband, Bablu, switched to the Trinamool Congress in 2009. Bablu was killed within a week when he defied the warning and went out to canvass for a Trinamool candidate for election to a local school's governing council. The family left their village and shifted to a safer area in the district after the murder.[32]

In the May 2006 state election, the LF won 16 of the 18 constituencies in the Hooghly district, and the CPM won in 12 of those. In May 2011 the LF won in two constituencies (and the CPM in one); Trinamool Congress won in 16 of the 18.

While conducting field research in the West Medinipur district in 2009 and 2010, I became acquainted with a warm and gracious Muslim farming family in Sijua, a village in the Salboni area. They are potato growers and also have a poultry farm. The middle-aged father joined the CPM in 1991 and subsequently became a member of the party's local committee. He quit the party before the 2008 *panchayat* elections. While he went into political hibernation, his older son, an ardent Mamata Banerjee fan, tried to start a Trinamool Congress unit in the village. The young man was picked up and taken to a shed, where he was blindfolded. His captors then fired more than a dozen blank shots inside the shed in a mock execution. A live bullet was then fired at his foot, leaving him with a permanent limp. The frantic father negotiated his son's release with the captors—former "comrades," he noted with a wry smile—and gave an undertaking that the young man would desist from political activity. He was then sent away to a different district of the state to ensure that there would be no repetition of his ordeal.

Despite major setbacks in many other districts of the state, the CPM swept the 2008 *panchayat* elections in the West Medinipur district, including the Salboni block (subdivision). In the 2009 national election, the ruling party and alliance suffered severe reverses statewide, but in the Jhargram parliamentary constituency, which includes Salboni, the CPM candidate secured nearly 300,000 more votes than his closest opposition rival, the highest margin of victory in the state. In April 2011, weeks before the May 2011 state election, I telephoned the family's younger son from Kolkata after seeing an opinion poll aired on a regional television channel that predicted that while the LF was facing defeat in the state, the CPM candidate in Salboni was projected to win with 61 percent of the vote. He responded that the opinion poll regarding Salboni was wrong because people were afraid to speak their mind and that in fact the opposition was ahead in the area.

The Trinamool Congress candidate won the Salboni seat in the state legislature in May 2011, narrowly defeating the CPM candidate. In the 2006 state election the LF won in 16 of the 19 constituencies in the West Medinipur district, and the CPM won 13 of those. In 2011 the LF won in 9 constituencies (and the CPM in seven), while 10 elected opposition candidates—8 from the Trinamool Congress, which emerged as the single largest party in the district.

The Regionalized Future

On July 21, 2011, the Trinamool Congress's annual "martyrs' day" rally in Kolkata's city center, organized on that day since 1994 by Mamata Banerjee to commemorate the 13 young men killed by police firing during the Youth Congress demonstration she led in central Kolkata on July 21, 1993, had a triumphal mood. Kohinoora Bibi, a 50-year-old widow from a village in West Medinipur's Keshpur area, attended the rally for the eighteenth consecutive year, with her 28-year-old son Shah Jahan. Her husband, Abdul Khaleq Ali, had been one of the 13 killed in July 1993. Unlike the others, he did not die of gunshot injuries but a teargas shell that exploded on his stomach and produced a wound that turned septic after a few days. For 17 years, Kohinoora Bibi said, "we attended the rally with tears in our eyes. . . . But this time is different. . . . We are joyous." Shah Jahan's second son was born a few days before the July 2011 rally. "I wanted a daughter," he said, "and had thought of naming her Mamata [Compassion]. But I couldn't. After all, I can't control my fate."[33]

Like all of the successful regional politicians who dominate India's democracy in the early twenty-first century, Mamata Banerjee cannot afford to take the people of her state for granted. Should her government stumble, and especially if it were to alienate the poor, rural majority of the population, the CPM, with deep roots in the soil of West Bengal, will be in a position to renew its fortunes. As in 1978 and 2008, the outcome of the state's five-year *panchayat* elections in July 2013 will be a bellwether of political trends. The one certainty is that the politics of West Bengal will be dominated for the foreseeable future by an explicitly regional (state-specific) party, the Trinamool Congress, and an effectively regional party, the CPM. That regionalization mirrors the transformation of India's democracy in the early twenty-first century.

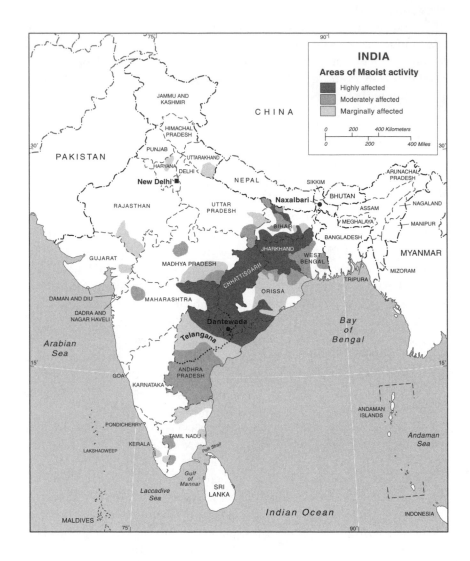

CHINA

JAMMU AND
KASHMIR

HIMACHAL
PRADESH

PAKISTAN

PUNJAB

UTTARAKHAND

HARYANA

DELHI

New Delhi

NEPAL

SIKKIM

BHUTAN

ARUNACHAL
PRADESH

Naxalbari

NAGALAND

RAJASTHAN

UTTAR
PRADESH

ASSAM

MEGHALAYA

MANIPUR

BIHAR

BANGLADESH

MYANMAR

GUJARAT

MADHYA PRADESH

JHARKHAND

WEST
BENGAL

MIZORAM

CHHATTISGARH

TRIPURA

DAMAN AND DIU

ORISSA

DADRA AND
NAGAR HAVELI

MAHARASHTRA

Bay
of
Bengal

Dantewada

Arabian
Sea

Telangana

GOA

ANDHRA
PRADESH

KARNATAKA

ANDAMAN
ISLANDS

PONDICHERRY

Andaman
Sea

LAKSHADWEEP

KERALA

TAMIL NADU

Palk Strait

Gulf
of
Mannar

Laccadive
Sea

SRI
LANKA

Indian Ocean

INDONESIA

MALDIVES

CHAPTER FOUR

The Maoist Challenge

THE ARMED men in jungle camouflage fatigues moved quietly in inverted *V* formation through the forest toward their target, a clearing located a mile inside the forest. The soldiers of the Combat Battalions for Resolute Action (COBRA), crack paramilitary units raised by the government of India and trained to take on India's Maoist insurgents in their jungle bases, had left their camp in a remote rural area of the state of West Bengal in eastern India at 2:30 A M. It was now nearly 4:30 A M, and they were closing in on the clearing with the help of handheld GPS devices. A tip-off had arrived a few hours earlier that an armed squad of the Communist Party of India (Maoist), which is waging an insurrection in a large swathe of the country, was camped out in that clearing.

As they crept up to the clearing, the lead commandos spotted the outlines of a tent. At that moment their element of surprise ran out, as the tent's sentry spotted them and opened fire. Within seconds the sentries of two other tents pitched in the clearing, which were not visible from the commando team's approach route, also opened fire. The six occupants of the first tent emerged and tried to engage the attackers, but they were hopelessly exposed to the commandos' line of fire and were cut down in a hail of bullets. The sentries and the dozen or so occupants of the other two tents managed to escape into the forest, firing intermittent bursts to keep the commandos at bay as they went.

As daylight broke, the commandos were able to inspect their "kill." The bullet-riddled bodies of five young men and one young woman lay in the clearing. One of the five males was identified within hours as a prominent local leader of the Maoists, known by his nom de guerre, Sidhu Soren. His was a prize kill. Since late 2008 he had emerged as a key grassroots leader of the Maoist insurgency in West Bengal. His death in July 2010 in the forests of Goaltore, an area of the state's West Medinipur district on the border with the neighboring Bankura district, was a major setback to the Maoists in their core area of operations in West Bengal. The killing of Sidhu Soren in an "encounter," as such incidents are referred to in India, made headline news in newspapers and on television channels across India. This encounter in a *saal* forest of eastern India—the *saal* is a tall tree found in eastern India and some other parts of the subcontinent—produced seven fatalities in all. The seventh was Ashis Tiwary, a young commando fatally shot by the Maoists. Maoist weapons recovered included a self-loading rifle, two .303 rifles, two 9mm. pistols, seven shotguns, two improvised explosive devices, and an Indian Small Arms System rifle, an Indian variant of the AK-47 and the standard-issue weapon of the Indian army's infantry forces. The INSAS rifle was the personal weapon of Sidhu Soren. Seven cell phones were also found.

The man known as Sidhu Soren was born 27 years earlier in a remote hamlet in the West Medinipur district. His real name was Bhuta Baskay. Persons with the surname Baskay belong to one of 11 extended clans that make up the Santal tribal people, an Adivasi (original inhabitant) community found in large numbers in rural and especially forested areas of eastern India, with the most sizable concentrations in parts of the states of West Bengal and Jharkhand. Other common Santal surnames, denoting clan identity, are Hansda, Murmu, Kisku, Hembrom, Marandi, Soren, Tudu, and Besra.

The day after the encounter, a police team arrived in Sidhu Soren's native village, a forest hamlet about 20 miles from the place where he died. This dirt-poor hamlet is accessible only on foot via a treacherous track punctuated by ponds and ditches and has no electricity. They handed his father, Jamadar Baskay, a daily wage laborer who lives with his family in a mud-walled hut with a tin roof, a typewritten piece of paper and left. Jamadar Baskay could not read it, as he is illiterate. He thought that this was another of the numerous police notices and summons that had been delivered to his home since Bhuta had left 10 years earlier to join the Maoist movement, just after sitting his school-leaving examinations, and put it away with the other documents. Jamadar and his wife, Bhuta's mother, Lakshmimani Baskay, realized what had happened when a journalist arrived later in the day and told them.

The parents had seen their son just once in the 10 years after he left. This was in late 2008, when the Maoists assumed center stage in a localized uprising in a sizable area of the rural tracts of the West Medinipur district—an area known as Jangalmahal (Abode of the Forests)—and "Sidhu Soren" surfaced from his underground life as a prominent face of the uprising. He made no attempt to contact them; it was they who traveled to an adjacent part of the district to meet him after hearing that he had appeared in public and was being regularly interviewed by television and print journalists. They managed to meet him after some difficulty. The meeting lasted no more than a few minutes, during which Bhuta, a wiry, ramrod-straight young man with a steely look in the eye who easily stood out in a crowd, inquired politely after their health and asked how his brothers and sisters were doing. He then left, and they never saw him again.

The parents' grief for their dead son was inconsolable, mixed with anger at those responsible for his death. They said that they would not "bend before the government," come what may, and insisted that their son was no criminal or terrorist but a patriot who had sacrificed his life for the emancipation of the poor and oppressed people of Jangalmahal, West Bengal, and India.[1]

The First Generation

Sidhu Soren was an activist of the third generation of India's Maoist movement. Its first phase began in 1967, triggered by a localized uprising among Santals in a rural area located in the northern part of the state of West Bengal, in the foothills of the eastern Himalayas. That episode became famous in India and abroad as the "Naxalbari" uprising, after the name of one of the three localities in which it occurred; was welcomed by the regime of Mao Zedong's China as "a development of tremendous significance"; and provided inspiration to a radical stream of Indian communists to form their own party and launch a revolutionary insurrection in 1969. Since that time the terms "Naxalite" and "Maoist" have been used interchangeably in India, with the former term more prevalent up to the end of the twentieth century. The first Maoist insurrection disintegrated rapidly and was over by 1972. The colloquial expressions "train wreck" and "crash and burn" would describe its trajectory accurately.

The Naxalites' grandiose vision of an India-wide revolution on the Chinese model—to be led by peasant armies that would establish liberated zones or base areas in the countryside and then encircle and seize the cities in a copybook application of Mao's operational doctrine of "people's war"—contrasted pitifully with the actual footprint on the ground of India's first Maoist insurrection. The insurrection that began in 1969 was able to mount significant rural campaigns in parts of only two of West Bengal's districts (two localities, Gopiballavpur and Debra, in the western part of the Medinipur district in 1969–1970 and a few localities of the Birbhum district in 1971), one district (Srikakulam) of the southern state of Andhra Pradesh in 1969–1970, and in a few pockets of the northern state of Bihar. These were localized outbreaks even within the states in which they occurred and no more than isolated events in the India-wide context, and all were suppressed in a matter of months by state police forces, backed up in some instances by paramilitary police sent by the Union government and in a few instances by detachments of the Indian army.

Their ambitions of a peasant-led revolutionary war having led nowhere, the Naxalites focused from 1970 onward in West Bengal—the state where their movement gained the most following, albeit mostly among high school, college, and university students—on an armed urban campaign. This juvenile campaign emphasized *khatam* (liquidation) of enemies of the people and primarily involved murders of low-ranking policemen and activists of other political parties—particularly the Communist Party of India (Marxist) (CPM), from which the Maoist wing had seceded in the late 1960s. The other activities were random throwing of crude bombs, intended to sow a climate of fear, and a "cultural revolution" campaign—vandalism of statues of heroes of the Indian anticolonial struggle and cultural icons, who were posthumously dubbed reactionaries deserving of extirpation from national history and collective memory. The anarchic spree caused mayhem during 1970–1971 in and around West Bengal's capital, Calcutta, but petered out in the face of a resolute and frequently brutal police counter-offensive amid mounting public disgust with Naxalite violence.

According to the program adopted at a congress in May 1970 of the Communist Party of India (Marxist-Leninist), the Maoist party that had formed in May 1969, India's first Maoist insurrection aimed "to overthrow" the "semicolonial" and "semifeudal" order masquerading as a democracy and replace it with a "people's democracy . . . a state guaranteeing democracy for 90 percent of the people and enforcing dictatorship over a handful of enemies," namely landed feudal elites and the upper bourgeoisie, who were described as a "comprador" class simultaneously allied to "U.S. imperialism and Soviet social imperialism" and the principal agent of "the plunder of our people." The 1970 program stated that "the party is confident . . . about the victory of the Indian revolution which, as Chairman Mao has predicted, will end the imperialist reactionary era in the history of mankind and ensure the worldwide victory of socialism." Within two years of this clarion call, the first Maoist insurrection lay in ruins. "The people" did not respond, and the insurrection remained limited to a few localized sparks that failed to ignite the prairie fires of the Indian revolution.[2]

The catastrophic failure of the 1967–1972 Maoist insurrection looks inevitable in retrospect, and stemmed from a complex of factors. The movement's simplistic theoretical propositions represented a reductive ideological framework inadequate for understanding India's vast and heterogeneous social landscape, and the nearly transcendent conception of "the people" (or 90 percent thereof) craving liberation from a semifeudal and semicolonial order could not provide the basis for a coherent revolutionary praxis. The slavish attitude toward Mao's China virtually guaranteed that many Indians would see the Naxalites as stooges of a hostile enemy country. At the time of the eruption of the first Naxalite insurrection Sino-Indian relations were completely broken, in the wake of the late 1962 border war between the two countries, in which India had been decisively defeated. The policies of the Indian government, headed by Jawaharlal Nehru, were substantially responsible for bringing on that debacle, but the Naxalite view, expressed in the 1970 party congress declaration, simply repeated Beijing's propaganda: "India's aggression against socialist China in 1962 and her continual provocations against China since then at the instance of U.S. imperialism and Soviet social-imperialism . . . prove beyond a shadow of doubt that India's ruling classes are faithful stooges of U.S. imperialism and Soviet social-imperialism."

This stance was part of a syndrome of Mao fixation: "the democratic revolution in India is taking place in the era of Mao Zedong. . . . Our revolution is part of the great proletarian cultural revolution which has consolidated socialism and proletarian dictatorship in China and turned China into the base area of world revolution. . . . The great, glorious and correct CPC [Chinese Communist Party] . . . headed by Chairman Mao and Vice-Chairman Lin Biao . . . has tremendously inspired the international proletariat. . . . We are a contingent of this great army of the international proletariat."[3] The chief Naxalite ideologue and proponent of the counterproductive *khatam* (liquidation) line, Charu Mazumdar, a middle-aged man who had been a district-level organizer of the CPM in the Naxalbari area of West Bengal until he broke away in 1967, was given to writing articles with titles such as "Chairman's China May Be Attacked: Hasten the Work of Revolution" (September 1969) and "China's Chairman Is Our Chairman, China's Path Is Our Path" (November 1969).[4]

The leaders of India's first Maoist insurrection seemed oblivious to the fact that the Chinese Communists gained mass support in the course of their struggle in significant measure because they came to be seen as more committed defenders of Chinese national pride and patriotism than their "Nationalist" Kuomintang rivals. They also appeared to be blind to the fact that the Chinese Communists had repeatedly organized and reorganized their party, built and rebuilt their mass base, and fought internal and external enemies for three grueling decades before their successful seizure of power in 1949. By contrast, the first generation of India's Maoist revolutionaries were led by men in a hurry, whose naïvete and delusions condemned their revolutionary project to catastrophic failure.

Indeed, the leaders of the 1967–1972 Maoist insurrection made almost no effort to build even the rudimentary infrastructure of a broadly based party to support their grandiose scheme of nationwide revolution. Of the 18 men "elected" to the CPI(ML)'s central committee at the May 1970 party congress, 14 were from just three states: West Bengal (seven), Andhra Pradesh (four) and Bihar (three). Of the seven members from West Bengal, six were from *bhadralok* backgrounds—well-educated urban, upper-caste Bengali Hindus. Of the four from Andhra Pradesh, three were from one district, Srikakulam (two of them were killed by police action in July 1970). The extraordinarily narrow social basis of the Naxalite leadership was equally evident in the CPI(ML)'s West Bengal state committee "elected" in January 1970. Of the 14 men on this committee, 11 were *bhadralok,* mostly former middle-level functionaries of the CPM. Just one member of the West Bengal state committee, a Santal leader from the Naxalbari area, belonged to a subaltern social group.[5]

The 1967–1972 Naxalite insurrection was not remotely a nationwide upsurge, nor was it led by members of subaltern social groups. Its defining feature was a *regional subculture of radicalism* particular to West Bengal, specifically the revolutionary fantasies of a section of the *bhadralok* class, among whom communist politics had appeared in the 1930s and 1940s and gained numerous adherents through the 1950s and 1960s. The ideologue Charu Mazumdar personified this strain of *bhadralok* radicalism gone wild. He clearly saw himself as the prophet of the imminent Indian revolution. As his exhortations grew more and more extreme in the course of 1970 and 1971, he frightened and alienated a steadily rising number of his closest colleagues. But by then the die was cast. The fledgling Maoist movement had embarked on a path of delusional adventurism and faced the full brunt of the government's response. Mazumdar himself was captured by police at a hideout in central Calcutta in July 1972 in failing health and died days later of cardiac arrest. The movement's main "cultural revolution" advocate—like Mazumdar a *bhadralok* radical in his fifties—had been captured in August 1971 in Calcutta and summarily shot by the police in a "fake" or staged encounter. Fake encounters be-came the state police's favored method of dealing with the Naxalite hard-core, and several thousand young men were killed in this way. The logic of *khatam* (liquidation) was turned against and devoured many of its ardent proponents and practitioners.

In the tiny handful of rural localities where the first-generation Mao-ists were able to mount short-lived campaigns of land seizure and liqui-dations of landlords, moneylenders, and officials—notably the Medini-pur and Birbhum districts of West Bengal and Srikakulam district in Andhra Pradesh—they were successful in mobilizing sizable numbers of the subaltern classes. These were predominantly people of Adivasi or tribal communities, the most impoverished and marginalized population in India then as now. A sizable number of Santals in the Naxalite-active zones of Medinipur and Birbhum, and of Girijan (Hill People) Adivasis in Srikakulam participated in the Naxalite campaigns. But in the vast India-wide context these local uprisings were no more than drops in the bucket. As a scholar of the Naxalite movement in rural West Bengal has written, "aside from a series of tactical and strategic blunders and a lack of [wider] mass support, the movement was doomed because the CPI-ML was no match for the ruthless organized power of the state. Given the cost to the tribal community—in casualties, arrested men-folk, con-fiscated food supplies and disrupted cultivation—failure to continue the struggle was a foregone conclusion."[6]

The biggest international story of the early 1970s in the subcontinent was the terminal crisis of Pakistan's unity that began in March 1971 and culminated nine months later in India's triumph in the December 1971 war with Pakistan and the liberation of East Pakistan, which held the bulk of the territory and population of the historic province of Bengal, which had been partitioned in 1947. The nine-month crisis and its dra-matic climax gripped the world's attention, and the outcome irrevocably changed the geostrategic balance in the subcontinent in India's favor (The Naxalite leadership opposed the Bangladesh struggle as an Indo-Soviet conspiracy, a position also held by the Nixon administration in the United States, and this aggravated their growing isolation in West Bengal and elsewhere in India.) On India's national political scene, the big devel-opment of the early 1970s was the rise of Indira Gandhi as the nation's dominant political figure riding the populist slogan "Garibi Hatao" (Abolish Poverty) in the March 1971 national election. In West Bengal, the political development of long-term significance was the arrival of the CPM—the party from which the Naxalites had seceded after branding it "revisionist" of revolutionary values—as a powerful, regionally based alternative to Congress in the state. The breakthrough the CPM achieved in rural West Bengal in the March 1971 national and state elections proved lasting and underpinned the continuous rule in West Bengal of the Left Front, dominated by the CPM, from 1977 to 2011.

India's first Maoist insurrection, in its death throes by late 1971, was relegated to the sidelines by the tumult sweeping West Bengal, India, and the subcontinent. But the story of the failed revolution was not inconsequential. In March 1973, 17,787 Naxalite prisoners were being held in jails in West Bengal alone (not counting detainees in other states), of whom 1,399 were minors under the age of 18. Several thousand more were dead, killed in real and fake encounters, while many others had escaped death or incarceration by fleeing abroad, including to the United States. In West Bengal, the hotbed of the doomed movement, the Naxalite rhetoric of revolution had attracted tens of thousands of students and youth in Calcutta and the small *(mofussil)* towns. Sons—and occasionally daughters—of wealthy, middle-class, and lower-middle-class families flocked to the Maoist banner, and they included many of the most talented of their generation. Their fate was a human tragedy of major proportions.

A decade after the first-generation Maoists were suppressed, the human dimension of the failed insurrection was brought vividly to life in a remarkable novel, *Kaalbaela* (Ominous Times), written by a young Bengali writer, Samaresh Majumdar. *Kaalbaela* has sold over 100,000 copies in Bengali and won a national book award in 1984. The main character, Animesh Mitra, arrives in Calcutta in the late 1960s to attend college, having grown up several hundred miles away in a middle-class family in a small town in the northern part of West Bengal, in an area of tea plantations close to Naxalbari. This youth of small-town origins is drawn into left-wing student politics and initially becomes an activist of the student organization of the CPM, before joining the Naxalites and becoming sucked into their insurrection. His revolutionary activities are unremarkable; he starts off writing wall graffiti and progresses to amateurish armed actions. Eventually captured by the police, he is subjected to brutal torture in captivity.

The thread of the novel is Animesh's love affair with Madhabilata, or "Lata," as he affectionately calls her, a fellow student he has met soon after his arrival in Calcutta. Madhabilata is completely apolitical and has no interest in revolution, Maoist or otherwise, but she likes Animesh and stands by him. In one of the novel's most harrowing passages, Madhabilata, pregnant, is brought to police headquarters in Calcutta and suspended by her wrists from the ceiling of an interrogation room in front of

Animesh while a police officer presses a lit cigarette to her swollen stomach. The purpose is to get Animesh to reveal the whereabouts of a top Maoist leader. Animesh, who has suffered severe torture and is very ill, is about to give in when Madhabilata tells him not to speak. He stays silent.

In the late 1970s Animesh is released after the Left Front government headed by the CPM, the Naxalites' archenemy, comes to power in West Bengal and announces an amnesty for the thousands of imprisoned Maoists. He has not seen Madhabilata since their meeting in the interrogation room and has spent the intervening years in the company of his cellmate in prison, a young man from an affluent Calcutta family who joined the Naxalites as an undergraduate in the city's most prestigious college. Unlike Animesh, who has become paraplegic from torture, this young man is physically all right but has suffered brain damage from torture and is in a mentally vegetative state. When Animesh is released, he finds Madhabilata waiting to take him home. She is a struggling schoolteacher and lives in a shantytown in a Calcutta suburb. In her one-room shack, the crippled Animesh comes face-to-face for the first time with their six-year-old son, who is in the first grade of school. As he converses for the first time with the child, Animesh rediscovers the will to live. The novel ends there.

Kaalbaela's Madhabilata is an iconic character of contemporary Bengali literature. Animesh, for his part, is unrepentant about the political path he chose. Lying on his mattress in a slum tenement, unable to stand, let alone walk, he muses on the choice he made: "the struggle against the British did not lead to a total revolution. For the first time after independence, an attempt was made to truly emancipate the Indian people. Mistakes were made but at least we tried. Those who will come after us will not repeat those mistakes."[7]

Kaalbaela's Animesh is a man of conscience, who was appalled by the desperate poverty, injustice, and oppression he saw around him since childhood and embraced what appeared to him to promise an alternative to a sham democracy. The outrage he felt was the driving force of India's first Maoist insurrection. The same sense of anger and betrayal would enable a second generation of the Maoist movement to rise from the embers of the first in the 1980s and 1990s and fire a third generation in the early twenty-first century. Belying Animesh's hopes, the second and third generations would replicate most of the limitations and mistakes of the pioneers.

The Second Generation

Just as the first generation was defined by a subculture of middle-class radicalism particular to West Bengal, the second generation evolved in regional landscapes specific to certain states of India. These sites were not in West Bengal, the nursery of first-generation Indian Maoism, where the movement was utterly broken and a parliamentary left-wing (and essentially regional) party, the CPM, came to power in 1977 and proceeded to entrench its hegemony for the next three decades. The sites where the second generation of Indian Maoism grew were in two other states of India: Bihar and Andhra Pradesh.

The rise of Maoism in Bihar began in Ekwari, a village in the Bhojpur district of the sprawling plains of central Bihar. Here Jagdish Mahato, a schoolteacher from the lowly—though not traditionally "untouchable"— Koeri caste, was influenced by the Naxalite struggle in neighboring West Bengal and tried to organize landless peasants against the village's landowning class. He was joined by Rameshwar Ahir, a "dacoit" turned political rebel from the middle-ranking but constitutionally "backward" Yadav caste who had served 12 years in prison for killing a policeman. Violence broke out, and in 1972 both Mahato and Nathuni Singh, a leader of the village's landowning Bhumihar caste, a Brahmin subcaste with a martial tradition, were killed. Ahir was killed in 1975. The outbreak in Ekwari was at that time an isolated incident but subsequently turned out to be the beginning of the spread of Maoism across the districts of the sprawling agricultural plains of central Bihar. In the 1980s most of these districts, particularly Bhojpur, Gaya, Jehanabad, Aurangabad, Nalanda, Rohtas, and some rural areas of the Patna district, where the eponymous state capital is located, became synonymous with Maoist activity and a bloody spiral of conflict on caste/class fault-lines.

The conflict that polarized Ekwari's landowning and landless communities from the early 1970s did not involve landlords with huge estates. The landowning Bhumihars of the village had been tenants of such a *zamindar* (big landlord) family based in the eastern part of the neighboring state of Uttar Pradesh, but following the abolition of *zamindari* estates after India's independence they emerged as independent *kisans* (farmers) with their own landholdings. These landholdings were not very large—a researcher found in 1995 that the biggest landowners in the village owned about 30 acres, the majority significantly fewer. Most of the landowning Bhumihars of Ekwari would normally be classified as "middle peasants" and a small proportion as "rich peasants." But there were two twists to the tale.

First, almost all the land in and around Ekwari was owned by the 250 or so Bhumihar households, who comprised about a third of the village's 9,000 inhabitants. The overwhelming majority of the other two-thirds were landless, their families dependent for subsistence on waged labor in the Bhumihars' fields. The landless majority of Ekwari belonged almost entirely to Dalit (literally: oppressed or downtrodden) castes, the traditional "untouchables" of the caste system who are constitutionally classified as "Scheduled Castes" (SC) in India. Second, the Bhumihar *kisans* of Ekwari did not touch the plow; they considered farming work beneath their status, and were thus dependent on the men and women of the landless Dalit castes, the *mazdoors* (laborers), for the cultivation of their fields.

In 1995–1996 Ekwari was described as "a village at war. The mood is tense, the class divide sharp and clear. . . . Since the Naxalite movement began [in the early 1970s] as many as 85 individuals have been killed on the side of the landowners, and an equal or perhaps larger number on the side of the poor."[8] In the village's Dalit *tola* (literally "quarter," but with strong "ghetto" connotations), separate and segregated by custom from the residential area of the upper-caste houses, most villagers supported the CPI(ML) Liberation, a Naxalite faction influential in the "Bhojpur belt" and often referred to as the "Liberation group" or simply "Liberation." The men leading the village's Bhumihar community were said to be members of the Ranveer Sena (Warlord Army), a Bhumihar militia, which carried out a series of massacres of Dalits in central Bihar through the middle and late 1990s and into the first years of the new century. The violence was not one-sided; in the late 1990s Sankh Singh, a Bhumihar leader of the village and the son of Nathuni Singh, killed in 1972, was murdered by Naxalites. In June 2012 Brahmeshwar Singh, the Ranveer Sena's founder, was shot dead in his village in Bhojpur district. He had been in jail from 2002 to 2011, when he was released due to lack of legally admissible evidence in most of the mass murder cases against him. Elderly by 2012, he was a well-educated man, having earned a master's degree in political science from Patna University in his youth.

The Naxalite-led struggle in central Bihar kicked off in the late 1970s, and over the two subsequent decades had a transformative effect on power relations in the countryside. The most important part of the struggle was waged by mobilizing the landless poor in mass fronts created by the Maoists: the Bihar Pradesh Kisan Sabha (Bihar State Peasants' Front) formed by the Liberation group and the Mazdoor Kisan Sangram Samiti (Agricultural Laborers' Struggle Society) formed by the other major Naxalite faction active in the region, the CPI(ML) Party Unity, usually referred to as the "Party Unity group" or just "Party Unity." The mass fronts employed a variety of agitation tactics and over time succeeded in realizing concrete gains such as higher wages for the agricultural laborers (often paid in kind, as food, rather than cash); an equal share *(batai)* for the owner and the tiller in sharecropping arrangements; access rights for Dalits to the village pond to bathe, wash clothes, or catch fish; and small plots taken from "common" land or privately held "surplus" land (above the legal landholding limit) for the landless to farm or build a modest dwelling. Where landed upper castes resisted, they were subjected to punitive actions, such as a "blockade" imposed on their land. For example, Sankh Singh's lands in Ekwari had been lying fallow for five years in 1995, due to a blockade and his inability to procure laborers from outside the village because of the Naxalites' strength in the area.

But the struggle was not solely or perhaps even primarily about material gains. The people mobilized in the Naxalite-led campaigns in central Bihar referred to their participation as *izzat ki ladai*, a struggle for respect and dignity *(izzat)* and freedom from being treated as subhuman, their everyday lot for generations if not centuries. Thus by the mid-1990s, after a decade and a half of Naxalite-led struggle, "instances of rape of low-caste women [had] decreased dramatically. Arbitrary beatings [were] no longer tolerated. Laborers [were] able to sell their labor to whomever they please[d]. Dalit children [were] able to go to school. Laborers [were] able to wear clean clothes, sit in front of their homes on *khatias* (string cots) and welcome their guests without interference from the landlords."[9] This was nothing short of a social revolution in central Bihar's countryside.

Such an assault on a long established and deeply rooted status quo could not be waged through the channels of electoral democracy. Before the Naxalite movement emerged in the region, the lot of the landless poor of central Bihar had not improved for over three decades under the Congress party's Union and state governments, which ruled continuously since 1947, except for brief periods in the late 1960s and late 1970s. Indeed, Jagdish Mahato of Bhojpur's Ekwari was radicalized after he was severely beaten by Bhumihars for trying to prevent them from casting the votes of the village's Dalits in the national and state elections of 1967, a form of collective disenfranchisement widely prevalent in Bihar until the late 1980s. Nor could the struggle be waged through nonviolent mobilization. When well-educated Naxalites, most from upper castes, of what would become the Party Unity group first came in 1979 to a village in central Bihar's Jehanabad district—a village that in the 1980s would provide the base for the group's emergence across the district, which was then a subdivision of the Gaya district—they were told by the Dalit villagers that the kind of struggle and change they envisioned would require *haathiyaar* (weapons). The landed class of the village would react violently to assertion by the downtrodden and despised and the unprecedented attack on their economic privilege, social superiority, and political dominance, and the local police would be on their side.

The bitter conflict that then unfolded in this Jehanabad village pitted the vast majority of the village's 118 households belonging to the Kurmi caste, who owned 95 percent of the land in and around the village, against the 134 households belonging to members of five Dalit castes, who owned no land at all. Unlike the Bhumihars, the Kurmis are not a "forward" caste—indeed, they are in the "Other Backward Classes" (OBC) category. Nitish Kumar, the reformist chief minister who has governed Bihar since late 2005 and is one of the nation's most highly regarded regionalist politicians, comes from a Kurmi family. In this Jehanabad village, however, there were almost no upper-caste households, and the Kurmis had the superiority and dominance usually enjoyed by upper castes. For the village's landless Dalit majority, this meant economic dependency bordering on bondage, social subservience, and everyday petty humiliation at the hands of landowning families, whom they referred to as their *maliks* (lords). The Kurmis were actually small landholders—the vast majority of the Kurmi households owned 2–3 acres of land, and only seven families owned more than 13 acres. But this made no difference to the relationship built on domination and subordination.

The Naxalites first entered the village at the invitation of a young Kurmi man who belonged to a socialist political party and disliked his compatriots' behavior. In 1981 the Naxalites called a strike for higher wages at a brick kiln owned by a Kurmi that employed Dalits as labor, and the village was plunged into warfare. Gun battles erupted between armed Naxalites and the kiln owner's hired goons. The Maoists beheaded a Kurmi villager and hung the severed head on a tree at the entrance to the village, and months later they killed the kiln owner. In response, in 1982 the Kurmi community in the area formed the Bhoomi Sena (Land Army), one of the first "self-defense" caste militias in Bihar, and the bloodshed spread and escalated. The Bhoomi Sena and the Maoist *dastas* (armed squads) fought a vicious tit-for-tat war in the area until 1985. Sizable numbers of Dalit recruits joined the Maoist armed squads. Rajubhai, a young Dalit villager, became the commander of the Party Unity group's *dasta* in the flashpoint village. The armed conflict was accompanied by reciprocal pressure tactics. At one point the Kurmis created a crisis in the Dalit camp by barring them from a plot of Kurmi-owned land used by the Dalits for the daily defecation routine. In November 1984 the village's Kurmis disassociated themselves from the Bhoomi Sena and formally "surrendered" to their adversaries, giving a written undertaking that they would not fight the *sangathan* any more. (The *sangathan,* literally "organization," is how the Dalits referred to the Naxalites—the term encompassed the shadowy leaderships of the Party

Unity and Liberation factions, their mass fronts—the Mazdoor Kisan Sangram Samiti and the Bihar Pradesh Kisan Sabha, respectively—and the armed wings.) Subsequently Rajubhai became the chairman of a village committee set up by the Maoists to supervise the recast Kurmi-Dalit relationship in the village.[10]

The rise in Bihar of the second generation of the Maoist movement made headline news in India and attracted attention abroad throughout the 1980s. This was partly due to the grave incidents of violence that became endemic in the Naxalite-active zones. Obscure villages and hamlets in the Bihar countryside became household names in India as sites of large-scale killings, in which women and children, even infants, were routinely slaughtered along with adult males. In a number of the worst instances there were several dozen fatalities in a single incident.

The perpetrators were often militias, organized by the landed social groups (usually upper-caste Bhumihar Brahmins and Rajputs), who attacked Dalits. But the Naxalite *sangathans* were also perpetrators, particularly the Party Unity group and another group, the Maoist Communist Center, which in addition to developing a footprint in the central Bihar districts frequented by the Party Unity and Liberation groups became especially active in several of the districts of southern Bihar. (These districts became the separate state of Jharkhand in November 2000.) The Party Unity group and the Maoist Communist Center showed no compunction in killing upper-caste men, women, and children, who were in some cases themselves people living in dire poverty, in response to the atrocities of the upper-caste militias, and the class war acquired an ugly casteist color as a result. Another brutal dimension was added by the emergence of turf wars between the Naxalite groups. It became usual for the Liberation, Party Unity, and Maoist Communist Center groups to murder each other's activists in battles for supremacy. The state police, when they intervened, usually did so against the Maoist rebels. In 1986 in Arwal, a village in central Bihar, 23 Dalit men and women who were taking part in a protest organized by the Mazdoor Kisan Sangram Samiti, the Party Unity group's mass front, were gunned down by the police. Numerous members of the various Maoist armed squads, mostly Dalits, were also killed in "encounters" with the police through the 1980s and 1990s. The tit-for-tat massacres of the Naxalites and the upper-caste militias and the bloody feuding of the Naxalite organizations turned much of the Bihar countryside into killing fields throughout the 1980s and 1990s, and these two types of violence have abated only in the new century.

The imprint of the first generation of the Maoist movement, which was centered on West Bengal, was evident in all three groups that emerged in Bihar. Naxalites released from West Bengal prisons in the late 1970s played a major role in the formation of the Party Unity group. The founders of the Maoist Communist Center—which was formally constituted in the mid-1970s—were a group of West Bengal Maoists led by the activist Kanai Chatterjee (a Bengali Brahmin). They coalesced in the late 1960s around the journal *Dakshin Desh* (The southern land; a reference to India's geographic location south of China). Unable to make headway in West Bengal during the first half of the 1970s, this maverick Naxalite faction, which stayed aloof from the original CPI(ML) that had self-destructed between 1969 and 1972, migrated to districts of southern Bihar (post-2000 Jharkhand) adjoining West Bengal. During the 1980s and 1990s the Maoist Communist Center acquired a reputation as the most violent of the Naxalite organizations active in Bihar. The general secretary of the Liberation group from 1975 until his death from cardiac arrest in 1998 was Vinod Mishra (b.1947). Mishra was born into a north Indian Brahmin family but became radicalized in the late 1960s while a student at an engineering college in Durgapur, an industrial town in West Bengal's Bardhaman district close to the border with southern Bihar/Jharkhand, at a time when insurrectionary Maoism was sweeping through West Bengal's campuses. He was the leader after 1975 of the Naxalite faction that became the Liberation group, taking over after the killing of the group's first leader, Subroto Datta, alias Jawahar, an ethnic Bengali based in Bihar. Mishra was succeeded as Liberation's leader in 1998 by Dipankar Bhattacharya (b.1960), a recruit to the second generation of the Maoist movement and a highly educated Bengali Brahmin from West Bengal.

In 1986 the Liberation group published a booklet documenting their struggle, *Report from the Flaming Fields of Bihar,* which attracted much attention in India and abroad. In his introduction, Vinod Mishra wrote: "Bihar is one of the most backward of Indian States, beset with rigid caste polarizations and devoid of any history of bourgeois reforms worth the name. . . . Well, these facts are indisputable. . . . [Yet] the same backward Bihar has proved to be a forward post of revolutionary democracy, with the lowest rung of society drawn into the vortex of peasant struggles. . . . None could enforce the peace of the graveyard on the flaming fields of Bihar."[11]

The revolutionary rhetoric notwithstanding, the Liberation group was the only one of the three Maoist organizations spawned in Bihar in the 1980s that evolved in the direction of an accommodation with India's "bourgeois" democracy. The evolution began early. In 1982 the (then) underground Liberation group floated a political front it called the Indian People's Front. In state elections in Bihar in 1985 this group put up candidates in 49 of the (then) 324 single-member constituencies constituting the state legislature. (After the division of Bihar in late 2000, 243 of these constituencies are in Bihar and 81 in Jharkhand, formerly southern Bihar.) None of the group's candidates won, but the move was significant. The Liberation group had added a third element to its repertoire of struggle to complement the dual strategy of mass mobilization and armed action: electoral participation. In the national election of November 1989, the Indian People's Front caused a nationwide sensation by electing an MP to the Lok Sabha in New Delhi. The victorious candidate was Rameshwar Prasad, a Dalit whose father had been a brick-kiln laborer. He won from the Arrah parliamentary constituency in central Bihar, polling nearly a third (178,211) of the 545,791 valid votes cast in the constituency and pushing to second place his closest rival from the Janata Dal, led by Vishwanath Pratap (V. P.) Singh, the party that otherwise swept these elections in Bihar and Uttar Pradesh. In state elections in Bihar in March 1990 the Indian People's Front won in 7 of the 324 constituencies, came second in 14, and came third in another 20. It thus demonstrated a presence in well over a tenth of (predivision) Bihar's political map.

This proved the high point of the Indian People's Front's electoral success, however. In the midterm national election of 1991, Rameshwar Prasad lost his seat in Parliament, finishing third among the candidates, with 117,262 votes. He failed to regain the constituency in subsequent national elections in 1996 and 1999 and finished third on both occasions, although he polled 146,398 and 141,399 votes (23 percent and 21 percent, respectively), demonstrating the enduring popular base of his party in its strongest bastions. Prasad was elected twice to Bihar's state legislature, in 1995 and February 2005, but lost from the same constituency on three other occasions (2000, November 2005, and 2010). From the Bihar state elections of 1995 onward, the CPI(ML) Liberation contested under its own name, shedding the label Indian People's Front, which was disbanded in 1994. But the CPI(ML) Liberation, the most moderate of the second-generation Maoist groups, failed to expand its electoral base. Indeed, its support seems to have waned in recent years. Prasad finished fourth in the most recent Bihar state election of late 2010 in the constituency he had won on two earlier occasions, in 1995 and early 2005, although he still received more than 15,000 votes, and in a parliamentary by-election in the Nalanda constituency of central Bihar in 2006 he got only 6 percent of the vote. The CPI(ML) Liberation exists on the margins of electoral politics in Bihar today.

The other two groups active in Bihar/Jharkhand—the CPI(ML) Party Unity and the Maoist Communist Center—remained resolutely "revolutionary," shunning bourgeois democracy. These groups are the spearhead of the contemporary Maoist insurgency in Bihar and Jharkhand. Since late 2004 they have operated under one banner, the Communist Party of India (Maoist). This party's other pillar is another second-generation Naxalite group (discussed below), born and developed in Andhra Pradesh. The CPI (Maoist) insurgency in Bihar and Jharkhand has some impact in adjoining areas of Orissa, West Bengal, and UP, particularly areas bordering Jharkhand state (where 18 of the 24 districts are "Maoist-affected").

While one strand of second-generation Maoism emerged during the 1980s in a regional landscape specific to Bihar, in India's north, the other strand developed several hundred miles away and quite separately during the same decade in a regional setting specific to Andhra Pradesh, in India's south.

The mobilization of Girijans (hill tribals) in Andhra Pradesh's Srikakulam district in the late 1960s was the only significant Naxalite-led movement in that state during the first Maoist insurrection. The Srikakulam campaign peaked in 1969 and was over by the second half of 1970, its top organizers killed by police action. But the suppression of this campaign obscured the broader revival in the late 1960s and early 1970s, under Maoist ideological influence, of Andhra Pradesh's notable tradition of subaltern struggles led by left-wing radicals.

The principal historical legacy was a widespread peasant uprising in the Telangana region that began in 1946 and lasted until 1951 and was led in part by activists of the undivided Communist Party of India, which went through a short phase of clandestine revolutionary activism in the late 1940s, just after India's independence. The Telugu-speaking state of Andhra Pradesh, which was fully formed in 1956, consists of three distinct regions: Telangana, Rayalaseema, and coastal Andhra. (Srikakulam is in the northeast corner of the state and the coastal Andhra region, just south of the border with Orissa.) The Telangana region was part of the princely state of Hyderabad in British-ruled India, with a Muslim dynasty ruling an overwhelmingly Hindu population of subjects. The Telangana uprising began in rural Telangana as resistance to exploitative landlords and princely state officials, who were predominantly upper-caste Hindus, particularly men of the Reddy community, and was eventually suppressed by the forces of the independent Indian state after the Hyderabad kingdom was absorbed into the Indian Union by Indian military action against the last princely ruler *(nizam)* in the autumn of 1948.

The movement left a legacy of peasant mobilization and guerrilla insurgency in the region. Most of the middle-aged Andhra communists who emerged as Naxalite leaders in the late 1960s and early 1970s had a history of participation as young men in the Telangana movement of the late 1940s. In the early 1960s Chandra Pulla Reddy, who was to emerge as a prominent Naxalite leader in Andhra Pradesh in the 1970s, led a march through the villages and forest tracts of the Karimnagar and Warangal districts, in the northern part of the Telangana region, to raise political consciousness among the area's landless agricultural laborers and tribal communities. Most of the Andhra Maoists—with the exception of the Srikakulam group—remained opposed to or aloof from the chaotically insurrectionary line of the West Bengal–centered CPI(ML) formed by the ideologue Charu Mazumdar and his associates. As a result, the Maoist tendency in Andhra Pradesh largely escaped the state repression that had decimated the West Bengal movement by 1972.

The Telangana region, particularly its northern districts, became the nursery of the Andhra-specific strand of the second generation of Indian Maoism. "The terrain . . . dotted with forests and hilly tracts," suited the Maoist model of guerrilla war, and the cover provided by terrain was to become important once the movement took off in the 1980s and escalated in the 1990s. But in the formative phase, the 1970s and the first half of the 1980s, the crucial factor was "a man-made environment of exploitation that drove bonded farm laborers to rebellion in 1973." The social structure of northern Telangana was built on the encompassing dominance of landed upper-caste communities over overwhelmingly Dalit landless labor—very similar to the central Bihar seedbed and laboratory of north Indian Naxalism. Dalits are a sixth of Andhra Pradesh's population, and at least 70 percent are landless families. "A familiar cycle" followed the initial uprisings, in which "several landlords died," as "the landlords, belonging to the upper-caste *velama* community, unleashed the police, who cracked down with mindless brutality."[12] By the late 1970s *ryothu coolie sanghams* (agricultural laborers' unions) formed by Naxalite activists had emerged in the troubled zones to organize the landless and agitate for higher wages and better working conditions.

This was paralleled by the emergence of a new generation of educated youth of broadly lower-middle-class background committed to the cause. One such young man was M. Lakshmana Rao (b. 1950), known by his nom de guerre, Ganapati (another name of the Hindu elephant-god, Ganesha), who is today the highest ranking leader of the contemporary, third-generation incarnation of India's Maoist movement. A schoolteacher in northern Telangana's Karimnagar district in the early 1970s, he subsequently opted to become a full-time revolutionary. Another was M. Koteswara Rao, alias Kishenji (1956–2011), a native of the same district, whose "hometown, Peddapalli, was the nerve center of the movement by bonded farm laborers."[13] Kishenji emerged as a top political and military leader of the third generation of India's Maoist movement in the early twenty-first century. He was killed in a gun battle with elite paramilitary commandos in a forest on West Bengal's border with Jharkhand in November 2011 (in the same district where Sidhu Soren had met an identical end a year earlier). A graduate in mathematics, Kishenji came from a modestly off, not very poor family, and his father had been a nationalist anticolonial activist as a member of a socialist group in the Congress party. Kishenji became a full-time revolutionary around 1979 and led an underground existence from then until his death.

Yet another recruit was Cherukuri Rajkumar, alias Azad (The Free), who was born in 1952 and rose to become a top Maoist leader. He had been the all-India official spokesperson of the Maoists for several years when he was killed in controversial circumstances in July 2010. The Maoists allege that he was arrested by an Andhra Pradesh police team in Nagpur, a large city in Maharashtra, taken to a forest in northern Telangana's Adilabad district, and shot dead. Ganapati, a "bespectacled, soft-spoken figure" who is India's "most wanted man," recalled his comrade's revolutionary beginnings after the death: "Azad was attracted to the revolutionary movement while studying in Warangal's Regional Engineering College. He played a role in the formation of the Radical Students' Union (RSU) in 1974 and was elected as the state president of RSU in 1978."[14]

Young men like Ganapati, Kishenji, and Azad formed the nucleus of the People's War Group, a second-generation Naxalite organization launched in 1980 in Andhra Pradesh under the leadership of Kondapalli Seetharamaiah (1915–2002), a veteran communist activist with a history of participation in the Telangana movement of the late 1940s. Seetharamaiah was from a prosperous farming family in the Krishna district in the coastal Andhra region, but he worked as a schoolteacher in the 1960s in northern Telangana's Warangal district. He was purged, and Ganapati took over the People's War Group's leadership after infighting in 1991. The Radical Students' Union provided a fertile recruiting ground for People's War Group cadres and significantly expanded the original nucleus of activists. In the late 1970s and early 1980s the Radical Students' Union, active on high school, college, and university campuses in the Telangana region and elsewhere in Andhra Pradesh, organized indoctrination trips for students styled as a "Go to the Villages" campaign on the model of Mao's China.

One such recruit was Vadkapur Chandramouli, who was born into a backward-caste artisan family in the Vadkapur village of Peddapalli *taluk* (subdivision) of the Karimnagar district and became a top Maoist military commander in Andhra Pradesh. According to his obituary, published in a Maoist journal after he was killed in December 2006, "Comrade Chandramouli contacted the party in 1981. At that time he was pursuing studies in a +2 junior college [eleventh and twelfth grades of high school]. Soon he started organizing the students in the Radical Students' Union. He participated actively in the "Go to the Villages" campaign, an annual campaign the party organized for revolutionary students. He became a professional revolutionary in 1982. From that time till the moment of his martyrdom his entire life in the intervening 25 years was dedicated solely to achieving the victory of India's New Democratic Revolution." The rugged-looking Chandramouli's petite wife, Karuna, a Maoist military leader and field nurse, died with him. Born into a left-leaning peasant family in Nawabpet village in the Karimnagar district, she joined the movement in 1985 and had worked as a "professional revolutionary" since 1986. It is not clear whether the encounter in the Visakhapatnam district of the coastal Andhra region was real or "fake."[15]

During the 1980s a regional subculture of radicalism with its epicenter in the districts of northern Telangana took hold in Andhra Pradesh under the aegis of the People's War Group. As K. Balagopal, a human rights advocate of Andhra Pradesh who was a sympathetic but not uncritical chronicler of the Naxalite movement there from the early 1980s until his death in 2009, analyzed the phenomenon: "unlike the rest of Andhra Pradesh where the Naxalites spread [later] through armed squads, in northern Telangana there was a clear period in the late 1970s and early 1980s when it was the mass organizations, mainly the agricultural laborers' associations and the youth and student fronts, that were the instrument for the spread of Maoism." The Maoists struck "fatally at the power relations of rural Telangana society" and were able to foster among "the poor, the Dalits and tribals . . . a voice of their own and the courage to speak out." This was very similar to the yearning for *izzat* (dignity) that fueled the Naxalite-led subaltern struggles in central Bihar during the same period. These struggles' most fundamental consequences, more so than their limited concrete gains, were the shift in the local dynamics of power and the redeeming of the humanity of the degraded. Among the Adivasi or tribal communities of Telangana, in a strategy that provided a template for subsequent Maoist activism among tribal groups in parts of the state of Chhattisgarh close to Telangana, People's War Group militants "encouraged tribals to cut down and cultivate reserved [state-owned] forests, forced a substantial increase in the wages paid by *tendu* leaf [used to make a coarse Indian cigarette] contractors [to the Adivasis who collected them in the forests] and put an end to the harassment Adivasis suffered at the hands of forest officials and the police."[16]

As in the "flaming fields" of Bihar, these struggles could not be waged through nonviolent means. Thus "in July 1985 the first incident of deliberate murder of a policeman by the Naxalites took place; this was in Jagtiyal, [a small town in] a "disturbed area" of Karimnagar [a district in north Telangana] where the police in collusion with armed Bharatiya Janata Party landlords had been subjecting Naxalite youth to savage torture."[17] According to Maoist folklore, both Ganapati and Kishenji participated in this incident. Thereafter the armed conflict in Andhra Pradesh escalated rapidly. By 1989 the threat posed by the People's War Group was so serious that a special anti-Naxalite force of the Andhra Pradesh police, the "Greyhounds," was formed. The police officer who founded the Greyhounds was shot dead by the Naxalites in January 1993 while jogging in the state capital, Hyderabad. Through the 1990s and into the new century a brutal war of attrition between the Maoists and the counterinsurgency apparatus unfolded in Andhra Pradesh.

Why did the second generation of India's Maoist movement emerge and develop in a fragmented fashion, in the geographies—separated by hundreds of miles—of Bihar in the north and Andhra Pradesh in the south? Three reasons come to mind.

The first factor was simply India's territorial vastness and more important the sheer plurality and diversity of its society. Just as this has driven the regionalization of India's democracy, it also accounts in substantial measure for the regionalized nature of the most significant radical challenge to that democracy.

The second factor was particular to India's Maoist movement. Since its inception in the late 1960s, it has been extraordinarily prone to schisms and splits. The original CPI(ML) formed in April–May 1969 was dominated by West Bengal radicals, and the bulk of the Andhra Pradesh Maoists did not join the party. When the party disintegrated in 1971–1972 it spawned a bewildering plethora of factions, many of which subsequently split into further factions. Differences over ideological emphasis, strategic direction, tactics, and personality and ego clashes fragmented the Maoist spectrum. (Some of the disputes were positively arcane; for example whether Lin Biao, Mao's designated successor from 1966 until his fall from grace and mysterious death in 1971, was a martyr or a traitor.)

In Bihar, three significant second-generation Maoist groups emerged in the 1980s: the CPI(ML) Liberation, the CPI(ML) Party Unity, and the Maoist Communist Center, which engaged in murderous turf wars with one another through the 1980s and 1990s and into the first years of the twenty-first century. In Andhra Pradesh the People's War Group emerged as the dominant Maoist movement in the 1980s, but there were other Maoist streams there in the 1970s that fell by the wayside due to organizational ineptitude and lack of leadership. The People's War Group consolidated its supremacy by killing activists of the smaller groups.

The third factor was specific to the regional landscapes of Bihar and Andhra Pradesh. In central Bihar and northern Telangana, the Maoist critique of India as a "semicolonial" and (particularly) "semifeudal" society ripe for revolution bore a plausible resemblance to the reality and resonated with parts of the populations. But the movements in these two hotbeds developed separately, driven by factors specific to each. In Bihar (and Jharkhand) the role of West Bengal Maoists who had survived the first insurrection and went to a neighboring region to rekindle and pursue the revolutionary agenda was critical in the formation of all the three groups and the birth of a regional subculture of radicalism. In Andhra Pradesh the Telangana movement of the late 1940s provided a powerful historical backdrop, and the Srikakulam campaign of the late 1960s a more recent reference point, for the emergence and entrenchment of a regional subculture of "people's war."

The Third Generation

The Communist Party of India (Maoist), the twenty-first-century incarnation of the Naxalite phenomenon, is an amalgamation of the regional subcultures of radicalism that took root in Bihar (which then included Jharkhand) and Andhra Pradesh during the last two decades of the twentieth century.

This party emerged in two stages in 1998 and 2004. In 1998, after five years of talks, the People's War Group of Andhra Pradesh and the CPI(ML) Party Unity of Bihar unified in an organization called the Communist Party of India (Marxist-Leninist)-People's War (CPI[ML]-PW). One consequence of the merger was a steep escalation in murderous clashes in central Bihar and the Naxalite-active districts of southern Bihar (which became the state of Jharkhand in November 2000) between cadres of the erstwhile CPI(ML) Party Unity and the Maoist Communist Center. The violent feud, subsequently referred to by the Maoists as a "black chapter," peaked in 2001–2002 and ended in 2004 when, after negotiations, the Maoist Communist

Center unified with the CPI(ML)-PW in an umbrella organization, which was renamed the Communist Party of India (Maoist).

In 2006 the Communist Party of India (Maoist) was described by India's prime minister as the gravest internal threat to the nation and its democracy. In early 2007 the Communist Party of India (Maoist) held a major party conference, styled as the "unity congress," in a jungle area somewhere in eastern India, probably in Bihar. The meeting was also called the ninth party congress, to emphasize the continuity with a convention of the original CPI(ML) in 1970, which was styled as the eighth congress of the communist movement in India. The 2007 meeting venue was named Charu Mazumdar-Kanai Chatterjee Nagar (City), in joint honor of Mazumdar, the ideologue of the 1967–1972 period, and Chatterjee, the founder of the Maoist Communist Center.

The objective behind the two-step emergence of the Communist Party of India (Maoist) is intuitively obvious: to unite regional Naxalite factions professing a broadly identical ideology and provide some semblance of a supraregional organizational apparatus—and a sense of national purpose—to a movement that had since its inception in the late 1960s held nationwide revolution as its goal. Without such unification, the Naxalites would remain scattered regional groups, and there would be little if any prospect of expanding the movement beyond the strongholds developed during the second generation. As early as 1981 Kondapalli Seetharamaiah, the first leader of the People's War Group, and Kanai Chatterjee, the founder of the Maoist Communist Center, had held talks aimed at eventual unification. It took nearly another quarter century for that to come to fruition.

The main initiative in the two-step unification process seems to have come from the People's War Group. Ganapati, the top People's War Group leader since 1991, serves as the general secretary, the key role in any communist *nomenklatura*, of the Communist Party of India (Maoist). Azad, another top People's War Group leader, served as the national spokesperson of the Communist Party of India (Maoist) until his death in July 2010. Kishenji, yet another top People's War Group leader, took the lead in efforts to expand the Maoist movement to other states—notably its original cradle, West Bengal—until his death in November 2011. All of these men were Telugu-speakers from the People's War Group seedbed of northern Telangana in Andhra Pradesh; Ganapati and Kishenji hail from the same district (Karimnagar), while Azad was converted to the cause as a university student in the neighboring Warangal district.

The ideological framework of the third generation of Indian Maoism is a recycled version of the first generation's, with almost no rethinking or renovation. This framework was outlined by Azad in an article he published in October 2006 in *Economic and Political Weekly,* a highly regarded journal of social science and public policy in India. The journal, known for its left-wing character, had published a special issue on India's contemporary Maoist movement in July 2006, and most of the articles were written by leftist scholars and analysts critical of the limitations and failings of India's democracy. But Azad felt the Maoists themselves had not been given a voice and submitted a "rejoinder" on behalf of his party.

Azad repeats the Charu Mazumdar argument of the late 1960s that India is a semicolonial, semifeudal country:

> semicolonial because the Indian ruling classes—big business, top bureaucrats and leading politicians running the Center and the states—are tied to imperialist interests [meaning above all the United States] . . . semifeudal as the old feudal relations have not been smashed, only a certain amount of capitalist growth has been superimposed on them. So also, Parliament is no democratic institution—[unlike] countries that have been through a democratic revolution, [and have] a bourgeois democracy—but has been instituted on the existing highly autocratic state and semifeudal structures as a ruse to dupe the masses. Consequently our beloved country, so rich in natural wealth, human power and ingenuity, has been reduced to a condition . . . worse than most of the countries of sub-Saharan Africa. In these sixty years of so-called independence the situation has not significantly improved compared to . . . the British Raj . . . for the general masses.

This statement is virtually copied from the CPI(ML)'s 1970 party program, which asserted:

> our beloved country is one of the biggest and most ancient countries of the world, inhabited by 500 million people. Ours is an agrarian country, a country of the peasant masses, hard-working and talented. They have rich revolutionary traditions and a glorious cultural heritage. . . . The sham independence declared in 1947 was nothing but a replacement of the colonial and semifeudal setup with a semicolonial and semifeudal one. . . . During these years of sham independence the big comprador-bureaucrat bourgeoisie and big landlord ruling classes have been serving their imperialist masters. . . . These lackeys of imperialism, while preserving the old British imperialist exploitation, have also brought the U.S. imperialist and Soviet social-imperialist exploiters to fleece our country.

According to Azad, this "semicolonial, semifeudal society under the grip of finance capital" can be saved only by "the new democratic revolution [which] entails the total democratization of the entire system and all aspects of life—political, economic, social, cultural, educational, recreational, etc. . . . A new social being has to emerge in the course of the revolutionary process."

Specifically, Azad wrote, "we Maoists stand for a people-oriented, self-reliant model of development. . . . We are of the opinion that all wealth generated within the country should stay here and not be allowed to be drained off abroad. . . . The vast wealth illegally and immorally appropriated by the imperialists, feudal elements and compradors should be seized and turned to use in developing the economy, first and foremost in agriculture and the rural areas, where the bulk of our people live." This will be accomplished "through land reforms, by the redistribution of land on the basis of 'land to the tiller' . . . coupled with large investments in agriculture, forestry and allied activities—poultry, goat-farming, fishery etc.—[which] will enormously expand the rural populace's purchasing power. This in turn will create a market for the basic necessities of life and will generate local industry, resulting in employment generation. With this employment generation the purchasing power will increase further, leading to more industry." "This is the most humane and peace-loving model of growth," Azad argued, "[as] stated in the party program and political resolutions issued from time to time," but "when we try and implement it the state comes down heavily on us." "It is not we who seek violence," but violent confrontation becomes inevitable because "the moneybags and their political representatives are unable to accept even the thought of such a transformation."

In its evocation of a rural utopia, this blueprint of revolutionary transformation has shades of the model the Khmer Rouge tried to implement in Cambodia between 1975 and 1979, and its advocacy of economic autarky is reminiscent of the extreme isolationism of Enver Hoxha's communist regime in Albania in its later years. But the model of the revolutionary state and society pertains to the future; in its present incarnation as a rural insurgency, India's Maoist movement most closely resembles the Sendero Luminoso (Shining Path) movement, which waged a bloody and ultimately failed Maoist insurgency aimed at seizing state power in Peru from 1980 to the mid-1990s.

In its content, the ideological framework of the third generation of Indian Maoism is virtually the same as the first generation's. There is the same transcendent conception of "the people" and "the masses," dupes of a fake democracy, awaiting deliverance. "The masses of the oppressed are with the Naxalites," according to Azad, while "a minority . . . [consisting of] the ruling elite and their hangers-on are with the state." The first-generation Maoists, too, had arrogated to themselves the right to speak in the name of "90 percent" of Indians. The exaltation of China during the Mao era and particularly the "Great Proletarian Cultural Revolution" that wreaked havoc in China in the second half of the 1960s

still occupies a central place in the contemporary Naxalites' creed of
"M-L-M" (Marxism-Leninism-Maoism). "All degenerate . . . ideas will
be fought against long after the revolution through cultural revolutions,"
Azad warned in his late 2006 essay. Contemporary Indian Maoist literature contains remarkably few references to the trajectory of post-Mao
China, beyond passing allusions to "Deng revisionism," which has led to
the "restoration of capitalism" in China.[18]

It is difficult to disagree with a left-wing critic of contemporary Indian
Maoism that "the Maoist grasp of theory is unbelievably primitive, a col-
lage of abstractions that bear little relation to reality at any level, [as]
analysis or strategy. 'Semifeudalism,' 'comprador bourgeoisie,' 'four-class
alliance,' 'protracted people's war' etc. are slavishly copied from Mao's
theorizations for China which will soon be almost a century old." The
static, hidebound ideological framework that guides the practice of
twenty-first-century Indian Maoism and its open totalitarianism worries
even some sympathizers. One such Indian writer expressed doubts about
the prospects of the movement after visiting in 2010 a remote area populated by Adivasis in the southern part of the state of Chhattisgarh where
Maoists rule the roost:

> it was clear that the Maoists will not resile from the goal of social transfor-
> mation in which they have invested. . . . [But] India is a vast country and
> diverse in multiple ways, including socioeconomic development. The condi-
> tions which prevail . . . in the 34 districts [of 640-plus nationwide] where
> the Maoists are relatively strong do not match conditions in other more
> populous parts. . . . Methods which work in one area may not apply let
> alone work in others. To make the leap from the forest strongholds . . . they
> will have to work out how they will negotiate . . . the diversity and plurality
> of India. . . . Political plurality has become as much if not more a hallmark
> of India as cultural diversity. . . . Thus I remain confused, if not uncon-
> vinced, by the path chosen by them.[19]

The much-publicized appearance of a third generation of Indian Maoism in the first decade of the twenty-first century obscured an important
fact: that the second-generation groups that coalesced as the Communist
Party of India (Maoist) in the middle of the decade had all stagnated or
even regressed by then in the zones of influence they had built during the
1980s. This was true in both Bihar and Andhra Pradesh.

When in 1995–1996 a researcher asked grassroots Naxalite activists
and supporters in central Bihar why they joined the movement, they mostly
replied that they did so to achieve *badal* (change) in their circumstances.
The terms *kranti* (revolution) or *nayee janwaadi kranti* (new democratic
revolution) figured far less frequently. The researcher concluded that while

"the Naxalite movement has a long-term agenda of achieving a [country-wide] revolution . . . people who join the movement . . . do not have [such a] textbook understanding of revolution. . . . At the village level, with few exceptions, there is little understanding of the formal ideology . . . [and] very few seem to have heard of Russia and China, leave alone Marx, Lenin and Mao."

By the mid-1990s, after a decade and a half of struggle, signs of exhaustion were discernible. Thus while "the outcome of these battles is much the same everywhere—feudal power has been undermined and the dignity of laborers restored, protracted violence has also left a long trail of blood and tears." Communities at the bottom of the heap in central Bihar's conflict zones saw Naxalite organizations like CPI(ML) Liberation and CPI(ML) Party Unity as the only forces in the 1980s ready to give them priority and stand up for their rights. These groups provided the only hope of challenging and changing for the better the oppressive, degrading conditions of their daily existence. But with the first phase of the battle (largely) won, the question "what next" came to the fore, and here the Naxalites were a part of the problem rather than the solution. In the second half of the 1990s and the first years of the twenty-first century,

> in the climate of tension and fear that prevails in central Bihar, development activity is extremely difficult. Naxalite leaders have taken little interest in enhancing the quality of life in the villages, arguing that all reform would have to follow revolution. Development efforts like building roads have often been hindered, for instance by extracting taxes from the contractors. The bottom-line is that Naxalite leaders are not interested in the "development" of the region. Some even consider that the more underdeveloped the region, the better the prospects of revolution. . . . Also darkness and inaccessibility, in the absence of roads and electricity, mean physical safety and some protection from state repression.

The researcher noted that "in the years following the merger with [Andhra Pradesh's] PWG [People's War Group] in 1998, there has been a marked decline in open and democratic forms of struggle and a greater focus on militaristic interventions in the erstwhile PU [Party Unity] areas."[20] Indeed, in 2012 Jugal Kishore Pal, alias Madanji, 56, a Naxalite leader for three decades in the Palamau district on the Jharkhand-Bihar border—first with the PU group and later the integrated Communist Party of India (Maoist)—left the movement and joined a regional political party in Jharkhand. He summarized why in 1982 he became a militant: "I belong to a backward caste [and I saw] inhuman treatment of lower caste people by upper castes all around me." His reasons for quitting were equally clear: "Of late, a vacuum has set in. There is a leadership crisis.

The organization has failed to retain public support, which is rapidly dwindling. Mere strength in arms cannot sustain a movement. You need people-centric issues."[21]

In 2003 another researcher found disillusionment with the struggle among Dalits in the village in Jehanabad district that in the first half of the 1980s was the launchpad for the Party Unity group's rise in central Bihar. They said

> that after the initial struggle and success against the Kurmis, the *sangathan* [organization] did nothing to raise wages, which for the last twenty years had remained at a dismal three kilograms of rice or wheat. They asked what anyone could do with three kilograms of rice, which fetched only 18 rupees in the village market. They pointed out that [by then] the minimum wage should have been at least five kilograms of grain, which would have marginally improved their economic condition. They also expressed their disappointment with the lack of development in the region. An educated Dalit man pointed out that the *sangathan* completely neglected education. . . . He further pointed out that the Party never used its influence to stop corruption at the *panchayat* [village cluster] or block [district subdivision] level. The local government officials and middlemen took 50 percent commission from various financial schemes extended to the poor peasants. He said that [far from challenging this] the *sangathan* itself took "commissions" from the projects sanctioned for rural development such as building roads, schools and community centers.[22]

To add insult to injury, the *sangathan*'s armed squads in the area had during the 1990s taken to staying and eating in the better-off Kurmi homes in the village and by 2003 had not set foot in the Dalit *tola* (quarter) on the village's southern edge for years. This picture of apparently revolutionary Maoist organizations becoming over time an integral part of the chain of institutionalized corruption and a de facto ally of village elites has also emerged in research on the Maoist Communist Center in Jharkhand (which was southern Bihar until November 2000). The Maoist Communist Center is, of course, the third constituent of the unified Communist Party of India (Maoist) formed in the autumn of 2004. In this account, the Maoist Communist Center's "revolutionary claims for the . . . liberation of the poor, indigenous [Adivasi] populations of rural Jharkhand" are misleading, and in fact "the MCC [Maoist Communist Center] is intimately linked to the politics of access to the economy of state patronage. In return for their cooperation in harboring and fostering the movement, recruits in areas under MCC control are offered privileged and protected access to state resources." These are usually "established rural elites," who are in some cases members of a relatively better-off layer of Adivasi communities, who see that tactical collaboration with the Maoists "will allow them to continue to capture state resources" and "maintain their [local] dominance."[23]

The only one of the three second-generation Naxalite organizations that emerged in Bihar in the 1980s that chose a path of engagement with India's electoral democracy—the Liberation group—is derided by the Communist Party of India (Maoist) as "revisionist." Yet when *panchayat* elections were held in Bihar in 2001 for the first time since 1978, "Liberation areas . . . saw impressive participation of people" and "a significant number of Dalit *mukhiyas* [village headmen] . . . local leaders who emerged over two decades of mobilization and action . . . replaced their upper-caste/class predecessors."[24] It is possible that the biggest contribution of the Naxalite-led movements in central Bihar during the 1980s and 1990s was to foster a relatively more egalitarian environment in which the kind of "development for all" agenda pushed by Nitish Kumar's state government, elected in late 2005 and reelected in late 2010, can operate with some success.

In Andhra Pradesh, the brutal war of attrition that began in the second half of the 1980s between the People's War Group and the state's police forces escalated through the 1990s and raged until the tide turned decisively in the police's favor in 2005–2006. In late 2009 Ganapati, the top People's War Group leader since 1991 and the general secretary of the Communist Party of India (Maoist) since its formation in late 2004, was asked why the Maoists had been defeated in the long war in his home state. He replied that "it was due to several mistakes on our part that we suffered a serious setback in most of Andhra Pradesh by 2006. . . . We have taken appropriate lessons from the setback suffered . . . in Andhra Pradesh." He pointedly evaded elaborating on the nature of these "mistakes" and the lessons drawn from them.[25]

A sustained campaign of state terror over two decades was instrumental in the making of the eventual Maoist debacle in Andhra Pradesh. As early as 1987, tribal hamlets in the east Godavari and Visakhapatnam districts of Andhra's coastal region were razed as collective punishment for harboring Naxalites. By 1997 a firsthand observer of the dirty war in Andhra Pradesh noted "an unprecedented escalation in . . . encounter killings [of Naxalite activists and supporters] . . . in the last six years."[26] This was to worsen; between 1997 and 2007 a civil liberties group in the state documented more than 1,800 deaths of Naxalite suspects in police operations, many in genuine "encounters" and many others in "fake" ones (that is, summary executions of captured and often tortured suspects). The counterinsurgency was aided by a steady stream of Maoist defectors who became auxiliaries of the state police's intelligence wing and the anti-Naxalite "Greyhounds" units. The Andhra Naxalites' bellicosity intensified in response to this onslaught—in October 2003 N. Chandrababu Naidu, the state chief minister belonging to the regionalist Telugu Desam Party, founded in 1982 by his father-in-law, N. T. Rama Rao, a trailblazer in the regionalization of India's politics, was injured in a Naxalite landmine attack. Naidu lost state elections in 2004 and was replaced by a Congress government that initially made moves to deescalate the bloodletting and open peace talks with the Naxalites. In the autumn of 2004, during a brief lull in the violence, a Maoist rally in the state capital, Hyderabad, drew 150,000 supporters. But fighting resumed in January 2005, and by the end of 2006 the Maoist hard core in the state was decimated. In mid-2007 the Maoist journal *People's March* published a list of 60 women cadres killed in real and fake encounters in Andhra Pradesh since early 2005. The journal claimed that these deaths were in addition to those of 180 women cadres killed during Chandrababu Naidu's chief ministership of the state (1995–2004).[27]

The ruthlessness of the counterinsurgency campaign partially explains the Maoist debacle in Andhra Pradesh. The other, equally vital part of the explanation lies in what a chronicler of the state's Maoist movement, himself a gradually disillusioned fellow traveler of the movement, referred to as the "real and disquieting ruthlessness" of the Maoists themselves. This was manifested in their systematic use of "terror as a political instrument," the "medieval forms of violence" meted out by so-called people's courts in their Telangana strongholds, and the complete lack of tolerance for any form of political pluralism where they gained dominance, all traits in evidence by the late 1980s and aggravated over the years by the infusion into the movement of cadres "more attracted by its weapons than its politics."[28]

It was surely these sorts of "mistakes" that Ganapati acknowledged in 2009 but would not elaborate on, let alone discuss. Instead, he emphasized: "in any protracted people's war, there will be advances and retreats. If we look at the situation in Andhra Pradesh from this perspective, you will understand that what we did there is a kind of retreat. Confronted with a superior force, we chose to temporarily retreat our forces from . . . Andhra Pradesh, extend and develop our bases in the surrounding regions and then hit back at the enemy."[29]

What this concretely meant was a drastic intensification of hostilities between the Maoists and the state in the southern part of the state of Chhattisgarh, close to the interstate border with Andhra Pradesh's Telangana region, where Maoists from Telangana had steadily built a presence since the early 1980s; a spike in Maoist activity in southern districts of the state of Orissa close to the interstate border with the coastal region of Andhra Pradesh; and an ambitious but failed attempt during 2008–2011 to open a new front in parts of West Bengal, the crucible of first-generation Indian Maoism.

Chhattisgarh was carved out as a full-fledged state of the Indian Union in November 2000 from 16 eastern and southeastern districts of the vast, sprawling north-central state of Madhya Pradesh (Central Province) at the same time that the districts of southern Bihar became the state of Jharkhand, leaving the (still vast and populous) expanses of northern and central Bihar as the "rump" Bihar. Unlike Jharkhand, which was created in response to a popular demand over several decades for statehood, led by activists from Adivasi communities but involving nontribal supporters as well, the rationale for Chhattisgarh is less clear and was probably based on a notion that smaller states foster administrative convenience.

Jharkhand and Chhattisgarh have important attributes in common. They have the highest proportions of Adivasi citizens among India's states, apart from six tiny—by Indian standards—states in India's north-eastern region bordered by China, Bhutan, Myanmar, and Bangladesh. More than a quarter of Jharkhand's 33 million people and about one-third of Chhattisgarh's 26 million belong to groups classified as "Scheduled Tribes" (India-wide, the ST are 8 percent of the population.) Jharkhand and Chhattisgarh also have rich endowments of mineral wealth, as well as natural resources such as timber, due to extensive forests that have been the traditional habitat of Adivasi communities, for centuries if not millennia.

Both of these young and naturally endowed states of India are in the frontline of the Maoist war of the early twenty-first century. The location of Chhattisgarh, a long sliver of territory smack in the geographic heart of India, is strategic, as the state has borders with Madhya Pradesh and Uttar Pradesh to the north, Jharkhand and Orissa to the east, Maharashtra to the west, and Andhra Pradesh to the south.

In the early 1980s, shortly after the formation of the People's War Group as a second-generation Naxalite revolutionary organization in Andhra Pradesh, two or three People's War Group *dalams* (squads), each consisting of no more than a half-dozen activists, entered the southern part of what is today Chhattisgarh from the contiguous Telangana region of Andhra Pradesh. This southern part of Chhattisgarh, known as the Bastar region, was a "princely state" ruled by a royal family under British "paramountcy" until India's independence—one of about 562 such

Figure 7.   Women Maoist guerrillas on patrol in Chhattisgarh, Bijapur district (July 2012). AFP/GETTY IMAGES.

principalities which existed in the subcontinent in 1947. (The northern slice of Bastar, Kanker, was a smaller princely state.) The Bastar region constitutes the bulk of Dandakaranya (roughly, Punishing Forest), an ancient name for the vast forested tracts of central India. The Bastar region is predominantly inhabited by Adivasi communities. Of the region's three administrative districts, according to the 2001 Indian census, 66 percent of the central Bastar district's 1.3 million people, 79 percent of the southern Dantewada district's 720,000 people, and 56 percent of the northern Kanker district's 650,000 people belonged to the ST. (Three more small districts have since been formed in the region, two carved from Dantewada district and one from Bastar district.) A medley of tribes who live in the region are sometimes collectively referred to as Gonds, and the region as Gondwana (Land of the Gonds). The local language, Gondi, is a spoken tongue—it does not have a script—although Chhattisgarhi, a variant of Hindi, is also prevalent, and Telugu is spoken and understood in areas close to Andhra Pradesh. (The Dantewada district has a 125-mile border with the Telangana region, mainly with Telangana's Khammam district.)

The first Naxalite squads that entered the Bastar region and the adjacent district of Gadchiroli in Maharashtra—also an overwhelmingly rural district where almost 40 percent of the 1.1 million people are Adivasis and another substantial chunk belong to the lowest castes (SC)—managed to impress the locals by imparting simple advice such as boiling water before drinking it. This drastically cut the incidence of water-borne disease and particularly infant mortality and won the revolutionaries credibility among the population. (As recently as 2001, just 30 percent of the Dantewada district's people could read or write.) Through the 1980s the Naxalite activists organized the Adivasis to confront the corrupt and abusive officialdom of the then Madhya Pradesh state's forest department. The activists successfully pressured the class of middlemen ("contractors") trading in forest products to pay higher wages for raw materials collected by the locals, such as *tendu* leaves and bamboo. In 1989 a mass front was launched under the label Dandakaranya Adivasi Kisan Mazdoor Sangathan (Dandakaranya Tribal Peasants' and Laborers' Organization). At this time the Naxalites had no more than 200 armed cadres in the entire "Dandakaranya belt" comprising the Bastar districts and Gadchiroli.[30]

Through the 1990s the Maoists expanded their social base and influence in the Bastar region by setting up village-level units known locally as *sanghams* (organizations). The *sanghams* gradually emerged as parallel institutions that sidelined the official *panchayat* (village-level governance) system of the government and, more important, challenged and undermined the traditional authority of the tribal chiefs and headmen, specifically those who would not cooperate with the Naxalites and be co-opted into the alternative "revolutionary" structures. This stirred conflict, and on two occasions, first in the early 1990s and again in the late 1990s, Mahendra Karma, a tribal politician belonging to the Congress party and a member of the state legislature elected from Dantewada, tried to organize *jan jagaran abhijans* (people's consciousness campaigns) against the expanding and deepening Naxalite presence. Karma had been a Naxalite in his youth but quit or was expelled from the movement in the early 1980s. The campaigns did not achieve much, and the Naxalites continued their base-building work.

They engaged in a civilizing mission, introducing among the Adivasis—skilled hunter-gatherers who also practiced slash-and-burn agriculture—more settled farming methods, sometimes involving cooperatives, and built small irrigation systems to support these initiatives. (In the mid-1990s just 3 percent of the land in the Bastar region had irrigation facilities.) They also undertook takeover and distribution among landless Adivasis of land, both forest land rich in resources and arable land, that had been under the control of the government or tribal chiefs. In 2010 the man heading the Maoists' Dandakaranya Special Zonal Committee, the movement's apex body in Bastar and Gadchiroli, a native Telugu-speaker from the Karimnagar district of Andhra Pradesh's Telangana region, the nursery of the People's War Group, claimed that 300,000 acres of land had been taken over and distributed among the land-poor and landless over the years. This is probably an exaggeration, but there is evidence of the Maoists taking over and distributing land in the region.[31]

For over two decades after the beginnings in the early 1980s, the Maoist movement in this remote and inaccessible region dominated by hills and forests and inhabited by marginalized communities attracted little attention. The spotlight during the 1980s and 1990s was on the second-generation Naxalite groups active in Bihar and Andhra Pradesh. This changed during the first half of the new century's first decade, as the protracted war in Andhra Pradesh between the Maoists and the counterinsurgency forces led by the state's police turned decisively against the Maoists. For over two decades the Maoists themselves saw their activities in Dandakaranya "as an adjunct to the movement in Andhra Pradesh."[32] Now hardened Naxalite leaders and cadres re-treated from Andhra Pradesh into the Bastar region (and Gadchiroli) to seek sanctuary and regroup. This development more or less coincided with the formation of the Communist Party of India (Maoist) around 2004, and the sideshow in Dandakaranya became a central arena of the third generation of Indian Maoism and its challenge to the authority of the Indian state.

The emergence of the Bastar region as a key base of instate and trans-
state Maoist operations presented a major problem for the state government of Chhattisgarh, run by the BJP. Conventional policing capacity in
the Bastar region was, and remains, very weak; in 2007, for example, the
districts of the Bastar region had a sanctioned police strength of 2,197,
but only 1,387 positions were actually filled. Contingents of the Union
government's well-trained, well-equipped Central Reserve Police Force
were moved into the region, but their effectiveness was limited, as they
were outsiders unfamiliar with local topography and society. The void
was partly filled by the emergence during 2005 in the Dantewada district
of an anti-Naxalite militia several thousand strong, the Salwa Judum
(Gondi: Purification Hunt). Its mastermind was Mahendra Karma, the
long-standing state legislator from the district belonging to the Congress
party. Salwa Judum appears to have originated in discussions during the
first half of 2005 between district-level politicians and administrative officials in Dantewada and mushroomed after an August 2005 decision
taken at the highest level of the government of Chhattisgarh "to provide
direct support to Salwa Judum in the form of logistics, arms and funding."[33] Its first crop of recruits consisted of a mix of Maoist defectors,
family members of victims of Maoist violence, and professional thugs
and criminals, all attracted by the prospect of loot. Tribal chiefs dispossessed by Naxalite campaigns, especially from the Dorla tribe—one of
two major tribal formations in the region, the other being the Koyas—
were an important source of support for Salwa Judum.

During the second half of 2005 and 2006, Salwa Judum gunmen went
on a rampage across the southern Dantewada district of the Bastar region.
The offensive apparently aimed to literally uproot the Maoists from the
district, as it targeted persons belonging to or associated with the Maoist-
initiated *sanghams,* villagers suspected of harboring Naxalite sympathies,
and villages that refused to join the Salwa Judum campaign. Reports of
wanton murders, gang rapes of girls and women, and arson of villages
proliferated. By March 2006 the Salwa Judum offensive had resulted in a
significant problem of displacement in the district, as 45,958 people fled
their villages and took shelter in camps. The largest of these camps, which
provided a source of further recruitment for the militia, particularly among
teenage boys, held 13,000 people as of late 2007. Several thousand more
fled across the interstate border into the Khammam district of Andhra
Pradesh's Telangana region, and an unknown number decamped to Naxalite bases in deep forests of the Bastar region. In June 2006, 644 of the
Dantewada district's 1,220 villages were declared to have been cleared of
Maoist presence by the state government of Chhattisgarh.

The Naxalites beefed up their own militia and carried out numerous counterattacks. In February 2006 they bombed a truck carrying Salwa Judum supporters and killed 27 people; in April they executed 13 men accused of Salwa Judum affiliations in a village after a "people's court" trial; and in July they attacked a camp guarded by Salwa Judum and killed 31 people. In July 2011 India's Supreme Court declared Salwa Judum illegal and unconstitutional, but by then a sizable part of the militia had been absorbed as auxiliaries in the CRPF's counterinsurgency campaign in a 5,000-strong force of "special police officers" (SPOs) paid a monthly wage of 1,500 rupees (not insignificant in a desperately poor area).

The continuing war is exacerbated by the area's "resource curse." The Dantewada district contains substantial iron-ore deposits, and both the Union-government-owned company that operates the existing mines and private Indian companies—notably the giant Tata and Essar groups—interested in prospecting rights and building steel-making plants are said to pay protection money to the Naxalites and the anti-Naxalite local warlords.

The counterinsurgency campaign has not eradicated the Maoist movement in Dantewada district and elsewhere in the Bastar region and may not have significantly weakened it. The Maoists have kept up a bitter insurgency in the Dandakaranya zone. Since 2007 the zone has seen the deadliest guerrilla attacks on counterinsurgency forces in three generations of Indian Maoism—part of a "tactical counteroffensive" by the rebels, who otherwise remain in "strategic defense" mode. One night in February 2007 about 2,000 Maoist militants and supporters raided the explosives storage facility of the Bailadila iron-ore mines in Dantewada district. They carried away 20 tons of high-grade ammonium nitrate, which has since turned up in "multiple roadside bombs" targeting CRPF convoys in the region. This means that the CRPF has a tough time securing even "major . . . roads," while "forested areas, secondary roads and areas . . . away from major roads are Naxalite-mined and remain inaccessible." In March 2007 the Maoists attacked a camp housing Chhattisgarh police and SPOs in Bijapur district, then newly carved out of a western pocket of Dantewada district. They killed 55 of the 79 personnel in the camp—39 SPOs and 16 police—before withdrawing with captured weapons. Six Maoists, including their local military commander, also died. A communique issued by the Dandakaranya Special Zonal Committee of the Communist Party of India (Maoist) hailed the raid as "the biggest attack in the history of the Indian communist movement to date."[34]

That was surpassed in April 2010, when the Maoists ambushed a CRPF column in the Dantewada district, killing 75 paramilitary troopers and a state policeman. The troopers had been camping in a forest for several days as part of an acclimation and "area domination" exercise and were attacked while returning on foot to their base. In June 2010 another ambush targeted a CRPF unit returning to their camp from a routine "road-opening" patrol—a perilous morning walk to make sure that a stretch of road is free of roadside bombs and mines that may have been planted during the night—in the Narayanpur district (carved out of the Bastar district, which lies in the heart of the eponymous region). Twenty-seven paramilitary troopers died.

All of these major incidents involved hundreds of attackers, whose numbers were estimated by wounded survivors as ranging from the middle to the high hundreds. The attackers were led by detachments of the People's Liberation Guerrilla Army, formed in December 2000. It consists of the crack Maoist fighting units equipped with the best weapons the radicals possess. (Its strength across the Maoist-active states is estimated at about 10,000 men and women, though this is impossible to verify.) According to the Maoist communique on the March 2007 raid on SPOs and police in Dantewada, 150 People's Liberation Guerrilla Army fighters were deployed in that operation. These leading assault units were supported by considerably greater numbers from the Maoist "people's militia," the second-line combatants whose strength across the Maoist-active states is estimated at about 100,000.

The Narayanpur/Bastar ambush of June 2010 took place at an entry point to Abujhmaad (roughly: Unknown Hills), a hilly, forested terrain of 4,000 square kilometers estimated to be inhabited by some 26,000 Adivasis spread across about 237 hamlets. (The area has never been properly surveyed because it is so remote and inaccessible.) The Maoists have nearly total control of Abujhmaad, and in March–April 2012 CRPF units, led by COBRA commandos stationed around the redoubt, could only make brief, probing forays into the area before withdrawing. The Gadchiroli district of Maharashtra adjoining Chhattisgarh's Bastar region is also part of the Maoists' Dandakaranya command and is the site of recurrent ambushes of police and CRPF personnel by the insurgents. In late March 2012, 13 CRPF troopers traveling in a motorized convoy were killed by a landmine blast when they "failed to follow a key part of the standard operating procedure for troop movements on rebel turf . . . that any vehicular movement in a high-risk zone must be preceded by a 'road-opening' team that travels on foot and makes sure the route is free of mines."[35]

As of 2013 the Maoists' writ runs partially or totally across a swathe of Dandakaranya amounting to "15,000–20,000 square kilometers—equivalent to a medium-sized European state."[36] In these areas the

Maoists operate what they call *janatana sarkars* (people's governments), rural communes engaged in subsistence agriculture and tending of forests. These have been referred to by Ganapati, the Communist Party of India (Maoist)'s general secretary, as "embryonic forms of new democratic people's governments [established] in some pockets" of the country.[37] They are examples of "the people-oriented, self-reliant model of development" based "first and foremost in agriculture and the rural areas, where the bulk of our people live," described in 2006 by Azad, the Communist Party of India (Maoist) spokesperson slain in 2010, as the core of the Maoists' revolutionary blueprint for the whole of India.

Popular support to the Maoist cause in Dandakaranya is rooted in four experiences. The first is oppression by the local representatives of the state. In 2011 a Maoist militiaman-cum-tour guide in the zone told a visitor in broken Hindi: "My family has been systematically tortured by the forest and revenue guards." This is a common complaint—"forest and revenue department officials have been harassing tribes in the region for decades over chopping of trees and killing of wild animals, which locals consider infringement of their rights. To make matters worse, the forest officers [often] settled the cases by taking money or . . . other benefits such as the company of tribal women."

Second is the improvement in people's livelihoods by Maoist initiatives. The same visitor met "a farmer" in a *janatana sarkar* area who "showed me his farmland and mud-and-thatch house and told me that he used to be a landless farm worker [until] six years ago. The Party gave him eight acres, five for farming and three for building a house. . . . He informed me that five families in his village got land [in this way]."

Third is long-standing neglect by the state of the basic needs of impoverished communities in remote areas. Thus "health care in Dandakaranya provided by the state government is nothing short of atrocious. There are few health centers and doctors are not available" most of the time. To fill the vacuum, Maoist "barefoot doctors," a few hundred boys and girls in their twenties, given paramedic training by the movement, "travel like missionaries from one hamlet to another with boxes full of medicine for common ailments like malaria, snakebite, dysentery, severe itching and fever. They are adored by the villagers." The same is true of schooling facilities. Government-funded schools in the region often did not function due to lack of teachers, until they were revived by the Naxalites. In rebel enclaves there are schools "where the government pays for teachers, assistants, cooks and meals, while the Maoists maintain the schools."

Fourth is the sense of agency and purpose imparted to some members of the younger generation in the region by the Maoists. One such young man, a 23-year-old paramedic, recounted his story: "earlier, nobody took me seriously. [Then] one day the Party's division secretary asked me if I would like to be a doctor. I thought he was joking but he sent me to a camp, manned by doctors from cities, where I was trained for two weeks. . . . Now the entire village, mine and others, runs after me. I [feel I] am doing something for my people, my land."

This is the context in which visitors to Maoist jungle camps in Dandakaranya are greeted by "very young girls with hair cropped like Audrey Hepburn in *Roman Holiday*, [who] ended their *laal salaam* [red salute] invariably with a giggle. . . . [Aged] between 15 and 30 years, the men and women wore rubber sandals, olive-green battle fatigues and carried guns of various makes." In the evenings there are occasional in-camp movie screenings that are very popular with local villagers, who "finish dinner early and come to watch the late-night show." This consists of a DVD played on a laptop computer. The top hits include *Do Bigha Zameen* (Two *bighas* of land; a *bigha* is one-third of an acre), a 1950s Hindi classic about peasant poverty and indebtedness in rural India; *The Axis of War*, about the Chinese communists' mid-1930s "long march"; *The Battle of Algiers*, the 1966 classic about the 1956–1957 Algerian urban insurgency against French colonialism; and *Enter the Dragon*, starring Bruce Lee. In the land of Bollywood, most villagers in these areas had never watched a movie before.

The Maoists' revolutionary macro-project is never far from the surface. A "Basic Communist Training School" set up in Dandakaranya in 2009 admits children aged 12–15 in batches of 30. The intensive six-month course covers languages (English and Hindi), math, and computer training, and the capstone is a two-week practical internship during which students join a work team to participate in hands-on development work. The course also includes an introduction to M-L-M (Marxism-Leninism-Maoism) and training in "use of different types of weapons." The trained and indoctrinated child-soldiers are then inducted into the movement.[38]

The early twenty-first-century Maoist mobilization among Adivasis in Dandakaranya has deep historical roots. The formation and territorial expansion of modern states has often produced cruel consequences for indigenous populations around the world. In Bastar, the policies of the British colonial state generated by the early twentieth-century conditions in which "life . . . seemed bleak to the local inhabitants, what with reservation of forests, restrictions on *penda* [shifting cultivation], introduction of grazing dues, increase in land revenue and greater demand for *begar* [forced labor]—all in the name of more efficient administration."[39] In 1910 a tribal uprising known as the Bhumkal revolt erupted in the princely state of Bastar and was suppressed by the British through police and military action. A prominent member of the princely state's royal family, the king's cousin and former *diwan* (vizier or prime minister), was on the side of the rebels. The Bhumkal revolt is a central part of local folklore and Adivasi memory a century later.

India's independence in 1947, the abolition of the princely states, and Bastar's integration into the Indian Union formally turned the Adivasis from colonial subjects into emancipated citizens. But the relationship between the new state authorities—above all the state government of Madhya Pradesh—and parts of the local population continued to be adversarial. Tensions came to a head in 1966, triggered by a government decision to impose a "levy" on paddy grown in Madhya Pradesh, under which cultivators had to provide a fixed amount of paddy for procurement by the government. (There were food shortages in the state and nationwide at the time due to droughts and hoarding, aggravated by the autumn 1965 war with Pakistan.) In Bastar the policy was unpopular and sparked opposition. In March 1966 protesting Adivasis gathered at the palace of the former princely family in the town of Jagdalpur. A confrontation ensued between Adivasis armed with bows and arrows and police. One policeman was killed by arrows and several others wounded. The police opened fire and killed at least 12 people, including the scion of the royal family, an eccentric man who had a long history of hostility toward the state authorities of Madhya Pradesh and the ruling Congress party.[40] Thereafter "a lull of fifteen years" followed, until "we entered this area [from Telangana/Andhra Pradesh]," in the words of the leader of the Maoists' Dandakaranya Special Zonal Committee.[41]

The tradition of resistance to intrusive and alien state power is not limited to the Gond tribes of central India. The pivotal event in the collective memory of the Santals of eastern India is the Hul, an insurrection that broke out in 1855–1856 in Santal-inhabited areas on both sides of the current border between West Bengal and Jharkhand. The Hul is commemorated annually as a cultural festival in the Santal calendar. The uprising targeted (nontribal) *zamindars* or big landlords, and usurious moneylenders, and was put down with much difficulty by the military forces of the British colonial authorities. (A year later, in 1857, some of these—Indian—military forces led a massive revolt against the British that convulsed the Gangetic plains of northern India.)

The leaders of the Santal Hul were four brothers, Sidhu, Kanu, Chand, and Bhairab, belonging to the Murmu clan who were fired by messianic zeal. Like the Gonds of central India, the Santals of eastern India subscribe to a cosmological view of the universe and are strongly animistic, with a tradition of worshiping forest spirits *(bongas)*. Sidhu and Kanu, the legendary leaders of the Hul, told their followers that "the *bongas* wished them to cast off the yoke of . . . oppression." When some of the Santals of West Bengal were attracted to the first Naxalite insurrection of the late 1960s and early 1970s—initially in the Himalayan foothills of Darjeeling district, where Naxalbari is located, and later in Medinipur and Birbhum districts—it was because "the strongly messianic character of the Naxalite movement" resonated with their traditional worldview and memories of past uprisings. Thus while "urban Bengali youths may have seen themselves as emulating the soldiers of Mao's Red Army . . . the Santal concept of liberation war" was based on an "identification with the Hul." In eastern India, this tradition of struggle is not limited to Santals. In 1900 the Mundas—an Adivasi community concentrated in today's Jharkhand—also rose against the British colonial state and its local Indian acolytes "under the messianic leadership" of the young man Birsa Munda.[42]

In West Bengal in the late 1960s and early 1970s, the first-generation "Naxalite cadres . . . were ultimately incapable of assuming the entire Santal cosmology . . . [but] continued to attempt to reconcile Santal grievances and aspirations with Marxist-Leninist explanations of the root causes of oppression and blueprints for an alternative society."[43] The Maoist revolutionaries of the second and third generations in Dandakaranya have pursued precisely the same strategy, but in a much more planned and patient style. The Communist Party of India (Maoist) national spokesperson Azad wrote in 2006 that "the Maoists have indeed sought to learn from the adivasi masses and have taken all that is positive in tribal culture, while doing away with the dross. So we have not only sought to preserve the Gondi, Santali and other [tribal] languages but developed them; we have preserved and adopted the folklore of the tribal peoples and their dance forms, infusing them with social content. We have encouraged and enhanced the elements of community and collective living, which were a natural part of their culture."[44] Indeed, the top Maoist organizer in Dandakaranya—like Azad a nontribal from the Telangana region of Andhra Pradesh—observed in 2010 that "the tradition of collective activity amongst the tribals acts as an enabling factor" because "when adivasis join [the movement] they do not join in small trickles but entire villages get mobilized at about the same time."[45]

Given the "connect" between Adivasi culture, memory, and tradition and the politics of salvation and redemption of the Maoist movement, it is not surprising that short-cut approaches such as Salwa Judum failed to uproot and eradicate the Maoists in Dandakaranya. A movement that has worked among the Gonds for three decades has been able to survive the onslaught launched by a state that to many in those communities—among the most marginalized in India's democracy—is identified with exploitation, cruelty, and neglect. As Edward Duyker, a scholar of Naxalite activism among the Santals of West Bengal in the 1967–1972 period, has observed, "the strongly messianic character of the Naxalite movement" appealed to some Santals not simply because it resonated with their own memories of insurrection led by messianic figures but because of their utterly peripheral position in society. He compared this to the Middle Ages in Europe, where millenarian movements "had their strongest hold among . . . peasants who were not simply poor but had no assured and recognized place in society at all."[46] It was surely this appeal of an early twenty-first-century brand of messianic ideology to the utterly peripheral that drew recruits like Bhuta Baskay alias Sidhu Soren, the son of a desperately poor Santal family in a remote hamlet of rural West Bengal, to the Maoist critique of India's democracy.

The war for the hearts and minds of the have-nots of India is complicated by the fact that "the mining and tribal maps of India are almost the same."[47] In other words, there is a great deal of coincidence between Adivasi-populated and mineral-rich areas. Since the deregulation of India's economy began in the early 1990s, the field of contenders seeking to exploit these mineral resources has gradually expanded. Mostly restricted until 2004 to state-owned companies, the field now includes big Indian private firms. In recent years the state-owned National Mineral Development Corporation has fought legal battles with the private Tata and Essar conglomerates over mining rights in the conflict zone of Chhattisgarh, and locals have protested the acquisition of land for steel-plant ventures of these conglomerates. The governments of mineral-rich states like Chhattisgarh, Jharkhand, and Orissa generally agree with the private businesses, Indian and foreign, that land acquisition is necessary for job creation and in the longer run beneficial for development in poor, "backward" areas. India's single largest foreign investment to date is a Korean company's proposal to set up a steel plant in Orissa, a plan that has run into tribal protests and environmentalist objections and been repeatedly stalled by the Congress-led Union government. (Orissa is governed by a strong regional party whose ascendancy has severely weakened the Congress party in the state.)

Critics see this as "predatory industrialization" that the "creation of [new] states like Chhattisgarh and Jharkhand has in effect worked to intensify" in the early twenty-first century.[48] The fear of dispossession often resonates with poor people whose past experience of state intervention in their lives, when it has occurred at all, has usually been deeply negative. The third generation of India's Maoist movement has recognized and cultivated the opportunity presented by such discontent (even while sometimes being complicit themselves, especially in Jharkhand, in the chain of corruption and protection rackets linking government and business interests). They have an expansive ideological critique of the oppressive Indian state, said to be in league with rapacious Indian and foreign capitalists and subservient to a "neoliberal" imperialist global order. While "increased exploitation of mineral resources by state-owned and private companies . . . underlies much of the discontent that feeds the insurgency," the crux of the problem is the absence of "a tradition of state engagement [with people] . . . [due to which] the encroachment of agents of resource extraction is not counter-balanced by institutions that can mediate with restive social groups."[49]

That sort of state engagement with citizens has been emerging, but belatedly and piecemeal. A forested area of 850 square kilometers known as Saranda, located on Jharkhand's southern border with Orissa, is inhabited by about 7,000 families of the Ho community, an Adivasi group, who live in 56 jungle hamlets. The area is said to have a quarter of India's iron-ore deposits, and a dozen state and private mining companies operate in its vicinity. The Saranda forest was a Maoist base for over a decade until 2011, when the militants were forced out by a huge counterinsurgency operation (although they remain present on its peripheries two years later). In late 2011 the Union government's rural development ministry unveiled an ambitious plan, to be implemented by the administrative authorities of the West Singhbhum district in which the area is located, for "holistic development of the erstwhile Maoist stronghold . . . [whose] tribal inhabitants have been victims of long years of official apathy and isolation . . . [and] where the administration's presence until now was practically nil." The plan visualizes the construction of about 4,000 houses—using "local designs acceptable to tribal people"—under a federally funded housing scheme for people below the official poverty line. Other provisions include old-age pensions for senior citizens, 10 schools to provide free education to children, mobile healthcare units, clean drinking water connections for all the villages, and a job-skills training program for local youth to be undertaken by the mining companies with funding from the Union government. The plan also visualizes the distribution of forest title deeds to the population. Under the "Scheduled Tribes and Other Traditional Forest Dwellers (Recognition of Forest Rights) Act" passed by Parliament in 2006, families living in forests for at least three generations are entitled to such recognition of ownership of forest land they have traditionally used for homestead and livelihood purposes.[50]

The closest analogue to India's contemporary Maoist movement emerged in the 1980s nearly a world away—in Peru in the southern Americas. This was the Sendero Luminoso (Shining Path) movement, formally the Communist Party of Peru-Sendero Luminoso, which waged a bloody and ultimately unsuccessful insurgency to seize state power in Peru between 1980 and the mid-1990s. The origins were similar; like the first generation of Indian Maoism, the Shining Path tendency was born of 1960s splits in the Peruvian communist spectrum between pro-Soviet and pro-China factions.

When multiparty elections were held in Peru in 1980, after a period of military rule that lasted for over a decade and during which significant propoor reforms were undertaken by leftist military officers between 1968–1975, the Shining Path tendency diverged from other Peruvian leftist parties in refusing participation in "bourgeois democracy." Instead the movement branded all other socialist and communist groups in Peru "revisionist" and embarked on an armed insurrection to achieve a "new democratic revolution" in the country. This insurrection took off around the time the second generation of Maoism/Naxalism was taking shape in India in the early 1980s. The Sendero Luminoso's ideological framework was the same as the one uncritically inherited by the second and third generations of Indian Maoism from the first generation. Thus Peru was a semicolonial country in the grip of "Yankee imperialism," and internally a semifeudal country, although in fact most landed estates *(haciendas)* had been abolished in Peru by the 1960s, like the old *zamindari* estates in India. The revolutionary overthrow of the established order in Peru would be achieved by a classic "people's war," which would create liberated zones and base areas in the countryside and then encircle and seize the cities— notably the capital, Lima, home to almost a third of the population. The Shining Path's revolution had a prophet similar to Charu Mazumdar in India's first-generation Naxalite upsurge: Abimael Guzman alias President Gonzalo, a middle-aged philosophy professor who was dubbed "the fourth sword of communism" (after Marx, Lenin, and Mao) and the "world's greatest living Marxist-Leninist" by his followers.

The Shining Path's insurrection began in 1982 in the most impoverished regions of Peru, inhabited predominantly by indigenous peoples, the equivalent of India's Adivasis. The movement's cradle and bastion was the highland region of Ayacucho in the heart of Peru's portion of the Andes, the north south mountain range that runs for several thousand miles close to the western coast of South America, from Venezuela to Argentina. Among the Quechua-speaking Indian communities of Ayacucho and its adjacent regions, Shining Path initially held "appeal to the desires in an impoverished countryside for a more just order." The cadres who sought to mobilize the Indian peasantry were mainly "high school and university students . . . from rural families," very similar to the Maoist cadres of Andhra Pradesh who formed the backbone of the movement there and in Dandakaranya. Guzman had taught during the 1960s at the provincial university in the Ayacucho region's eponymous capital city, where he developed a following. The "harshness of rural life in Apurimac, Ayacucho and Huancavelica—three of the poorest departments [regions] in an impoverished country—partially explains the initial receptivity to Shining Path's call for radical change."[51]

The movement gained traction in the Andean highlands of Peru because of a brutal counterinsurgency crackdown conducted in 1983–1984 by the Peruvian army that indiscriminately targeted Indian communities thought to be harboring Shining Path guerrillas, particularly in Ayacucho. Between 1980 and 1991, there were 11,969 deaths in the violence that engulfed the remote regions in the center-south of Peru, and 7,481 of these were in the Ayacucho region. Of these 7,481 deaths, more than half (4,148) occurred in 1983 and 1984, when the Peruvian army went on a rampage in Ayacucho in a manner similar to Salwa Judum in Chhattisgarh's Dantewada district in 2005–2006.[52] The Shining Path retaliated in kind; in 1983 its cadres massacred 80 Indian peasants in a rural Ayacucho community that had refused to join the movement.

Like India's third-generation Maoist movement, Shining Path did "best in extremely poor and historically marginal areas of the country characterized by a weak state presence."[53] But the "people's war" ran into serious difficulties by the end of the 1980s in its Andean strongholds. This was partly the result of an intelligently ruthless—as opposed to indiscriminately violent—counterinsurgency strategy adopted by the Peruvian army after 1985. The revised approach "recognized the need to combine intimidation and persuasion in a so-called 'integral strategy' which included 'sociopolitical development' and 'civic action' to build support among the peasantry."[54] The integral strategy continued to rely heavily on coercion. Through the second half of the 1980s, several hundred thousand villagers were regrouped by the army into "strategic hamlets" so as to isolate Shining Path and were organized into a network of "civil autodefense committees" (CACs), known locally as *rondas*. The *ronderos* were equipped with basic firearms such as shotguns and old rifles. But unlike Chhattisgarh's Salwa Judum, these anti–Shining Path vigilantes were not allowed to go on a rampage but were assigned a defensive function against insurgent attacks while the army undertook offensive operations (in a selective, targeted way). Some *ronda* leaders were disillusioned veterans of the Shining Path movement. The disillusionment had spread among rural communities by the end of the 1980s and was the crucial factor in turning the tide of Peru's internal war.

The fundamental reason for the spreading disillusionment was the revolutionary movement's "totalitarian political project." In its guerrilla zones, Shining Path aimed to "not only construct a new state but a new society, controlled by the party in its most minute details." Anyone perceived to disagree with this project faced lethal retribution—often brutal public executions after "people's trials" in kangaroo courts. As "resistance from within its own bases of support" grew against the "total domination" imposed by the movement, Shining Path reacted by "intensifying the climate of terror" and launching "indiscriminate attacks . . . not only against communities organized into CACs but against neutral civilian populations with no direct connection to the conflict." By the late 1980s the Maoist insurgents and not the army had become the chief perpetrator of massacres. By contrast, the army "did not seek total control of everyday life, as Shining Path did." By the end of the 1980s "decisive sectors of the peasantry opted for a pragmatic alliance with the armed forces" as the lesser of two evils.[55]

Shining Path launched its promised urban offensive focused on Lima in 1991, after "President Gonzalo" announced that the phase of strategic defense (and tactical offense) was over, "strategic equilibrium" with the state had been achieved, and the time was ripe for the decisive stage of people's war, the "strategic offensive." But by this time the Maoist movement had actually been severely weakened in its base areas and was in disarray. The urban campaign, whose prime targets were activists of moderate left-wing parties active in Lima's shantytowns, achieved some impact but then ran out of steam. A devastating blow to insurgent morale was delivered in September 1992 by the capture of Abimael Guzman from an apartment in an upscale Lima neighborhood. By late 1993 some of the most tenacious rebel communities in the Andean highlands had surrendered en masse, and by the mid-1990s the revolutionary war was effectively over, its surviving practitioners reduced to scattered remnants.

The saga of Peru—whose population size is about the same as Chhattisgarh or Jharkhand—shows that the kind of messianic, millenarian movement represented by India's Maoists contains the seeds of its own downfall. While a Peru-type outcome is unlikely on an India-wide scale, the totalistic vision of revolutionary transformation of India's Maoist leaders, and the organic connection of that project to the practice of violence, has already resulted in ominous setbacks in particular regions to the third generation of Indian Maoism. One example is of course Andhra Pradesh. The other and even more recent example is West Bengal, the crucible of first-generation Indian Maoism, where a spectacular Maoist ascendancy in certain rural areas in 2009–2010 turned rapidly into decline and retreat.

West Bengal occupies a special place in the Indian Maoist imagination. This is the state of Naxalbari and the founding myth of the movement, of Charu Mazumdar the pioneer ideologue, and the main site of the first, doomed insurrection. After that insurrection ended in 1972, however, the Naxalites and their ideology were relegated to marginality in the state. In public memory in West Bengal, the first Naxalite uprising became predominantly associated with senseless violence, broken lives, and a dream of revolution that turned into a nightmare, the central themes of the bestselling 1980s novel *Kaalbaela*. In 1977 the Communist Party of India (Marxist), the party the Naxalites had condemned as sellouts to bourgeois democracy and bitterly split from in the late 1960s, came to power in West Bengal at the head of the Left Front and proceeded to govern the state for a record-setting 34 years. The main, mass-based opposition during those decades was first the Congress party and after 1998 the regionalist Trinamool Congress. The Naxalites of the second and third generations were nowhere in the picture.

After a hiatus of nearly four decades, the unlikely resurgence of Maoist revolutionary politics in West Bengal made headlines across India and beyond in 2009–2010. This was sparked by events in late 2008 in the West Medinipur district, where in 1969–1970 the first-generation Maoists led rebellions of the rural poor in the locales of Debra and Gopiballavpur. (In 2002 the vast Medinipur district, then India's most populous district with nearly 10 million people, was bifurcated for administrative convenience into "West Medinipur" and "East Medinipur." The West Medinipur district's population is about 6 million in 2013, of whom 88 percent live in rural communities.) By 2008 the Left Front government had become unpopular because of its repression of peasant protests against acquisition of farmland for industrial projects to be set up by big business. The two flashpoints were Singur, in the Hooghly district near Kolkata, and Nandigram, in the East Medinipur district.

With the state on the political boil, the government persisted with the remnants of its industrialization strategy. The state's chief minister, a junior minister of steel in the Union government, and a leading out-of-state business tycoon were returning in a convoy after the ceremonial laying of a foundation stone for a steel-and-thermal power plant in the rural Salboni area of the West Medinipur district—to be built by the Jindal Group, the tycoon's company—when Maoist militants exploded a roadside bomb close to the town of Medinipur, the district's center of administration, higher education, and commerce. The dignitaries escaped unscathed, but the outraged state government ordered police raids on villages in the district suspected to be harboring Maoist militants. These raids were conducted in a heavy-handed way. Beatings, arbitrary arrests, and other abuses triggered a backlash among the local population.

When the British East India Company acquired control of the Medinipur district in 1760, "it was one of the first districts in India to come under British rule. In the western half of the district they found a continuous jungle, broken by patches of cultivation." From the first decade of the twentieth century through the 1940s, Medinipur became famous as a center of anticolonial nationalist activity, which took the form of mass mobilizations as well as armed actions. But independence did not uplift the lives of the inhabitants of the jungle terrain, especially "a poor miserable proscribed race of men called Santals," as they were described by a British official in the early nineteenth century.[56] Some of these Santals were drawn to and participated in the 1969–1970 Naxalite movement in the area. The 2002 bifurcation of Medinipur district carved out the West Medinipur district covering nearly 10,000 square kilometers. The western half of this new district, corresponding to the terrain historically known as Jangalmahal (Abode of the Forests), which also takes in contiguous parts of the neighboring Bankura district, became a war zone between third-generation Maoists and the state during 2009–2010.

For a decade before the escalation, the Maoists had had a low-profile presence in parts of the West Bengal districts of West Medinipur, Bankura, and Purulia—a third district that, like West Medinipur, has a large Adivasi population and a border with Maoist-active zones of Jharkhand. There had been occasional ambushes of police and murders of local politicians, usually belonging to the ruling CPM, in these areas through the first decade of the twenty-first century. The Maoists had also been quietly recruiting among local youth. Sidhu Soren, the Maoist militant killed in July 2010, had disappeared 10 years previously, while in his late teens, to join what some locals refer to as the *bon party* (party that lives in the forest). In late 2008, after years of preparation, the Maoists sensed an opportunity to dramatically escalate their activities in Jangalmahal and open a new regional front in their "people's war." The People's Committee

Against Police Atrocities was formed as the public front of the escalated campaign. Lalmohan Tudu, a local Santal politician who had previously been with the CPM, became its chair, and Chhatradhar Mahato (born 1964), another local activist, became its spokesperson. Mahato had previously been affiliated with the Congress party and then the Trinamool Congress, but his younger brother had been an underground Maoist militant for some years. Tudu was shot dead by the CRPF while visiting his village in February 2010; Mahato was arrested in September 2009 and has been in jail since then. Mahato's brother was killed in a gun battle with the CRPF in March 2011.

The People's Committee emerged within weeks as the de facto authority across a swathe of West Medinipur district. Its members kept the police out of extensive rural areas by cutting up roads or blocking them with felled trees. The state government, reeling from accusations of police brutality in Singur, Nandigram, and Jangalmahal, chose not to confront the challenge. It was not until seven months later, in June 2009, that "joint forces" comprising the Union government's CRPF and the state police entered the no-go areas. During that period the Maoists had a free run of most of the western half of the West Medinipur district. They used the time to stamp their dominance on these areas. The Sidhu Kanu Gana Militia (Sidhu Kanu People's Militia), named after Sidhu and Kanu, the leaders of the Hul uprising of 1855–1856, was formed to enforce the writ of the People's Committee. Hundreds of young men and some young women from the villages of the area were recruited into the Maoist ranks. They were overwhelmingly Adivasis belonging to the Santal community or from the Mahato community, a socioeconomically disadvantaged group numerous in the area. The Mahatos have historical affinities with the Santals. They were classified as a tribal community until 1935, when they were delisted, but "are actually semitribals who . . . retain their tribal characteristics" though they are formally classified as an OBC group.[57] The Santals and groups like the Mahatos have a long history of joint political action. In the nineteenth-century Hul rebellion, "the Santals and such low-caste Hindus . . . made common cause," and to a limited extent this was also true of the first-generation Naxalite revolts in rural West Bengal.[58]

By early 2009, heavily armed Maoist camps dotted the forested tracts of West Medinipur. The importance the third generation of the Maoist movement was giving to their newest guerrilla zone was revealed by the fact that Kishenji, a top Maoist political and military leader of Telangana origins, assumed overall charge of the Jangalmahal campaign. The movement came to be known across India as the "Lalgarh movement" after

Lalgarh, a tiny township at the center of a cluster of West Medinipur villages where some of the initial People's Committee planning and organizing took place.

During visits to Jangalmahal, the underlying causes of the eruption became clear to me, the first being abject poverty. Unlike much of the rest of West Bengal, the soil in Jangalmahal is uneven and relatively infertile, and even subsistence agriculture is difficult in parts because of lack of irrigation facilities. In Bandarboni, a village of 2,000 people inhabited mainly by the Shabar tribe, people live in mud-and-thatch hovels in near-destitution all year. The hovels are flooded during the monsoons, and there is no road to the village except a barely usable path covered with sticky mud. The nearest paved road is three miles away, and sick people need to be bodily carried to that point and then put on transport to the hospital in Jhargram, a town of 60,000. There is a primary health center that is closer, but neither doctors nor medicines are usually available there. The villagers have not heard of various government schemes that entitle them, as people below the official poverty line, to assistance to build habitable houses and their senior citizens and widows to pensions. In September 2011, with the Maoist movement in steep decline in the zone, the only political graffiti in Bandarboni belonged to Maoist front organizations. Across Jangalmahal, many of the new recruits to Maoist armed squads in 2009 who died in encounters with the CRPF-led forces in 2010 were young Adivasi men and women from "families that starve for half the year."[59]

During travels in Jangalmahal in 2010, I was told by people of various generations, social groups, and political leanings in the conflict zone of the West Medinipur district that initially—roughly late 2008 through mid-2009—"80 to 90 percent" of the locals were positively inclined toward the protest movement. When I asked why, the usual response was that they, particularly the very poor, felt cheated by the supposedly "propoor" government led by the CPM, in power in West Bengal since 1977, which had failed to deliver improvements in their living conditions and prospects while using them as a captive "vote bank" for three decades. Moreover, any signs of dissent or opposition activity attracted harsh "punishment."

Thus the landless family of Alo Tudu, a teenaged Santal girl, was one of the very few in her West Medinipur village who would not support the ruling party. They were socially ostracized as a result, and Alo was once beaten for refusing to join a CPM rally. She enthusiastically joined the "Lalgarh movement" as soon as it began and in January 2010 left home to become a fighter in a Maoist armed squad. Alo was killed in June 2010, aged 18, in a jungle encounter with the counterinsurgency forces. Suman

Maity, a nontribal man in his early twenties from another West Medinipur village, joined the Maoist underground in March 2009 and rose to
become a junior commander. His father had been a CPM supporter but
switched allegiance to a faction of the Jharkhand Party, an Adivasi-based
party in Jangalmahal. Their home was then vandalized by CPM cadres,
and the father was taken to the local police station on a trumped-up
charge and severely assaulted. Maity survived the underground life and
was captured during a counterinsurgency operation in the zone in November 2011.[60]

During 2009 and 2010 the Jangalmahal tracts of West Medinipur were
engulfed by a firestorm of violence. The Maoists were emboldened by their
initial successes; the Communist Party of India (Maoist) national leader
Ganapati said in late 2009 that "the Lalgarh upsurge exceeded our expec
tations." They went on a killing spree in the zone in an effort to turn their
new-found dominance into absolute control. Their main targets were
members and supporters of the CPM, who were singled out in a campaign
to uproot its formidable grassroots organization from the zone. Between
200 and 300 local CPM loyalists were killed by the Maoists, most during
the peak of the terror in 2009 and 2010. But the slaughter was by no means
restricted to CPM loyalists. One of the first to be killed, in late 2008, was
Sudhir Mandi, a popular local politician belonging to a Jharkhand Party
faction who had a clean, corruption-free image; he was a poor Adivasi with
almost no land of his own who lived in a mud-and-thatch hut and eked out
a meager living selling forest products. Other victims included Rabindra-
nath Mahato, 59, the headmaster of a rural primary school near the town
of Jhargram who was hacked and shot to death in July 2010 on the
grounds of his school for disobeying a Maoist *diktat* to send his students
to a People's Committee march. He was one of 15 local teachers killed by
Maoist hit squads between 2008 and 2011, in most cases in full view of
terrified schoolchildren. During 2009 and 2010 bloodied corpses appeared
almost daily on roads in the area, usually deliberately dumped in places
where they would be seen by significant numbers of people. Some were
simply abducted and murdered; others were subjected to kangaroo courts
in Maoist-controlled villages and executed, usually while begging for their
lives, after being denounced as enemies of the people and the revolution.
The victims were sometimes alleged by the Maoists to be spies and informers, and the vast majority of the dead were poor people belonging to
Adivasi and low-caste communities.[61]

The terror campaign occasionally extended to whole villages. One
night in December 2009 about 20 armed Maoists riding on motorbikes
entered Salpatra, a mostly Muslim village near the town of Jhargram. All

the 75 households were rounded up and marched to a nearby forest, where they were ordered to form a "village committee" of six men and three women that would operate under Maoist supervision and regularly provide rice to the insurgents. The frightened villagers complied, but their ordeal had just begun. One night in June 2010 the villagers were rounded up again and taken to a paddy field where a "people's trial" was held. One man, Mehfuz Ali, was denounced as a CPM loyalist and bound hand and foot. When another man, Nirmal Nayek, a low-caste Hindu, asked the Maoists not to kill the condemned man, he too was tied up, and the two men were beaten for an hour. They were then shot dead in front of the other villagers. The villagers fled en masse the next morning; they claim that the Maoists expressly ordered them to leave. Two elderly Muslim women stayed behind, in the belief that their gender and age would protect them from harm. Both, Amena Bibi and Momena Bibi, were found dumped a few days later in a nearby canal with marks of torture on their bodies. In March 2012, nearly two years later, the traumatized villagers had still not returned home.[62]

After mid-2009 the beleaguered CPM started to organize its own armed militia in the war zones of the West Medinipur district. These armed squads came mainly from three sources. First were party loyalists who had fled their villages in the face of the Maoist onslaught. Second were thuggish party cadres from the much less affected eastern half of the West Medinipur district, where the CPM had for many years dominated the population and swept *panchayat,* state, and national elections using strong-arm methods, including murdering activists of opposition parties like the Trinamool Congress. Third were party goons from other West Bengal districts, particularly neighboring East Medinipur. The CPM armed squads became known in popular jargon as *harmads* (bandits), a term coined by the CPM's bête noire, the Trinamool Congress leader Mamata Banerjee. By the second half of 2010, dozens of heavily fortified camps housing *harmad* squads dotted the war zones of West Medinipur. The presence of these squads in villages added a further element of insecurity in the lives of a terrorized population. In January 2011 a *harmad* squad based in a nontribal village near Lalgarh opened fire on villagers after an altercation, killing nine villagers, including several women, and seriously injuring at least a dozen others.

Until mid-2010 the Maoists appeared to have the upper hand in the brutal conflict raging across the western half of West Medinipur. In October 2009 a police station was attacked, two policemen shot dead, and the officer-in-charge abducted. In February 2010 a large Maoist squad, including many women cadres, stormed a camp housing men of the Eastern Frontier Rifles, a small paramilitary police force of West Bengal's state government, killing 24 of them.

During the second half of 2010 the tide of the war turned against the Maoists. This began soon after a horrific incident in the zone in May 2010. Several carriages of a passenger train traveling from Kolkata to Mumbai derailed after midnight in a forested area close to the town of Jhargram. Saboteurs from the Maoist "people's militia" had damaged the tracks in support of a Maoist *hartal* (shutdown) call in Jangalmahal. The derailed carriages were hit in the darkness by a goods train coming at high speed from the opposite direction. The carriages were mangled, and 149 people died.

In June and July 2010 two successful nocturnal ambushes were made by the CRPF-led counterinsurgency forces on Maoist forest camps in which 14 insurgents were slain, including Sidhu Soren. This showed that the counterinsurgency was starting to receive pinpoint information about their adversaries' movements and whereabouts.

A very significant development took place in July 2010, when about 10,000 inhabitants of a cluster of villages around the town of Jhargram held a mass meeting and vowed to resist the Maoists. These were not *harmads* but ordinary peasants who had had enough of Maoist terror. The majority of the gathering consisted of angry women. They waved weapons belligerently—not firearms but stout sticks made from tree branches, bamboo staves, and sharp tools used for chopping and cutting in the kitchen or harvesting crops. The epicenter of this people's uprising against the practitioners of "people's war" was the village of Radhanagar.[63]

One afternoon in September 2010 I decided to return from the town of Jhargram to Medinipur, the largest town (170,000 people) in West Medinipur and its administrative seat. I traveled along a route that would take me through the "Radhanagar belt." Jhargram was bustling with market activity, but there was tension in the air. A few days earlier a senior CPM organizer in the town had been shot by a Maoist hit squad and had just died of his injuries in a Kolkata hospital. I had just driven beyond Jhargram's municipal limits and entered the rural hinterland when a bus full of passengers approached at speed from the other direction. Its driver did not slow down, but as he passed he honked furiously, leaned out of his window, and made a hand gesture that was clearly a warning not to proceed further. I stopped, surmising that perhaps the CRPF had discovered a roadside improvised explosive device, a frequent occurrence on the roads around Jhargram at the time, and traffic was stalled.

A few minutes later a car came careering from the opposite direction, headed toward Jhargram. As it passed I saw a young man covered in blood slumped on the rear seat. After another 15 minutes, plumes of smoke, clearly from one or more major fires, became visible about a mile ahead.

The bloodied young man, who was declared "brought dead" by doctors at the hospital in Jhargram, was Srikanta Mondal, 24, a resident of Radhanagar. That afternoon he had stepped out of his workplace, a secondary school for girls in the neighboring village of Sebayatan where he worked as a clerical assistant, when he noticed three young men loitering in front of the school. Apprehensive, he made a call from his mobile phone to his parents in Radhanagar, who ran to Sebayatan. When they arrived they saw their son, astride his motorbike, being accosted by the trio, who were accusing him of tearing down posters of the People's Committee Against Police Atrocities. Srikanta was denying this, and the parents, too, intervened and entreated the trio to let him go. The trio produced pistols and first shot at the parents, who were both hit and fell down. They then shot Srikanta several times at point-blank range, got on his motorbike, and rode off. The parents were lucky to escape death; the father, Haelu Mondal, received a bullet wound in one arm, and another bullet grazed the head of the mother, Sabita Mondal. Some of the girl students of the school witnessed the incident. As news of the shooting spread, enraged villagers attacked and set ablaze 15 houses of alleged People's Committee supporters in Sebayatan and an adjacent village, Joynagar; there were no deaths or injuries from the arson.

Srikanta belonged to a fairly typical poor Indian rural family. The father, Haelu, is landless and struggles to make a living transporting people in a cycle-rickshaw and doing painting and decorating jobs in the houses of better-off families. Because of the family's poverty, Srikanta, an only child, finished high school at a later than normal age, and in 2008 his secondary diploma secured him the modest job he had. He had received death threats for participating with hundreds of other able-bodied locals in night patrols organized to keep Maoist armed squads out of the area's villages.[64]

Santosh Rana, the main organizer of the 1969–1970 Naxalite rural insurrection in the Medinipur district's Gopiballavpur area, which is south of Jhargram, on the banks of the Subarnarekha River and close to the interstate border with Orissa, wrote in 2009 that "the [Indian] Maoists hold a grossly wrong understanding of the nature of people's power . . . that absolute power in their hands is equivalent to people's power."[65] The same fallacy caused the (self-)destruction of the Shining Path movement in Peru. The pursuit of absolute power over people—in the name of "the people"—inevitably leads to violence against all except those who believe absolutely in the cause. And there is nothing unusual about the Maoists' brutal modus operandi in Jangalmahal. At the other end of India's so-called Red Corridor, in Maharashtra's Gadchiroli district, the same pattern of murdering political opponents (and civilians) is apparent. There the victims, often targeted by small squads consisting of teenage boys, belong to parties like Congress and the regionalist Nationalist Congress Party. At least 16 elected *panchayat* members and other local community leaders were "executed" in Gadchiroli during 2012.

The third generation of India's Maoist movement have evidently learned nothing from the fates of their kindred movement in South America and the first generation of their own movement. The tragedy suffered by the Mondal family helps explain why the Maoist tide in Jangalmahal ebbed after just two years. In the state election of May 2011, which toppled West Bengal's CPM-led regime from power after 34 years, most of the constituencies in the war zones of West Medinipur elected Trinamool Congress candidates. Chhatradhar Mahato, who shot to fame as the spokesperson of the Maoists' People's Committee Against Police Atrocities before being arrested in September 2009, contested the election from jail as an independent "people's candidate." He stood from the Jhargram constituency, one of the 294 single-member electoral districts making up the state legislature. Mahato finished a poor third, with 13 percent of the vote, behind the victorious Trinamool Congress candidate (45 percent) and the second-placed CPM candidate, who got 35 percent. He still got a substantial bloc of votes, however—20,037 out of 155,520 votes cast in Jhargram, a turnout of 84 percent of the eligible electorate.

After coming to power in Kolkata, the new chief minister of West Bengal, the Trinamool Congress leader Mamata Banerjee, was quick to announce a slew of development projects for the poverty-stricken areas of Jangalmahal. By that time, the Maoist surge had already ebbed. (Among the applicants to a scheme to recruit local youth into the state police was Nilu Baskay, the younger brother of the slain Maoist action squad commander Sidhu Soren.) The Maoists responded to her initiatives by murdering two popular local leaders of the Trinamool Congress in Jhargram's rural hinterland in August and September 2011.

In November 2011 the remnant Maoist insurgency in Jangalmahal suffered a body blow when COBRA commandos tracked down and killed Kishenji, the revolutionary from Andhra Pradesh's Telangana region who headed the campaign to open a new front of the "people's war" in West Bengal. Kishenji was killed in a gun battle in a West Medinipur forest close to the interstate border with Jharkhand. A year later it emerged that his whereabouts had been given to the security forces by four local young men, all post-2008 Maoist recruits, who were "disillusioned with the movement and tired of the relentless killings." After Kishenji's death, young men in the former war zone who had left during the violence to work as laborers in other states trickled back to their villages. As one returnee put it: "I wouldn't say our lives are happy, but the menace is gone."[66] Across India, Maoist violence declined in relative terms during 2012.

It is absolutely correct that in urban India "Maoist sympathizers abstract from the profound deformities of the movement to engage in solidarity with it at any cost," by accepting at more or less face value the "almost mystical identity between the Maoists and 'the people' " that is the basis of the Maoists' self-image and propaganda. It is equally correct that it is "pure naïvete," or indeed much worse, to collapse India's Maoists and India's Adivasis into one category and believe that "the victory of the one would mean the emancipation of the other."[67]

Yet the third generation of India's Maoist movement survives and in its strongholds poses a real challenge to the Indian state. That is because the Maoist argument of how India's democracy has failed much of the *demos* is not a fiction. In the West Medinipur district, the Maoists are not extinct. By September 2011, a year after young Srikanta Mondal was killed in cold blood, the rebels were in headlong retreat in the zone. Their armed squads could no longer roam and strike at will, and the spate of killings of 2009–2010 gradually declined to a trickle. (In 2012 dozens of local Maoist militants, including women cadres, surrendered.) Maoist calls for *bandhs* (general strikes/shutdowns) and *abarodhs* (road blockades) paralyzed Jangalmahal in 2009 and 2010; by the second half of 2011 these calls were ignored by the populace. But another type of Maoist activity continued: the provision of basic health care, primary schooling, and other forms of assistance to communities in need.

Thus in Aguibani, a hamlet in the Gopiballavpur forests in the southern part of West Medinipur, a one-room health clinic with brick walls and an asbestos roof was chock-a-bloc in the autumn of 2011 with women and children from the area's villages. The clinic, open daily, is attended twice a week by qualified doctors and on other days by paramedics. The women and their children, including infants, receive free treatment and medicines, courtesy of "the movement." The facility is a godsend for locals, who are mostly from the Mahato community, because the nearest government health care center—which opens erratically, is poorly staffed, and often does not have medicines for common illnesses—is a 10-mile walk away, and the hospital in Jhargram is 25 miles away. Meanwhile in Balarampur, a village in the Binpur area in the northwest of the district, two teachers from the movement provided free after-school tuition to Adivasi children in the village's primary school building, their services warmly appreciated because the regular teachers are of poor quality and the children cannot get help at home because most parents are illiterate. And in Bandarboni, the miserably poor village inhabited by the Shabar tribe, a work team organized by the movement had built an embankment to prevent the swollen monsoon waters of the Kangsabati River from flooding the residents' hovels, something never done at government initiative.[68]

The Future

The leaders of India's contemporary Maoist insurrection appear to be convinced of the absolute correctness of their path and their solution. A May 2011 statement of the Central Committee of the Communist Party of India (Maoist), which called on "the people of the world to condemn the brutal murder of Osama bin Laden . . . [by the] warmonger, butcher and bloodthirsty Obama," added: "CPI (Maoist) firmly reiterates that Marxism-Leninism-Maoism is the only ideology that can end all kinds of exploitation and oppression" and "achieve the complete liberation" of "nations and peoples crushed under tyrants, bourgeois dictatorships going by the name of 'democracies,' and imperialism." The statement declared that "the upsurges in the Arab world including the struggle of the Palestinian people . . . would go nowhere unless they get consolidated into People's Wars against imperialism, feudalism and comprador-bureaucratic capitalism."[69]

In July 2009 the Central Committee of the Communist Party of India (Maoist) published a long "open letter" addressed to the leadership of the United Communist Party of Nepal-Maoist. Nepal's Maoists waged an insurgency for a decade starting in 1996 and were regarded as a sister party by the Indian Maoists throughout that time. The letter, formally couched as an appeal, reads like a denunciation in a "people's court." The nub of the complaint is that Nepal's Maoist movement, "instead of adhering to the Marxist-Leninist understanding on the need to smash the old state and establish the proletarian state, and advance towards the radical transformation of society . . . [eventually] chose to reform the existing state through an elected constituent assembly and a bourgeois-democratic republic. It is indeed a great tragedy that it has come to this position in spite of having had de facto power in most of the countryside." The letter asserted that "by abandoning the base areas, disarming the people's army, discarding the path of PPW [protracted people's war]

and adopting the parliamentary path," Nepal's Maoists had taken "a political line which is against the basic tenets of M-L-M . . . in essence nothing but a right-opportunist and revisionist line." Moreover, the change of
course had not been justified in tactical terms: "the most objectionable
part is your projection of these tactics as a theoretically developed position that you think should be the model for revolutions in the twenty-
first century." The letter called on Nepal's Maoists to remember "the
slogans of the Great Proletarian Cultural Revolution: fight self, refute
revisionism, practice Marxism." It does not seem to have occurred to the
letter's authors that the missive might be viewed by Nepal's Maoists as
arrogant, "big brother" interference in their affairs, a sensitive issue for
many Nepalese vis-à-vis India.[70]

The top leader of India's Maoist insurrection, Ganapati, asserted in
late 2009 that "the present stage of strategic defense [of the people's war]
will last for some time. It is difficult to predict how long it will take to
pass this stage and go to the stage of strategic equilibrium or strategic
stalemate."[71] It was wise of him to not hazard a guess (although other
Maoist leaders have expressed hope that the struggle will move into the
final phase of "strategic offensive" by the middle of the century and the
revolution will reach fruition around 2060).

India's Maoist revolutionaries of the early twenty-first century are
little more than a loose, possibly unstable federation of regional movements that emerged in some parts of the country during the 1980s and
1990s. The leadership of the movement that aspires to transform India
into a "people's democracy" is not remotely representative of the vast
diversity of India's society. Nearly one-half of the Central Committee of
the Communist Party of India (Maoist), about 15 of approximately 32
members, are from one of India's 650 districts: Karimnagar in Andhra
Pradesh's Telangana region, the cradle of second-generation Maoist militancy in that southern state. Ganapati, who is in his sixties, is also from
this district (as was P. V. Narasimha Rao, who was India's prime minister
from 1991 to 1996 and unshackled the nation's economy from state control).[72] There are just three or four Adivasis on the central committee,
and very few women. There are signs that the domination of Andhra
militants is causing friction and regional fissures within the movement,
for example with Oriya cadres in Orissa. (In August 2012 the top Maoist
leader there, an ethnic Oriya, was expelled from the party.) Intra-regional
fissures are appearing as well, with lethal consequences. In March 2013,
10 Maoist cadres including a senior commander were killed in a clash
near Jharkhand's border with Bihar with members of a breakaway faction that has links with the Jharkhand police.

While the course of history is, as Ganapati recognizes, "difficult to predict," it is possible that this millenarian movement will wither away over time, and long before the Indian democratic republic reaches its centennial milestone around the middle of the twenty-first century. In that event, the movement should be remembered for its one positive contribution—the role it played in the early twenty-first century in foregrounding poverty as the central problem and challenge for India's democracy.

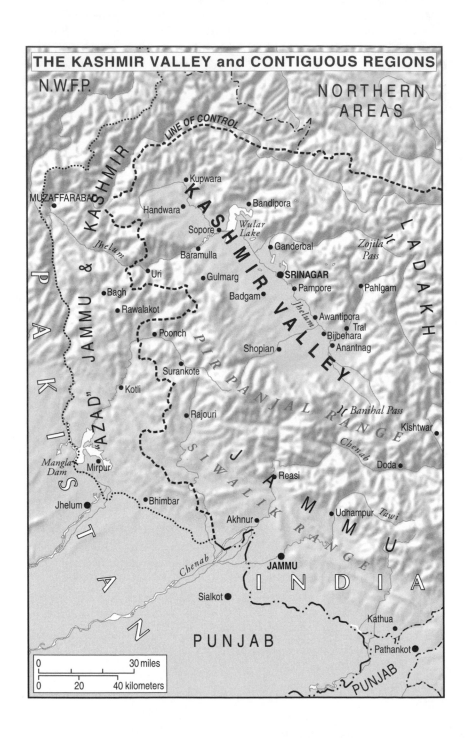

THE KASHMIR VALLEY and CONTIGUOUS REGIONS

N.W.F.P.

NORTHERN AREAS

LINE OF CONTROL

K A S H M I R

MUZAFFARABAD

KASHMIR VALLEY

• Kupwara

Handwara •

• Bandipora

Sopore •

Wular Lake

• Ganderbal

Zojila Pass

L A D A K H

Baramulla •

Jhelum

• Uri

• Gulmarg

SRINAGAR

• Pampore

• Pahlgam

J A M M U   &

• Bagh

• Rawalakot

Badgam •

Jhelum

• Awantipora

• Tral

P A K I S T A N

"A Z A D"

• Poonch

P I R   P A N J A L   R A N G E

Shopian •

Bijbehara •

• Anantnag

• Surankote

• Kotli

• Rajouri

S I W A L I K   R A N G E

Banihal Pass

Kishtwar •

Chenab

Doda •

Mangla Dam

• Mirpur

J A M M U

• Reasi

Jhelum •

• Bhimbar

Akhnur •

R A N G E

• Udhampur

Tawi

Chenab

JAMMU

I N D I A

Sialkot •

Kathua •

P U N J A B

Pathankot •

PUNJAB

0 ———————— 30 miles

0 —— 20 —— 40 kilometers

CHAPTER FIVE

The Kashmir Question

IN THE early evening of Friday, June 11, 2010, Tufail Ahmad Mattoo, 17, was walking home in Srinagar, the capital city of the Kashmir Valley. In the final year of secondary school, he had a busy schedule. He had just finished a session at a coaching center for a medical school entrance examination.

The walk home through Srinagar's bustling streets that summer evening would be Tufail's last. At Rajouri Kadal, a congested locality in the old city of Srinagar that is known for wildcat demonstrations by groups of youths who suddenly emerge from lanes and by-lanes to confront patrols of the Jammu & Kashmir police and the Indian Union government's Central Reserve Police Force, tasked with keeping order in restive neighborhoods, Tufail was caught up in such a fracas. The detachment of the J&K state police fired tear-gas shells to disperse their adversaries. One shell hit Tufail's head as it exploded. The impact split the boy's skull open, and his brain spilled out. He died instantly.

Tufail's death ignited a summer of rage in the Kashmir Valley. Over the next three and a half months, until late September, the Kashmir Valley was convulsed by stone-pelting protests as tens of thousands of people, predominantly teenage boys and young men in their twenties, confronted the state police and the CRPF across the Valley day after day, week after week. When the extraordinary eruption of public disorder subsided in the autumn, about 120 protesters were dead, shot by the police and the CRPF and occasionally by Indian army personnel. About 1,500 stone-throwers sustained serious injuries, and several hundred police and CRPF personnel were also injured. The vast majority of the dead and seriously injured stone-throwers were males aged between 15 and 30—that is, persons who had been children, infants, or unborn when the Kashmir Valley had descended into a maelstrom of violence 20 years earlier, in 1990, when an insurgency and uprising against Indian rule marked the beginning of a brutal conflict that lasted a decade and a half before subsiding.

Tufail Mattoo's family, middle-class people, with no strong political beliefs, wished their son to be buried in a family graveyard plot. But that was not to be. On June 12, 2010, Tufail's body was carried in a procession of thousands chanting slogans for *azaadi* (freedom) from India through Srinagar and buried in the "martyrs' graveyard" in the old city's Eidgah neighborhood, where a few thousand slain insurgents and other political activists have been laid to rest since 1990. The crowds fought pitched and running battles with the police and the CRPF before, during, and after the funeral. The stone-throwers' uprising sparked by Tufail's death spread and intensified over the next three months, and its fury, reported worldwide by international media and daily, often in graphic detail, by Indian television channels and newspapers, shocked India's political establishment and urban middle class, who had come to believe that a steep decline in insurgency since 2004 meant that "normalcy" had returned to Kashmir. The eruption subsided in the autumn, worn down by severe restrictions on public assembly and freedom of movement. But it had shown that a political problem still existed in the Kashmir Valley and that a new generation of its youth were as aggrieved with Indian authority as the generation that had produced thousands of Kalashnikov-wielding militants during the first half of the 1990s.

Tufail Mattoo's family, neighbors, friends, and teachers all recalled his most endearing trait: his gentleness. "What a polite boy he was," a woman neighbor said sotto voce. Indeed, photographs of Tufail taken at the Srinagar schools where he studied—the Little Angels' School, where he did elementary schooling, the Radiant Public School, where he did middle schooling and finished tenth grade, and the Government Higher Secondary School, where he was a twelfth-grader when he died—all show a slightly built boy with sensitivity writ large on his face. "Tufail was an extremely gentle boy," the headmaster of Radiant Public School recalled. "There were 120 students in that [tenth grade] class in 2008, and Tufail was the most polite one. All I can say is that his gentleness made him very different from other students."

Tufail's parents were too shattered to engage with the avalanche of public and media attention, but an uncle who flew in from Oman to attend his last rites recalled Tufail's compassion for the less fortunate.

Three months before his death Tufail bought a jacket, which he wore for a couple of days, until he happened to walk past a boy of the same age shivering in the winter cold in Amira Kadal, in the heart of downtown Srinagar. "He took off the jacket and handed it to the boy," the uncle remembered; "I just watched him." A schoolmate confirmed that Tufail had "some sort of obsession with the needy. Whenever he spotted a person in need, he would try to help." Tufail's interests were "playing cricket, reading books and driving." His family had ordered a car as his eighteenth birthday present. This likeable teenager from a middle-class family might have made a fine doctor, had he passed that entrance examination. Instead he will be remembered as Shaheed (Martyr) Tufail Ahmad Mattoo, a notable name in Kashmir's pantheon of "martyrs."[1]

The Kashmir question is usually viewed through the lens of the international dispute over the territory's ownership between India and Pakistan, which has existed since 1947. This perspective necessarily foregrounds the religious dimension and the Hindu-Muslim conflict that led to the subcontinent's partition in 1947. The Indian standpoint is that the avowedly secular Indian Union needs the Indian state of J&K, the only one of the Union's 28 states that has a majority of Muslims in its population—about two-thirds—to be complete. This standpoint is contested by the Pakistani claim that as a Muslim-majority territory that is more territorially contiguous to Pakistan than to India, most, if not all, of the disputed entity ought to belong to Pakistan, an explicitly Muslim nation-state. These competing ideological claims have produced diametrically opposed positions on the sovereignty dispute. The Indian position is that the whole of the disputed territory is an "integral part" *(atut ang)* of India and emphasizes the legal fact that the last ruler of the princely state of Jammu and Kashmir acceded his domain to India in October 1947. In this view the parts of the former princely state that have been under Pakistan's control since the end of the first India-Pakistan war over Kashmir in January 1949 rightfully belong to India, although in practice Indian governments since the mid-1950s have been content with the territorial status quo, as about three-quarters of the population of the disputed entity live on the Indian side of the de facto border, known as the Ceasefire Line until 1972 and the Line of Control since then, that divides the former princely state between the two countries. The typical Pakistani view is that the territorial status quo is a grave injustice to Pakistan as well as to the people living under Indian jurisdiction, who have not had the opportunity to choose whether to be part of India or Pakistan. (A United Nations–supervised referendum, or plebiscite, was to settle the sovereignty dispute in the early 1950s, and India and Pakistan blame each other for its nonoccurrence.) In Pakistani nationalist rhetoric, the former princely state is Pakistan's "jugular vein" *(shah rug)*, most of which has been usurped by India.

The typical Pakistani view of the Kashmir question as a case of Muslims oppressed in and by Hindu-majority India has a mirror-image counterpart in India: that a perennial problem exists in India's only Muslim-majority state because the state's Muslims, or a large proportion thereof, have always been and continue to be congenitally disloyal to the ideal of the secular Indian nation-state and are a fifth column for Pakistan. Thus, this story goes, it is no wonder that they are the perpetual malcontents of Indian democracy and troublemakers who waged an armed revolt from 1990 and have persisted after the decline of the insurgency in sporadically expressing their disloyalty through other means, such as the mass rioting of 2010.

This reification of religion and religious difference is grossly misleading. The violence that engulfed the Indian state of J&K through the 1990s and well into the first decade of the new century was not due to the fact that the majority of the state's people had a religious faith that was at once different from the majority of other citizens of India and the same as that of the vast majority of Pakistan's population. The insurgency against Indian authority was rooted instead in the gradual radicalization, over a period of four decades from the 1950s through the end of the 1980s, of a distinct *regional* identity and political tradition specific to the Kashmir Valley. Religion has been and continues to be an important constitutive element of this regional identity, not least because the Kashmir Valley is an overwhelmingly Muslim region, and appeals couched in religious idioms have figured prominently in political struggles and mobilizations since the beginnings of mass-based politics in the Valley in the early 1930s.

Yet the regional identity of the Kashmir Valley, like all the regional identities evolved over historical time that together make up the rich and diverse social mosaic of contemporary India, is not one-dimensional but complex and multifaceted. It draws on deep wellsprings of a common culture shaped over centuries, in which a language-based heritage is a vital constitutive element. Kashmiri, a Dardic variant of the Indo-Aryan family of languages that retains Sanskritic features from the pre-Islamic era in Kashmir, is the native tongue of the vast majority of the Valley's people. A religious faith rooted in a particular Kashmiri form of Islam is another such element.

The regional identity of the Kashmir Valley is *not* qualitatively different from numerous other regional identities that are quite at peace in and with the Indian Union. That the Kashmir Valley is not at such peace is because the Valley's people were continuously, and eventually deeply, alienated from the Indian Union due to authoritarian control and intervention imposed on them by the Center (New Delhi). As a result, the Indian state of J&K, and particularly the Kashmir Valley, where the majority of the state's population lives, was denied the democratic and quasi-federal development that became the norm, and the fundamental source of strength, of the Indian Union. This *post*-1947 history explains why the Kashmir Valley is the Achilles' heel of India's democracy in the early twenty-first century: a weak spot that tarnishes an otherwise vibrant democracy that is today unmistakably evolving as a federation of distinct and diverse regional polities.

This chapter focuses primarily on the Kashmir Valley, a region of about 7.5 million people. I give less attention to, though I do not ignore, the other two regions of the Indian state of Jammu & Kashmir—the Jammu region of about 5.5 million people, which lies south of the Valley and whose social composition and political dynamics are different from the Valley's, and the Ladakh region, a sparsely populated mountain desert of 300,000 people that lies northeast of the Valley. Likewise, I refer only when necessary to the two regions of the former princely state that lie across the Line of Control, have a total population of under 5 million, and are referred to as "Pakistan-occupied Kashmir" in India: "Azad" (Free) J&K, a long sliver of territory comprising mainly western Jammu districts whose cultural character is close to contiguous areas of Pakistan's Punjab province, and Gilgit and Baltistan to its north and northeast, a vast and sparsely populated high-altitude wilderness similar to Ladakh and referred to in Pakistan as the Northern Areas.

A Regional Identity

Walter R. Lawrence was a British official who was deputed to the Kashmir Valley as "settlement commissioner" in 1889. His job was to reform the land revenue system of this region of the princely state of Jammu and Kashmir, which had been established in 1846 as a vassal principality of the British colonial power, ruled by a Hindu dynasty originally from the Jammu region. When the British departed India in 1947, there were about 562 such principalities, covering 45 percent of the subcontinent's land area, governed by an assemblage of Hindu, Muslim, and Sikh vassal rulers. This extraordinary network developed through the nineteenth century formed the pillar of the British practice of "indirect rule" in India. Jammu and Kashmir was one of the largest princely states in territory and population, along with Hyderabad in the south (where, in a mirror image of Jammu and Kashmir, a Muslim dynasty and ruling elite presided over a subject population of which Hindus comprised the large majority).

Walter Lawrence spent six years in the Kashmir Valley and in 1895 published his book *The Valley of Kashmir.* He wrote: "if one looks at the map of the territories of His Highness the Maharaja of Jammu and Kashmir, one sees a white footprint set in a mass of black mountains. This is the valley of Kashmir, known to its inhabitants as *Kashir.* Perched securely among the Himalayas at an average height of about 6,000 feet above the sea, it is about 84 miles in length and 20 to 25 miles in breadth. North, east and west, range after range of mountains guard the valley from the outer world, while in the south it is cut off from the Panjab by rocky barriers 50 to 75 miles in width." The Valley's population was then 814,241, of whom "52,576 are Hindus, 4,092 are Sikhs, and the rest are Musalmans, who thus form over 93 percent."[2]

The Valley of "Kashir" has an ancient lineage as a cultural and political unit. In the eighth century Lalitaditya, the king of Kashmir, built an imperial domain centered on the Valley that encompassed a swathe of the plains of northern India and parts of Tibet, Afghanistan, and Central Asia. An epic chronicle of Kashmir from antiquity to the eleventh century was composed around 1149 by Kalhana, the son of a minister in the royal court. Written in Sanskrit, the classical language of pre-Islamic India, the chronicle is called *Rajatarangini* (The flow of kings) and has 7,826 verses divided into eight books. *Rajatarangini* was translated into English in 1900 by Marc Aurel Stein, a British explorer and scholar, as "A Chronicle of the Kings of Kashmir."[3]

Islam arrived in the Kashmir Valley in the fourteenth century and spread rapidly. The conversion of all but a tiny fraction of the population from Hinduism was due to the proselytizing of wandering Sufi mystics. A crucial figure was Mir Sayyid Ali Hamadani, a Persian Sufi from Hamedan in western Iran. Hamadani, known in Kashmir as Shah Hamdan, made three visits to the Valley during the 1370s and 1380s with hundreds of disciples, many of whom settled in Kashmir. A mosque commemorating him, the Khanqah-e-Maula, was built in Srinagar in the 1390s on the bank of the Jhelum River. It still stands on the original site in an imposing eighteenth-century version.

Kashmir's Sufi heritage is, however, identified above all with an indigenous saintly figure, Sheikh Nooruddin Noorani. This mystic, also known among Muslims and non-Muslims in the Valley by the Sanskritic (and Hindu-sounding) name Nund Rishi (Nund the Saint), was born around

1377 in a village south of Srinagar and lived until about 1440. His life was deeply influenced by Lalleshwari (c. 1320–1392), a woman mystic of the Hindu Shaivite sect, which was influential in Kashmir at the time; its followers worship the deity Shiva. Lalleshwari, known as Lal Ded in the Valley and venerated as a saint, expressed her spirituality through poetry composed as couplets in the Kashmiri language. She can be regarded as the founder of the Kashmiri literary tradition. Her influence on Sheikh Noorani was so great that he has been referred to as a "Muslim Shaivite" who "translated Islam into Kashmir's spiritual and cultural idiom."[4] He could be called the Kashmir Valley's patron saint and is referred to as Alamdar-e-Kashmir (The Standard-Bearer of Kashmir). His mausoleum-shrine is in Charar-e-Sharief, a small town about 20 miles southwest of Srinagar. In 1995 the shrine and most of the town were razed by fire during a gun-battle between Indian army troops and insurgents who had holed up in the holy premises, sparking anguish in the Valley. The shrine has been reconstructed and continues to be a center of pilgrimage for Kashmiri Muslims as well as the Valley's Hindus and Sikhs.

Sheikh Noorani's syncretistic philosophy set the tone of Islamic belief and practice in the Kashmir Valley, and the specifically regional variant of Sufism he pioneered is the dominant religious tradition at the popular level in the Valley to this day. One of those influenced by his preaching was Zain-ul-Abidin, the greatest of Kashmir's indigenous medieval rulers *(sultans)*, who reigned from about 1423 to 1474. A square in the center of Srinagar, Badshah Chowk, is named after Zain-ul-Abidin, who is known as Badshah (Great Ruler). He reversed the intolerant policies of his father, Sultan Sikandar, who had persecuted Hindus, especially Brahmins who would not convert, and vandalized ancient Hindu and Buddhist monuments. The son reinstated religious tolerance, got Hindus who had fled the Valley to return by abolishing the *jiziya* (a tax on non-Muslims), restored grants paid to learned Brahmins, and had Kalhana's *Rajatarangini* translated into Persian.

The legacy of Nund Rishi and Zain-ul-Abidin is writ large six centuries later in the everyday practice of the dominant faith in the Kashmir Valley. The towns and villages are full of *ziarats,* shrines dedicated to Sufi saints, some of whom are women. These "Muslim saints are worshipped like Hindu gods and godlings." Relic worship, which has its roots in Buddhism, was influential in pre-Islamic Kashmir although persecuted by some of the later Hindu monarchs.[5] It endures most famously in the gleaming-white Hazratbal shrine on the outskirts of Srinagar, where a hair believed to be from the head of the Prophet Mohammad is preserved. The Kashmiri literary tradition pioneered by Lal Ded has also found illustrious exponents, from the late sixteenth-century female singer and poet Habba Khatun, whose compositions are suffused with longing and loss, to the innovative twentieth-century poet Ghulam Ahmad Mahjoor.[6]

A narrative of victimhood prevalent in the Kashmir Valley stresses a history of subjugation going back over four centuries to 1586, when the Valley was annexed by the Mughal Empire, which ruled from Delhi. The Mughal emperors' main interest in the Valley was as a summer resort where they repaired to escape the heat and dust of the plains. During the first half of the seventeenth century the Mughals laid out beautiful gardens overlooking Srinagar's Dal Lake that are preserved to this day. By the middle of the eighteenth century the Mughal Empire was in advanced decline. In 1752 marauders from Afghanistan led by a warrior-king of the Pashtun Durrani tribe conquered the Valley. Afghan rule lasted until 1819, when forces loyal to Ranjit Singh (1780–1839), a Sikh warlord, captured the Kashmir Valley. In the early nineteenth century Singh established an extensive kingdom across northwestern India that mostly covered large parts of the present-day Punjab and Khyber-Pakhtunkhwa (North-West Frontier Province) provinces of Pakistan, with its capital in Lahore, close to Pakistan's border with India.

The Princely State

The succession of conquerors and occupiers notwithstanding, the period and overlordship truly relevant to understanding the Kashmir Valley since 1947 is the princely state of Jammu and Kashmir created in 1846 under British tutelage and suzerainty. The founding ruler of the princely state was Gulab Singh (1792–1857), a warrior belonging to a Rajput (Jamwal) caste of the Dogra ethnic group, who live in large numbers now, as then, in the southern parts of the Jammu region. Gulab Singh rose to prominence as a commander in Ranjit Singh's army. After the Sikh monarch's death in 1839, his expansive kingdom began to disintegrate due to lack of leadership and internal feuding. Gulab Singh became an ally of the British—strictly speaking the East India Company, which moved to assume direct or indirect control over the huge and disparate areas of Ranjit Singh's domain. In return for Gulab Singh's collaboration, the British gave him the Kashmir Valley, a remote region they were not interested in directly administering and garrisoning. This was accomplished in 1846 under the Treaty of Amritsar. (Amritsar, a city in India's Punjab province, is close to the post-1947 India-Pakistan border, is a short distance from Lahore, and is famous for Sikhism's holiest shrine, the Golden Temple.)

The Treaty of Amritsar was preceded by the Treaty of Lahore, signed on March 9, 1846, between the British and an effete son of the valiant Ranjit Singh. A clause of this treaty ceded "perpetual sovereignty" over "the hill countries" of the Sikh kingdom, "including the provinces of Cashmere and Hazarah," to the British. A week later, on March 16, the Treaty of Amritsar was signed, which stipulated: "The British Government transfers and makes over, for ever, in independent possession, to Maharaja [Great King] Gulab Singh and the heirs male of his body, all the hilly or mountainous country . . . being part of the territories ceded to the British Government by the Lahore state." This meant above all the agriculturally fertile, naturally scenic and populous Valley of Kashmir, as well as the sparsely populated and rugged region of Gilgit to its northwest (Gilgit is part of Pakistan's "Northern Areas"). In return Gulab Singh paid the Company 75 lakh (7.5 million) rupees—a considerable sum in India even today but a real bargain for the territory and souls he acquired as subjects—acknowledged "the supremacy of the British Government," and agreed, "in token of such supremacy, to present annually to the British Government one horse, twelve perfect shawl goats of approved breed (six male and six female), and three pairs of Kashmir shawls."[7]

Gulab Singh already had control of the Jammu region, a mix of plains, foothills, and mountainous tracts, and had also acquired the vast and scantily populated high-altitude zones of Ladakh and Baltistan through military expeditions led by one of his colleagues. Thus the acquisition of the Kashmir Valley (and Gilgit) completed the territory of the new entity: the princely state of Jammu and Kashmir. C. E. Tyndale Biscoe, a British missionary who worked as an educator in the Kashmir Valley in the early twentieth century—one of Srinagar's best schools is named after him— noted the polyglot nature of the sprawling entity, a menagerie of diverse regions and communities, in a book published in 1922: "to write about the character of the Kashmiris is not easy, as the country of Kashmir, including the province of Jammu, is large and contains many races of people. Then again, these various countries included under the name of Kashmir are separated . . . by high mountain passes, so that the people of these various states differ considerably . . . in features, manner, customs, language, character and religion."[8]

The eternity promised by the British to Gulab Singh and his successors by the Treaty of Amritsar lasted 101 years, until 1947. After the founder's death in 1857, Ranbir Singh ruled until 1885, Pratap Singh until 1925, and Hari Singh, the last maharaja, held court until events in the autumn of 1947 literally imploded the princely state. The hundred-year reign of the tinpot monarchy appointed as subcontractors of the Raj was an unmitigated disaster for the peasantry of Muslim faith who made up the overwhelming majority of the Valley's population.

Walter Lawrence wrote: "when I first came to Kashmir in 1889, I found the people sullen, desperate and suspicious. They had been taught for many years that they were serfs without any rights. . . . Pages might be written by me on facts which have come under my personal observation, but it will suffice to say that the system of administration had degraded the people and taken all heart out of them." Lawrence was especially horrified by the practice of *begar*, forced labor with no compensation, routinely inflicted on the mass of peasant serfs. He was careful to absolve the ruler of personal culpability: "the peasants, one and all, attributed their miseries to the deputies through which the Maharajas ruled, and they have always recognized that their rulers were sympathetic and anxious to ensure their prosperity. But the officials of Kashmir would never allow their master to know the real condition of the people." Who were these venal officials? Lawrence was particularly critical of princely state officials belonging to the Kashmiri Pandit community, the tiny religious minority (4–5 percent) of Brahmin caste indigenous to the Valley:

> In a country where education has not yet made much progress it is only natural that the State should employ the Pandits, who at any rate can read and write. . . . They are a local agency, and as they have depended on office as a means of existence for many generations, it is just and expedient to employ them. Still it is to be regretted that the interests of the State and the people should have been entrusted to one class of men, and still more to be regretted that these men, the Pandits, should have systematically combined to defraud the State and to rob the people. . . . Though this generosity in the matter of official establishments was an enormous boon to the Pandit class, it was a curse and misfortune to the Musalmans of Kashmir. . . . I have no wish to condemn the Pandits. . . . But . . . it is necessary to grasp the fact that official morality has, generally speaking, been non-existent.[9]

Walter Lawrence was not the first outsider to be mortified by the abject circumstances of the vast majority of the Kashmir Valley's people under the princely state. In a book titled *Cashmere Misgovernment*, published from Calcutta in 1868, Robert Thorp wrote: "in no portion of the treaty made with Gulab Singh was the slightest provision made for the just or humane government of the people of Cashmere and others upon whom we forced a government which they detested."[10] Indeed, Lawrence was sent to Kashmir as part of a British attempt to reform governance after a famine devastated the Valley between 1877 and 1879, but the Raj's intervention had to wait until Ranbir Singh died in 1885 and was replaced by a relatively more pliable successor, Pratap Singh. In 1890

Colonel R. Parry Nisbet, the "resident" (term for the top British supervisor in princely states) in Jammu and Kashmir, wrote to his superiors that "Kashmir [should] no longer be governed solely to benefit the ruling family and the rapacious horde of Hindu officials and Pandits, but also for its people, the long suffering indigenous Muhammadans."[11]

That proved to be a forlorn hope. In his chronicle of Kashmir at the turn of the nineteenth and twentieth centuries, Lawrence trumpeted his efforts to improve the conditions of the peasantry of the Valley, but the high-minded reformism of the white man had practically no effect on the brutal realities of power and penury in the princely state. A similar effort in the 1930s, after popular resistance to the established order emerged, proved ineffectual with a regime incapable of reform. In 1929 Sir Albion Bannerji, a Bengali (and Christian) civil servant who served as the princely state's "foreign and political minister" in the late 1920s, resigned in disgust after two years. He explained to the Associated Press: "Jammu and Kashmir state is laboring under many disadvantages with a large Muhammedan population absolutely illiterate, laboring under poverty . . . in the villages and practically governed like dumb-driven cattle. There is no touch between the Government and the people, no suitable opportunity for representing grievances and the administrative machinery requires overhauling from top to bottom. . . . It has at present little or no sympathy with the people's wants and grievances."[12]

Tyndale Biscoe, fired by missionary zeal, was more optimistic. He wrote in 1922: "if we Britishers had to undergo what the Kashmiris have suffered, we might also have lost our manhood. But thank God, it has been otherwise with us and other Western nations, for to us instead has been given the opportunity of helping some of the weaker peoples of the world, the Kashmiri among them. May we ever be true to our trust. Gradually are the Kashmiris rising from slavery to manhood. . . . I trust they will become once more a brave people, as they were in the days of old when their own kings led them into battle."[13]

Biscoe's narrative is full of anecdotes of peasant-paupers living in conditions resembling slavery in the countryside of the Kashmir Valley, and the capital, Srinagar, which is set in a beautiful natural setting of lakes and mountains, appears as a fetid city inhabited largely by illiterate and wretched people. Indeed, in a book titled *Kashmir Then and Now,* published in 1924, Gawasha Nath Kaul, a Kashmiri Pandit, painted a Dickensian picture of Srinagar: beggars, thieves, and prostitutes abounded along with disease and filth, and "90 percent of Muslim houses [were] mortgaged to Hindu *sahukars* [moneylenders]." The overall situation was, according to Kaul, "frightful."[14] Until 1924, the Kashmiri historian

Mohammad Ishaq Khan writes, "there was not a single newspaper printed or published in the State of Jammu and Kashmir."[15] Until 1920 a death sentence was mandatory for a state subject who killed a cow, an act of sacrilege in Hindu orthodoxy; in 1920 this was reduced to 10 years in prison, and later to 7 years.

According to a census conducted in 1941, 77 percent of the princely state's inhabitants were Muslims, 20 percent were Hindus, and 3 percent others, mostly Sikhs. But local Muslims were barred from becoming officers in the princely state's military forces and were almost nonexistent in the civil administration. In 1941 Prem Nath Bazaz, one of a handful of Kashmiri Pandits who joined the popular movement for change that emerged during the 1930s and swept the Valley in the 1940s, wrote: "the poverty of the Muslim masses is appalling. Dressed in rags and barefoot, a Muslim peasant presents the appearance of a starving beggar. . . . Most are landless laborers, working as serfs for absentee landlords. . . . Rural indebtedness is staggering."[16]

This political regime and social order revolted Walter Lawrence, Albion Bannerji, and Tyndale Biscoe. But the challenge to it could not come from well-meaning outsiders. It had to arise from within the society. It did arise from 1931 onward, and its principal agent was Sheikh Mohammad Abdullah.

The Rise and Fall of Sheikh Abdullah

He was born in 1905 into a modestly off family in Soura, then a village near Srinagar and today a neighborhood of the city. The family were late converts to Islam; they were Brahmins until the late eighteenth century, when they were influenced by a saintly Sufi. From the late nineteenth century, conditions in the princely state led to significant migration of people from the Kashmir Valley to the neighboring Punjab province of "British"—as distinct from "princely"—India. In the 1920s an association of Kashmiri migrants formed in Lahore started offering scholarships to enable young Muslim males from the princely state to acquire higher education in institutions in "British" India. One beneficiary was Sheikh Abdullah, who graduated from Lahore's Islamia College and then earned a master's degree in chemistry in 1930 from the Aligarh Muslim University, situated in Aligarh, a town in the western part of postindependence India's Uttar Pradesh state. This university was founded in 1875 as the "Mohammedan Anglo-Oriental College" to provide the subcontinent's Muslims with access to modern, particularly Western, education. Abdullah returned to the Valley to work as a schoolteacher and in 1930 established the Reading Room Association in Srinagar, where a small number of educated young Muslim men gathered to discuss social issues. Physically a very tall man but with a gentle, sensitive face, he is the most important political leader the Kashmir Valley has ever produced.

The turning point came on July 13, 1931. The trial of a Muslim sparked a protest in downtown Srinagar that was fired on by the maharaja's police. He was charged with making public remarks in a mosque condemning the princely state's regime and inciting fellow Muslims to violence. The firing killed 22 demonstrators and triggered unprecedented disorder in the city. Rioters sacked a commercial quarter of Srinagar populated predominantly by Kashmiri Pandits and Hindu traders from the Punjab. Until then the absence of popular protest against the conditions prevailing in the Valley was attributed to "the exceptionally docile nature of the peasantry in the Vale," consistent with Tyndale Biscoe's theory of a people whose "manhood" had been crushed by oppression.[17] But in 1931 Albion Bannerji's "'dumb-driven cattle' raised the standard of revolt. The people were never to be cowed again by police action. The women joined the struggle and to them belongs the honor of facing cavalry charges [by the maharaja's police] in Srinagar's Maisuma bazaar."[18] Eight decades after the eruption of 1931, Maisuma, an old neighborhood in the historic center of Srinagar, has changed remarkably little. It is still a warren of wooden houses built in traditional Kashmiri style inhabited by working-class and lower-middle-class people. The tradition of political struggle has also continued. During the first half of the 1990s Maisuma was a stronghold of gun-wielding proindependence insurgents, and in recent years its winding streets teem with stone-throwing youths of the postinsurgency generation who emerge from alleys to confront J&K police and CRPF personnel.

The British government appointed a commission to inquire into grievances and suggest measures for redress. From the early 1930s popular politics, and resistance, grew in the Kashmir Valley, and the princely state's regime during its last two decades in power swam against ever stronger currents of the tide of history. Abdullah attracted attention as a fiery orator. Initially he was one leader among several of the All Jammu and Kashmir Muslim Conference (hereafter Muslim Conference), a political party formed in October 1932 to provide direction to the nascent mass movement. His rhetoric was pungent; according to a report by the regime's spies on a "seditious speech" by him in a village in 1933, he urged the crowd to "take revenge" and "turn out Hindus."[19]

By the late 1930s Abdullah's politics had evolved in a more mature, inclusive direction. In 1938, after internal debate and primarily at the initiative of Valley activists grouped around him, the Muslim Conference resolved to "end communalism by ceasing to think in terms of Muslims and non-Muslims" and invited "all Hindus and Sikhs who believe in the freedom of their country [Jammu and Kashmir] from the shackles of an irresponsible rule" to join the popular struggle.[20] The reasons for this mutation may have included the presence of a tiny handful of Pandits (and Sikhs) in the rising popular movement in the Valley and the growing influence of left-wing thinking among some of Abdullah's colleagues. A powerful underlying factor may have been the Valley's syncretistic Sufi heritage. In 1939 the Muslim Conference was formally renamed the All Jammu and Kashmir National Conference (JKNC) to reflect the shift. The transition was not unproblematic. In 1941 Muslim religious and social conservatives, mostly from the Jammu region but including anti-Abdullah elements in the Valley, broke away and revived the Muslim Conference. This faction was increasingly drawn to the campaign for Pakistan led by the All-India Muslim League and its leader Mohammad Ali Jinnah as the 1940s progressed. The call to Jammu and Kashmir's religious minorities to participate alongside Muslims in the popular struggle also evoked a poor response. In the Valley, the vast majority of Pandits remained aloof and were often hostile, and the few Pandits who did join achieved unusual political prominence precisely because of their deviant status in their own community.

Just as the movement for Pakistan—founded on a religion-based concept of nationhood and political self-determination—gained momentum in the subcontinent, the dominant tendency of the Kashmir Valley's popular movement, led by Abdullah, moved in the opposite ideological direction. In 1940 Jawaharlal Nehru, the Congress leader who would go on to be India's first prime minister from August 1947 until his death in May 1964, visited the Valley on Abdullah's invitation. Nehru had a familial connection with Kashmir, as his forebears were Kashmiri Pandits who had migrated from the Valley to the plains of northern India. He was also a man of socialistic and republican convictions whose natural sympathies lay with the struggle against despotic feudalism in Kashmir. In 1944 Jinnah visited the Kashmir Valley. While the Muslim Conference and the JKNC competed to organize a grand welcome for him, he chose to address the annual gathering of the former party and declared the Muslim Conference to be representative of "99 percent" of Jammu and Kashmir's Muslims.[21]

Later that year, in September 1944, the JKNC leadership met in the northern Valley town of Sopore and adopted "Naya [New] Kashmir," a detailed charter for a post-princely-state social and political order. In a diplomatic feint, this manifesto did not abolish the hereditary monarchy but reduced it to purely ceremonial status. Power would be vested in a legislature called the National Assembly, to be elected by universal adult franchise, and executive authority would be exercised by a cabinet responsible to that assembly. There would be decentralization of administration to districts, *tehsils* (subdivisions of districts), towns, and even the village level. Recognizing the multilingual character of Jammu and Kashmir, the manifesto designated Urdu the lingua franca of the future. (Kashmiri was the dominant tongue only in the Valley and some hilly areas of the Jammu region contiguous to the Valley inhabited by Kashmiri-speaking Muslims, and Dogri-speakers were largely concentrated in the Jammu plains). Kashmiri, Dogri, Punjabi, Hindi, Balti, and Dardi would all be "national languages."

The document's most significant section had to do with the transformation of the agrarian economy. The Naya Kashmir charter called for the abolition of parasitic landlordism without compensation, distribution of land among tillers, and the establishment of cooperative farms. This confirmed the leftist turn in the JKNC's politics and the presence of a sizable cohort of socialists and even communist (pro-Soviet) fellow travelers in the organization. (On taking control of Srinagar in late 1947, one of the party's first acts was to name the city's central square Lal Chowk, Red Square, after the Moscow original.) In 1945, after the end of World War II and the release of Congress leaders jailed by the British for anticolonial nationalist activities during the war, the JKNC's annual convention was attended by Nehru, as well as Maulana Abul Kalam Azad, Congress's most prominent Muslim figure, and Khan Abdul Ghaffar Khan (1890–1988), known as the Frontier Gandhi because of the mass popularity of his pacifist (and Congress-aligned) anticolonial movement among the Pathans (Pashtuns) of the North-West Frontier Province.

Despite the secular (and socialist) turn in the JKNC's line, the movement's mobilization strategy and its mass appeal among the Kashmir Valley's people continued be rooted in a *Muslim* idiom of politics, derived from and tailored to the Valley's *regional* culture, six centuries old, of Sufi-inspired Islam. The charismatic Abdullah's style personified this. His crowd-pulling prowess owed much to his ability to enthrall predominantly illiterate audiences by reciting beautifully from the holy Koran. During the 1940s his political rise was built on the control his followers managed to acquire over most of the Valley's mosques, and consequently their congregations, at the expense of religious preachers of the traditional variety. Asked toward the end of his life, in 1978, how he managed to outmaneuver and marginalize the traditional clergy *(mullahs)* he chuckled and replied: "By becoming a mullah myself."[22]

When Sheikh Abdullah launched a civil disobedience movement against the princely state's regime in May 1946, and led the resistance to an invasion of the Kashmir Valley from Pakistan in October–November 1947, his headquarters was in the Hazratbal shrine on the shores of Srinagar's Nageen Lake, revered by the Valley's people as the shrine housing a hair believed to be from the head of the Prophet Mohammad. (In 1990 control of Hazratbal passed to proindependence insurgents fighting Indian rule, until they were evicted in 1996 by Indian security forces after a bloody gun battle.) The general secretary of the JKNC party was a cleric, Maulana Mohammad Sayyid Masoodi, who doubled up as the editor of *Khidmat,* the party's paper. Masoodi, who was influential in Valley politics through the 1960s, was "highly respected by the people for the depth of his views and the sobriety of his judgment."[23] In December 1990, aged 87, he was shot dead in his home in Ganderbal, a town north of Srinagar, by gunmen from a pro-Pakistan Kashmiri insurgent group who were young enough to be his grandchildren.

The other pillar of the JKNC's strategy and mass appeal was the hope it held out to the craving for social emancipation among the Valley's mass of impoverished peasants, who lived and toiled in conditions of serfdom. The party's flag, depicting a plow, the peasant's essential implement, imprinted in yellow against a red background, signified the peasant base that constituted its bedrock support.

With World War II over and British withdrawal from India increasingly looking imminent, in April 1946, exactly 100 years after the establishment of the princely state, the JKNC launched the "Quit Kashmir" movement, a campaign of mass demonstrations and civil disobedience against the princely state's authorities. Abdullah declared: "the time has come to tear up the Treaty of Amritsar. . . . Sovereignty is not the birthright of Maharaja Hari Singh. Quit Kashmir is not a question of revolt. It is a matter of right."[24] The drive to replace the hereditary kingship and its autocratic regime with popular sovereignty had overtones of a decisive offensive of mobilized people's power, and it was modeled on the Quit India movement, which Congress launched against India's British Raj in August 1942, at a critical stage of World War II. The Quit India movement is a landmark episode in India's struggle for freedom. The movement spread like wildfire across (nonprincely) India, and (poorly) armed freedom fighters in some parts of the country were able to create "liberated zones." The movement was put down through mass arrests of Congress leaders, including almost the entire apex leadership, and of key organizers in different parts of the country, and continuing resistance was suppressed through brutal violence by the Raj's police and military forces against rank-and-file freedom fighters and the civilian populations supporting them in the strongholds of the movement. Jinnah's Muslim League, a key collaborator with the British government during World War II, derided the uprisings as "not directed for securing the independence of all constituent elements in the life of the country but to establish Hindu raj [rule] and [to] deal a death-blow to the Muslim goal of Pakistan." The Jammu and Kashmir Muslim Conference echoed this stance. Abdullah's JKNC, however, strongly condemned the repression unleashed by the colonial power.[25]

Of the regions of Jammu and Kashmir, the Quit Kashmir movement had by far the greatest impact in the JKNC's bastion, the Kashmir Valley. The princely state's authorities responded with large-scale arrests of the party's top leaders and key organizers across the Valley. Abdullah himself was promptly arrested and spent 16 months in prison until his release on 29 September 1947, a month and a half after the birth of two independent "Dominions" in the subcontinent, India and Pakistan. Some JKNC organizers managed to escape detention by going underground. Speaking in Lahore, the Jammu and Kashmir Muslim Conference's most prominent leader, Ghulam Abbas, a native of the Jammu region, derided the Quit Kashmir movement as "an agitation started at the behest of Hindu leaders." By June 1946 the movement wilted under intense repression, and the atrocities of the (overwhelmingly non-Muslim) police and military forces of the princely state "in the Valley caused tremendous commotion, leaving bitter memories of cruelties firmly implanted in the minds of the normally peaceful Kashmiris."[26] Thereafter a lull fraught with a sense of simmering crisis ensued in the Valley. This lasted until the autumn of 1947, when Jammu and Kashmir, and particularly the Kashmir Valley, emerged as the prime bone of contention between the newly independent states of India and Pakistan.

The hundreds of princely states were naturally an issue in the decolonization, amid partition, of the subcontinent. In July 1947 Lord Mountbatten, the last British viceroy of India, urged a gathering of princely rulers in Delhi to decide without delay, preferably before mid-August, whether to join India or Pakistan after evaluating two criteria: their territory's geographic embedding in or contiguity to India or Pakistan, and the wishes of their population of subjects.

This was reasonable advice, and on its basis the accession of the large majority of princely states to India and the rest to Pakistan was the inevitable outcome, as most princely states lay within the borders of India and had non-Muslim majorities. Problems arose with only two princely states, bounded by India with Muslim rulers and predominantly Hindu subjects. In Junagadh in western India, a small princely state that was later incorporated into the state of Gujarat formed in 1960, a Muslim ruler presiding over a population that was over 80 percent Hindu acceded his kingdom to Pakistan and then fled to Pakistan. In the princely state of Hyderabad in southern India, most of which would become part of the state of Andhra Pradesh in 1956, the Muslim ruler stalled for a year, amid mounting violence by his regime against a population that was 87 percent Hindu, until the Indian army was sent in and settled the matter in September 1948.

Mountbatten's common-sense formula could not resolve the status of Jammu and Kashmir, however. This princely state was contiguous to both India and Pakistan, although its contiguity to Pakistan, to its west and northwest, was more extensive than with India to the south and southeast. The princely state's transport, trading, and cultural links were also more extensive with western Punjab and the Frontier Province, which became part of Pakistan in 1947 (for example, the Jhelum Road, so called after the river, connecting Srinagar with Rawalpindi). The princely state's religious demographics, 77 percent Muslim, also counted at least superficially in favor of Pakistan. But the wishes of the population were not obvious, despite that demographic fact. This was primarily because the princely state's largest popularly based political movement, led by the JKNC with mass support in the Kashmir Valley and pockets of influence in the Jammu region, had developed a secularist and socialist orientation and was ideologically much closer to and more compatible with India's Congress party than Pakistan's Muslim League.

Jammu and Kashmir's last maharaja, Hari Singh, and his coterie of advisers were concerned above all with the preservation of the dynastic throne and privileges. On August 15, 1947, a day after Pakistan's birth, his regime concluded a "standstill agreement" with the government of Pakistan, normally a precursor to accession. This was a strange dalliance between the leaders of the new Muslim sovereign state on the subcontinent and a despotic regime that had systematically oppressed its Muslim majority for a century and whose police and military had committed atrocities against Muslims in the Kashmir Valley and elsewhere in the princely state in 1946 and the first half of 1947. But it was explicable. Hari Singh and his coterie calculated that their interests were more likely to be entertained by Pakistan's leaders than India's, who were known to hold princely rulers in contempt as British stooges and had friendly ties with the princely state's largest political opposition, the JKNC. Pakistan's leaders knew that though geographic contiguity and religious demographics favored their case, a legally valid accession would have to be signed by the princely ruler.

The dalliance steadily unraveled, and broke down in the first half of October 1947. It was derailed by developments on the ground. In spring 1947 a localized revolt against the maharaja's regime flared in the Jammu region's Poonch district, which is today bisected by the Line of Control between J&K and Pakistan's so-called "Azad" Kashmir. The rebellion was met with atrocities by the princely state's overwhelmingly non-Muslim security forces against the overwhelmingly Muslim population of Poonch but was not suppressed. Poonch, along with nearby west Punjab and Frontier Province districts, had been a prime recruiting ground for imperial Britain's Indian army, and of 71,667 men from the princely state who served in British forces during World War II, 60,402 were Poonchis. These demobilized soldiers put up fierce resistance to the princely state's forces. After mid-August the rebellion renewed, this time with a definite pro-Pakistan character. By the beginning of October the rebels gained control of almost all of Poonch, and on October 3, 1947, a collection of pro-Pakistan *sardars* (clan chiefs) of western Jammu districts—Poonch, Mirpur to its south, and Muzaffarabad to its north—proclaimed a provisional Azad (Free) Jammu and Kashmir government in Rawalpindi, Pakistan. On the same day, the maharaja's government cabled Pakistan's foreign ministry in Karachi, accusing the government of Pakistan of complicity in crossborder attacks being conducted along several hundred kilometers of the border between Pakistan's Punjab province and the Jammu region of the princely state, from Rawalpindi in the north to Sialkot in the south. On October 18 an even more acrimonious cable, which alleged that the government of Pakistan had imposed an economic blockade on Jammu and Kashmir in violation of its obligations under the "standstill agreement" of mid-August, signaled an irretrievable breakdown in relations.

The decisive chapter of the struggle for Jammu and Kashmir then unfolded. On October 21, 1947, a motorized armed force consisting mainly of Pashtun tribesmen entered Jammu and Kashmir from the Frontier Province's Hazara district, located north and northwest of the princely state. Although many were motivated by the prospect of loot and rape, they were "led by experienced military leaders familiar with the terrain and equipped with modern arms, [and] they poured down . . . at 5000-strong initially, with a fleet of transport vehicles numbering about 300 trucks."[27] After taking the town of Muzaffarabad, later the capital of Pakistan's "Azad Kashmir" region, they headed for the Kashmir Valley. Meeting almost no resistance from the princely state's forces, they seized

Baramulla, the largest town in the northwestern part of the Valley, just 20 miles by road from Srinagar. On October 24 the maharaja's administration sent an urgent message to New Delhi requesting immediate military assistance to repel the raiders.

Nehru and his colleague Vallabhbhai Patel (1875–1950)—a dour, conservative Congress leader from Gujarat who as India's home (interior) minister supervised the integration of princely states into India—were willing to oblige but correctly determined that intervention by Indian army troops without prior accession of Jammu and Kashmir to India might be regarded internationally as an Indian invasion of a neutral territory. Accordingly, on October 26 the last maharaja signed the formal "instrument of accession" to India, which made the princely state legally part of the Indian Union and ceded to the government in New Delhi jurisdiction over external defense, foreign affairs, and currency and communications. On October 27 Mountbatten, the governor-general of the Indian "Dominion," accepted the accession but noted that once the raiders were expelled and order restored, the accession should be ratified by "a reference to the people" of Jammu and Kashmir.

On the morning of October 27, the first Indian army units arrived in Srinagar by airlift, to a warm welcome from the leaders of the JKNC. They deployed immediately and found that units of the raiding force had penetrated the outskirts of Srinagar. Within a few days they also "discovered that they were dealing with an organized body of men armed with medium and light machine-guns and mortars," led by "commanders thoroughly conversant with modern tactics and use of ground" and supported by "considerable engineering skill."[28] More than a half century later, in the summer of 1999, the Indian army would face much the same situation in the mountainous Kargil district of the Ladakh region, where they were taken by surprise by Pakistani military units who had crossed the Line of Control during the winter months in a meticulously planned operation and occupied ridges and peaks on the Indian side of the Line.

The hostilities of late 1947 turned swiftly in favor of the Indians. Within a week the Indian units pushed back the raiders from the vicinity of Srinagar. Then, reinforced by armored cars that had arrived by road via the Banihal Pass, which connects the Kashmir Valley with the Jammu region, they went on the offensive. Baramulla was retaken on November 8, and Uri, a smaller town on the western edge of the Valley that has straddled the border between the Kashmir Valley and "Azad Kashmir" ever since, was taken on November 14. By the time the harsh Himalayan winter of 1947–1948 set in and fighting wound down, the raiders had been driven to the peripheries of the Kashmir Valley.

Two factors were crucial in this outcome. First, the Indian counteroffensive benefited enormously from the support of an auxiliary force—the JKNC organization in the Kashmir Valley. Thousands of volunteers enrolled in a "National Militia" that the JKNC quickly put together, and these locals were invaluable to the Indian campaign. Second, some of the raiders had committed atrocities as they advanced. Baramulla was pillaged, and the fighters who had come ostensibly to liberate their coreligionists perpetrated brutalities, particularly on women, there and in other northern Kashmir Valley towns such as Handwara. The terror unleashed in the name of liberation deeply unsettled the people in these areas, and their memories of savage executions and rapes would linger for several decades.

The leaders of Pakistan were furious at the turn of events. Kashmir, meaning above all the Valley, had been an integral part of the idea of Pakistan since the term "Pakistan" was coined by an Indian Muslim student at Cambridge University in 1933. (The K denoted Kashmir, the P Punjab, the S Sind, and the "tan" Baluchistan.) In late November 1947 Liaquat Ali Khan, Pakistan's prime minister, denounced the JKNC's leader: "Sheikh Abdullah has been a paid agent of Congress for two decades and with the exception of some gangsters he has purchased with Congress money, he has no following among the Muslim masses [of Kashmir]."[29] In fact, after his release from jail in late September, Abdullah had told a huge gathering on the premises of Srinagar's Hazratbal shrine on October 5 that the question of accession to India or Pakistan was secondary to the imperative of establishing a government legitimate in the eyes of the people. However, after the force from Pakistan entered the Valley, overran its northwestern areas, and approached Srinagar, he traveled to Delhi. He arrived there on the evening of October 25, and on October 26–27, when the maharaja's accession to India was sealed, he was staying at Prime Minister Nehru's residence. On October 27 he told the daily *Times of India* that the attack had to be resisted because failure would mean the coercive absorption of the Valley into Pakistan.

Abdullah could not have behaved otherwise in late 1947. The Valley was his home region and power base, and he had every reason to believe from experience that he would have no place in Jinnah's scheme of things if the Valley passed into Pakistan's control. A veteran political activist from the city of Jammu has written that the Valley's people were "outraged" by the Pakistani attempt to first secure accession by wooing the hated princely ruler and when that failed "to decide the issue by force." He argues that the deeply rooted regional identity of the Kashmir Valley, evolved over centuries and rekindled through political struggle in the 1930s and 1940s, "was obviously a misfit in the monolithic structure of Pakistan, which did not recognize any identity other than that based on religion. The federal-democratic and secular framework of India . . . promised a better guarantee for the defense and growth of Kashmiri identity."[30]

While the fighting temporarily subsided, the conflict was internationalized when in January 1948 the Indian government complained to the United Nations about Pakistani aggression on a territory that had acceded to India. In response, the UN Security Council established the United Nations Commission for India and Pakistan. In April 1948, as winter snows melted and hostilities resumed, the Security Council adopted a resolution that the Commission was "to proceed at once to the Indian subcontinent and there place its good offices . . . at the disposal of the Governments of India and Pakistan . . . both with respect to the restoration of peace and order and the holding of a plebiscite" to decide Jammu and Kashmir's final status. The reference to a plebiscite was consistent with the Indian stand at the time; on 2 November 1947 Nehru had announced his "pledge . . . not only to the people of Kashmir but to the world . . . [to] hold a referendum under international auspices such as the United Nations" to ascertain whether a majority of the erstwhile princely state's population favored India or Pakistan. He repeated this several times up to 1952. The April 1948 UN Security Council resolution called on the government of Pakistan to "secure the withdrawal" of the invading tribesmen and other nonresidents from the regions of the princely state under Pakistan's control, and once this was done the government of India was urged to reduce its forces in Jammu and Kashmir "progressively to the minimum strength required for the support of civil power."[31]

As in many bitter conflicts, events on the ground evolved very differently from the UN's high-minded intentions. Over the spring and summer of 1948, the Indian army, by now fighting the regular Pakistani army in what had become a war between the militaries of sovereign states, made further advances, retaking the strategic town of Rajouri in the Jammu region and consolidating gains in the Kashmir Valley. The final act of the first India-Pakistan war occurred in the autumn of 1948, when Pakistani forces made a thrust toward the Valley from the north, using the mountainous areas of Gilgit and Skardu as the base. The thrust was repulsed by Indian light tanks in a battle at the Zojila Pass, which connects the Valley with Ladakh. The Indians then took the western Ladakh towns of Dras and Kargil in November and secured the strategic road link between the Valley and the eastern Ladakh district of Leh, populated mainly by Buddhists of Tibetan stock. When a cease-fire came into effect on January 1, 1949, the Indians were in control of the bulk of the population and territory of the former princely state, including almost all of the Kashmir Valley—139,000 out of 223,000 square kilometers, about 63 percent. This is the territorial status quo that prevails to this day, with very minor changes from subsequent military conflicts, notably the third India-Pakistan war of December 1971. The UN-supervised plebiscite never materialized. Pakistanis see this as evidence of Indian duplicity; Indians argue that Pakistan failed to fulfill the first condition set out by the UN for holding the plebiscite, the withdrawal of Pakistani regular and irregular forces from the territory of the former princely state of Jammu and Kashmir.

The British official Walter Lawrence noted in 1895 that "the people of the valley [of Kashmir] . . . have retained their peculiar nationality unimpaired" despite three centuries of rule by outside powers: first the Mughal Empire, then the Durrani Afghans, succeeded by the Sikh monarchy of Ranjit Singh, and then the princely state of Jammu's Dogra elite. He attributed the stubborn resilience of the distinct regional identity and culture formed in the Valley in the late medieval era to "the isolation of Kashmir," its remote location. He did foresee, on the eve of the twentieth century, that this isolation would not last with the advent of modern communications. He could not have foreseen that within a half century the remote, isolated Kashmir Valley would become the crux of contention between the nationalisms of India and Pakistan. But he presciently warned that once this remote region and its historically insular people were no longer cocooned from the wider subcontinent, "the revolution which will follow the more rapid communication with India is one which will require wise guidance and most careful watching."[32]

Sheikh Mohammad Abdullah became the prime minister of the Indian state of J&K in March 1948 and governed it in the style of an uncrowned monarch until his fall from power in August 1953. He was at once the Valley's first indigenous "sultan" in nearly four centuries and, in retrospect, the first truly autonomous regional leader of the polity of postindependence India, with a well-knit party and significant mass base. He had thrown in his lot with India in clear preference to Pakistan, but due to his stature he did not see the relationship between New Delhi and his regime in dominant-subordinate terms. He felt that Srinagar could deal with Delhi on more or less equal terms.

The maharaja's accession limited New Delhi's jurisdiction over Jammu and Kashmir to three subjects: defense, foreign affairs, and communications. This was normal practice in accession agreements and usually did not preempt further integration of princely states into India (or Pakistan). Jammu and Kashmir was, however, an unusual case because of the international dispute and UN resolutions calling for a plebiscite and the presence of a mass-based political movement within, the JKNC. In October 1949 India's Constituent Assembly inserted Article 306A into India's Constitution, specifying that the Center's jurisdiction over Jammu and Kashmir (effectively the 63 percent of its territory on India's side of the Ceasefire Line) would remain limited to the three subjects specified in the original instrument of accession. After India shed "dominion" status and became the Republic of India on January 26, 1950, Article 306A became the basis for Article 370 of the Indian Constitution, which enshrined the same degree of autonomy for J&K in the Indian Union. This gave the Indian state of J&K a statutory degree of autonomy not enjoyed by any other unit of the Indian Union, an arrangement known as "asymmetric autonomy" or "asymmetric federalism" in comparative political science. Under Article 370, which remains in India's Constitution, India's Parliament can legislate even regarding the three categories of subjects assigned to the Center only "in consultation with the Government of Jammu and Kashmir state," and regarding other matters of governance on the Union List with "the final concurrence of the Jammu and Kashmir Assembly."

Sheikh Abdullah was adamant that this asymmetric autonomy was the sine qua non of J&K's membership of the Indian Union. He articulated this in an important address he gave on August 11, 1952, to J&K's Constituent Assembly, which had been constituted in November 1951 to frame a J&K state constitution, in itself unusual, because other Indian states do not have their own constitutions and the Republic of India's 1950 Constitution is supreme across the country. He noted that his priority was to ensure "maximum autonomy for the local organs of state power, while discharging obligations as a unit of the [Indian] Union." He pointedly added: "I would like to make it clear that any suggestion of arbitrarily altering this basis of our relationship with India would not only constitute a breach of the spirit and letter of the [Indian] Constitution, but might invite serious consequences for the harmonious association of our state with India." This language—especially the use of words like "relationship" and "association"—was different from a flowery speech he had made to the first session of the Assembly, nine months earlier, in November 1951: "the real character of a state is revealed in its Constitution. The Indian Constitution has set before the country the goal of secular democracy based on justice, freedom and equality for all without distinction. . . . The national movement in our State naturally gravitates towards these principles. . . . This affinity in political principles, as well as past associations and our common path of suffering in the cause of freedom, must be weighed properly while deciding the future of the

State." The last phrase is a reference to the UN-administered plebiscite, then a live proposition, and can be read as entirely supportive of India's position on Kashmir. In the same speech Abdullah criticized Pakistan's failure to enact a constitution and ridiculed Pakistan, especially its (then) western half, as a den of feudal landlords. He also dismissed the idea of independence for part or all of the former princely state of Jammu and Kashmir as utopian.[33]

In his August 1952 speech in Srinagar, Abdullah was reporting the outcome of talks on the autonomy issue held in Delhi in June and July between a J&K delegation led by him and Indian government officials headed by Nehru. During these talks, the J&K team stuck strongly to the "maximum autonomy" position. They blocked the other side's proposals for J&K's financial and fiscal integration with the Indian Union, rejected a suggestion to extend the fundamental rights provisions of the Indian constitution to J&K, and turned down a proposal to make India's Supreme Court the ultimate court of appeal for civil and criminal cases that came up before J&K courts (as is normal for Indian states). They made a few concessions, agreeing to fly India's national flag in the "supremely distinctive" position alongside the J&K state flag in J&K, and they agreed to the Indian Supreme Court's arbitration in the event of disputes between the state and the Center or with another state of the Indian Union. The talks resulted in an unwritten—and as it turned out within a year, tenuous—modus vivendi that was separately reported by the leaders to their respective legislatures. Nehru's comments to India's Parliament, elected a few months earlier in the country's first Lok Sabha election, had a tone of weary resignation; he said that he wanted "no forced unions," and if J&K were to decide "to part company with us, they can go their way and we shall go our way."[34]

Abdullah's stance on "maximum autonomy" was not an altruistic defense of the identity of his base—meaning essentially the Valley. He had a compelling personal motive: keeping maximum power in his own hands. This drive for absolute power was revealed by the manner in which the J&K Constituent Assembly was "elected" in late 1951. It was to have 75 members—43 from the Kashmir Valley, 30 from the Jammu region, and two from Ladakh. (In a token gesture, a further 25 seats were kept vacant for representatives of the regions across the Ceasefire Line.) Of the 45 seats allotted to the Valley and Ladakh, JKNC candidates were declared elected "unopposed" to 43 seats one week before the election date. In the two remaining seats, non-JKNC candidates who filed papers "withdrew under pressure subsequently," according to Josef Korbel of the UN Commission for India and Pakistan. In the Jammu region's 30 seats, the Praja Parishad (Subjects' Forum), a Hindu organization led by former officials of the maharaja's administration and landlords dispossessed by the Abdullah regime's radical land reforms (described below), decided to contest 28 seats. Thirteen of its candidates were arbitrarily disqualified, and the Parishad then withdrew the rest of its candidates in protest and in anticipation of a completely rigged election that it would be pointless to enter. The Parishad would have won a few seats in Hindu-dominated southern and southeastern Jammu districts if allowed to run for them. Two other non-JKNC candidates standing in the Jammu region's remaining two seats also pulled out. In the Jammu region's Muslim-majority areas and in the Valley, almost all anti-Abdullah leaders owing allegiance to the Muslim Conference were in exile across the Ceasefire Line, but the JKNC's 100 percent sweep was still a farce.

The 75-seat Constituent Assembly thus consisted entirely of JKNC members. In this scheme of things, maximum autonomy for J&K translated into maximum power for Abdullah and his men. New Delhi turned a blind eye. Nehru reportedly told a political activist from Jammu that while Abdullah's suppression of all opposition—including dissenting members of the JKNC—was undemocratic, because "India's Kashmir policy revolved around Abdullah, nothing should be done to weaken him."[35] Between 1948 and 1953, only one slogan could be heard in the Kashmir Valley: "One Leader, One Party, One Program!" (referring to Abdullah, the JKNC, and their "Naya [New] Kashmir" agenda of 1944, respectively).

Abdullah's confidence, even brazenness, was based on one political fact: the mass support and indeed adulation he enjoyed in the Kashmir Valley. He had already achieved near-iconic status among the Valley's people by 1947 for his leadership of the struggle against feudal autocracy. (His top lieutenants, Bakshi Ghulam Mohammed, Mirza Afzal Beg, G. M. Sadiq, Maulana Masoodi, Ghulam Mohiuddin Karra, and Syed Mir Qasim, had also become household names there.) On July 13, 1950, the anniversary of the bloody protest in Srinagar in 1931, Abdullah's regime "introduced the most sweeping land reform in the entire subcontinent." Up to then, almost all of J&K's arable area of 2.2 million acres was owned by 396 big landlords and 2,347 middling landlords, "who rented to peasants under medieval conditions of exploitation."[36] In the Valley, Kashmiri Pandits, under 5 percent of the Valley's population, owned over 30 percent of the land. (The Abdullah regime softened the blow for the Pandits by allowing them to retain their fruit orchards and reserved 10 percent of state government jobs for them, a share several times the Pandit community's proportion of the J&K population.)[37] Between 1950 and 1952, 700,000 landless peasants in J&K became peasant-proprietors, as over a million acres of expropriated land were transferred to them. The majority of the beneficiaries were Muslims in the Valley, but one-third were low-caste Hindu cultivators in the Jammu region. By the early 1960s there were 2.8 million smallholding peasant households in the state.

The transformation of rural J&K had far-reaching consequences. It elevated Abdullah to nearly divine stature among the Kashmir Valley's peasantry, a lay addition to the Valley's pantheon of Sufi saints. Already literally lionized by his followers as Sher-e-Kashmir (The Lion of Kashmir), he now became the Valley's Baba-e-Qaum (Father of the Nation). In the mid-1950s Daniel Thorner, a scholar of agrarian affairs, visited the Valley. He found that despite "defects in implementation, many tillers have become landowners and some land has even gone to the landless. The peasantry of the Valley were not long ago fearful and submissive. Nobody who has spent time with Kashmiri villagers will say the same today."[38]

The land reforms catalyzed an intense opposition to the Abdullah regime in the Hindu-dominated southern districts of the Jammu region. The Praja Parishad had been formed in late 1947 at the initiative of former officials in the princely state's administration based in the city of Jammu, J&K's second largest city after Srinagar and the state's winter capital. These elements, smarting at their displacement from power by a new ruling elite of Valley Muslims, began agitating against Abdullah's regime in 1949. They were joined by upper-caste Hindu landlords dispossessed by the land reforms. (In contrast to the Valley's Pandits, there were no sweeteners for Hindu landlords in the Jammu region.) After the dubious J&K Constituent Assembly election process of late 1951, the Praja Parishad launched a campaign of protest meetings, marches, and civil disobedience against the Abdullah regime in the Jammu region's southern districts that steadily intensified through 1952 and the first half of 1953. The campaign demanded "full integration of Jammu & Kashmir State with the rest of India like other acceding [princely] States and safeguarding of the legitimate democratic rights of the people of Jammu from the communist-dominated and anti-Dogra government of Sheikh Abdullah," in the words of Balraj Madhok, a leader of the movement who later became the all-India president of India's Hindu nationalist party, the Bharatiya Jan Sangh (forerunner of the BJP; founded in 1951 and renamed in 1980).[39] Its rallying cry was "Ek Vidhaan, Ek Nishaan, Ek Pradhaan!" (One Constitution, One Flag, One Premier!) for all of India—a reference to separate constitution-making by the J&K government, the existence of a J&K state flag alongside the Indian national tricolor, and Abdullah's title of "Prime Minister."

Abdullah reacted with a combative speech in April 1952 in Ranbirsinghpora, a small town named after the second ruler of the princely state on the Jammu district's border with Pakistan's Punjab province. In this heartland of Jammu Hindus, he described the demand for full integration—that is, revocation of J&K's asymmetric autonomy within the Indian Union—as "unrealistic, childish and savoring of lunacy."[40] He asserted that the agitation had backing from not just the Hindu nationalist party but unnamed elements in the Congress party and Union government. The speech was widely reported in the Indian press and deepened the controversy. The Delhi talks in the summer of 1952 between Abdullah and Nehru were intended by the Indian government to calm things down and to elicit concessions from the J&K government that might dampen the clamor for "full integration" while upholding the asymmetric autonomy framework. That did not happen.

In April 1953 Abdullah appeared to consider compromise with his internal enemies. The basic principles committee of his handpicked J&K Constituent Assembly proposed devolution of power to regions within J&K within the framework of the state's asymmetric autonomy. In addition to the state legislature, the Kashmir Valley and Jammu regions would each have directly elected assemblies with authority to legislate on specified subjects, as well as separate ministerial councils for regional affairs. Ladakh too would have an elected council to exercise local autonomy. It was even proposed to change J&K's name to "Autonomous Federated Unit of the Republic of India." The Jammu agitators refused to take the bait and stuck to their "full integration" stance, supported by the spiritual and political leader of eastern Ladakh's Tibetan Buddhist community, who disliked the meteoric rise of a Valley-based Sunni Muslim ruling elite and feared the implications of the land reform policy for the Buddhist clergy's immense landholdings in eastern Ladakh. Areas of the Jammu region with Kashmiri-speaking Muslim majorities and strong JKNC support—mostly the current districts of Doda, Kishtwar, and Ramban, mountainous tracts contiguous to the southeastern Valley—also refused to be part of an autonomous Hindu-majority Jammu region.

In May 1953 Abdullah switched to confrontation. In that month the internal situation in J&K worsened when Shyama Prasad Mukherjee, a leading Hindu nationalist politician from West Bengal and the founder in 1951 of the Bharatiya Jan Sangh, entered J&K in solidarity with the "full integration" agitation and was arrested. He died of apparently natural causes the following month while detained in the Kashmir Valley. In May the JKNC's apex body, its working committee, appointed a subcommittee to examine constitutional options for the future of J&K (and the disputed territory of the former princely state as a whole). On 9 June 1953 this subcommittee submitted its report, outlining four possible options, all involving a plebiscite and independence for part or whole of the disputed territory. The first and recommended option called for a plebiscite across the entire disputed territory but differed from the UN Security Council resolutions by suggesting that the population should be given not two but three options: become part of India, part of Pakistan, or an independent state. Abdullah refused to back down during July 1953 in correspondence with Nehru and India's education minister, Abul Kalam Azad. Instead, he announced he would convene the JKNC's working committee and general council in late August to discuss the recommendations, and planned to hold a public rally on the issue in the Valley on August 21, coinciding with a Muslim religious celebration.

On August 9, 1953, Sheikh Mohammad Abdullah was formally dismissed as prime minister of J&K—by Karan Singh, the 22-year-old son of the last maharaja and the ceremonial head of state, a titular position styled *sadr-e-riyasat*, acting "in the interest of the people of the state." Abdullah had already been taken into custody in a predawn raid by state police under the Jammu & Kashmir Public Security Act, a draconian law used until then to persecute his opponents. He would remain incarcerated for the next 22 years, until 1975, barring brief spells in 1958, 1964–1965, and 1968. On August 9 and 10, 33 JKNC leaders—including Afzal Beg, a cabinet minister in the deposed J&K government—were also taken into detention under this Public Security Act. Bakshi Ghulam Mohammed, deputy prime minister and home (interior) minister and one of Abdullah's top lieutenants for two decades, took over as the prime minister of J&K. Of Abdullah's closest lieutenants, only Afzal Beg and Maulana Masoodi remained loyal. Most others—Bakshi Ghulam Mohammed, G. M. Sadiq, and Mir Qasim—became the leaders of a new, New Delhi–sponsored regime in J&K.

On August 10, Bakshi Ghulam Mohammed issued his first statement as prime minister, in which he denounced Abdullah as an oppressive leader who had become a tool of (unspecified) foreign conspiracies to undermine J&K's ties with India. In September 1953 Nehru justified the change of government in J&K on the floor of India's Parliament on the grounds that Abdullah had lost the confidence of the majority of his cabinet, which consisted—in addition to Abdullah and Afzal Beg—of Bakshi Ghulam Mohammed, the Kashmiri Pandit Shyamlal Saraf, and Giridharilal Dogra from Jammu, and by his actions caused "distress to the people." Nehru was never to offer any reason for Abdullah's arrest and protracted incarceration. In

October 1953 large majorities of J&K Constituent Assembly members (60 of 75) and JKNC general council members (90 of 110) ratified the new leadership in specially convened sessions.[41]

The extraordinary events of August 1953 bore telltale signs of a carefully planned putsch, instigated by and executed on behalf of the government in New Delhi. To the Nehru government, Abdullah's behavior had crossed red lines, and he could no longer be tolerated. The intrigue capitalized on rifts in the leadership of the JKNC party and its government. For the Hindu members of Abdullah's cabinet, Shyamlal Saraf and Giridharilal Dogra, allegiance to India was probably the decisive factor. For G. M. Sadiq, the leading cryptocommunist in the JKNC leadership and speaker (president) of the J&K Constituent Assembly, the changing position of the Soviet Union on the international dispute over Kashmir may have been a factor, as also for D. P. Dhar, the Kashmiri Pandit deputy home (interior) minister in Abdullah's government and another communist fellow traveler. In 1948 the Soviet propaganda organ *New Times* hailed Abdullah as the leader of "a progressive and democratic mass movement" but condemned the intervention of "Indian reactionaries" in Kashmir. By 1953, after Stalin's death and amid growing Soviet interest in India's emerging foreign policy posture of "nonalignment" with either superpower bloc, while Pakistan gravitated toward the United States, the same paper was calling the Kashmir question an "internal affair" of India and decrying "imperialist efforts to turn the Valley into a strategic bridgehead."[42] For Bakshi Ghulam Mohammed, personal ambition was probably the motive—the lure of stepping out of Abdullah's shadow and supplanting him.

The problem was that August 1953 also marked the beginning of bitter feelings of estrangement, arising from regional pride and sentiment, among the population of the Kashmir Valley toward the Indian Union as embodied by the Center in New Delhi. For most people in the Valley, Sheikh Abdullah was the hero who led the struggle that had brought them emancipation from the princely state's yoke and the messiah who gave the peasant masses land, dignity, and deliverance from generations of serfdom.

Mir Qasim, a prominent JKNC leader in Anantnag, the southern Valley district, joined the putschist group and was immediately made a minister in Bakshi's cabinet. Qasim, who later served as J&K's chief minister from 1971 to 1975, recalled in his memoirs, published in 1992, that the coup d'état "gave rise to a grim situation and a bitter sense of betrayal in Kashmir. . . . The news spread like wildfire, giving rise to widespread agitations and protest marches. In [the town of] Anantnag, where the news reached a day late, I sat in my [law] chamber for three days, watching wave after wave of protest marches surge past. Some people were killed in police firing." On August 12, Qasim and G. M. Sadiq left Anantnag for Srinagar with a police escort: "on our way to Srinagar we passed through [the small towns] Kulgam, Shopian and Pulwama and saw the people's angry, rebellious mood." In Kulgam, crowds gathered at a graveyard were burying people killed in police firing. When they saw Qasim with a police escort, they asked him: "So you are also with them?" "In Shopian we faced a graver situation," Qasim wrote, "here a 20,000-strong crowd menacingly surged towards where we were staying, to attack us." When they arrived in the capital, "Srinagar was in chaos. Bakshi Saheb's own house, despite the police guard, was under attack. He was nervous and wanted to step down as prime minister in favor of Mr Sadiq."[43]

Wearing the martyr's crown, Abdullah would dominate the Valley's politics in absentia throughout his 22 years in captivity. He was let out on three occasions—for brief periods in 1958 and 1968 and a year in 1964–1965. His short-lived public appearances invariably triggered mass euphoria in the Valley. Thus on April 18, 1964, according to Indian newspaper accounts, Abdullah "entered Srinagar and was greeted by a delirious crowd of 250,000 people. Srinagar was a blaze of color, and everyone seemed [to be] out on the streets to give Abdullah a hero's welcome. . . . Addressing a gathering of 150,000 people on 20 April, Abdullah said that in 1947 he had challenged Pakistan's authority to annex Kashmir on grounds of religion, and now he was challenging the Indian contention that the question had been settled." In March 1968, "almost the entire population of Srinagar turned out to greet him" as he arrived in the Valley, the *Times of India* reported, adding that hundreds of thousands of people were chanting "Sher-e-Kashmir zindabad [long live the Lion of Kashmir], our demand plebiscite." Days later, addressing 100,000 supporters in Anantnag, south of Srinagar, Abdullah warned that "repression will never suppress the Kashmiri people's urge to be free." Indeed, Mir Qasim wrote in his 1992 memoirs that the Jammu & Kashmir Plebiscite Front, an organization formed by Abdullah's supporters in 1955, had since its formation "reduced the [official] National Conference to a nonentity in Kashmir's [the Valley's] politics."[44]

Abdullah overplayed his hand in 1953. But his fall from power, engineered beyond any reasonable doubt by Nehru's government, was fundamentally because he was a mass-based regionalist leader whose stature among his own people and assertive style were at odds with the vision of centralized power and top-down authority in the corridors of official New Delhi.

To put the 1953 (and post-1953) events in J&K in context, it is important to remember that in the early 1950s Nehru wanted to renege on

Congress's commitment during the struggle for independence that free India would be constituted as a decentralized union of linguistic states, and he instead pushed the idea of a powerful Center presiding over four "administrative zones" on grounds of "security and stability." He reluctantly climbed down from this agenda in 1953 in the face of popular protest, and from the mid-1950s the Indian Union gradually formed on the basis of the states' autonomy, a process largely completed by the late 1960s. But in J&K, the focus of a sovereignty dispute with Pakistan, the "security and stability" perspective prevailed, and a virtual dictatorship of the Center was imposed on the state after 1953.

Six decades on, India's politics revolves around powerful regional leaders who have a mass base in one state of the Indian Union. But Abdullah was a regionalist leader ahead of his times. In 1951 his J&K government announced a "nation-building" program to bring together the diverse communities of J&K in an official publication released to celebrate its achievements in its first three years in office, particularly land reform. This sort of terminology was bound to raise alarm, if not hackles, in Nehru's New Delhi.[45]

Integration

The top-down implementation of J&K's "integration" with India after 1953 was dictated from New Delhi and executed by client governments in Srinagar run by stooge Valley politicians with no legitimacy in the eyes of the Kashmir Valley's people: Bakshi Ghulam Mohammed from 1953 to 1963, G. M. Sadiq from 1964 to 1971, and Mir Qasim from 1971 to 1975. This process built up a toxic reservoir of anger and discontent in the Valley. This succession of puppets could not have survived in office if Abdullah had been at liberty to lead popular resistance, hence his banishment from public life for 22 years, of which he spent nearly 20 in prison. The policy of remote control from New Delhi could only be effected by turning J&K—and particularly the Kashmir Valley—into a police state where civil liberties and democratic institutions and processes were systematically subverted and destroyed. Thus as the rest of India evolved as a plural and competitive democracy with a substantial degree of autonomy for its states, the Kashmir Valley became an enclave ruled by crude authoritarianism and repression.

In February 1954 the J&K Constituent Assembly gave its consent, in the absence of a small number of dogged Abdullah loyalists, to a slew of integrative measures. Bakshi Ghulam Mohammed called it "fulfilling the formalities of our unbreakable bonds with India." Speaking in the national

Parliament, Nehru welcomed the move as "representing the wishes of the people of Kashmir."[46] In May 1954 a constitutional order was issued in the name of the president of India (the titular head of state) that brought J&K within the purview of legislation passed by Parliament on most subjects on the Union List, placed J&K's financial and fiscal relationship with the Center on the same footing as that of other states, and gave India's Supreme Court full jurisdiction in J&K. The fundamental rights of citizens guaranteed by the Indian Constitution were also extended to J&K, but with an escape clause: these rights could be suspended at any time by the state government on grounds of "security," and no judicial appeals against such decisions would be allowed. The 1954 developments were the beginning of the end for J&K's asymmetric autonomy as enshrined in Article 370 of India's constitution.

During October–November 1956, the J&K Constituent Assembly was presented with a draft state constitution, which was rapidly approved by 67 of the 75 members. (Of the rest, four were in jail, and another four boycotted the proceedings.) The preamble stated that "the state of Jammu and Kashmir is and shall be an integral part of the Union of India."[47] The state constitution came into effect on January 26, 1957, India's Republic Day. On January 24, 1957, the UN Security Council passed a resolution reiterating its 1948–1951 resolutions calling for the sovereignty dispute to be resolved "in accordance with the will of the people expressed through the democratic method of a free and impartial plebiscite conducted under the auspices of the United Nations" and stated that any action taken by the J&K Constituent Assembly "would not constitute a disposition of the State in accordance with the above principle."[48] But by 1957 the UN's role in the Kashmir dispute was fading into irrelevance as events in Kashmir unfolded differently.

In May 1954 Pakistan formally entered the United States' orbit, when an agreement was signed in Karachi providing for American military hardware to be supplied to Pakistan. In September 1954 Pakistan joined the South-East Asia Treaty Organization, and in September 1955 it became a member of the Central Treaty Organization, another U.S.-sponsored regional security alliance. Pakistan's motivation was to fortify itself militarily and strategically against India. The United States welcomed Pakistan's cooperation with its overriding strategic priority, "containment" of the Soviet Union. Around the same time, India formalized its stance of "nonalignment" with either superpower bloc.

In response to these developments, the Soviet Union moved closer to neutrality-minded India. In December 1955 the Soviet leaders Nikita Khrushchev and Nikolai Bulganin visited India and traveled to Srinagar.

In Srinagar, Premier Khrushchev said: "the people of Jammu and Kashmir want to work for the well-being of their beloved country—the Republic of India. The people of Kashmir do not want to become toys of imperialist powers. This is what some powers are trying to do by supporting Pakistan on the so-called Kashmir question. It made us very sad when imperialist powers succeeded in bringing about the partition of India. That Kashmir is one of the States of the Republic of India has already been decided by the people of Kashmir." Marshal Bulganin referred to Kashmir as "this northern part of India" and discerned that its population felt "deep joy" in being "part of the Indian people."[49] Fortified by this support, Nehru told Parliament in March 1956 that the plebiscite was "beside the point" and emphasized "Pakistani aggression in Kashmir and the legality of Kashmir's accession to India."[50] In April he disclosed that a year earlier, in May 1955, he had offered Pakistan's prime minister a permanent, de jure division of the former princely state along the 1949 Ceasefire Line. That the offer was made, and summarily rejected, reveals India's contentment and Pakistan's grievance with the territorial status quo. In February 1957 the Soviet Union for the first time vetoed a UN Security Council resolution on Kashmir, and would do so regularly thereafter.

Meanwhile, on August 10, 1955, Abdullah's followers in the Valley, purged from the JKNC, floated an opposition organization, the Jammu & Kashmir Plebiscite Front. Afzal Beg, in and out of prison, became its first president, and its other leaders included Maulana Masoodi, who had been removed as the JKNC's general secretary in 1953 for opposing Abdullah's ouster and incarceration. As the Plebiscite Front began to mobilize the people, on August 23 the J&K government banned public meetings, "to prevent clashes between supporters and opponents of the Government." Mass detentions of Plebiscite Front activists followed. Indeed, "between 19 November 1955 and 29 September 1956 four presidents of the Plebiscite Front were arrested" one after another.[51]

In the Kashmir Valley, Bakshi's 10-year regime became synonymous with, and is remembered for, organized thuggery and blatant election fraud. In 1957 the J&K Constituent Assembly was dissolved and elections were held to form a state legislature. The official JKNC won 69 of its 75 seats. Of the Kashmir Valley's 43 seats, 35 were won by official candidates without any contest, either because no candidates filed nomination papers or because all papers other than those of the official candidates were ruled invalid. Token contests in the other eight seats pitted official candidates against politically unknown persons. The opposition in the J&K state legislature constituted in 1957 consisted of five Praja

Parishad members who won from Hindu-majority areas of the Jammu region. The results in state elections in 1962 were a replica of 1957: the official JKNC won 68 of the 74 seats. (The Praja Parishad got three, and three went to independents, including the chief Buddhist lama of Ladakh.) Of the Valley's 43 seats, 32 were decided without any contest, and Bakshi and his cabinet colleagues G. M. Sadiq, Mir Qasim, and Khwaja Shamsuddin were all elected unopposed.

The man responsible for deciding whether nomination papers were valid was Abdul Khaleq Malik, a Bakshi henchman, and those blessed by him in this way are remembered even today in the Valley's political lore as "Khaleq-made MLAs" (members of the legislative assembly). Nehru wrote to Bakshi after the 1962 state elections: "it would strengthen your position if you lost a few seats to bona fide opponents." The farcical situation was of Nehru's making. When in 1954 an attempt by the Praja Socialist Party, a leftist all-India party, to open a branch office in Srinagar was thwarted by Bakshi's thugs, Nehru's reaction was to accuse the Praja Socialist Party of "joining hands with the enemies of the country." According to a Jammu-based activist who met Nehru in Delhi to request that pro-Abdullah elements be allowed some political space to operate as an opposition in the Valley, Nehru agreed that Bakshi was an unsavory character but "argued that India's case [on Kashmir] now revolved around him and so . . . Bakshi's government had to be strengthened." The activist recalls Nehru saying that the Valley's politics "revolved around personalities" and there was "no material for democracy there."[52]

Bakshi Ghulam Mohammed outlived his usefulness to his masters in New Delhi after a decade as J&K's "prime minister," during which time he came to personify a regime hated in the Valley. In late 1963 an attempt was made to dilute the embarrassment and the anger, and he was compelled to step down. But he managed to stave off the New Delhi–backed prime ministerial candidacy of G. M. Sadiq, his rival within the ruling clique, with whom he had been locked in conflict since 1957, after failing to appoint anyone from the Sadiq faction to cabinet posts after the 1957 state elections. Bakshi was replaced as prime minister by one of his more obscure cabinet colleagues, Khwaja Shamsuddin, who lasted four months in the office, from October 1963 to February 1964.

Winters tend to be relatively quiet in the Kashmir Valley because of the biting cold weather and frequent snowbound conditions. But the winter of 1963–1964 saw the Valley explode in popular protest.

The unrest was sparked by the mysterious disappearance of the holy hair of the Prophet Mohammad from Srinagar's Hazratbal shrine in late

December 1963. The vanished relic reappeared just as mysteriously a week later, but in the meantime the Valley had been convulsed by agitation and protest. It was an eruption of mass fury against the government of India and its local proxies, who were suspected by the public of malfeasance or negligence in the relic affair. The release of pent-up resentment of over a decade of repression generated an uprising that surpassed the Quit Kashmir movement of 1946 and would itself be surpassed for intensity a quarter century later, in the winter of 1989–1990, when an uprising-cum-insurgency against Indian authority would engulf the Valley.

The few leaders of popular standing not in prison, notably Maulana Masoodi and Ghulam Mohiuddin Karra, who had been the chief of the Srinagar city organization of the JKNC in the 1940s before falling out with Sheikh Abdullah, had a difficult time controlling and calming the people. Yet

> Masoodi and Karra warned against violence. . . . Both did wonderful work pacifying excited Muslim crowds during the critical days, when a small mistake could have soaked the Valley in blood. But for Masoodi [a senior cleric], authentication of the restored relic would have been impossible and placed the Indian authorities in tremendous difficulty. Karra's speeches, characterized by balance and caution, produced a moderating influence. . . . In a mass meeting at Zadibal [a quarter of Srinagar inhabited by the Valley's Shia minority] he advised Kashmiris that while denouncing Hindu communalism in India they should not overlook the atrocities of Muslim fanatics in East Pakistan [a reference to early 1964 riots targeting the Hindu minority of East Pakistan].[53]

The intelligence reports from the Valley were most alarming, and the outpouring of rage unnerved at least some in New Delhi's officialdom as well as destabilizing the proxy regime in the Valley. The inept Shamsuddin was replaced in late February 1964 as prime minister of J&K by G. M. Sadiq, and a decision was made by the Sadiq government and its handlers in New Delhi to take the calculated risk of releasing Sheikh Abdullah in order to calm down the people. This was the context of Abdullah's release and triumphant return to Srinagar in April 1964. In late April he went to Delhi to meet Nehru, who was ailing and died weeks later, on May 27, 1964. In May he was allowed to go to Pakistan to meet with the Pakistani military dictator, Ayub Khan. The steadfast loyalists Beg and Masoodi accompanied Abdullah to both Delhi and Pakistan.

The "Srinagar Spring" dissipated within months. The Indian government was worried and alarmed by Abdullah's defiant rhetoric on "self-determination" and the mass response this evoked in the Valley. Over a decade in prison seemed to have steeled rather than broken his resolve. The Sadiq government, packed with Sadiq loyalists like Mir Qasim and D. P. Dhar, came under pressure not just from the Kashmiri street, dominated by Abdullah, but from the deposed Bakshi Ghulam Mohammed, who tried to organize a no-confidence motion against Sadiq in the state legislature with Abdullah's tacit support. In September 1964 Bakshi was arrested under the Defense of India Rules—a draconian law inherited from the British Raj, who used it liberally against Indian freedom fighters—and sent to the same prison in the Jammu region where Abdullah had been consigned 11 years earlier. (Bakshi was released after a few months on health grounds.) Then, in the winter of 1964–1965, the most drastic episode yet of J&K's "integration" into India unfolded.

In December 1964 India's home (interior) minister announced in Parliament that the Center had decided to bring J&K under the purview of Articles 356 and 357 of the Indian Constitution. These articles empower the Center to dismiss elected state governments if it determines that there has been a breakdown of governance in the state and to assume the state government's legislative mandate (President's Rule), respectively. They are the most antifederal features of India's Constitution and would gain particular infamy during the 1980s, when Indira and Rajiv Gandhi's governments sought to topple democratically elected state governments run by regionalist opposition parties. In March 1965, the Center's powers of control and intervention were consolidated in J&K when the J&K Assembly passed an amendment to the state constitution replacing the post of *sadr-e-riyasat*, the nominal head of state elected by the state legislature, with a governor appointed by New Delhi, as in other Indian states. Another amendment changed the title of J&K's head of government from "prime minister" to "chief minister," as in other Indian states. This round of "integration" effectively marked the end of the asymmetric autonomy given to J&K under Article 370 of the Constitution.

The most breathtaking "integrative" development occurred in January 1965. On January 3 the working committee of the JKNC, meaning the ruling Sadiq group, with Mir Qasim the party general secretary, announced that it would dissolve its identity and become the state branch of the Congress party. The Congress's working committee, the party's highest body, accepted the decision with alacrity, suggesting a carefully choreographed plan.

The "people of the Valley reacted with unprecedented anger," and their "protests were again suppressed with brute force and large-scale arrests." In mid-January Abdullah delivered a vitriolic speech to a mammoth rally at the Hazratbal shrine calling on the people to resist the imposition of

Articles 356 and 357 and reject the absurd and insulting attempt to eradicate the identity of Kashmir's historic regionalist political movement. "Violence and arson took place in some parts of Srinagar," particularly targeting shops and businesses owned by Pandits and other Hindus, as soon as crowds dispersed after the meeting. By March, mass arrests of Plebiscite Front leaders and activists were taking place, and in May 1965 Abdullah himself was arrested under the Defense of India Rules on his return from a tour abroad.[54]

The turmoil in the Valley encouraged the Pakistani military to launch a large-scale cross–Ceasefire Line infiltration in August 1965, with the aim of instigating a general uprising in the Valley. The several thousand armed men who crossed the Ceasefire Line into the Valley were a mix of Pakistani professional soldiers and volunteers from the "non-Kashmiri speaking AJK ["Azad" Jammu and Kashmir] territories" under Pakistan's control since the late 1940s. Such an invasion had been in preparation ever since October–November 1962, when the Indian army had suffered a demoralizing military defeat in a border war with China, an emerging ally of Pakistan. Pakistan had ceded to China a remote and barren mountainous tract of its part of the former princely state of Jammu and Kashmir, bordering China's Xinjiang province, in 1963. The planners of the 1965 operation "had taken for granted the fullest cooperation of the local Muslims but this was not forthcoming, at any rate not on the expected huge scale." The operation failed due to the paucity of local support and a hard fight-back by the initially surprised Indian army. This was the first of two Pakistani incursions into the Indian side of the former princely state. The second came in 1999 when Pakistani military units crossed the Line of Control (as the Ceasefire Line had been renamed in 1972), in an operation initially undetected by the Indians, and seized ridges and peaks in the remote Kargil district of Ladakh. It was a counterproductive attempt to spark an international crisis that would force India into negotiations and concessions on Kashmir. As later in 1999, when the Pakistani move elicited broad international condemnation as reckless and rife with dangers of escalation between nuclear-armed adversaries, the 1965 operation not only flopped but boomeranged on Pakistan when the Indian government decided to broaden the conflict to the India-Pakistan international border, triggering a 22-day inconclusive war in September 1965. Pakistan's chronic revisionism vis-à-vis the Ceasefire Line/Line of Control has remained frustrated to this day.

The lesson of 1965 was that the Kashmir Valley's Muslims, however aggrieved with India, were not going to take the bait offered by Pakistan. Though embittered, they were also "reluctant to bring about change through warfare and bloodshed."[55] That would change a quarter century later, in the early 1990s, when many thousands from a new generation of the Valley's young men took up arms, with Pakistan's material support, against Indian authority, and a brutal cycle of violence ensued that inflicted enormous suffering and trauma on the Valley's people and society for over a decade and a half.

In June 1966 Jaya Prakash Narayan, an anticolonial freedom fighter and veteran socialist leader, wrote a confidential letter to India's new prime minister, Indira Gandhi. (A decade later, in the mid-1970s, the aged Narayan would play an important role in mobilizing opposition, notably among youth, to her autocratic policies and especially her infamous 19-month Emergency.) In the 1966 letter Narayan wrote: "we profess democracy, but rule by force in Kashmir. . . . We profess secularism, but let Hindu nationalism stampede us into trying to establish it by repression. Kashmir has distorted India's image in the world as nothing has done. . . . That problem exists not because Pakistan wants to grab Kashmir, but because there is deep and widespread political discontent among the people."[56]

But in the Kashmir Valley, it was back to the pathetic "politics as usual" by then. In elections to the state legislature in 1967, the majority of seats, 39 of 75, were filled without any contest. Congress candidates, meaning nominees of the ruling Sadiq-Mir Qasim group, which had metamorphosed into the Pradesh (State) Congress of J&K, were "elected unopposed" in over half, 22, of the Valley's 42 constituencies. One of these victors was Shamsuddin, formerly prime minister of J&K for four shambolic months in 1963–1964, who was declared elected unopposed from the town of Anantnag after the papers filed by five other candidates were rejected as invalid. In all, 118 candidates were disqualified from contesting, nearly half, 55, on the grounds that they had failed to take the compulsory oath of allegiance to India and the rest with no reason given. The Congress won a four-fifths majority in the state legislature—60 of the 75 seats.

The 1967 national and state elections in India were the country's most competitive after independence: the hegemonic Congress party saw its parliamentary majority sharply reduced and suffered outright defeats or serious reverses in state elections across northern, eastern, and southern India to an assortment of opposition parties, almost all of which were explicitly or effectively regionalist in character. As noted earlier, these elections were an important juncture in India's gradual evolution as a robust multiparty and semifederal democracy. In J&K, the dreary farce of rigged elections continued. For the first time, following the integrative measures enacted in 1965, the state elected six members to the Lok

Sabha (three from the Valley, two from the Jammu region, and one from Ladakh). Congress won five of these six seats, two uncontested: Anantnag, in the southern Valley, and Ladakh. In the Jammu region, where Congress won both constituencies, opposition parties of all-India orientation, the leftist Praja Socialist Party and the Hindu nationalist Bharatiya Jan Sangh, "severely criticized electoral irregularities." The abuses common to both sets of polls in J&K, state and national, included "large-scale rejection of nomination papers, arrests of [opposition] polling agents, advance distribution of ballot papers to Congress workers, absence of opposition agents at time of counting, and rampant use of official machinery to the advantage of the ruling party."[57]

The only opposition candidate to win election to India's Parliament in 1967 from J&K was Bakshi Ghulam Mohammed, who stood from the Srinagar constituency. His platform was regional patriotism. In particular, he claimed to be running in order to save the identity of the Valley's historic political movement, the JKNC, now that his rival faction had forsaken that identity and been absorbed into Congress as a provincial unit. A commentator on state politics from the city of Jammu remembers being told in Srinagar by officials sent from New Delhi to "supervise" the elections in J&K—mainly operatives of intelligence agencies—that their instructions were that "Bakshi had to be defeated in the national interest."[58] Their efforts failed. It is probable that "Bakshi Ghulam Mohammed would not have won a free election at any point during his ten years in office."[59] But now the groundswell of support for Bakshi the regional patriot was so strong that he managed to win from Srinagar. Always the joker in the pack of Valley politicians, Bakshi lived up to his chameleon and turncoat reputation until his death in 1972. In March 1971 he sought reelection to the Lok Sabha from Srinagar as a Congress candidate. This was the national election that saw the rise of Indira Gandhi as the dominant figure in India's politics on a left-populist platform. Her party won a resounding majority in the Lok Sabha and five of the six constituencies in J&K. The exception was Srinagar, a congested capital city where outright rigging is more difficult than in the Valley's district towns and rural areas. Here Bakshi, the regime-sponsored candidate, was heavily defeated by a journalist known to be a Plebiscite Front sympathizer who stood as an independent.

In December 1970 the Plebiscite Front announced that it would put forward candidates in the Lok Sabha election imminent in March 1971 and the state election due in 1972. The decision had been in the offing. In 1969 Plebiscite Front candidates had run for local bodies in the Valley, albeit not under the Plebiscite Front's name, and swept the polls. Mir

Qasim, who had just taken over as J&K's Congress chief minister on his mentor Sadiq's death, was aghast at the prospect of Plebiscite Front participation in the national and state elections. As he wrote in his memoirs, "if the elections were free and fair, the victory of the Front was a foregone conclusion" in the Valley. Indira Gandhi was also displeased at the prospect. Speaking in the city of Jammu on December 23, 1970, she was unequivocal that attempts to enter the Lok Sabha or the J&K legislature with the intent of "wrecking the Constitution" would not be tolerated. Asked by journalists how this could be prevented, she replied: "Ways will be found."[60]

On January 8, 1971, "externment orders" were served on the senior Plebiscite Front leaders Afzal Beg and Ghulam Mohammad (G. M.) Shah, Abdullah's son-in-law, requiring them to leave J&K. During the night of January 8–9, "at least 350 officials and members of the Front were arrested under the [Jammu & Kashmir] Preventive Detention Act in a series of police raids." On January 12 the Center declared the Plebiscite Front illegal under the India-wide Unlawful Activities (Prevention) Act, as it had "on diverse occasions by words, either spoken or written, and signs and visual representations . . . asserted a claim to determine whether or not Jammu and Kashmir will remain part of India."[61] In the state elections of 1972, the ruling Congress party got 57 of the 75 seats in the J&K Assembly. For the first time, the Kashmir Valley wing of the Jama'at-i-Islami (Islamic Rally), a fundamentalist movement that has wings in Pakistan, Bangladesh, and both sides of the Line of Control in Kashmir, elected five Assembly members from Valley constituencies, apparently after an understanding with Qasim that they would help oppose the Plebiscite Front.

In 1968 Sheikh Abdullah said: "the fact remains that Indian democracy stops short at Pathankot [the last town in India's Punjab before the Jammu region]. Between Pathankot and the Banihal [a mountain pass linking the Jammu region with the Valley] you may have some measure of democracy, but beyond Banihal there is none. What we have in [the] Kashmir [Valley] bears some of the worst characteristics of colonial rule."[62] Indeed, the relationship between the Kashmir Valley and the Indian Union was utterly poisoned by the policy of force and fraud deployed between 1953 and 1975. The toxic legacy of that period provided the backdrop to the outbreak of a protracted insurgency in the Valley in 1990.

The Return of Sheikh Abdullah

When Sheikh Abdullah finally made his peace, in 1975, with those in power in New Delhi, it was on New Delhi's terms. In November 1974 his faithful associate Afzal Beg and a senior bureaucrat representing the government of India inked a short agreement subsequently known as the "Delhi accord" and sometimes as the "Indira-Abdullah accord." It asserted that "the State of Jammu and Kashmir which is a constituent unit of the Union of India shall, in its relation with the Union, continue to be governed by Article 370 of the Constitution of India." But there was no restoration in substantive terms of the asymmetric autonomy enshrined in Article 370. Instead, the agreement specified that "provisions of the Constitution of India already applied to the State of Jammu and Kashmir without adaptation or modification are unalterable." This meant that almost all of the 28 "integrative" constitutional orders issued from New Delhi and the 262 Union laws made applicable to the state between 1953 and the mid-1970s would stand. The only concession the Center made was minor:

> With a view to assuring freedom to the State of Jammu and Kashmir to have its own legislation on matters like welfare measures, cultural matters, social security, personal law and procedural laws, in a manner suited to the special conditions in the State [a coy reference to its Muslim-majority population, unique among India's states], it is agreed that the State Government can review laws made by Parliament or extended to the State after 1953 on any matter relatable to the Concurrent List [subject to the joint jurisdiction of the Center and the states] and may decide which of them, in its opinion, needs amendment or repeal. Thereafter appropriate steps may be taken under Article 254 of the Constitution of India. The grant of President's assent to any such legislation [passed by the J&K Assembly] would be sympathetically considered.

A committee was later set up to examine this matter; its recommendations were never made public.

The Delhi accord was especially careful to protect "the appointment, powers, functions, duties, immunities and privileges of the Governor" of J&K, an appointee of New Delhi since 1965. It specified that "no law made by the Legislature of the State of Jammu and Kashmir seeking to make any change" in the Governor's role and prerogatives "shall take effect" without the assent of the president of India (effectively, the Center). Abdullah formally accepted the agreement in February 1975, after unsuccessfully holding out for the restoration of the "prime minister" title to J&K's head of government, and its contents were then made public by Indira Gandhi. Abdullah was then reinstated as the state's chief minister, after Mir Qasim stepped down. In March both houses of India's Parliament approved the Delhi accord; the only opposition came from Hindu nationalists, then a small presence in Parliament, who demanded

Figure 8. Sheikh Abdullah addresses a public meeting in Srinagar, Kashmir
Valley (1975). POPPERFOTO/GETTY IMAGES.

the abrogation of Article 370 and objected to "appeasement" of the separatist Abdullah. After returning to the Valley, Abdullah dissolved the Plebiscite Front formed in 1955 and resumed leadership, after 22 years, of the Jammu & Kashmir National Conference. (The two men who had usurped the JKNC mantle in 1953, Bakshi and Sadiq, were dead, and Qasim, a Congress leader since 1965, faded into political oblivion.)[63]

This turn of events in 1975 signaled Abdullah's abandonment of the "self-determination" platform he had upheld for over two decades. He never again spoke using the rhetoric he used in the 1950s and 1960s. He may have calculated that after India's historic victory in the December 1971 India-Pakistan war and the breakup of Pakistan with the formation of Bangladesh, the strategic balance in the subcontinent had shifted so decisively in India's favor that it made sense to conclude a rapprochement with New Delhi. It is also possible that he was worn down by advancing age—he turned 70 in 1975—and by two decades of incarceration. (He had a major heart attack in 1977 and died in 1982.) He was faced with the prospect of dying in jail or in enforced exile from his homeland, the Kashmir Valley.

Abdullah returned to the Valley amid massive acclaim and celebration. The ordinary people of the Valley were delighted to have their "Lion" back, not just free but in charge, as the long era of the jackals finally came to an end. His stature was so commanding that any regime headed by him was guaranteed to have wide legitimacy in the Valley. When he died in September 1982, having dominated the Valley's politics for 50 years, his funeral procession was gigantic. It may have been the largest funeral procession ever seen for a political leader in India and the subcontinent, although the Valley is not particularly populous nor Srinagar a very large city by Indian and subcontinental standards.

Under the surface, however, things were not hunky-dory in the Valley after Abdullah's return. In 1995 I interviewed Abdul Qayyum Zargar, who as secretary to Afzal Beg in 1975 had had inside knowledge of the Delhi accord's making and aftermath. He was living in his hometown, Doda, and was now middle-aged. Doda, which is nestled amid rugged mountains in the northeastern part of the Jammu region, close to the southeastern part of the Valley, is inhabited predominantly by Kashmiri-speaking Muslims, who are about 80 percent of its population. (The rest are Hindu.) The district of Doda was at the time J&K's largest in area—11,500 square kilometers—and had a population consisting of 57 percent Muslims, mostly Kashmiri-speakers like the Valley's majority population, and 43 percent Hindus. The district has since been trifurcated for administrative convenience (into Doda, Kishtwar, and Ramban districts). At the time of this interview, the undivided Doda district was in the grip of a brutal cycle of insurgency and counterinsurgency that pitted armed militants, mainly locals with a sprinkling of Pakistani radicals, against the Indian army and paramilitary police forces, with the horror all the more stark in the picturesque setting of nature. And in the Valley, lacerated by violence since 1990, Sheikh Abdullah's grave, near Srinagar's Hazratbal shrine, was under guard by Indian paramilitary police to prevent its desecration by a young generation of angry militants who had come to see him as a sellout to "India."

Zargar recalled that at the time, 20 years earlier, the terms of the 1975 accord had caused consternation and resentment among Plebiscite Front/National Conference activists across the Valley and other strongholds like the Jammu region's Doda-Kishtwar zone. Many activists saw the agreement as not an honorable compromise they could live with but abject capitulation by their leader, an unconditional surrender rather than a negotiated truce. It took tremendous persuasion, according to Zargar, to convince the disgruntled rank and file not to openly oppose the agreement. The appeal to them was couched in sentimental terms: they should fall in line because Sheikh Saheb's (Respected Sheikh's) personal prestige was at stake, and he had suffered so much for the *awaam* (people). While this was largely effective, not everyone was persuaded. A significant number of politically minded younger men who had been born after 1947, grown up through the oppressive 1950s and 1960s, and come of age in the 1970s, charted an alternative path to keep the call for "self-determination" alive. One was Shabir Shah, who cofounded the People's League, a group based in the southern half of the Valley (with some influence in Doda) and paid the price by spending 20 years in jail until late 1994. Some of these men, joined by an even younger generation of men born in the 1960s who were radicalized during the second half of the 1980s, emerged as leaders of the Valley's insurgency in the late 1980s and early 1990s.

The Sheikh Abdullah of 1975–1982 was a lion in winter and, in retrospect, the 1975 deal was a way station en route to the armed struggle for *azaadi* (freedom) that convulsed the Valley in the 1990s. But for some time—up to 1984—the political rehabilitation of Abdullah and by extension of the regional base he represented resulted in a fragile stability in the Valley.

Once state elections were held in 1977, after the nationwide Emergency imposed by Indira Gandhi in June 1975 ended, the JKNC won a clear majority in the J&K legislature, 47 of the 76 seats. This majority was built on their overwhelming victory in the Kashmir Valley, where their candidates won in 40 of the 42 constituencies. (The other two seats went to a short-lived J&K branch of the Janata Party that had defeated Congress in the post-Emergency national election. In the Valley this was led by Maulana Masoodi, who had become estranged from Abdullah.) In the Jammu region (32 seats), Congress and the Janata Party won 11 constituencies each, and the JKNC came third, with seven wins. The State Assembly elected in 1977 was J&K's first ever legislature that was substantially representative of its people and diverse communities, and the government formed by Abdullah was the first in a quarter century with any legitimacy in the Valley.

In 1981 Sheikh Abdullah anointed his eldest son, Farooq Abdullah, a doctor and political novice, as his successor. This was in the already well-established, if deeply problematic, tradition of hereditary succession and political dynasties in the subcontinent. In June 1983 Farooq led the JKNC to its second consecutive victory in state elections. As in 1977, the JKNC won 47 of the 76 seats in the J&K Assembly: 38 of 42 constituencies in the Valley, 8 of 32 in the Jammu region, and one of the two in Ladakh. Congress emerged as a large opposition, with 26 seats in the new house—23 from the Jammu region, two in the Valley, and one in Ladakh. It seemed that at last a "normal" polity was taking root in J&K, a popularly elected government with a majority mandate facing a strong opposition. The fact that the party in government was a regional party specific to the state and the main opposition a national party (indeed, *the* national party) with a base across India also constituted a healthy balance between the Kashmir Valley's autonomist regionalism and the nationally oriented perspective favored by the majority of the Jammu region's electorate.

Countdown to Insurgency

The promise was subverted within a year by ruthless intervention from the Center. Prior to J&K's June 1983 state elections, Farooq Abdullah had angered Indira Gandhi by opening channels with opposition parties in power in the southern states of Andhra Pradesh and Karnataka, and the eastern state of West Bengal. In West Bengal the Left Front, led by the CPM, had ousted Congress from power in June 1977. In January 1983 Indira had been badly jolted when Congress was routed in state elections in Andhra Pradesh by the fledgling regional party the Telugu Desam, led by N. T. Rama Rao. At the same time Congress had been defeated in Karnataka, like Andhra a Congress bastion, by the regional incarnation of the Janata Party whose implosion into factions in 1979 had enabled Indira Gandhi's return to power in New Delhi in the midterm national election three years earlier. After winning the J&K state elections, Farooq enraged Indira Gandhi further by participating in opposition "conclaves" with the chief ministers of Andhra Pradesh, West Bengal, and Karnataka that were intended to build a coordinated anti-Congress front in national elections due in late 1984. As the chief minister of a state government run by a regional party he led, Farooq Abdullah had much in common with the opposition chief ministers of these states and their regionalist parties, above all a tense relationship with the Congress-ruled Center. (The parties in power in Andhra Pradesh and Karnataka were explicitly regionalist or state specific, while in West Bengal the CPM, nominally a national party, had grown and eventually won power essentially as a state-specific alternative to Congress.)

For J&K's democratic integration with the Indian Union, Farooq's initiative to come out of the insular cocoon of the Kashmir Valley and play a role in all-India politics was a very positive development. But Indira Gandhi saw this behavior as hostile provocation. In the national elections of 1977 and 1980, Congress and JKNC had run candidates as de facto allies in J&K, sharing out the state's six Lok Sabha constituencies. This reflected an implicit element of the 1975 pact that had restored an emasculated Sheikh Abdullah to office in J&K: an agreement that the JKNC would not be party to challenges to Congress's nationwide primacy. Now his son had broken that understanding.

In the J&K state elections of June 1983, Indira Gandhi campaigned energetically in the Jammu region, appealing to Jammu Hindus' long-held resentment of the greater political importance of the Kashmir Valley. The campaign yielded rich dividends for Congress in the Jammu region, and by early 1984 it was becoming clear that she had used the J&K state elections as a laboratory to test an India-wide strategy she was developing for the national election due in late 1984. This strategy involved appealing to Hindu majoritarian sentiment to support her party and government's defense of "national unity and integrity" against assorted "separatist" ethnic and ethnoreligious tendencies: in the northeastern state of Assam, among Sikhs in Punjab, and among Kashmiri Muslims in J&K—rather implausibly, given Farooq and his father's commitment to the Indian Union.

In June 1984, with the national election a few months away, Indira escalated her anti-"separatist" strategy by sending the Indian army into Sikhism's holiest site, the Golden Temple complex in Amritsar, to evict a group of armed radical Sikhs in a bloody battle, sparking a chain of events that worsened the Punjab crisis and fed a Sikh insurgency there through the early 1990s. In the same month, Farooq Abdullah's government, barely a year into its six-year term, was dismissed by yet another intervention from the Center: 12 of the 47 JKNC legislators defected and formed a new J&K government with the support of the Congress contingent in the state legislature. All 12, mainly back-benchers, became ministers in the new government. Ghulam Mohammad (G. M.) Shah, Sheikh Abdullah's son-in-law and a former Plebiscite Front leader, who had nursed ambitions of inheriting the sheikh's political mantle, became the chief minister.

The chief executor of this putsch was J&K's New Delhi-appointed governor, Jagmohan. He had earned Indira Gandhi's trust—and public notoriety—a decade earlier when he had served as a controversial administrator in Delhi during the Emergency of 1975–1977. He was dispatched as governor to J&K three months before the putsch, after the previous governor apparently refused to connive in Congress's unconstitutional and antidemocratic conspiracies. Once installed, Jagmohan dismissed Farooq Abdullah, denied him the opportunity to try and prove his majority on the floor of the legislature, and rejected his appeal for fresh elections.

It was a surreal replay of 1953, with Indira Gandhi, Farooq Abdullah, Jagmohan, and G. M. Shah playing the roles of Jawaharlal Nehru, Sheikh Abdullah, Karan Singh, and Bakshi Ghulam Mohammed, respectively. As in 1953, furious protests erupted in Srinagar and across the Valley. These were suppressed by detachments of the CRPF, whose personnel were airlifted into Srinagar the night before the coup. (Nearly three decades later, the CRPF still discharges the thankless task, along with the J&K police, of maintaining order in Srinagar and other Valley towns.) In August 1984 exactly the same modus operandi was used in the failed coup to topple N. T. Rama Rao's recently elected Telugu Desam Party government in Andhra Pradesh. In 1985 Farooq Abdullah wrote that the plot to depose his government was "hatched in 1 Safdarjang Road, New Delhi," the prime minister's residence, and "directed by Mrs Gandhi."[64]

The developments of 1984 marked the beginning of the end of the fragile stability that had prevailed in the Valley for nearly a decade. The outrageous removal of a government with popular legitimacy and its replacement by a motley collection of opportunist stooges, along with the use of repression to put down protests, touched an all-too-familiar chord with the Valley population's experience of New Delhi's shenanigans and rekindled their simmering rebellious streak, particularly among students and youth. There was already anger in the Valley, especially among the young, at the Union government's hanging, on 11 February 1984, of the pro–Kashmir independence militant Maqbool Butt (1938–1984). Originally from a village in the Valley's northern Kupwara district close to the

Line of Control, he was executed in Delhi's Tihar prison for having allegedly killed a policeman during a bank robbery in 1976.

In the national sympathy wave after Indira Gandhi was assassinated, when Congress won its highest ever proportion of the Lok Sabha, its landslide victory stopped at the Banihal Pass. All three parliamentary constituencies in the Valley elected pro-Farooq candidates with huge majorities. (As recounted earlier, Congress's landslide was also defied in Andhra Pradesh, Punjab, and Assam.)

G. M. Shah's tenure as chief minister was a farcical episode even by J&K's standards. He earned the sobriquet "curfew chief minister" because of the high frequency of curfews imposed in the Valley to prevent protest demonstrations during his 20 months in office. Indeed, the Valley was under curfew orders for 72 of his first 90 days as chief minister. His lame-duck reign came to a pathetic end in March 1986 when localized violence against members of the minority Pandit community occurred around a town south of Srinagar and his government was dismissed by the Center under Article 356 of the Indian Constitution, citing a breakdown of law and order in the state. J&K was then brought under direct central rule, which meant that Governor Jagmohan became the state's de facto ruler.

Farooq Abdullah, a political greenhorn known for his impulsive temperament, committed political hara-kiri in November 1986 when he reached an understanding with the government in New Delhi. In a fresh twist to the political circus going on since 1984, he was reinstated as J&K's chief minister pending new state elections, which were fixed for March 1987. In return, he agreed to run in those elections in alliance with the Congress party, led by Rajiv Gandhi, which at the time looked unassailable in India's politics. Under the deal's terms, the JKNC would field candidates in only 45 of J&K's 76 constituencies, mostly in the Valley, while Congress would contest the other 31 seats, mostly in the Jammu region.

Farooq justified his volte-face as a hard political reality he had "come to accept": "if I want to implement programs to fight poverty and run a government, I will have to stay on the right side of the Center."[65] This logic was seen in the Valley as abject surrender to New Delhi's bullying and evoked nearly universal scorn. By deciding to capitulate to Rajiv Gandhi's party and government in return for his restoration to office, Farooq abandoned the platform of regional pride and patriotism that was the lifeblood of the JKNC's mass appeal in the Valley. He simply did not have the stature and authority that had enabled his father to paper over a similar capitulation to Indira Gandhi in 1975. When Farooq turned this page on his defiance of New Delhi, he lost ownership of the Valley's deeply rooted and overwhelmingly popular political tradition of standing up for regional identity and rights. That field was now open to others to fill. There was also a related problem. The JKNC and Congress had won 73 of the 76 seats in the J&K Assembly in the mid-1983 state elections (47 and 26, respectively.) With the former governing and opposition parties now in the same camp, a yawning void opened up in the opposition space. Jammu & Kashmir's democratic development had been crippled since the early 1950s by the (forced) absence of a legal and institutionalized opposition, with the partial exception of the 1977–1984 interlude, and the Rajiv-Farooq accord threatened to bring about the revival of this fundamentally antidemocratic feature of the state's politics.

The winter of 1986–1987 saw an extraordinary democratic mobilization in the Kashmir Valley, as a broad and heterogeneous spectrum of individuals and groups came together to build a regionalist opposition force to contest the March 1987 state elections. This coalition came to be popularly known as the Muslim United Front. As a mainstream Indian news magazine published from Delhi observed during the campaign, the Muslim United Front was an improvised "*ad hoc* bloc" of various religious, civil society, and political groups "with no real unifying ideology." One element was the fundamentalist Jama'at-i-Islami, which had a small popular base but good organization; another was the J&K People's Conference, a regional party with a base in the Valley's northern Kupwara district, formed in 1978 by Abdul Ghani Lone, a very nonfundamentalist politician who had begun his career in the Congress party. (Lone, a "self-determination" advocate from 1990, was badly beaten by Indian paramilitary police during a demonstration in the early 1990s and repeatedly jailed, and was shot dead at a public meeting in Srinagar in 2002 by pro-Pakistan gunmen who viewed him as too moderate.) Another influential Muslim United Front figure was Qazi Nissar, the charismatic *mirwaiz* (high priest) of the southern half of the Valley. He was arrested by the Indian government after insurgency engulfed the Valley and jailed from 1990 to 1992. In 1994 he was shot dead in his home near the town of Anantnag by gunmen from a pro-Pakistan armed group, Hizb-ul Mujahideen (Party of Holy Warriors), a close affiliate of Jama'at-i-Islami, after he publicly criticized them for a spate of murders they had committed of pro–Kashmir independence activists.

The Delhi-based magazine noted that the Muslim United Front's base was as diverse as its leaders, comprising "educated youth, illiterate working-class people, and farmers who express anger with the Abdullahs' family rule, government corruption, and lack of economic development."

It observed that "the Valley is sharply divided between the party machine that brings out the traditional vote for the JKNC and hundreds of thousands who have entered politics as participants for the first time under the umbrella provided by the MUF." One of the 12 JKNC legislators who defected in 1984, a Pandit woman who in late 1991 was kidnapped by a group of insurgents and held captive for 45 days, says in her memoirs that in early 1987 there was a "wave" in favor of the Muslim United Front in the Valley. The movement's grassroots campaign was exceptionally energetic because it attracted an army of youthful volunteers, young men born during the 1960s.[66]

On March 23, 1987, the Valley went to the polls. The same Indian magazine reported "rigging and strong-arm tactics all over the Valley," "massive booth-capturing [forcible takeover of polling stations] by gangs," and "entire ballot boxes pre-stamped in favor of JKNC," while numerous citizens were "simply not allowed to vote." The bureaucracy administering the polls "worked blatantly in favor of the JKNC-Congress alliance," and "the police refused to listen to any complaint." Once counting began, a pattern emerged of supervising officials "stopping the counting as soon as they saw opposition candidates taking a lead."[67] It was another episode of J&K's hallowed history since 1951 of farcical elections. The JKNC-Congress alliance took an overwhelming majority in the state legislature: 66 of the 76 seats. (The JKNC won 40 of the 45 constituencies it contested and Congress 26 of 31.) Muslim United Front candidates won in just four constituencies, including the towns of Anantnag and Sopore, although according to the official results the opposition alliance got one-third of the statewide vote (which meant that its official vote in the Valley was much higher than one-third). The Muslim United Front won no constituencies in Srinagar. One of its defeated candidates was Mohammad Yusuf Shah, a Jam'aat-i-Islami member who stood from Amira Kadal, the downtown Srinagar constituency covering the Lal Chowk and Maisuma areas. (This was Shah's third foray into electoral politics; he had also contested state polls in 1977 and 1983.) One of his chief campaigners was Mohammad Yasin Malik, a previously apolitical young man in his twenties from a typical working-class family in the Maisuma neighborhood.

A familiar cycle of repression and punishment followed the elections. Shah and Malik were among the hundreds and possibly thousands of opposition activists picked up in mass arrests across the Valley as the election concluded. Most of those arrested were kept in prison until late 1987 or early 1988, and many were tortured in custody. In May 1989 Malik, by then a leader of the Jammu and Kashmir Liberation Front, which would launch an insurgency for an independent state in the second half of 1989, spoke to the same Indian magazine in a Srinagar location. He said he had recently returned from across the Line of Control, with weapons and training, along with Ashfaq Majid Wani, another Muslim United Front volunteer who had been arrested and tortured in 1987. Wani (born 1967), the son of an upper-middle-class Srinagar family, was killed in late March 1990 during a Srinagar encounter with Indian forces when a grenade he was priming to throw exploded in his hand. His funeral attracted 500,000 mourners who defied curfew orders.

Malik (born 1966), who was captured in August 1990, survived the underground life, years of incarceration over the next two decades, and assassination attempts by the pro-Pakistan Hizb-ul Mujahideen. In mid-1989 he recalled his imprisonment in 1987: "they called me a Pakistani bastard. I told them I wanted my rights, my vote was stolen. I am not pro-Pakistan but have lost faith in India." Yusuf Shah spoke to another Indian magazine in the autumn of 1992. By then he was the commander of Hizb-ul Mujahideen, operating under the nom de guerre Syed Salahuddin. He said he had taken up the gun because experience had convinced him that "slaves have no vote in the so-called democratic set-up of India."[68]

The most likely scenario had there been a free and fair election in 1987 was that the Muslim United Front would have won most of the constituencies in the Kashmir Valley and a few in the Jammu region and emerged as a large opposition in the J&K legislature, holding at least 30 of the 76 seats. The Muslim United Front's unity might not have lasted, given its ad hoc character and heterogeneous composition. Instead the second Farooq Abdullah government, with no legitimacy in the eyes of the bulk of the Valley's people, took office, and the Valley sank into a morass of frustration and radicalization. In June 1988 protests against a hike in the electricity tariff were fired on by police in Srinagar, and people were killed. In late July 1988 the first Jammu and Kashmir Liberation Front bomb attacks occurred in the city. General strikes and "black days" were observed across the Valley in 1988 and 1989 on India's Independence Day (August 15), Republic Day (January 26), the anniversaries of the 1931 Srinagar protests and the 1947 arrival of Indian troops in the Valley (July 13 and October 27), and the anniversary of the 1984 execution of the Jammu and Kashmir Liberation Front leader Maqbool Butt (February 11).

In August 1989 the Jammu and Kashmir Liberation Front's small band of underground militants began a campaign of targeted killings of members of the political establishment and men working as employees and agents of the extensive surveillance and intelligence-gathering apparatus in the Valley. The first victim was Mohammad Yusuf Halwai, a JKNC official in Srinagar who had been prominent in rigging the 1987 election in the city. He was shot dead by masked gunmen on a downtown street. On the same day, "many shops in Srinagar were closed in protest against the opening of a session of the State Assembly and police clashed in some districts with rock-throwing crowds."[69] Over the next six months, these targeted killings claimed the lives of about 100 men, approximately three-fourths of whom were Muslims and the rest Kashmiri Pandits.

In late November 1989 India's ninth national election after independence was held. This was the watershed election in India's evolution as a democracy that marked the end of over four decades of single-party dominance and ushered in the regionalization of India's polity of the next two decades. In the Kashmir Valley, the election was a decisive point in the people's estrangement from the Indian Union. Almost nobody voted. In Srinagar the JKNC candidate was "elected unopposed," as no other candidates filed nomination papers. In the other two parliamentary constituencies, Baramulla and Anantnag, the JKNC candidates won with 94 percent and 98 percent of the votes polled. The turnout in both constituencies was 5 percent of the electorate, partly achieved through stuffing of ballot boxes at selected polling stations. (Turnout was also abnormally low, at 39 percent, in one of the Jammu region's two Lok Sabha constituencies, the result of a negligible turnout among the Kashmiri-speaking Muslims of the Doda-Kishtwar zone.) The *Kashmir Times*, a respected daily newspaper in the state published from the city of Jammu, editorialized: "let the image of Indian democracy not be tarnished further in Kashmir."[70]

In the second half of January 1990, mass demonstrations demanding *azaadi* (freedom) from India broke out across the Kashmir Valley. Hundreds of thousands took to the streets in Srinagar, and tens of thousands marched in other towns like Baramulla, Sopore, and Anantnag. Farooq Abdullah's government was then dismissed from the Center under Article 356 of the Indian Constitution, citing a breakdown of law and order in the state.

War

I have recounted elsewhere the brutal and complicated saga of the war in J&K as it has evolved over the two decades since 1990.[71] In recent years, the story has also been told by writers who are from the Kashmir Valley, notably Basharat Peer, as a mix of autobiographical reminiscence and reportage, and Mirza Waheed, in the form of documentary fiction.[72]

According to official statistics, 43,460 people were killed in violence in J&K between January 1990 and April 2011. The large majority of these deaths occurred in the Kashmir Valley. Nearly half the victims, 21,323, are classified as "militants" (i.e. insurgents). Another 5,369 were members of the security forces: the Indian army, the CRPF and the Border Security Force, and the J&K police. The rest, 16,868, are classified as "civilians," of whom 13,226 are said to have been killed by militants and 3,642 by security forces.

Groups in the Kashmir Valley advocating "self-determination" commonly cite a death toll of civilians and insurgents combined of 80,000–100,000 over the same period. This may be implausibly high, but the official figures and their categorized breakdown of deaths also deserve scrutiny and skepticism. They do not include, for example, the "disappeared": persons taken away during the conflict, mostly by security forces, and never seen again. This number is somewhere between the low and high four digits. It is also unlikely that all of the 21,000-plus dead classified as "militants" were in fact insurgents. Anecdotal and circumstantial evidence suggests that a portion of these are civilians passed off as militants. And the breakdown of civilian fatalities is suspect; the number killed by militants is probably substantially inflated and the number killed by security forces substantially deflated. Yet even if the official figures are taken at face value, it is clear that at a minimum, apart from "the 4,000 or so *jawans* [soldiers] of the Army, BSF [Border Security Force] and CRPF and 5,000-odd *mehmaan mujahideen* [guest fighters] from Pakistan, 34,000 Kashmiri men and women" met violent deaths between 1990 and 2011.[73] The count of 34,000 is almost certainly an underestimate, and the probable actual figure is somewhere between 40,000 and 50,000, the vast majority in the Kashmir Valley.

Some elements of the official statistics are very revealing of the trajectory of the armed conflict. Thus the security forces killed 539 civilians in 1990, the year insurgency took off in the Kashmir Valley. Most of these civilians were agitated but unarmed people who marched in the huge *azaadi* demonstrations that year in Srinagar and other Valley towns and were gunned down in the hundreds by CRPF and Border Security Force personnel, all men from outside the state, who were as unnerved as they were enraged by an entire society in the throes of uprising. During 1991, 844 insurgents were killed in fighting with the security forces, of whom 842 were residents of J&K and who were overwhelmingly natives of the Valley, evidence of the wildfire spread of armed struggle in the Valley after the repression and atrocities of 1990. Among the dead militants were 72 young men who were intercepted and eliminated by Indian army

troops on the Line of Control on a single day in May 1991 while returning from Pakistan's "Azad" Kashmir with weapons and training, at the
start of the summer infiltration and fighting season.

A decade later, 1,612 militants were slain across the state in 2000. The
majority were locals native to J&K and mostly the Valley. But a sizable minority were Pakistani religious radicals who belonged to groups who were
closely linked to the Pakistani military's Directorate for Inter-Services Intelligence and who began to infiltrate across the Line of Control in the mid-
1990s to fight in the Valley and open new theaters of war in the Jammu region, especially the Rajouri and Poonch districts abutting the Line of
Control. Led and dominated by radicalized locals during the first half of the
1990s, the insurgency mutated over the decade into a protracted war in
which Pakistani religious zealots assumed a major role. By late 2002,
15,937 insurgents had died in confrontations with security forces since
1990. The deaths of "only" 5,386 militants in the next eight and a half
years, until April 2011, reveals the steady waning of the insurgency in the
course of the first decade of the twenty-first century, with a steep downward
graph of incidents and fatalities starting in 2004, when the regime of Pervez
Musharraf in Pakistan curbed support for the Kashmir "jehad." Despite the
intrusion of Pakistani radicals that escalated from the mid-1990s, over the
period 1990–2011 fewer than a quarter of the militants killed in combat
were *not* natives of the Indian state of J&K; these outsiders were overwhelmingly Pakistanis, most from that country's Punjab province. This fact
reveals the extent of anger toward Indian authority among the majority of
the state's population, above all in the Kashmir Valley.

Between 1989 and 2002, 55,538 incidents of violence arising from the
armed conflict were officially recorded in the war zones of J&K, the large
majority in the Kashmir Valley.[74] While statistics such as these give an
insight into the intensity of the violence that gripped the Valley after
1990, the magnitude of the trauma that percolates through the Valley's
society is not readily quantifiable. Hundreds of "martyrs' graveyards"
dot the Valley's towns and villages, the resting place of militant and civilian fatalities alike. Alongside the dead are the living relics of counterinsurgency: the survivors of torture. Starting in 1990, "interrogation centers" run by the paramilitary police and the army sprang up in Srinagar
and elsewhere in the Valley. Most of those who had the misfortune of
being inmates of such facilities were detained in "crackdowns"—
roundups in which the entire male population of a *mohalla* (urban neighborhood) or village was screened and suspects, often identified by masked
mukhbirs (informers) accompanying the troops, taken away. Many never
returned. Many others did, but commonly in a broken state (mentally,

physically, or both). The peak of the "excesses"—official jargon for summary executions, torture, and other violations—occurred during the peak of the insurgency (1990–1995), but serious abuses continued on a relatively diminished scale thereafter. In the second half of 1990 the government of India declared the Valley a "disturbed area" and subject to the Armed Forces Special Powers Act, which is descended from a law that the British had used in 1942–1943 to crush the Quit India movement launched by Indian freedom fighters and that Nehru's government first used in the late 1950s against rebellious tribes of the Naga people on the India-Myanmar border. These "emergency" regulations remain in force more than two decades later.

While loved ones in many families in the Valley have been killed in the violence or have suffered serious traumas such as torture during detention, many others have not. Yet even those fortunate to be spared a major familial tragedy have not escaped the harshness of counterinsurgency. During the first half of the 1990s the Valley was saturated with paramilitary and army forces, and checkpoints were common. Srinagar became a "bunker city," as almost every street had a bunker manned by paramilitary police, and the other major Valley towns were the same. (Between 1990 and 1993 the central market squares of the capital and other towns—Srinagar's Lal Chowk and equivalents in Sopore and Handwara in the northern Valley, Bijbehara in the southern Valley, and Doda in the Jammu region—were severely damaged by paramilitary personnel, mainly from the Border Security Force, who ran amok after being targeted by militants, and scores of civilians were killed in these incidents.) New army camps appeared across the rural areas of the Valley after the insurgency began. The result was a suffocating, prison-like atmosphere in which citizens regardless of age, gender, or political orientation have been subject to petty humiliation and abuse at checkpoints, at camps, and at the hands of ubiquitous roving patrols. Since the mid-1990s the oppressive atmosphere has gradually eased, but the essentials remain in place.

The Legacies

One legacy of this experience is the bitter resentment toward Indian authority that is widespread, almost pervasive, in the Valley's society. It is important to realize that this resentment is *not* a post-1990 development, though it has certainly deepened and sharpened since then. It dates back to 1953 and has been transmitted from generation to generation over six decades. The rage of the stone-pelters has a long lineage in the Valley's collective consciousness.

There are two other significant legacies of the violence that over-whelmed the Valley in the 1990s. The first is profound disillusionment with the "gun culture" introduced into the Valley by militancy. This disillusionment became manifest by the mid-1990s, as the mass enthusiasm of the first years of the *azaadi* uprising dissipated. Once the initial euphoria wore off, the Valley's people came to the (literally) painful realization that freedom, understood by most as independence, was not around the corner and the price of waging armed struggle was relentless repression and suffering with no end in sight. In the early 1990s it was fashionable to become a "freedom fighter," and droves of angry young men enlisted in a variety of militant *tanzeems* (groups) that sprouted across the Valley. This first phase also saw the exodus from the Valley, in controversial circumstances, of the bulk of the Pandit community, who numbered approximately 140,000 when the insurgency began. About 100,000 Pandits left the Valley for Jammu and Delhi in the space of a few weeks in February–March 1990. From 1990 to 1992, the Jammu and Kashmir Liberation Front dominated the insurgency, and its ideology of independence, however far-fetched, had mass resonance among the people. From 1993 on, however, the Kashmiri armed group Hizb-ul Mujahideen, who were backed by Pakistan's Inter-Services Intelligence, gained ascendancy in the insurgency, and the Jammu and Kashmir Liberation Front faded away by the mid-1990s. The attempt by Hizb-ul Mujahideen to impose their own understanding of *azaadi*, represented by the slogan "Kashmir Banega Pakistan" (Kashmir Will Be Part of Pakistan), on the Valley's people by means of the killing and intimidation of other guerrilla groups and civilians caused the insurgency to lose popular appeal and triggered a backlash: some members of Jammu and Kashmir Liberation Front and other armed groups changed sides and joined the Indian counterinsurgency campaign as auxiliaries, seeking protection, vengeance, or profit (or all three). In the second half of the 1990s a brutal civil war was fought between Hizb-ul Mujahideen cadres and these pro-India armed groups made up of surrendered insurgents.

In 1999 the insurgency in the Valley entered a new phase. Pakistani religious radicals, especially those belonging to the Lashkar-e-Taiba (Army of the Pious) assumed center stage and carried out scores of frontal assaults by two-man *fidayeen* (daredevil) teams, effectively suicide squads, against army and paramilitary camps, police stations, and other official installations. The *fidayeen* campaign, which peaked in 2001 and gradually fell off after 2003, caused problems for the counterinsurgency forces but was always a Pakistani rather than Kashmiri initiative. Some residents of the Valley harbored and helped the

Pakistani militants who came across the Line of Control, and the Lashkar-e-Taiba and a smaller *jehadi* group, Jaish-e-Mohammad (Army of the Prophet), recruited a small number of young Kashmiri men as cadres. But the role and participation of Valley people remained marginal in the campaign waged by these organizations, led by Pakistanis and headquartered in Pakistan.

The other legacy is disenchantment with Pakistan. During the second half of the 1980s, as the Valley festered with discontent, it was common for people to hold a positive view of Pakistan. In the first years of the insurgency, most people in the Valley saw Pakistan as a friendly big brother and strategic ally in their struggle. This started to change from 1993, once the Hizb-ul Mujahideen gained dominance in the insurgency and tried to take over the movement by using terror against fellow Kashmiris. The Hizb-ul Mujahideen's rise was due to vigorous sponsorship by Inter-Services Intelligence handlers, who simultaneously worked to undermine and weaken the proindependence Jammu and Kashmir Liberation Front. A large-scale reaction gradually grew in the Valley against heavy-handed and malign Pakistani interventions executed through local agents. The shambolic failure of democratization in Pakistan through the 1990s and Pervez Musharraf's Kargil misadventure in 1999 increased Kashmiris' skepticism.

Over the past decade, Pakistan's crisis-ridden existence has rendered it unappealing to the Valley's people. Pakistan's dire economic situation and prospects, its unstable civil-military relationship, and above all the blowback from the radical Islamists nurtured by the Pakistani military and Inter-Services Intelligence to push its interests in Afghanistan and Kashmir have made Pakistan's stocks in the Valley plummet to an all-time low. In the autumn of 2009, a polling agency conducted an extensive opinion survey on both sides of the Line of Control on behalf of the Royal Institute of International Affairs, a London think tank. This broadly credible survey found overwhelming support for the idea of independence in the Kashmir Valley, ranging from 75–95 percent in various districts. It also reported the percentage of Valley residents who wish to be part of Pakistan to be in the low single digits.[75]

The Kashmir Valley's relationship with the political institutions of J&K is complex. In 1996 the government in New Delhi deemed the insurgency sufficiently contained that elections to constitute a new state legislature and government could be held. These elections, which restored the JKNC and Farooq Abdullah to office, saw generally low turnout in the Valley and were marred by security forces coercing people to vote in rural areas. But there was some genuine participation by voters who felt that the restoration of a semblance of civilian government might dilute the oppressive weight of military and paramilitary forces on their lives. In state elections in 2002, turnout was again generally low albeit uneven, ranging from moderate to very low across Valley constituencies, a result of complicated local factors and dynamics. Forced voting occurred again in some rural areas, on a lesser scale than in 1996, and some fraud was perpetrated by JKNC members. But the 2002 state elections also saw some genuine participation in the Valley, mainly due to the emergence of a new regional party, the People's Democratic Party, committed to India but with a "propeople" stance on human rights and the aspiration to autonomy or "self-rule." (The PDP was formed in the late 1990s by Mufti Mohammad Sayeed, formerly a Congress leader in the southern part of the Valley since the 1960s.)

In both 1996 and 2002, election boycott calls given by political groups seeking "self-determination," reinforced by militant violence, achieved considerable impact in the Valley but were not totally effective. State elections in November–December 2008 saw moderate to high voter turnout in most parts of the Valley, with the notable exception of the city of Srinagar, where a boycott call prevailed. The regional parties the JKNC and the People's Democratic Party were the two main contestants, with Congress playing an also-ran role. There was almost no forced voting. The turnout was counterintuitive because a few months earlier, in July–August 2008, the Valley had seen the first mass demonstrations against Indian rule since 1994, even as militant violence declined to negligible levels. As Lashkar-e-Taiba launched its infamous terror attack in Mumbai in late November 2008, executed by 10 Pakistanis who had arrived by a sea route from Karachi, people in the Kashmir Valley were preoccupied with voting.

The Valley has learned to combine pragmatic electoral participation with a dogged attachment to the cause of *azaadi*. Its politics is overwhelmingly dominated by regional forces, in which establishment parties like the JKNC—now led by Sheikh Abdullah's grandson, Omar Abdullah—and the People's Democratic Party exist alongside a spectrum of political factions that advocate "self-determination." The stone-throwing uprising of 2010 sparked by the death of the teenager Tufail Mattoo revealed that the Achilles' heel of India's democracy remains as volatile as ever. The simmering anger in the Valley was accentuated in February 2013 by the hanging in Delhi's Tihar prison of Afzal Guru, a Valley native convicted of being an accomplice to a terrorist attack by Pakistani religious radicals, in December 2001, on the building where India's Parliament sits in New Delhi.

Figure 9. The Taj Mahal Hotel, Mumbai, on fire after a terrorist attack (November 2008). AFP/GETTY IMAGES.

The Future

Despite the tortured history and uncomfortable present of their relationship, the Kashmir Valley will have to live with the Indian Union, and the Indian Union will have to live with the Kashmir Valley.

A key driver of their uneasy coexistence is likely to be economic. For decades the Valley's traditional shawl and handicrafts trade has depended on the Indian market—customers in cities across India—and the Valley's tourism industry, comatose for many years from 1990, has revived since the decline of insurgency; its main clientele consists, as before, of masses of visitors from all over India. There is an additional factor peculiar to the early twenty-first century. Six decades ago the Kashmir Valley's population was overwhelmingly comprised of peasants newly emancipated from generations of serfdom. Now, as in India as a whole, there is a large and growing urbanized middle class, not just in Srinagar but in middle-sized and small towns across the Valley. The sons and daughters of the post-1990 generation—avid users of Facebook and Twitter, like their peers across the world—subscribe as strongly as their grandparents and parents to a Kashmiri identity, many males are experienced stone-pelters, and the vast majority will tell any opinion pollster that their preferred resolution to the Kashmir question is independence. Yet many aspire to higher education, professional training and careers outside the insular and often claustrophobic confines of the Kashmir Valley—in "India," where options "from air hostess to aerospace engineer" exist.[76]

The political relationship between the Indian Union and the Kashmir Valley is likely to remain unsettled for the foreseeable future. The Kashmir question in its totality has multiple dimensions: the India-Pakistan dispute, the cross–Line of Control aspect relating to the two parts of the divided former princely state, the internal tensions in the Indian state of J&K between the Valley and Hindus in the Jammu region, and the fractured and fractious politics of the Valley itself. All of these dimensions have an impact on the relationship between the Valley and the Union.

Moreover, the Kashmir question—meaning above all the "problem" of the Valley, the Union's most troublesome region, where "separatist" sentiment is deeply rooted and widespread—is a very sensitive issue in India's politics and difficult and risky for any political leadership in New Delhi to engage. The only Indian political leader of the post-1989 era who showed flashes of vision and initiative on the issue is Atal Behari Vajpayee, the moderate Hindu nationalist who was India's prime minister from 1998 to 2004. There is also a military command and a civilian bureaucratic establishment which sees the issue purely as a matter of national defense and security narrowly defined and is protective of the status quo, even if that status quo is fundamentally unstable and volatile.

It is noteworthy, nonetheless, that the real damage to the relationship between the Valley and the Union was inflicted from New Delhi between 1953 and 1989, i.e., in a now bygone era in which one party (and one political dynasty) dominated India's politics and an overweening Center lorded it or at least held the upper hand over states. In India's evolution as a democratic federation of regional (state-based) polities in the early twenty-first century, there is a glimmer of possibility of a positive reconstruction of the Valley-Union relationship. Any such reconstruction would require both sides to modify dogmatic positions and go beyond formulaic proposals. Were the glimmer of possibility to be acted on, it will attenuate the Achilles' heel of the world's largest democracy, and help India's emergence on the global stage.

The Future of India's Democracy

NDIA has a long history of being a "polycentric polity." Indeed, "Indian history can be read as an alternation between subcontinental empires and regional kingdoms, where regional kingdoms are understood as the relatively more homogenous forms . . . and empires are understood as aggregations of ethnically and culturally diverse polities." A relatively recent episode of this cycle of alternation happened during the eighteenth century, when the power and reach of the Mughal dynasty—which dominated most of the subcontinent from its capital in Delhi for about 150 years between the second half of the sixteenth century and the early eighteenth century—declined drastically. The result was "an emerging sense of regional identity which buttressed political and to a degree economic decentralization," and ironically this was partly because "different regions of the empire [had] gained in strength in the wake of relative peace and political stability under the Mughal system in the seventeenth century."[1]

Prior to the Mughals, the Tughlaq dynasty ruled much of the subcontinent for most the fourteenth century. The Tughlaqs divided their domain into 25 provinces. When Tughlaq power disintegrated at the end of the fourteenth century, many of the satraps of the provinces under Tughlaq suzerainty declared themselves sovereign rulers, and a host of regional sultanates came into being. In the words of one scholar, "the ancient natural divisions, which more or less represented the provinces of the empire, became independent kingdoms, such as for instance Malwa, Gujarat, Bengal, Jaunpur."[2] From the late sixteenth century the Mughals, who were of Central Asian Turkic origin, reinstated a Delhi-based empire over most of the subcontinent. But they too organized their vast and heterogeneous domain into numerous provinces *(subahs)*. Akbar, the greatest of the Mughal monarchs (reigned 1556–1605), established 15 new provinces as his domain expanded to encompass territory from Kabul to Bengal and Kashmir to the Deccan. The decline of Mughal power in the eighteenth century and the ensuing fragmentation of territorial control and political authority made for nearly a hundred years of growing political fluidity in an increasingly fractured subcontinent—until the first half of the nineteenth century, when the British East India Company expanded from its zones of control around the maritime trading centers of Calcutta, Madras, and Bombay to incrementally impose the writ of the British Raj on India.

That disunity, fragmentation, and a variety of rivalries among Indian kings, chieftains, and elites in different regions were cunningly exploited by the Company and led to this outcome is precisely why the Indian freedom movement that emerged and grew in the first half of the twentieth century strongly emphasized the need for a shared national identity and a sense of unity. The British conquest and colonization of India generated its own internal borders—the Bengal, Bombay, and Madras "presidencies" (huge administrative jurisdictions) evolved distinct identities and policies and even had separate armies until 1895. The patchwork of several hundred "princely states" of varying sizes and populations that the British created through the nineteenth century, governed by vassal Indian rulers who acknowledged British "paramountcy," eventually covered nearly half of the subcontinent's land area. British power over India rested on two operational principles: "indirect rule" and "divide and rule."

Thus "the propensity to organize India's governance into large regional units" goes back many centuries, and "regional political and administrative units, units that might be more or less autonomous, [are] an abiding aspect of India's political experience." When the sun set on the Raj after World War II, the colonial framework was replaced by "a new form of organization," the Indian Union, "that combined the relative autonomy of the regional kingdom and the encompassing and aggregating role of an empire."[3] This outcome was set in motion in 1920 when Mahatma Gandhi, who took up the reins of the anticolonial struggle after his return from South Africa and during the 1920s led its transformation into a mass movement, overhauled the organizational structure of the Indian National Congress. He replaced the provincial party committees based on British administrative demarcations with 20 Pradesh [State] Congress Committees, formed on the (approximate) territorial boundaries of the nation's major ethnolinguistic communities. Over the next two decades, this vision of India as a democratic union of autonomous ethno-linguistic states became the Congress party's blueprint for the independent nation-state. I have narrated how this vision prevailed in the 1950s, due to popular demand and protest, over Nehru's preference for a powerful central government that would exercise top-down authority over a few administrative zones modeled on the British paradigm.

The regionalization of India's polity over the past two decades, which gathered rapid momentum after the end of Congress's long domination of the nation's democracy in the watershed elections of November 1989 and the proliferation of mass-based parties and leaders based within a particular state of the Indian Union, is a still spreading and deepening process. Does this represent the return of history?

The contemporary transformation of India's democracy does carry strains and echoes from the past but is also fundamentally different in three crucial ways.

The first point of difference is that post-1947 India is not an empire. It is a twentieth-century nation-state underpinned by a widely (though not universally) shared sense of a national identity among its diverse peoples. This national identity was forged in the crucible of the struggle for freedom from colonial rule and has been consolidated since 1947 by the broad (though not unqualified) success of the Indian way of reconciling diversity with unity and community with nation. In 1978 the Indian film director Shyam Benegal made a riveting movie about the Great Revolt of 1857–1858, called the Sepoy Mutiny by the British and retrospectively the First War of Independence by twentieth-century Indian nationalists, which convulsed northern India and came close to driving the British out of the subcontinent. In the climactic scenes of the movie, *Junoon,* Hindu and Muslim soldiers of the Company's army who have rebelled against their masters are seen undertaking desperate cavalry charges against the British forces. As they sweep toward their adversaries in battle formation, the Hindu and Muslim horsemen carry differently colored flags signifying their religious faiths—saffron and green, respectively, two of the three colors in post-1947 India's national tricolor—and shout two different sets of war cries based on Hindu and Islamic idioms ("Har-Har-Mahadev" and "Allah-u-Akbar"). It took nearly a century before the next sizable set of British-trained Indian soldiers defected to the cause of India's freedom. These were the men who joined the Indian National Army, formed with Japanese support in Southeast Asia during World War II and led between 1943 and 1945 by the legendary Indian nationalist Subhas Chandra Bose. They had a common war cry, "Jai Hind!"

(Victory to India), which became independent India's national slogan, and a common flag, the Congress tricolor with the *charkha* (spinning wheel popularized by Gandhi) set in the center, on which the saffron-white-green flag of independent India is modeled.

The second point of difference is that the rise and growing dominance of regional (state-based) power in India's politics is not, as in the historical past, the result of governors and generals in the provinces opportunistically throwing off the suzerainty of a weakened central (and "imperial") authority. The regionalization of India's politics in the last decade of the twentieth century and the first and second decades of this century has developed democratically through the popular will, because the demos in more and more Indian states has chosen to vote for state-specific parties and politicians. (And in many states today, from Tamil Nadu and Andhra Pradesh to West Bengal and UP and Bihar, multiple regional political formations compete against each other to win popular support and political power.) This is emphatically *not* the scenario of Yugoslavia in the early 1990s, where differences between largely, though not entirely, territorially concentrated ethnonational communities festered in an authoritarian, one-party political framework, papered over by the shallow slogan "Brotherhood and Unity," and triggered civil war and the breakup of the state once the one-party regime lost cohesiveness and collapsed.

For all the flaws and vices of many of contemporary India's regional(ist) political figures, the regionalization of India's politics is a democratic outcome that has emerged through the dynamic evolution of India's democracy over six decades. It is a bottom-up federalization of the polity driven by the will of the demos. The latest rising star in India's regionalized political landscape is the YSR Congress, a breakaway party from Congress in Andhra Pradesh that is named after the state's former Congress chief minister, Y. S. Rajasekhara Reddy, who governed from 2004 until he was killed in a helicopter crash in 2009. The party is led by the deceased leader's son, who faces serious criminal charges of accumulating vast amounts of money and assets through blatant corruption during his strongman father's term in office. But that has not prevented the new regional party from gaining mass popularity among the electorate in Andhra Pradesh at the expense of Congress.

The third point of difference is derived from the first two. In the polycentric polities of India's medieval and early modern past, "a center [held] together and dominat[ed] subordinate [regional] polities with which it share[d] power."[4] This may be an approximately accurate description of the Indian Union as it existed from 1947 to 1989 as well. But in the post-November 1989 era of regionalization and the growth of mass parties based in one state of the Union, a decentered democracy has developed in which the state polities, always the building blocks of the Union, call the shots over the Center. They form distinct and autonomous arenas of political contestation that determine the shape and composition of coalition governments in New Delhi.

It is apt that the essence of India, its diversity, defines the nature of its democracy. But the transformation of India's democracy has major implications and presents significant challenges for the nation's political and social equilibrium, economic and developmental prospects, and emerging position as a key player in a multipolar world.

The two rising giants of Asia, China and India, have completely different political systems and political cultures but face challenges of a remarkably similar nature. India has a much more widespread problem of acute poverty, and China has far superior infrastructure (especially highways and roads). But both are grappling with the problems of social inequality and interregional disparities in levels of prosperity.[5] China's mantra is "Harmonious Development," and India's is "Inclusive Growth." Both are clever, glib slogans.

China and India face the common problem of scandalous levels of corruption among politicians and bureaucrats, including those holding high office: bribe-taking, embezzlement, and various forms of plunder of public resources. India's problem of graft is well known, while China's problem has been labeled a "corruption epidemic" by scholars and termed a matter of "life and death" for the system's legitimacy among the people by both Jiang Zemin and Hu Jintao, the top leaders of China's party-state in 1992–2002 and 2002–2012. As China undertook its decennial leadership transition in late 2012, the outgoing premier, Hu Jintao, warned that corruption "could prove fatal" to the party-state, echoing Jiang Zemin's warning of "self-destruction" given 10 years earlier.[6]

China and India both face stubborn challenges to state authority from discontented nationalities with a territorial base. China has the Tibetans, as well as the Uighurs of Xinjiang province. India has an unresolved problem with the people of the Kashmir Valley, as well as with some communities in the nation's northeastern borderlands wedged between China, Bhutan, Myanmar, and Bangladesh. The political and military establishments of both countries see these rebellious peoples within as a particularly sensitive issue, partly because of the international ramifications; while Tibetan opposition to China has networks of supporters in "the West," Kashmiri dissidence has a self-interested advocate in Pakistan.

Due to its spectacular rates of economic growth over two and a half decades, China is already having to cope with a massive population of rural migrants who live and work in the nation's burgeoning urban centers. The total migrant population is around 250 million people, about half of whom are young people born in the post-1979 era of economic reform.[7] The pace of urbanization in India is much slower in comparison, but India also faces a mass rural-to-urban influx over the next two decades. This is likely to put a great deal of pressure on the inadequate, creaky infrastructure of India's cities and breed new social problems.

Finally, neither China nor India has yet worked out a coherent, holistic strategy to cope with its enhanced weight and rising importance in the international system and global geopolitics. China, whose weight and importance in this respect significantly exceeds India's, has coined a maxim, "Peaceful Rise," in lieu of a strategy. India lacks a strategic foreign policy vision adequate to its status, and needs, in the early twenty-first century. It has been pointed out that India's foreign policy "software," that is, its professional diplomatic service and the caliber of international affairs and strategic studies expertise in its universities and nascent think tanks, is woefully short of the standards that can be reasonably expected of a "rising power."[8] And both China's and India's (near) futures are inextricably tied to the wider world. While both avoided being hit hard by the economic crisis that has gripped the Euro-Atlantic world since 2008, they are not immune to its effects, when combined with the internal structural problems and policy-making bottlenecks in both countries. India's economic growth, eye-catching since about 2003, slowed in 2008–2009 and again in 2011–2012 and 2012–2013, amid persistent inflation in food prices. China, too, is faced with an economic slowdown of uncertain magnitude and consequences.[9]

In coping with this gamut of challenges, China has the advantage of a more disciplined and efficient state than India's, because the Chinese state is authoritarian, hierarchical, and command-driven (although that is not in itself a guarantee of efficacy in the longer run).[10] India's democracy, by contrast, resembles a cacophonous bazaar, and its decentered, regionalized character in the early twenty-first century complicates the question whether the Indian state has the capacity to successfully cope with extant and emerging challenges.

The answer to that question depends largely on the arbiters of India's democracy in the early twenty-first century—the nation's powerful regional politicians, men and women who enjoy a mass base in one state of the Indian Union, especially the dozen most populous states, which

Figure 10.   Thousands of young people, protesting the gang-rape in Delhi of a 23-year-old woman from a working-class family, confront riot police in the center of New Delhi (December 2012). INDIA TODAY GROUP/GETTY IMAGES.

contain about four-fifths of the nation's population. The era of nation-wide leaders is definitively in the past, rendered obsolete by the transformation of India's democracy.

The capacity of this democracy to cope with India's many challenges is critically contingent on three factors. The first is the ability of the powerful leaders of state polities to provide competent and (relatively) corruption-free governance that delivers tangible socioeconomic development and opportunities for a better life to their populations. It is crucial in the early twenty-first century for regionalist leaders governing the states to break out of and transcend the boundaries of caste, religion, and political partisanship, although mobilizations on such fault-lines may have facilitated their political ascent in the first place, so as to govern in the broad interest of the entire populations of their states.

The most intelligent of contemporary India's state-based elected leaders, and not only those who belong to explicitly regional (state-specific) parties, have realized that this is the winning formula of the future, as electorates across the country are becoming progressively less susceptible to "primordial" instincts and appeals and more discerning on issues of performance, and fair-minded as well as forward-looking governance. The youthfulness of India's population, and therefore its electorate, is a factor in this evolution, as is the gradually increasing participation of women in political life. The reservation by laws enacted in various states of seats and positions for women in *panchayat* bodies in rural India and municipal bodies in urban centers over the past two decades has aided this development, but a deeper factor is the slow breaking of the social shackles of gender. In the twenty-first century, the turnout of women voters in elections, particularly state elections, has grown significantly, even in northern states like UP and Bihar, traditionally known for low participation of women voters and even more for the paucity of female elected public officials in the towns and villages. In the next one to two decades, successful political strategies and campaigns in India will increasingly be those that appeal to "new" or rising constituencies—women, youth (roughly the 18–35 age cohort), and the growing numbers aspiring to a "middle-class" existence—rather than simply the "old" constituencies defined by caste or religion or ethnicity. However, this will happen unevenly across the country, subject to much specificity and variation across states, and in the context of the nation's regionalized political landscape.

The second critical factor is the ability of regional political leaders to adopt a national perspective when necessary and needed. In the important work *Democracy and Difference,* published two decades ago, a British political philosopher wrote: "none, I imagine, would want to flee the abstractions of an undifferentiated humanity only to end up in its opposite; none would favor the kind of politics in which people only speak for their own group identity and interests, and never address any wider concerns."[11] Similarly, one can argue that none would want to escape from a monolithic notion of Indian identity and citizenship and its political corollary, parties spuriously claiming to encompass and represent the nation (of which Congress embodied one variant through a vacuous "centrism" and the BJP another through a politically unsustainable construct of Hindu identity) only to end up in ghettoes defined by the boundaries of ethnicity, language, caste, or for that matter the political units known as states. Even as Indian democracy blooms in all its diversity in the early twenty-first century, certain kinds of policy need to be based, as in all federal systems, on a judgment of the best interest of the whole nation, on matters ranging from structural economic reforms to foreign policy. Even as India's rise is contingent on the strength of its constituent parts—confident states that can deliver decent governance, in the form of effective antipoverty programs, multipronged socioeconomic development and opportunity, especially good-quality education and jobs—the prospects of the parts are linked to each other, and the ultimate political community is the nation as a whole.

Shared decision-making on matters of national scope and importance can only be realized through *concertacion,* a political term familiar in Spanish-speaking countries in Iberia and Latin America that can be translated idiomatically as the skill of pact-making between different (and often rival) segments of the political class. India is still some way from developing effective *concertacion,* but it is the third critical factor that will determine the efficacy of India's democracy in the near-term future. A notable example of failure to forge such consensual decision-making was when in 2012 the Union home (interior) ministry—held by Congress, the senior partner in the coalition government in New Delhi, like other major ministries including finance, defense, and external (foreign) affairs—attempted to establish what was to be called the National Counter-Terrorism Center, loosely modeled on the national-level government body of the same name formed in the United States after the attacks of September 11, 2001.

Intuitively, this should not have been difficult or politically contentious, given the reality and seriousness of the terror threat to India, as revealed above all by the November 2008 assault on Mumbai. However, the proposal was stymied by strong opposition from the chief ministers of West Bengal, Bihar, Tamil Nadu, and Orissa, all leaders of regional parties based in those states, with the West Bengal party then the second-largest constituent of the coalition government in New Delhi. All felt they had not been appropriately consulted in the making of the proposal and that the counter-terrorism center, as visualized by Congress, would encroach unacceptably on the states' jurisdiction over law enforcement. They were not alone in their dissent. Another vociferous objector, who cited the same reasons, was the BJP chief minister of Gujarat, a de facto regionalist kingpin who has hawkish views on national security and counterterrorism. Other critics included the chief minister of J&K, who represents the state's oldest regional party, formed more than seven decades ago and part of the governing coalition at the Center; the BJP chief minister of Chhattisgarh, a state affected in parts by a strong Maoist insurgency; and even the Congress chief minister of Assam, a state with a recent history of secessionist insurgency. An Indian newspaper editorialized in May 2012:

the NCTC [the counter-terrorism center] impasse mirrors a larger breakdown. On NCTC, the Congress did not just refuse to talk to the States, it also did not work the lines of communication at the Center. But it is the Congress's inability or unwillingness or both to strike a dialogue with the States that is likely to come back to haunt. Quite simply, the party has failed to acknowledge that in its new [postregionalization] phase, federalism is not just the virtual exorcism of Article 356 from the Center's arsenal [the constitutional provision used by Congress governments for decades to dismiss elected opposition governments in the states]. Federalism today requires the Center to engage the States on all major decisions with nationwide consequences, such as the now stillborn NCTC.[12]

In the post-1989 era, the people of India have progressively empowered regional(ist) parties and leaders. As a result, India's democracy has steadily transformed into a full-blooded federation of state-based polities. It is now up to the empowered regionalists, and the next generation of regional(ist) leaders who will come after them, to live up to the needs and expectations of the people of the world's largest democracy.

Notes

Introduction

1. Seymour Martin Lipset, "Some Social Requisites of Democracy: Economic Development and Political Legitimacy," *American Political Science Review* 53, 1 (1959), 69–105. See also Lipset, *Political Man: The Social Bases of Politics* (Garden City, N.Y.: Doubleday, 1960), especially chapter 2 ("Economic Development and Democracy") of part 1 ("The Conditions of the Democratic Order").
2. John Stuart Mill, *Considerations on Representative Government* (New York: Liberal Arts Press, 1958 [1861]), 230, 232–233.
3. K. S. James, "India's Demographic Change: Opportunities and Challenges," *Science* 333 (2011), 576–580; *Global Trends 2030: Alternative Worlds* (Washington, D.C.: National Intelligence Council, 2012).
4. "India setting up foreign aid agency," *Hindustan Times*, July 17, 2011 (internet ed.); "India's middle-class population to rise, key driver for Asia's rise by 2050," *Times of India*, May 5, 2011 (internet ed.).
5. "Why Does the UK Give Aid to India?," BBC News Online, March 1, 2011; "Twenty years on, job half done," *Hindustan Times*, July 24, 2011, 8–9; "Ghare ghare jaler cheye mobile pounchhochhe druto" [Mobiles reaching homes faster than water], *Anandabazar Patrika* [Bengali], March 15, 2012 (internet ed.).
6. "The Great Indian divide," *Hindustan Times*, December 18, 2011, 9.
7. "The poverty line debate," *Hindustan Times*, October 2, 2011, 10–11.

1. From Independence to 1989

1. Since the name of the Communist Party of India (Marxist), or CPI-M, is usually referred to in India as the CPM, the latter abbreviation is used throughout the text.

2. For the statistics quoted here, see David Butler, Ashok Lahiri, and Prannoy Roy, *India Decides: Elections 1952–1995* (New Delhi: Books and Things, 1995).

3. M. J. Akbar, *India, the Siege Within: Challenges to a Nation's Unity* (New Delhi: Roli Books, 2003), 95.

4. D. A. Low, introduction to Low, ed., *The Political Inheritance of Pakistan* (London: Macmillan, 1991), 16.

5. Lloyd Rudolph and Susanne Rudolph, *In Pursuit of Lakshmi: The Political Economy of the Indian State* (Chicago: University of Chicago Press, 1987), 50.

6. The term "Congress system" was used in Rajni Kothari, *Politics in India* (Boston: Little Brown, 1970).

7. Christophe Jaffrelot, *India's Silent Revolution: The Rise of the Lower Castes in North India* (London: Hurst, 2003), 68, 83, 87.

8. Kathinka Froystad, *Blended Boundaries: Caste, Class and the Shifting Faces of "Hinduness" in a North Indian City* (New Delhi: Oxford University Press, 2005), 247.

9. See Joya Chatterji, *The Spoils of Partition: Bengal and India, 1947–1967* (Cambridge: Cambridge University Press, 2007).

10. David Forgacs, ed., *The Antonio Gramsci Reader* (New York: Schocken Books, 1988), 255.

11. Balveer Arora and Nirmal Mukarji, "The Basic Issues," in Nirmal Mukarji and Balveer Arora, eds., *Federalism in India: Origins and Development* (New Delhi: Vikas, 1992), 7.

12. Balveer Arora, "Adapting Federalism to India," in Balveer Arora and Douglas Verney, eds., *Multiple Identities in a Single State: Indian Federalism in Comparative Perspective* (New Delhi: Konark, 1995), 71; Akbar, *India, the Siege Within,* 74, 79.

13. Akbar, *India, the Siege Within,* 80–81.

14. Daniel Elazar, *Exploring Federalism* (Tuscaloosa: University of Alabama Press, 1987).

15. Arora, "Adapting Federalism to India," 71; S. Guhan, "Federalism and the New Political Economy in India," in Arora and Verney, *Multiple Identities in a Single State,* 268.

16. See Butler, Lahiri, and Roy, *India Decides.*

17. On the "green revolution" and its implications for politics, see Francine Frankel, *India's Green Revolution: Economic Gains and Political Costs* (Princeton: Princeton University Press, 1971), and Francine Frankel, *India's Political Economy, 1947–1977: The Gradual Revolution* (Princeton: Princeton University Press, 1978).

18. Gurmit Singh, *A History of Sikh Struggles* (New Delhi: Atlantic Publishers, 1991), 39.

19. See Butler, Lahiri and Roy, *India Decides,* for the detailed results.

20. Ibid.

21. See Sanjib Baruah, *India against Itself: Assam and the Politics of Nationality* (Philadelphia: University of Pennsylvania Press, 1999).

22. Walter Andersen and Shridhar Damle, *The Brotherhood in Saffron: The Rashtriya Swayamsevak Sangh and Hindu Revivalism* (New Delhi: Vistaar, 1987), 231–232.

23. Farooq Abdullah, *My Dismissal* (New Delhi: Vikas, 1985), 1–2.

24. Paul Brass, *Ethnicity and Nationalism: Theory and Comparison* (New Delhi: Sage, 1991), 210, 212.

25. Seema Mustafa, "Uttar Pradesh Government Took Sides in Ayodhya Dispute," in Asghar Ali Engineer, ed., *The Babri Masjid-Ramjanambhoomi Controversy* (New Delhi: Ajanta Books, 1990), 117.

26. Rudolph and Rudolph, *In Pursuit of Lakshmi,* 194–197.

27. Zoya Hasan, "Changing Orientation of the State and the Emergence of Majoritarianism in the 1980s," in K. N. Panikkar, ed., *Communalism in India: History, Politics and Culture* (New Delhi: Manohar Books, 1991), 147.

28. Akbar, *India, the Siege Within,* 311.

29. See Andrew Davison, *Secularism and Revivalism in Turkey: A Hermeneutic Reconsideration* (New Haven: Yale University Press, 1998).

30. An early authoritative study of the nature of India's "secular state" is Donald E. Smith, *India as a Secular State* (Princeton: Princeton University Press, 1963).

31. Atul Kohli, *The State and Poverty in India: The Politics of Reform* (Cambridge: Cambridge University Press, 1987), 108.

32. Arora, "Adapting Federalism to India," 91.

33. Nirmal Mukarji and George Mathew, "Federal Issues, 1988–1990," in Mukarji and Arora, *Federalism in India,* 282.

34. A. G. Noorani, "Congress Agreed to Ram Shilanyas," in Engineer, *Babri Masjid-Ramjanambhoomi Controversy,* 151.

35. Bruce Graham, *Hindu Nationalism and Indian Politics: The Origins and Development of the Bharatiya Jan Sangh* (Cambridge: Cambridge University Press, 1990), 254; Andersen and Damle, *Brotherhood in Saffron,* 248.

2. The Transformation since 1990

1. David Forgacs, ed., *The Antonio Gramsci Reader* (New York: Schocken Books, 1988), 144–146.

2. Dag Erik Berg, *Dalits and the Constitutional State: Untouchability, Dalit Movements and Legal Approaches to Equality and Social Justice for India's Scheduled Castes* (Ph.D. diss., University of Bergen, Norway, 2011).

3. Christophe Jaffrelot, *India's Silent Revolution: The Rise of the Lower Castes in North India* (London: Hurst, 2003), 343–344.

4. Ibid., 346.

5. Francine Frankel, "Middle Classes and Castes in India's Politics: Prospects for Political Accommodation," in Atul Kohli, ed., *India's Democracy: An Analysis of Changing State-Society Relations* (New Delhi: Orient Longman, 1991), 255, 259.

6. *Indian Express,* September 8, 1990, 1.

7. See K. R. Malkani, *Principles for a New Political Party* (Delhi: Vijay Pustak Bhandar, 1951).

8. V. D. Savarkar, *Hindu Rashtra Darshan* (Bombay: Veer Savarkar Prakashan, 1984), 7, 10, 78–79, 196.

9. Ashis Nandy, "The Politics of Secularism and the Recovery of Religious Tolerance," in Veena Das, ed., *Mirrors of Violence: Communities, Riots and Survivors in South Asia* (New Delhi: Oxford University Press, 1990), 70, 78, 83.

10. M. S. Golwalkar, *Bunch of Thoughts* (Bangalore: Vikram Prakashan, 1968), 437–438.

11. Ibid., 18, 108–110.

12. Savarkar, *Hindu Rashtra Darshan*, 109–111.

13. H. V. Seshadri, *RSS: A Vision in Action* (Bangalore: Jagaran Prakashan, 1988), 242–248.

14. See Craig Baxter, *The Jan Sangh: A Biography of an Indian Political Party* (Philadelphia: University of Pennsylvania Press, 1969), 270–289.

15. Bruce Graham, *Hindu Nationalism and Indian Politics: The Origins and Development of the Bharatiya Jan Singh* (Cambridge: Cambridge University Press, 1990), 255.

16. See Ornit Shani, *Communalism, Caste and Hindu Nationalism: The Violence in Gujarat* (Cambridge: Cambridge University Press, 2007), 77–88.

17. M. S. Golwalkar, *We, or Our Nationhood Defined* (Nagpur: Bharat Prakashan, 1947), 55–56. This tract was first published in 1938 or 1939.

18. Unless otherwise noted, the term "constituency" will denote "parliamentary constituency" hereafter.

19. An useful collection of articles on the Ayodhya issue is S. Gopal, ed., *Anatomy of a Confrontation: The Ramjanambhoomi-Babri Masjid Dispute* (New Delhi: Penguin Books, 1991).

20. S. Guhan, "Federalism and the New Political Economy in India," in Balveer Arora and Douglas Verney, eds., *Multiple Identities in a Single State: Indian Federalism in Comparative Perspective* (New Delhi: Konark, 1995), 237–238.

21. Ibid., 238.

22. Thomas Blom Hansen, *The Saffron Wave: Democracy and Hindu Nationalism in Modern India* (Princeton: Princeton University Press, 1999), 20–21; Alexis de Tocqueville, *Democracy in America* (London: Harper and Row, 1966).

23. See Ajoy Bose, *Behenji: A Political Biography of Mayawati* (New Delhi: Penguin Books, 2008).

24. Forgacs, *Antonio Gramsci Reader*, 217–219.

25. Sonia Gandhi, "Inaugural address of the Congress president," September 4, 1998. All India Congress Committee, www.congresssandesh.com/AICC/president/speech/pachmarhi_camp.htm (accessed March 27, 2013).

26. See Kingshuk Nag, *Battleground Telangana: Chronicle of an Agitation* (New Delhi: HarperCollins, 2011).

27. "Supreme Court puts Government under hammer," *Hindustan Times,* February 3, 2012, 1.

28. Vir Sanghvi, "On to the next campaign," *Hindustan Times,* December 21, 2012, 10. See also Ashok Malik, "Hate him or love him, Modi has worked

for Gujarat," *Hindustan Times,* October 10, 2012 (internet ed.), and Ashok Malik, "Capitalist hero: How Modi made reforms work for Gujaratis," *Hindustan Times,* November 1, 2012 (internet ed.).

29. "Jairam playing politics, Maya writes to PM," *Indian Express,* October 29, 2011 (internet ed.).

30. "Jaya attacks Center, says communal violence bill is fascist," *Hindustan Times,* October 22, 2011 (internet ed.).

31. "Haripur happy Mamata said "No" to N-plant," *Sunday Guardian,* September 25, 2011, 6.

32. "Chief Ministers united on increasing states' powers: Mamata leads the struggle," *Ananda Bazar Patrika* [Bengali], January 1, 2012, 1.

33. "Mamata is game for third front," *Hindustan Times,* September 27, 2012, 1.

34. Seshadri, *RSS,* 9.

35. Paranjoy Guha Thakurta and Shankar Raghuraman, *A Time of Coalitions: Divided We Stand* (New Delhi: Sage, 2004), 393.

36. See Jaffrelot, *India's Silent Revolution,* 377–386.

37. "Bihar's virtuous cycle," *Hindustan Times,* August 10, 2010, 2.

38. "Blog talk: Caste won't be a factor in polls, says Nitish," *Hindustan Times,* September 16, 2010, 3.

39. "Interview with Nitish Kumar," *Hindustan Times,* October 11, 2010, 3.

40. A sympathetic biography of Nitish Kumar is Arun Sinha, *Nitish Kumar and the Rise of Bihar* (New Delhi: Penguin Books, 2011). A thoughtful appraisal of the achievements and limits of Nitish Kumar's approach appeared in a two-part article by Amitava Gupta, "Sarkar kaaj korbey, Biharey ekhon Bishwaser hawa" [The people of Bihar believe in this government] and "Nitisher unnayaner sarak kon gantabye pounchobe" [Where will Nitish's road to development lead], in the Kolkata-based Bengali daily newspaper *Ananda Bazar Patrika,* January 6–7, 2011.

41. Sankarshan Thakur, "Nitish: Bihar's mood is *dil maange more* [the heart wants more], we have raised people's expectations," *Telegraph,* November 24, 2012 (internet ed.).

42. "*Sadbhavana:* A prayer for togetherness," *Hindustan Times,* September 17, 2011, 7.

43. "Cumbersome food bill could crumble under its own weight," *Hindustan Times,* December 26, 2011, 9.

3. Democracy in West Bengal

1. For a history of Bengal from antiquity to 1971, see Nitish Sengupta, *Land of Two Rivers: A History of Bengal from the Mahabharata to Mujib* (New Delhi: Penguin Books, 2011).

2. See Sugata Bose, *His Majesty's Opponent: Subhas Chandra Bose and India's Struggle against Empire* (Cambridge, Mass.: Harvard University Press, 2011).

3. David Butler, Ashok Lahiri and Prannoy Roy, *India Decides: Elections 1952– 1995* (New Delhi: Books and Things, 1995), 317.

4. For a detailed account of the refugees in West Bengal, see Joya Chatterji, *The Spoils of Partition: Bengal and India, 1947–1967* (Cambridge: Cambridge University Press, 2007), 105–158.

5. See Paul R. Greenough, *Prosperity and Misery in Modern Bengal: The Famine of 1943–44* (New Delhi: Oxford University Press, 1983).

6. Edward Duyker, *Tribal Guerrillas: The Santals of West Bengal and the Naxalite Movement* (New Delhi: Oxford University Press, 1987), 71.

7. Ibid., 72–73.

8. Arild Engelsen Ruud, "Land and Power: The Marxist Conquest of Rural Bengal," *Modern Asian Studies* 28, 2 (1994), 358.

9. Atul Kohli, *The State and Poverty in India: The Politics of Reform* (Cambridge: Cambridge University Press, 1987), 118.

10. Ruud, "Land and Power," 364.

11. Ibid., 375.

12. Ibid., 359, 361, 369, 379.

13. Kohli, *State and Poverty in India,* 108, 117, 139.

14. Ibid., 100, 110–111, 118.

15. Ibid., 114, 140.

16. Ross Mallick, *Development Policy of a Communist Government: West Bengal since 1977* (Cambridge: Cambridge University Press, 1993), 70.

17. Ibid., 55–56.

18. Ruud, "Land and Power," 373; Kohli, *State and Poverty in India,* 118.

19. Mallick, *Development Policy of a Communist Government,* 55.

20. Kohli, *State and Poverty in India,* 129–130.

21. Mallick, *Development Policy of a Communist Government,* 216.

22. Mamata Banerjee, *My Unforgettable Memories* (New Delhi: Roli Books, 2012), 40, 76. For an insightful biography of Banerjee, see Monobina Gupta, *Didi: A Political Biography* (New Delhi: HarperCollins, 2012).

23. Anirban Choudhury, "Deaths in 1993 rally," *Hindustan Times,* July 22, 2010, 1 (Kolkata Metro sec.).

24. Banerjee, *My Unforgettable Memories,* 108–109.

25. Dwaipayan Bhattacharyya, "Left in the Lurch: The Demise of the World's Longest Elected Regime?," *Economic and Political Weekly* 45, 3 (2010), 51.

26. Kohli, *State and Poverty in India,* 121–122.

27. Chatterji, *Spoils of Partition,* 136–139; Snigdhendu Bhattacharya, "Ghosts of Marichjhapi," *Hindustan Times* (Kolkata ed.), April 25, 2011, 2.

28. Bhattacharya, "Ghosts of Marichjhapi."

29. Ravik Bhattacharya, "The misery bowl," *Hindustan Times* (Kolkata ed.), April 29, 2011, 2.

30. Sumanta Ray Chaudhuri, "Left in the lurch," *Hindustan Times* (Kolkata ed.), April 23, 2011, 2.

31. Prime Minister's High-Level Committee, *Social, Economic and Educational Status of the Muslim Community of India: A Report* (New Delhi: Cabinet Secretariat, Government of India, 2006).

32. Arnab Mitra and Snigdhendu Bhattacharya, "Reign of red terror loses bite," *Hindustan Times* (Kolkata ed.), April 17, 2011, 5.

33. Naresh Jana, "To Trinamool rally, with a smile," *Telegraph,* July 20, 2011 (internet ed.).

4. The Maoist Challenge

1. Caesar Mandal, "Top Maoist, five aides shot in Lalgarh: Soren an irreplaceable loss for the rebels," *Times of India* (Kolkata ed.), July 27, 2010, 1, 2; Caesar Mandal, "Sidhu joined Maoists in school," *Times of India* (Kolkata ed.), July 28, 2010, 3.
2. The program of the CPI(ML) adopted by the party congress of May 1970, reproduced as app. 2 in Edward Duyker, *Tribal Guerrillas: The Santals of West Bengal and the Naxalite Movement* (New Delhi: Oxford University Press, 1987), 173–179.
3. Ibid.
4. A list of Charu Mazumdar's writings, compiled as app. 2 of Sumanta Banerjee, *India's Simmering Revolution: The Naxalite Uprising* (London: Zed Books, 1984), 323–325.
5. The information in this paragraph is from Ashim Chatterjee, *Ei Samayer Dalil O Anyanyo* (Kolkata: Ananda, 2011), 78–79. The point about social backgrounds is mine.
6. Duyker, *Tribal Guerrillas,* 163.
7. Samaresh Majumdar, *Kaalbaela* (Kolkata: Ananda, 2008). The 2008 edition is the fifteenth reprint of the novel, which was first published in 1983.
8. Bela Bhatia, "The Naxalite Movement in Central Bihar," *Economic and Political Weekly* 40, 15 (2005), 1541.
9. Ibid., 1544.
10. George J. Kunnath, "Smouldering Dalit fires in Bihar, India," *Dialectical Anthropology* 33 (2009), 309–325.
11. Communist Party of India (Marxist-Leninist)-Liberation, *Report from the Flaming Fields of Bihar* (Calcutta: Prabodh Bhattacharya, 1986).
12. G. S. Radhakrishna, "Fertile Kishen Nagar," *Telegraph,* November 28, 2011 (internet ed.).
13. Ibid.
14. Comrade Ganapati, "Nobody Can Kill the Ideas of Azad! Nobody Can Stop the Advance of the Revolution!," *People's March* 11, 5 (2010), 3.
15. "Red Homage to Comrade Chandramouli and Comrade Karuna," *People's March* 8, 4 (2007), 25–28.
16. K. Balagopal, "Maoist Movement in Andhra Pradesh," *Economic and Political Weekly* 41, 29 (2006), 3183; K. Balagopal, "Naxalite Terrorists and Benign Policemen," *Economic and Political Weekly* 32, 36 (1997), 2255; Jairus Banaji, "The Ironies of Indian Maoism," *International Socialism* 128 (2010), 139.
17. K. Balagopal, "Chenna Reddy's Spring," *Economic and Political Weekly* 25, 12 (1990), 591.
18. Azad (Cherukuri Rajkumar), "Maoists in India: A Rejoinder," *Economic and Political Weekly* 41, 41 (2006), 4379–4383. The full text of the 1970 CPI(ML) program is in Duyker, *Tribal Guerrillas,* 173–179.

19. Banaji, "Ironies of Indian Maoism," 146; Gautam Navlakha, "Days and Nights in the Heartland of Rebellion," April 1, 2010, Sanhati, http://sanhati .com/articles/2250/, 40–41 (accessed April 1, 2013).

20. Bhatia, "Naxalite Movement in Central Bihar," 1540, 1542, 1547, 1548.

21. "Maoists joining mainstream to cleanse system legally," *Hindustan Times* (Kolkata ed.), September 28, 2012, 7.

22. Kunnath, "Smouldering Dalit fires in Bihar, India," 320–322.

23. Alpa Shah, *In the Shadows of the State: Indigenous Politics, Environmentalism and Insurgency in Jharkhand, India* (Durham, N.C.: Duke University Press, 2010), 162–183.

24. Bhatia, "Naxalite Movement in Central Bihar," 1548.

25. "We Shall Certainly Defeat the Government: Ganapati," *People's March* 10, 11 (2009), 5.

26. K. Balagopal, "A Tale of Arson," *Economic and Political Weekly* 22, 29 (1987), 1171; Balagopal, "Naxalite terrorists and benign policemen," 2257.

27. "List of Mahila [women] comrades killed in AP during the last 2.5 years," *People's March* 8, 5 (2007), 30.

28. Balagopal, "Chenna Reddy's Spring," 591; Balagopal, "Naxalite Terrorists and Benign Policemen," 2254; K. Balagopal, "Andhra Pradesh: The End of Spring?," *Economic and Political Weekly* 25, 34 (1990), 1885; K. Balagopal, "People's War and the Government: Did the Police Have the Last Laugh?," *Economic and Political Weekly* 38, 6 (2003), 515.

29. "We Shall Certainly Defeat the Government," 5.

30. People's Union for Civil Liberties, "Bastar: Development and Democracy," *Economic and Political Weekly* 24, 40 (1989), 2239; Navlakha, "Days and Nights in the Heartland of Rebellion," 18–20.

31. Navlakha, "Days and Nights in the Heartland of Rebellion," 20; Suvojit Bagchi, "34 days with Maoists inside the forest," *Sunday Guardian*, November 27, 2011, 11. For the Maoist view of their revolutionary project in the region, see Tugge, "Dandakaranya: Two Paths of Development," *People's March* 8, 12 (2007), 3–6.

32. Navlakha, "Days and Nights in the Heartland of Rebellion," 37.

33. Jason Miklian, "The Purification Hunt: The Salwa Judum Counter-insurgency in Chhattisgarh, India," *Dialectical Anthropology* 33 (2009), 447.

34. Miklian, "Purification Hunt," 443, 456; "Ranibodili Raid: An Answer to White Terror," *People's March* 8, 7 (July 2007), 17.

35. "Mine detection lapse kills troopers on Maoist turf," *Telegraph*, March 28, 2012, 6.

36. Bagchi, "34 days with Maoists inside the forest."

37. "We Shall Certainly Defeat the Government," 5.

38. Bagchi, "34 days with Maoists inside the forest"; Suvojit Bagchi, "I don't know how many Naxals I've killed," *Sunday Guardian*, December 4, 2011, 11; Suvojit Bagchi, "In two weeks, I was a paramedic," *Sunday Guardian*, December 11, 2011, 11; Suvojit Bagchi, "Life in an Indian Maoist jungle camp," *BBC News Online*, March 7, 2011; Navlakha, "Days and Nights in the Heartland of Rebellion," 12.

39. Nandini Sundar, *Subalterns and Sovereigns: An Anthropological History of Bastar, 1854–2006* (New Delhi: Oxford University Press, 2007), 132.
40. Ibid., 212–224.
41. Navlakha, "Days and Nights in the Heartland of Rebellion," 18.
42. Duyker, *Tribal Guerrillas,* 33–34, 149, 161–162.
43. Ibid., 109.
44. Azad, "Maoists in India," 10.
45. Navlakha, "Days and Nights in the Heartland of Rebellion," 19–20.
46. Duyker, *Tribal Guerrillas,* 162.
47. Bagchi, "In two weeks, I was a paramedic."
48. Sundar, *Subalterns and Sovereigns,* 289.
49. Adnan Naseemullah, "Variable State-Building and Insurgency," unpublished paper, London School of Economics and Political Science, 2011.
50. "Center's Saranda blueprint ready," *Telegraph,* October 29, 2011 (internet ed.).
51. Orin Starn, "Villagers at Arms: War and Counterrevolution in the Central-South Andes," in Steve J. Stern (ed.), *Shining and Other Paths: War and Society in Peru, 1980–1995* (Durham, N.C.: Duke University Press, 1998), 229, 247.
52. Nelson Manrique, "The War for the Central Sierra," in Stern, *Shining and Other Paths,* 193.
53. Jo-Marie Burt, "Shining Path and the 'Decisive Battle' in Lima's *Barriadas,*" in Stern, *Shining and Other Paths,* 267.
54. Starn, "Villagers at Arms," 237–238.
55. Carlos Ivan Degregori, "Harvesting Storms: Peasant *Rondas* and the Defeat of Shining Path in Ayacucho," 136, 147, and Ponciano del Pino H., "Family, Culture and Revolution: Everyday Life with Sendero Luminoso," 167, 183, 189, both in Stern, *Shining and Other Paths.*
56. Duyker, *Tribal Guerrillas,* 28.
57. Santosh Rana, "A People's Uprising Destroyed by the Maoists," August 23, 2009, Kafila, http://kafila.org (accessed April 1, 2013).
58. Duyker, *Tribal Guerrillas,* 138.
59. "Where development has stopped," *Hindustan Times,* September 17, 2011 (Kolkata ed.), 5; Mandal, "Sidhu joined Maoists in school."
60. Mandal, "Sidhu joined Maoists in school"; "CPM torture made youths join rebels," *Hindustan Times* (Kolkata ed.), December 25, 2011, 5.
61. "We Shall Certainly Defeat the Government," 4; Rana, "A People's Uprising Destroyed by the Maoists"; "Unabated terror: Head-teacher killed for not sending students to Maoist march," *Anandabazar Patrika,* July 24, 2010, 1.
62. Pronab Mondal, "Fear is the sole inhabitant of Salpatra," *Telegraph,* March 5, 2012 (internet ed.).
63. "Resistance to Maoists gets stronger," *Hindustan Times,* July 24, 2010 (Kolkata ed.), 4.
64. "School worker killed by Maoists near Jhargram, parents injured," *Anandabazar Patrika,* September 23, 2010, 1.
65. Rana, "A People's Uprising Destroyed by the Maoists."

66. Pronab Mondal, "The Kishen trackers," *Telegraph,* November 24, 2012 (internet ed.); Kingshuk Gupta and Debraj Ghosh, "Kishenji Nei" [No more Kishenji], *Anandabazar Patrika,* November 24, 2012 (internet ed.).

67. Banaji, "Ironies of Indian Maoism," 143–144.

68. Pronab Mondal, "Maoists fill welfare shoes in lull," *Telegraph,* September 10, 2011, 10.

69. Central Committee of the CPI (Maoist), [untitled statement], May 4, 2011, reprinted in *People's March* 12, 2 (2011), 38–39.

70. Central Committee of the CPI (Maoist), "Open Letter to the Leadership of the United Communist Party of Nepal-Maoist (UCPN-M)," July 20, 2009, reprinted in *People's March* 10, 11 (2009), 9–27.

71. "We Shall Certainly Defeat the Government," 8.

72. Radhakrishna, "Fertile Kishen Nagar."

5. The Kashmir Question

1. Lydia Polgreen, "A youth's death in Kashmir renews a familiar pattern of crisis," *New York Times,* July 11, 2010, A1; Samaan Lateef, "Family, friends, teachers recall Tufail," *Greater Kashmir,* June 14, 2010, 1. On the turmoil in the Kashmir Valley between June and September 2010 see Sumantra Bose, "Kashmir's Summer of Discontent Is Now an Autumn of Woe," *BBC News Online,* September 21, 2010.

2. Walter R. Lawrence, *The Valley of Kashmir* (London: Henry Frowde, 1895), 12, 284.

3. M. A. Stein, *Kalhana's Rajatarangini: A Chronicle of the Kings of Kashmir* (Mirpur: Verinag, 1991).

4. Balraj Puri, "*Kashmiriyat:* The Vitality of Kashmiri Identity," *Contemporary South Asia* 4, 1 (1995), 56, 60–61. See also Mohammad Ishaq Khan, *Kashmir's Transition to Islam: The Role of Muslim Rishis* (Delhi: Manohar, 1994).

5. Puri, "Kashmiriyat," 61.

6. See T. N. Raina, ed. and trans., *The Best of Mahjoor: Selections from Mahjoor's Kashmiri Poems* (Srinagar: Jammu & Kashmir Academy of Art, Culture and Languages, 1989).

7. Sumantra Bose, *Kashmir: Roots of Conflict, Paths to Peace* (Cambridge, Mass.: Harvard University Press, 2003), 15; Mridu Rai, *Hindu Rulers, Muslim Subjects: Islam, Rights, and the History of Kashmir* (Princeton, N.J.: Princeton University Press, 2004), 26.

8. C. E. Tyndale Biscoe, *Kashmir in Sunlight and Shade* (London: Seeley, Service, 1922), 77.

9. Lawrence, *Valley of Kashmir,* 2–3, 401.

10. Robert Thorp, *Cashmere Misgovernment* (Calcutta: Wyman Brothers, 1868), 54.

11. Rai, *Hindu Rulers, Muslim Subjects,* 174.

12. Prem Nath Bazaz, *The History of the Struggle for Freedom in Kashmir* (Karachi: National Book Foundation, 1976), 140–141.

13. Biscoe, *Kashmir in Sunlight and Shade,* 79–80.

14. Cited in M. J. Akbar, *India, the Siege Within: Challenges to a Nation's Unity* (New Delhi: Roli Books, 2003), 221–222.

15. Mohammad Ishaq Khan, *History of Srinagar, 1846–1947: A Study in Socio-cultural Change* (Srinagar: Cosmos, 1999), 193.

16. Prem Nath Bazaz, *Inside Kashmir* (Mirpur: Verinag, 1987) (originally published from Srinagar in 1941), 252–253.

17. Alastair Lamb, *Crisis in Kashmir, 1947 to 1966* (London: Routledge and Kegan Paul, 1966), 28.

18. Khan, *History of Srinagar,* 192.

19. Rai, *Hindu Rulers, Muslim Subjects,* 273.

20. Lamb, *Crisis in Kashmir,* 31.

21. Bose, *Kashmir,* 22.

22. Akbar, *India, the Siege Within,* 250.

23. Khan, *History of Srinagar,* 198.

24. Akbar, *India, the Siege Within,* 227–228.

25. Jyoti Bhushan Dasgupta, *Jammu and Kashmir* (The Hague: Nijhoff, 1968), 66.

26. Ibid., 70.

27. Ibid., 95.

28. Ibid., 113.

29. Ibid., 109.

30. Puri, "Kashmiriyat," 57, 62.

31. Lamb, *Crisis in Kashmir,* 46–48; Dasgupta, *Jammu and Kashmir,* 395–398.

32. Lawrence, *Valley of Kashmir,* 203.

33. Saifuddin Soz, *Why Autonomy for Kashmir?* (New Delhi: Indian Centre for Asian Studies, 1995), 128; A. G. Noorani, *The Kashmir Question* (Bombay: Manaktalas, 1964), 101; Prem Nath Bazaz, *Kashmir in Crucible* (New Delhi: Pamposh, 1967), 136–137.

34. Noorani, *Kashmir Question,* 61.

35. Balraj Puri, *Kashmir: Towards Insurgency* (Delhi: Orient Longman, 1993), 45–49.

36. Dasgupta, *Jammu and Kashmir,* 188–189.

37. Rai, *Hindu Rulers, Muslim Subjects,* 283–284.

38. Daniel Thorner, *The Agrarian Prospect in India* (Bombay: Allied, 1976), 50.

39. Dasgupta, *Jammu and Kashmir,* 195.

40. Ibid., 196.

41. Bose, *Kashmir,* 66.

42. R. K. Jain, ed., *Soviet–South Asian Relations,* vol. 1, *1947–1978* (Atlantic Highlands, N.J.: Humanities Press, 1979), 3–4.

43. Syed Mir Qasim, *My Life and Times* (Delhi: Allied, 1992), 68–70.

44. Dasgupta, *Jammu and Kashmir,* 323; Shaheen Akhtar, "Elections in Indian-Held Kashmir, 1951–1999," *Regional Studies* 18, 3 (2000), 87; Qasim, *My Life and Times,* 106.

45. *Jammu and Kashmir, 1947–1950: An Account of the Activities of the First Three Years of Sheikh Abdullah's Government* (Jammu: Ranbir Government Press, 1951).

46. Josef Korbel, *Danger in Kashmir* (Princeton, N.J.: Princeton University Press, 1954), 246; Dasgupta, *Jammu and Kashmir,* 212–213.

47. Noorani, *Kashmir Question,* 73.

48. Dasgupta, *Jammu and Kashmir,* 408.

49. Jain, *Soviet–South Asian Relations,* 15–20.

50. Dasgupta, *Jammu and Kashmir,* 223–224.

51. Ibid., 227–228.

52. Akbar, *India, the Siege Within,* 258; Puri, *Kashmir,* 45–49.

53. Bazaz, *Kashmir in Crucible,* 100.

54. Puri, *Kashmir,* 31–32; Dasgupta, *Jammu and Kashmir,* 333.

55. Bazaz, *Kashmir in Crucible,* 99–104.

56. Akbar, *India, the Siege Within,* 267.

57. Akhtar, "Elections in Indian-Held Kashmir," 37.

58. Puri, *Kashmir,* 49.

59. Alastair Lamb, *Kashmir: A Disputed Legacy, 1946–1990* (Karachi: Oxford University Press, 1992), 209–210.

60. Qasim, *My Life and Times,* 132; Akhtar, "Elections in Indian-Held Kashmir," 87.

61. Akhtar, "Elections in Indian-Held Kashmir," 38–39.

62. *Speeches and Interviews of Sher-e-Kashmir Sheikh Mohammad Abdullah* (Srinagar: Jammu and Kashmir Plebiscite Front, 1968), vol. 2, 13.

63. The full text of the Delhi accord is in Qasim, *My Life and Times,* 138–140.

64. Farooq Abdullah, *My Dismissal* (New Delhi: Vikas, 1985), 1–2.

65. Interview in *India Today,* November 30, 1986.

66. Inderjit Badhwar, "Testing the Accord," *India Today,* March 31, 1987, 26; Khemlata Wakhloo, *Kashmir: Behind the White Curtain, 1972–1991* (Delhi: Konark, 1992), 321.

67. Inderjit Badhwar, "A Tarnished Triumph," *India Today,* April 15, 1987, 40–43.

68. "Kashmir: Valley of Tears," *India Today,* May 31, 1989; interview in *Illustrated Weekly of India,* October 10–16, 1992, 4.

69. "Senior NC member killed," *Free Press Kashmir,* August 21, 1989.

70. *Kashmir Times,* November 30, 1989.

71. Sumantra Bose, *The Challenge in Kashmir: Democracy, Self-Determination and a Just Peace* (New Delhi: Sage, 1997); Bose, *Kashmir,* and *Contested Lands: Israel-Palestine, Kashmir, Bosnia, Cyprus, and Sri Lanka* (Cambridge, Mass.: Harvard University Press, 2007), 154–203.

72. Basharat Peer, *Curfewed Night: A Frontline Memoir of Life, Love and War in Kashmir* (London: Harper Press, 2010); Mirza Waheed, *The Collaborator* (London: Viking, 2011).

73. "State data refutes claim of 100,000 killed in Kashmir," *Times of India,* June 20, 2011 (internet ed.).

74. *Kashmir Times,* December 5, 2002, 1.

75. Royal Institute of International Affairs, *Kashmir: Paths to Peace* (London: Chatham House, 2010).

76. "From air hostess to aerospace engineer, Kashmir youth look for new professions," *Times of India,* November 8, 2011 (internet ed.).

Conclusion

1. Lloyd I. Rudolph and Susanne H. Rudolph, "Federalism as State Formation in India: A Theory of Negotiated and Shared Sovereignty," *International Political Science Review* 31, 5 (2010), 557; Muzaffar Alam, *The Crisis of Empire in Mughal North India*, 2nd ed. (Delhi: Oxford University Press, 2012), 14.

2. Parmatma Saran, *The Provincial Government of the Mughals, 1526–1658* (Allahabad: Kitabistan, 1941), 36.

3. Rudolph and Rudolph, "Federalism as State Formation in India," 558–559.

4. Ibid., 557.

5. "Inequality in China: Rural Poverty Persists as Urban Wealth Balloons," BBC News Online, June 29, 2011; "China: What Happened to Mao's Revolution?," BBC News Online, June 8, 2012; "China among World's Most Unequal Countries," Agence France-Presse (Shanghai), December 10, 2012; "China Inequality Causes Unease: Pew Survey," BBC News Online, October 16, 2012.

6. David Shambaugh, *China's Communist Party: Atrophy and Adaptation* (Washington, D.C.: Woodrow Wilson Center Press, 2008), 166; "China Congress: Hu Jintao Opens Party Meeting on Leadership Change," BBC News Online, November 8, 2012.

7. "Second Generation Migrants: The Rise of China's Hidden Class," *China Weekly* 25 (2010), 12–25.

8. Daniel Markey, "Developing India's Foreign Policy Software," *Asia Policy* 8 (2009), 73–96. On the past, present, and future of India's role in subcontinental, Asian, and world politics, see David Malone, *Does the Elephant Dance? Contemporary Indian Foreign Policy* (Oxford: Oxford University Press, 2011).

9. Keith Bradsher, "Having ridden out the storm, China sees a slowdown coming," *International Herald Tribune*, May 25, 2012, 1.

10. On China's vulnerabilities, see Susan Shirk, *China, Fragile Superpower: How China's Internal Politics Could Derail Its Peaceful Rise* (Oxford: Oxford University Press, 2007).

11. Anne Phillips, *Democracy and Difference* (University Park: Pennsylvania State University Press, 1993), chapters 5, 8.

12. "States versus Center," *Indian Express*, May 7, 2012 (internet ed.); see also "NCTC: Center-state feud continues," *Indian Express*, May 5, 2012 (internet ed.).

Glossary of Names and Terms

Abdullah, Farooq: Chief minister of Jammu & Kashmir, 1982–1984, 1986–1990, and 1996–2002. Son of Sheikh Mohammad Abdullah.

Abdullah, Omar: Chief minister of Jammu & Kashmir, 2009–. Son of Farooq Abdullah.

Abdullah, Sheikh Mohammad (1905–1982): The Kashmir Valley's most important political leader in the twentieth century; the dominant figure in the Valley's politics for nearly 50 years.

Adivasi (Original Inhabitant): This term refers to India's tribal peoples, who make up about 8 percent of the nation's population. They are constitutionally classified as Scheduled Tribes.

Advani, Lal Krishna (L. K.): A top Hindu nationalist political leader, born in 1927.

Akali Dal (roughly: Party of Believers): Sikh regionalist political party in Punjab.

Anna Dravida Munnetra Kazhagam (Anna's Dravidian Progress Party; ADMK): Common name of one of two major regionalist parties in Tamil Nadu. Formed in 1972 by M. G. Ramachandran, a film star turned politician, who broke away from the parent party, the Dravida Munnetra Kazhagam. The breakaway party took the name of C. N. Annadurai (1909–1969), a Tamil leader, who founded the Dravida Munnetra Kazhagam in 1949.

Asom Gana Parishad: Regionalist political party in Assam, formed in the mid-1980s.

Ayodhya: Small town in eastern Uttar Pradesh where a religious site claimed by both Hindus and Muslims became the flashpoint for a major political dispute in the early 1990s.

"Azaadi" (Freedom): Popular political chant in the Kashmir Valley.

Azad (1952–2010): Nom de guerre of Cherukuri Rajkumar, a top Maoist leader from Andhra Pradesh; killed in 2010.

Bahujan Samaj Party (Party of the Social Majority; BSP): Political party formed in the mid-1980s to represent the interests of India's Dalits ("The Oppressed," referring to the communities that were considered "untouchable" under the ritual caste system and are constitutionally classified as Scheduled Castes). The party's founder was Kanshi Ram, a Dalit activist. In the 1990s it developed a mass base among Dalits in Uttar Pradesh. It is one of two large regional parties in Uttar Pradesh, the other being the Samajwadi Party.

Bakshi Ghulam Mohammed: Prominent political figure in the Kashmir Valley who between 1953 and 1963 acted as the main agent of Jammu & Kashmir's integration into the Indian Union, a top-down process imposed by and from New Delhi.

Banerjee, Mamata (born 1955): Founder and leader of the Trinamool Congress, a regional party formed in West Bengal in late 1997 after a split that decimated the Congress party in the state. Chief minister of West Bengal, May 2011–. She previously held cabinet portfolios in the Union government, including the important railways ministry.

Basu, Jyoti: Veteran communist leader who was chief minister of West Bengal from 1977 to 2000. A leader of the Communist Party of India (Marxist).

Beg, Afzal: Prominent political leader in the Kashmir Valley from the 1940s through the 1970s and a close associate of Sheikh Abdullah.

Bhadralok: Term in Bengali referring to the social class of well-educated, usually upper-caste, urbanized Bengali Hindus.

Bharatiya Jan Sangh (Indian People's Organization): India's Hindu nationalist political party, formed in 1951.

Bharatiya Janata Party (BJP): India's Hindu nationalist political party, launched in 1980 as the slightly relabeled successor to the Bharatiya Jan Sangh.

Bhattacharya, Buddhadev (born 1944): Chief minister of West Bengal from November 2000 to May 2011. A leader of the Communist Party of India (Marxist).

Bhindranwale, Jarnail Singh: Young radical Sikh preacher who emerged as the leader of a Sikh secessionist movement in Punjab during the early 1980s; killed in 1984.

Biju Janata Dal (Biju People's Party): Regional party formed in Orissa in 1997 and named after Biju Patnaik, a renowned political leader of the state. The party is led by his son Naveen Patnaik and has been the ruling party in Orissa since 2000.

Border Security Force: One of the two largest paramilitary police forces of the Union government, the other being the Central Reserve Police Force. Established to police India's borders, but has been deployed in counterinsurgency operations as well. Has about 240,000 personnel.

Bose, Sarat Chandra (1889–1950): Prominent leader of the Indian independence movement nationally and in the province of Bengal. A distinguished lawyer and the older brother of Subhas Chandra Bose.

Bose, Subhas Chandra (1897–1945): Legendary leader of the Indian independence movement. President of the Indian National Congress in 1938 and 1939 and the leader of the Indian National Army from 1943 to 1945. Popularly referred to as Netaji (The Leader) in the subcontinent.

Center: Term commonly used in India to denote the Union government in New Delhi.

Central Reserve Police Force (CRPF): One of the two largest paramilitary police forces of the Union government, the other being the Border Security Force. Has between 250,000 and 300,000 personnel, including some specially trained and equipped elite battalions. Extensively deployed in counterinsurgency operations and in the frontline of the conflict with Maoist guerrillas in several states alongside state police forces. Also deployed in urban centers of the Kashmir Valley.

Communist Party of India (CPI): India's first communist party, formed in the 1920s. Weakened by a major split in 1964, it has a minor presence in India's politics.

Communist Party of India (Maoist): Formed in 2004 by the amalgamation of regional Maoist factions active in Andhra Pradesh, Bihar, and Jharkhand, this party is committed to bringing about a communist revolution in India through "protracted people's war" and is waging a rural insurgency of uneven and variable impact across a swathe of India's states. Its movement has a presence in nearly one-third of the country's 650 administrative districts.

Communist Party of India (Marxist) (CPM): The largest communist party that operates within the framework of India's democracy, formed by splitting from the parent Communist Party of India in 1964. Usually referred to in India as "CPM." Has a sizable base in only 3 of the Union's 28 states: West Bengal (where it ruled continuously from 1977 to 2011), Kerala, and Tripura.

Communist Party of India (Marxist-Leninist); abbreviated "CPI(ML)": Party formed in 1969 by a radical wing of the Communist Party of India (Marxist) who wished to pursue an insurrectionary line rather than operate within the confines of "bourgeois" democracy. Inspired by Mao's China and especially the Cultural Revolution, they launched amateurish insurrections in a few parts of India, notably West Bengal. This party was crushed by 1972, and the remnants splintered into many factions.

Communist Party of India (Marxist-Leninist)-Liberation; abbreviated "CPI(ML) Liberation": Second-generation Maoist faction that grew in Bihar in the 1980s. The most moderate of the Maoist groups, it has put up candidates in state, national, and local elections in Bihar starting in 1985 and is not part of the current Maoist insurgency.

Communist Party of India (Marxist-Leninist)-Party Unity; abbreviated "CPI(ML) Party Unity": Another second-generation Maoist faction that developed in Bihar in the 1980s. Unlike the Communist Party of India (Marxist-Leninist)-Liberation, this party repudiates parliamentary democracy and is one of the constituents of the contemporary Communist Party of India (Maoist).

Congress: Shortened name of the political party founded as the Indian National Congress in 1885, which led the anticolonial mass mobilization under the leadership of Mahatma Gandhi and others during the last three decades of the British Raj in India. The hegemonic party of India's democracy for more than four decades, from independence in 1947 until late 1989, the party is now an emasculated version of its formerly dominant self, having been reduced to a marginal or weak position in numerous states across the country. Since the early 1970s, except for the period 1991–1997, Congress has been led and controlled by the direct descendants of Jawaharlal Nehru, India's first prime minister, who served from 1947 to 1964: first by his daughter, Indira Gandhi, and then by her son Rajiv Gandhi. The party leader since 1998 is Sonia Gandhi, Rajiv's widow, who was born Antonia Maino in Italy. Congress has been the leading constituent of coalition governments at the Center since mid-2004.

Dalit (The Oppressed; The Downtrodden): Term used to describe the communities who comprised the ritual "untouchables" of the caste system's hierarchical order. These communities, constitutionally classified as Scheduled Castes in India, make up about a sixth of the nation's population. Over the last two decades "Dalit" has replaced the term Mahatma Gandhi coined, Harijans (Children of God), which Dalit activists view as patronizing.

Dandakaranya (Punishing Forest): Ancient name for the vast forested tracts of central India. Parts of Dandakaranya are now a major base of operations for Maoist insurgents.

Dasgupta, Promode: Bengali communist and main organizational architect of the Communist Party of India (Marxist) in West Bengal. Died while visiting Beijing in November 1982.

Desai, Morarji: Conservative Congress leader from Gujarat who was sidelined by Indira Gandhi's rise in the late 1960s. In 1977 he became India's first non-Congress prime minister and served until 1979.

Dravida Munnetra Kazhagam (Dravidian Progress Federation; DMK): One of the two major regionalist parties in Tamil Nadu, the other being its offshoot the Anna Dravida Munnetra Kazhagam. In 1967 the Dravida Munnetra Kazhagam won power in Tamil Nadu by defeating Congress and since then has alternated in power there with the Anna Dravida Munnetra Kazhagam, which was formed in 1972. The Dravida Munnetra Kazhagam traditionally stood for political autonomy based on an assertion of Tamil ethnolinguistic identity, and its support base is rooted among intermediate Tamil castes. The long-standing party leader is M. Karunanidhi (born 1924), a film scriptwriter turned politician.

Emergency: Period from June 1975 through January 1977 when Prime Minister Indira Gandhi clamped a dictatorial regime on India, citing an "emergency" on grounds of internal disorder. The Emergency was marked by mass arrests of opposition leaders and activists and members of the free press. The only period in the history of India's democracy when civil liberties and democratic freedoms were violated outright on a nationwide scale. In national elections held in March 1977 after the Emergency regime was relaxed, the ruling Congress party was severely defeated.

Ganapati (born 1950): Nom de guerre of M. Lakshmana Rao, general secretary of the Communist Party of India (Maoist). He is from Andhra Pradesh's northern Telangana region. Ganapati is one of many names for the elephant-god Ganesha.

Gandhi, Indira (1917–1984): Prime minister of India, 1966–1977 and 1980–1984. Only child of Jawaharlal Nehru, who was India's first prime minister from 1947 to 1964. Assassinated on October 31, 1984.

Gandhi, Mohandas Karamchand (1869–1948): Known as Mahatma (Great Soul), he led the transformation of Indian anticolonial nationalism into a mass movement during the 1920s. The top leader of India's independence movement for nearly three decades. Assassinated on January 30, 1948.

Gandhi, Rahul (born 1970): Son of Rajiv and Sonia Gandhi who entered politics in 2004 and became a general secretary of the Congress party. Widely seen as aspiring to inherit the legacy of the Nehru-Gandhi political dynasty. Appointed vice-president of the Congress party in 2013. His mother is the party's president.

Gandhi, Rajiv (1944–1991): Prime minister of India from November 1984 to November 1989. Older of two sons of Indira Gandhi. Assassinated on May 21, 1991.

Gandhi, Sanjay (1946–1980): The younger son of Indira Gandhi. Primarily remembered for his leading role during the 1975–1977 Emergency. Killed in June 1980 when a small plane he was flying for recreation crashed in Delhi.

Gandhi, Sonia (born 1946): Leader of the Congress party since 1998 and chair since 2004 of the United Progressive Alliance, the Congress-led coalition ruling at New Delhi. Widow of Rajiv Gandhi; born Antonia Maino in Italy.

"Garibi Hatao" (Hindi: Abolish Poverty): Populist slogan that propelled Indira Gandhi's ascent to dominance of India's politics in the early 1970s.

Golwalkar, Madhav Sadashiv: Hindu nationalist who headed the Rashtriya Swayamsevak Sangh, the core organization of India's Hindu nationalist *sangh-parivar* (family of organizations), from 1940 to 1973. Known as Guruji (Revered Teacher) to his followers.

Gonds: Term used to describe traditionally forest-dwelling Adivasi (tribal) communities of central India. Some Gonds are active in the Maoist insurgency.

Greyhounds: Specialized anti-Maoist police force established in Andhra Pradesh in 1989. Played a critical role in severely weakening the Maoists in Andhra Pradesh by the first decade of the twenty-first century.

Harmad (roughly: "bandit"): Term used to describe armed militias of the ruling Communist Party of India (Marxist) active in West Bengal from 2007 to 2011.

Hindutva: The ideology of Hindu nationalism. Holds that the large majority of Indians (about 80 percent) are united by a Hindu identity that ought to override all other identities and differences of region, ethnicity, language, and caste.

Indian Administrative Service: The professional bureaucracy of the Indian state. Descended from the Indian Civil Service, which was known as the "steel frame" of the British Raj in India. An Indian Administrative Service career has lost some of its luster in the last two decades, primarily because of

alternative opportunities opened up by economic liberalization, but continues to be an attractive option for many. Indian Administrative Service
recruits are in charge of the administrative machinery in India's 650-odd
districts, where they are known as "district magistrates" in colonial-era
terminology and more informally as "collectors." The service's officers staff
various ministries and departments of the Union government and the state
governments.

Indian National Army: Anticolonial army raised with Japanese support in
Southeast Asia during World War II. Its 40,000-plus troops were composed
in nearly equal proportions of Indian officers and soldiers of the colonial
army of British-ruled India who had surrendered to the Japanese and
volunteers drawn from the 3-million-strong population of Indian origin
living in Southeast Asia. Included a women's regiment of about 1,500
volunteers. Commanded from 1943 to 1945 by the Indian nationalist leader
Subhas Chandra Bose.

Indian People's Front: Political front floated in Bihar in 1982 by the Communist Party of India (Marxist-Leninist)-Liberation, the most moderate of the
second-generation Indian Maoist groups and then an underground organization. Disbanded in 1994 when its parent organization decided to assume a
legal existence.

Jammu and Kashmir Hizb-ul-Mujahideen (Party of Holy Warriors; JKHM):
Pro-Pakistan insurgent group formed in Jammu & Kashmir in 1989.

Jammu and Kashmir Liberation Front: Proindependence Kashmir organization
originally founded in 1964 in Pakistan-controlled Kashmir. Launched the
insurgency in the Kashmir Valley in 1989–1990 and dominated it until 1993.

Jammu and Kashmir National Conference (JKNC): Jammu & Kashmir's
dominant regional party, founded in the late 1930s in the Kashmir Valley.

Jammu and Kashmir People's Democratic Party: Regional party formed in the
late 1990s in Jammu & Kashmir. Like its rival the Jammu and Kashmir
National Conference, it has a pro-India orientation but seeks "self-rule"
within the Indian Union.

Jammu and Kashmir Plebiscite Front: Mass organization set up by supporters
of Sheikh Abdullah in the Kashmir Valley in 1955. Disbanded in 1975.

Janata Dal (People's Party): Federation of anti-Congress factions that coalesced
in northern India, particularly the states of Uttar Pradesh and Bihar, in the
late 1980s. Played a vital role in ending four decades of Congress hegemony
in India's politics. Splintered into regional parties beginning in the early
1990s. The Rashtriya Janata Dal and the Janata Dal-United in Bihar, the
Samajwadi Party in Uttar Pradesh, the Biju Janata Dal in Orissa, and the
Janata Dal-Secular in Karnataka are all offshoots of the Janata Dal.

Janata Dal-United: Regional party in Bihar descended from the Janata Dal. Has
been the ruling party in Bihar, with the Hindu nationalist Bharatiya Janata
Party as its junior ally in a coalition government, since late 2005.

Janata Party (People's Party): Loose alliance of anti-Congress parties based
predominantly in northern and western India that coalesced in opposition to
the Emergency regime of 1975–1977 and routed Congress across northern

India in national elections in March 1977. Unlike the Janata Dal of the late 1980s, the Janata Party included the Hindu nationalist party the Bharatiya Jan Sangh (forerunner of the Bharatiya Janata Party) as a constituent. Formed the first-ever non-Congress government in New Delhi in 1977 but in the second half of 1979 fell apart amid factional and personal feuds. Midterm national elections in January 1980 returned Indira Gandhi and Congress to power.

Janatana Sarkar (People's Government): Term used by the Maoists to describe rudimentary administrative structures established by them in pockets of territory controlled by their movement in central India.

Jangalmahal (Abode of the Forests): Term used to describe forested tracts of the West Medinipur, Bankura, and Purulia districts in the southwestern part of West Bengal. Socioeconomically underdeveloped area with a large Adivasi population; zone of the Maoist insurgency in West Bengal between 2008 and 2011.

Jayalalitha, J. (born 1948): The leader of the Anna Dravida Munnetra Kazhagam in Tamil Nadu after the death of the party's founder, M. G. Ramachandran, in late 1987. Chief minister of Tamil Nadu in 1991–1996, 2001, 2002–2006, and May 2011–. Before entering politics, she was a successful actress in Tamil cinema.

Jotedar: Term used in rural West Bengal to denote medium and large landowners.

Kanshi Ram (1934–2006): Leading Dalit activist; founded the Bahujan Samaj Party in 1984.

Karunanidhi, M. (born 1924): Long-standing leader of the Dravida Munnetra Kazhagam party in Tamil Nadu. Chief minister of Tamil Nadu in 1969–1971, 1971–1976, 1989–1991, 1996–2001, and 2006–2011. Formerly a scriptwriter in Tamil cinema.

Kishenji (1956–2011): Nom de guerre of M. Koteswara Rao, a top Maoist leader. Native of the Telangana region of Andhra Pradesh. Killed in West Bengal in November 2011.

Konar, Harekrishna (1915–1974): A leader of the Communist Party of India (Marxist) in West Bengal; spearheaded land reform there in the late 1960s and early 1970s.

Krishak Sabha (Peasants' Front): The mass organization of the Communist Party of India (Marxist) in agrarian West Bengal.

Kumar, Nitish (born 1951): Chief minister of Bihar since late 2005; has won praise for policies promoting good governance and socioeconomic development. A leader of the Janata Dal-United, a regionalist party based in Bihar. Belongs to the intermediate Kurmi caste, an Other Backward Classes community.

Lal Ded: Fourteenth-century female mystic and poet in the Kashmir Valley. Regarded as the progenitor of the Kashmiri literary tradition. Also known as Lalleshwari.

Lalgarh: Tiny township in the West Medinipur district of West Bengal that in late 2008 and early 2009 emerged as the epicenter of a Maoist-backed rural uprising by Adivasi and low-caste communities.

Lashkar-e-Taiba (Army of the Pious): Pakistani radical Islamist organization that became active in the Kashmir Valley from the mid-1990s and conducted a campaign of suicide attacks there that peaked between 1999 and 2003. Plotted and perpetrated the terrorist attack that killed 166 people in Mumbai, India's commercial capital, in late November 2008.

Left Front (LF): Alliance of communist and socialist parties dominated by the Communist Party of India (Marxist). Was in power in West Bengal as a coalition government led by the Communist Party of India (Marxist) continuously for 34 years, from 1977 to 2011.

Line of Control: The de facto border dividing the Indian and Pakistani parts of Jammu and Kashmir. Is approximately 742 kilometers long and originated as a ceasefire line in 1949.

Lok Sabha (House of the People): Directly elected lower chamber of India's Parliament. Normally constituted through a nationwide election every five years. Has 543 members, who represent single-member electoral districts known as parliamentary constituencies across the country. The candidate who wins the single largest share of the popular vote polled in each constituency is elected as a Member of Parliament-Lok Sabha. The number of Lok Sabha constituencies allocated to each of India's 28 states (and seven small entities known as Union Territories) depends primarily on the size of their populations. Thus the more populous a state, the greater its number of Lok Sabha constituencies (and seats in the directly elected chamber of Parliament), and vice versa. The Lok Sabha is the key legislative body in India's democracy, and the Lok Sabha election is the pivotal event in the calendar of India's democracy. There were 15 Lok Sabha elections between 1952 and 2009 (including several midterm elections), and the sixteenth is due in April–May 2014. All citizens aged 18 and above are eligible to vote in elections to the Lok Sabha (and in elections to state legislatures, known as Legislative Assemblies or Vidhan Sabhas, as well as in local elections).

Longowal, Harcharan Singh (1932–1985): A senior leader of the Akali Dal, the Sikh regional party of Punjab; assassinated in August 1985.

Mandal Commission: Formally the Second Backward Classes Commission but widely known as the Mandal Commission after the name of its chair, B. P. Mandal, a politician from Bihar. Five-member commission appointed by the Janata Party government in power in New Delhi in late 1978 to identify the socioeconomically disadvantaged sections of India's population and recommend policies for their advancement. Recommended in its report submitted in late 1980 that 27 percent of jobs in the Union government and the same proportion of places in institutions of higher education supported by that government be reserved for the Other Backward Classes, a vast and heterogeneous layer of intermediate or middle castes sandwiched between the upper or "forward" castes and the Scheduled Castes (Dalits, who already had reservations in government jobs and education guaranteed to them in independent India). In August 1990 the report was retrieved from the cold storage to which the Congress governments of Indira and Rajiv Gandhi had consigned it for a decade when V. P. Singh, the new (and short-lived) prime minister, announced that its recommendation would be implemented. This sparked an intense reaction from upper castes in northern India and triggered a political crisis with far-reaching ramifications for the evolution of India's democracy.

Maoist Communist Center: Underground leftist revolutionary group that emerged in Bihar, which then included Jharkhand, during the 1980s. One constituent of the federated Communist Party of India (Maoist).

Masoodi, Maulana (1903–1990): Prominent figure in the Kashmir Valley's politics from the 1940s through the 1970s; assassinated in December 1990.

Mayawati (born 1956): Leader of the Bahujan Samaj Party. Belongs to a Dalit family of the *chamar* caste. Chief minister of Uttar Pradesh in 1995, 1997, 2002–2003, and 2007–2012.

Mazumdar, Charu (1918–1972): Main ideologue of India's first Maoist insurrection in the late 1960s and early 1970s. Arrested in Calcutta in July 1972; died in police custody.

Modi, Narendra (born 1950): A leader of the Hindu nationalist Bharatiya Janata Party. Chief minister of Gujarat, 2001–. He is controversial because India's only large-scale outbreak of communal (interreligious) violence since 1992–1993 took place under his watch in Gujarat in 2002. Gujarat's 9 percent Muslim minority suffered pogrom-like attacks during the violence. In the last few years he has been trying to reinvent his image and projects himself as a hardworking chief minister who works for all of Gujarat's people.

Mountbatten, Lord: Last British viceroy of India; assassinated in 1979 while vacationing off the coast of Ireland by the Provisional Irish Republican Army.

Mukherjee, Ajoy: First non-Congress chief minister of West Bengal. Headed United Front coalition governments there in 1967 and 1969–1970. During World War II he was a prominent leader of an anticolonial uprising in the Medinipur district of Bengal.

Muslim United Front: Coalition of diverse opposition groups in the Kashmir Valley who came together to run candidates in the Jammu & Kashmir state elections of 1987. The election was rigged to the detriment of this coalition, and thus began the countdown to insurgency that erupted in 1990.

N. T. Rama Rao (1923–1996): Founder of the Telugu Desam Party (Telugu Homeland Party) of Andhra Pradesh in 1982; popularly known by his initials, NTR. Was previously a successful lead actor ("hero") of Telugu cinema. Chief minister of Andhra Pradesh, 1983–1989 and 1994–1995.

Naidu, N. Chandrababu (born 1950): Son-in-law of N. T. Rama Rao; leader of the Telugu Desam Party from 1995. Chief minister of Andhra Pradesh, 1995–2004.

Nandigram: Cluster of villages in the East Medinipur district of West Bengal where a popular agitation flared in 2007 against the plans of the state government, led by the Communist Party of India (Marxist), to acquire about 10,000 acres of farmland to set up a petrochemical industry hub. The agitation was a crucial episode in the unraveling of three decades of communist supremacy in West Bengal.

Narayan, Jaya Prakash (1902–1979): Anticolonial freedom fighter and socialist opposition leader in independent India. His leadership of protests against

Indira Gandhi's government in the mid-1970s was a major factor in Indira's decision to impose the Emergency in mid-1975.

National Democratic Alliance (NDA): Alliance of diverse political parties formed in 1998 with the Hindu nationalist Bharatiya Janata Party as the central constituent. Held power in New Delhi from 1998 to 2004. Its formation was a milestone in the evolution of coalition politics in India's democracy. It continues to be one of the two major multiparty alliances in Indian politics; the other is the Congress-led United Progressive Alliance.

Nationalist Congress Party: Regional political party of Maharashtra, formed in 1999 by a breakaway faction of the state's Congress party.

Naxalite: Term used to describe Maoist revolutionaries in India since the late 1960s. The term derives from Naxalbari, a rural area in the northern part of West Bengal where Maoists were active in a local uprising of Adivasi peasants in 1967.

Nehru, Jawaharlal (1889–1964): A top leader of the Indian independence movement and independent India's first prime minister; held office from 1947 until his death in 1964.

Noorani, Sheikh Nooruddin (c. 1377–1440): Sufi mystic who is the Kashmir Valley's patron saint. Kashmir's Sufi heritage is identified with his influence. Also known by the Hindu-sounding name Nund Rishi (Nund the Saint).

Operation Barga: Program to register sharecropping peasants *(bargadars)* carried out between 1978 and 1985 by the Left Front government—led by the Communist Party of India (Marxist)—of West Bengal. The program aimed to make sharecroppers aware of their legal rights vis-à-vis the owners of the land they farmed as tenants. Registered over 1.3 million sharecroppers and entrenched Communist Party of India (Marxist) power in the West Bengal countryside.

Other Backward Classes (OBC): Vast, heterogeneous layer of middle or intermediate caste communities between the upper or "forward" castes (Brahmins, Rajputs, Kayasths, etc.) and the Scheduled Castes (comprised of Dalit communities). The Yadav and Kurmi communities are among the most numerically and politically prominent castes in northern India categorized as Other Backward Classes, especially in Uttar Pradesh and Bihar. See also "Mandal Commission."

Panchayat: The system of elected village-based governance in rural India. The precise form varies somewhat across states but typically follows a three-tiered structure. The base tier usually consists of an elected council for a cluster of villages, which in turn elects a *pradhan* (headman or headwoman). A middle tier often consists of an elected body at the "block" (subdistrict) level, and the upper tier of an elected body at the district level. (India has about 650 administrative districts, and each district is subdivided into a variable number of blocks.) *Panchayat* elections are entered in most states by political parties that field slates of candidates, although independent candidates can and do stand as well.

Pandits: The small Hindu minority of the Kashmir Valley; about 3 percent of the Valley's population according to the national census of 1981.

Patel, Vallabhbhai (1875–1950): Prominent leader of the Indian independence movement and deputy prime minister and home (interior) minister of India after independence. A native of Gujarat.

Patnaik, Biju (1916–1997): Legendary political leader of Orissa. Initially in the Congress party but from the late 1960s onward a regionalist politician. Chief minister of Orissa in 1961–1963 and 1990–1995.

Patnaik, Naveen (born 1946): A son of Biju Patnaik. Leader of the regionalist Biju Janata Dal of Orissa, named in honor of his father and launched in 1997; has been chief minister of Orissa since 2000.

Pawar, Sharad (born 1940): A senior politician of Maharashtra. Chief minister of Maharashtra in 1978–1980, 1988–1991, and 1993–1995. Has also held cabinet portfolios in the Union government. Leader since 1999 of the Nationalist Congress Party, a significant regional party in Maharashtra.

People's Committee Against Police Atrocities: Maoist front organization floated in the West Medinipur district of West Bengal in late 2008 and locally influential during 2009–2010.

People's Liberation Guerrilla Army: The elite fighting force of the Communist Party of India (Maoist) and estimated to consist of at least 10,000 men and women.

People's War Group: Second-generation Maoist organization founded in Andhra Pradesh in 1980. Its core zone of activity was in some districts of the Telangana region in the northern part of the state. Grew in Andhra Pradesh through the 1980s and 1990s but by the first decade of the twenty-first century was severely weakened in the state. A key constituent of the federated Communist Party of India (Maoist).

Praja Parishad (Subjects' Forum): Organization formed in the late 1940s in the city of Jammu in the southern part of Jammu & Kashmir by former officials of the princely state (1846–1947) of Jammu and Kashmir and local Hindu nationalists. From 1949 to 1953 the Praja Parishad agitated in and around the city of Jammu for the revocation of the asymmetric autonomy of Jammu & Kashmir within the Indian Union.

Qasim, Mir: Prominent political figure in the Kashmir Valley in the 1950s and 1960s and chief minister of Jammu & Kashmir from 1971 to 1975.

Quit India movement: Campaign of civil disobedience and mass protest initiated by the leadership of the Indian National Congress on August 9, 1942, against the British Raj in India. The uprising was crushed by brutal police and military action and mass arrests of Congress leaders and organizers. Although initiated with the support of Mahatma Gandhi, who advocated nonviolent resistance, the Quit India movement sparked uprisings by (poorly) armed freedom fighters in some parts of India. A few "liberated zones" established by these fighters held out until 1944.

Quit Kashmir movement (1946): Movement of civil disobedience and mass protest initiated by the Jammu and Kashmir National Conference and its leader, Sheikh Abdullah, to overthrow the feudal and despotic regime of the princely state of Jammu and Kashmir. Had a major impact in the Kashmir Valley, the stronghold of the Jammu and Kashmir National Conference. Modeled on Congress's Quit India movement of 1942.

Rajya Sabha (House of the States): The indirectly elected upper chamber of India's Parliament. Has 250 members, almost all of whom are elected, to serve six-year terms, by members of the Vidhan Sabhas, the directly elected legislatures of the states of the Indian Union. The composition of the Rajya Sabha thus approximately reflects the strengths of political parties in the states of the Union. The number of Rajya Sabha seats allocated to each state is roughly proportionate to its population, but less populous states tend to be slightly overrepresented.

Ramachandran, M. G. (1917–1987): Popular actor in Tamil cinema turned politician; referred to by his initials as MGR. Was a leader of the Tamil regionalist Dravida Munnetra Kazhagam party for over two decades but split from it in 1972 and founded the Anna Dravida Munnetra Kazhagam as an alternative regionalist party. Chief minister of Tamil Nadu, 1977–1987.

Ranveer Sena (Warlord Army): Armed militia formed by landowning Bhumihar Brahmins in the central Bihar countryside in the 1990s to fight Dalit landless laborers mobilized by Maoist groups. Responsible for a number of massacres of Dalits in central Bihar villages between the mid-1990s and the first few years of the twenty-first century.

Rao, P. V. Narasimha (1921–2004): Prime minister of India, 1991–1996; veteran Congress politician from Andhra Pradesh who previously served as foreign minister, home (interior) minister, and defense minister in Union governments through the 1980s. Chief minister of Andhra Pradesh, 1971–1973. As prime minister, undertook measures to rescue India from a dire economic and fiscal crisis in mid-1991 and set in motion a process of structural reforms to unshackle the economy from state control.

Rashtriya Janata Dal (National People's Party): Regional party based in Bihar. Formed in 1997 by Laloo Prasad Yadav, a Bihar politician who served as the state's Janata Dal chief minister from 1990 to 1997 and continued as de facto chief minister until 2005, ruling through his wife, whom he managed to get appointed chief minister after he was forced to formally step down after being indicted on corruption charges.

Rashtriya Swayamsevak Sangh (National Volunteer Organization; RSS): Core organization, founded in 1925, of the Hindu nationalist *sangh-parivar* (family of organizations). The Bharatiya Janata Party is its affiliated political party, and the Vishwa Hindu Parishad (World Hindu Forum) is its affiliate in religious affairs. Exists to promote its ideal of India as a Hindu Rashtra (Hindu nation-state) and the ideology of Hindutva. The Rashtriya Swayamsevak Sangh leadership is based in the city of Nagpur in Maharashtra, and the organization has local branches *(shakhas)* across India. Its membership of several million is all male, with an affiliated women's organization. Has cultivated a militia-style character since its inception in the late colonial period; members wear khaki shorts regardless of age and conduct carefully choreographed marches and parades. Most senior Bharatiya Janata Party leaders have been socialized in the Rashtriya Swayamsevak Sangh, many as full-time *pracharaks*, volunteer preachers of Hindutva values, and the Rashtriya Swayamsevak Sangh exercises a strong influence on the Bharatiya Janata Party.

Sadiq, G. M.: Prominent political figure in the Kashmir Valley from the 1940s through the 1960s. Prime minister of Jammu & Kashmir, 1964–1965; chief minister of Jammu & Kashmir, 1965–1970.

Salwa Judum (Purification Hunt): Gondi-language name of an anti-Maoist vigilante militia that was formed with official support in 2005 in the Dantewada district of Chhattisgarh.

Samajwadi Party (Socialist Party; SP): One of the two major regional parties of Uttar Pradesh, the other being the Bahujan Samaj Party. Founded in late 1992 by Mulayam Singh Yadav. Its base since that time has consisted predominantly of Uttar Pradesh's Yadav community, a lower-middle caste classified as an Other Backward Classes group, and of Muslims, who comprise about 18 percent of the state's population. Won a legislative majority in UP state elections in 2012 and replaced the Bahujan Samaj Party, which had won a legislative majority in 2007, as Uttar Pradesh's ruling party.

Santals: Adivasi community who live in eastern India, with the largest concentrations in parts of West Bengal and Jharkhand.

Savarkar, Vinayak Damodar (V. D.): Early Hindu nationalist who in the 1920s coined the term Hindutva and propounded the ideology of Hindu nationalism. He was a native of Maharashtra.

Scheduled Castes (SC): The "lowest" castes of the ritual caste hierarchy are constitutionally classified as Scheduled Castes. These groups make up about a sixth of India's population and are often referred to as Dalits. Nearly 15 percent of the Lok Sabha's 543 constituencies are reserved for Scheduled Castes contestants only, and variable proportions of the state legislative assemblies are similarly reserved. (The proportion depends on the proportion of Scheduled Castes people in the state's population.) Persons of Scheduled Castes identity are also entitled to reserved jobs in Union and state government employment and to reserved places in public institutions of higher education.

Scheduled Tribes (ST): Constitutional classification of India's tribal communities. These groups make up about 8 percent of India's population and are often referred to collectively as Adivasis. Nearly 8 percent of the Lok Sabha's 543 constituencies are reserved for Scheduled Tribes contestants only, and variable proportions of the state legislative assemblies are similarly reserved. (The proportion depends on the proportion of Scheduled Tribes people in the state's population.) Persons of Scheduled Tribes identity are also entitled to reserved jobs in Union and state government employment and to reserved places in public institutions of higher education.

Shastri, Lal Bahadur (1904–1966): Prime minister of India from June 1964 until his death in January 1966. A Congress leader from Uttar Pradesh; was India's second prime minister and the only Congress prime minister during the 42 years (1947–1989) of Congress dominance of India's democracy who was not from the Nehru-Gandhi family. Also served as the nation's home (interior) minister from 1961 to 1963 and displayed sterling leadership qualities during the 1965 war with Pakistan.

Shining Path (Spanish: Sendero Luminoso): Maoist movement that waged a violent and ultimately failed insurrection to capture state power in Peru between 1982 and the mid-1990s. The closest analogue to India's contemporary Maoist movement in origins, ideology, strategy, and tactics.

Shiv Sena (Army of Shivaji): Regional party in Maharashtra named after Shivaji, a valorous Maratha warrior-king of the seventeenth century. Formed in 1966 with a "son-of-the-soil" ideology, asserting the rights of native Maharashtrians over those of migrants to Mumbai and other cities from out of state. Has been a sizable force in the state's politics, with a base among middle- and lower-middle-class native Maharashtrians, for over two decades; has been aligned with the Hindu nationalist Bharatiya Janata Party during this time.

Singh, Chaudhary Charan (1902–1987): Uttar Pradesh politician who for several decades was the main leader of the Jats, an intermediate-caste farming community concentrated in western Uttar Pradesh. Was in the Congress party for most of his life but became an opposition leader from 1967. Served very briefly as India's prime minister in 1979.

Singh, Gulab: Warrior from the Jammu region who founded the princely state of Jammu and Kashmir (1846–1947).

Singh, Hari: Descendant of Gulab Singh and the last ruler of the princely state of Jammu and Kashmir.

Singh, Manmohan (born 1932): Prime minister of India, May 2004–. Trained as an economist and a technocrat by background. Was India's finance minister from 1991 to 1996, when the deregulation and liberalization of the nation's economy was set in motion under the premiership of P. V. Narasimha Rao.

Singh, Vishwanath Pratap (V. P.): Prime minister of India, December 1989–November 1990. An Uttar Pradesh Congress politician for most of his life. Born in 1931 into a minor princely family; died in 2008. Chiefly remembered for his leading role, after his controversial exit from Congress in 1987, in the coordinated opposition campaign of 1988–1989 that defeated Congress in the Lok Sabha election of November 1989 and ended the party's four-decade hegemony in India's politics. His short-lived but tumultuous term as prime minister is chiefly remembered for the caste conflict ignited by his announcement that the Mandal Commission's recommendation on job and educational quotas for Other Backward Classes communities would be implemented. Was also chief minister of Uttar Pradesh from 1980 to 1982; served as finance minister in the Union government from January 1985 to January 1987 and as defense minister from January to April 1987.

Singur: Rural area of West Bengal close to the capital, Kolkata: a cluster of villages in the Hooghly district. Was gripped from the second half of 2006 by farmers' protests against acquisition by the state government, led by the Communist Party of India (Marxist), of nearly 1,000 acres of farmland for a small-car plant to be built by the automobile-making arm of India's privately owned Tata group of companies. The Tata group moved the project to Gujarat in late 2008 due to the protest movement—a crucial episode in the unraveling of more than three decades of communist supremacy in West Bengal.

Telangana: The northern region of Andhra Pradesh and one of three regions that make up the state. (The other two are coastal Andhra and Rayalaseema.) Some Telangana districts were a hotbed of Maoist activity from the 1970s through the first half of the first decade of this century. A popular demand for full statehood for Telangana grew in the late 1960s and has reemerged in the last few years. If realized, Telangana will be the twenty-ninth state of the Indian Union. The capital of Andhra Pradesh, Hyderabad, lies in Telangana and is the main bone of contention in the dispute.

Telugu Desam Party (Telugu Homeland Party): Regionalist party launched in Andhra Pradesh in 1982 by N. T. Rama Rao, a movie actor turned politician. The ruling party of Andhra Pradesh from 1983 to 1989 and from 1994 to 2004. Now a sizable opposition party led by N. Chandrababu Naidu. Telugu is the dominant language of Andhra Pradesh.

Trinamool Congress (Grassroots Congress): Regional party formed in West Bengal in late 1997 by Mamata Banerjee, then the most popular leader of the Congress party in the state. The main opposition party in West Bengal from 1998 onward and its ruling party since May 2011.

United Front: The anti-Congress coalition governments formed in West Bengal in 1967 and 1969–1970.

United Front: The non-Congress, anti–Bharatiya Janata Party coalition government in New Delhi between June 1996 and December 1997.

United Liberation Front of Assam: Armed secessionist organization in Assam, founded in 1979; waged a significant insurgency in the early 1990s and again in the late 1990s. Much weakened since then by splits, defections, and arrests but still active.

United Progressive Alliance (UPA): Alliance of diverse political parties formed in mid-2004 with the Congress party as central constituent. Has run a coalition government in New Delhi since May 2004 and was reelected in the April–May 2009 Lok Sabha election. (The two terms in office are often referred to in India as UPA I and UPA II.) One of the two major multiparty alliances in Indian politics, the other being the BJP-led National Democratic Alliance.

Vajpayee, Atal Behari (A. B.): Prime minister of India, 1998–2004 (and very briefly in 1996). Born in 1924. Lifelong Hindu nationalist but known for his civil and moderate style and widely respected in India. Elected to the Lok Sabha nine times starting in 1957. Foreign minister in the Janata Party government in New Delhi from March 1977 to July 1979. Effectively retired from politics after 2004.

Vidhan Sabha (Legislative Assembly): The directly elected state legislature in each of the 28 states of the Indian Union; endowed with extensive lawmaking powers and competencies. (Two of the seven "Union Territories," including Delhi, the national capital territory, also have directly elected legislatures.) All citizens aged 18 and above are eligible to vote in elections to their state's Vidhan Sabha, which normally take place every five years. Members are elected from single-member electoral districts known as assembly constituencies. The candidate who wins the single largest share of the votes cast in an assembly constituency is elected to represent that constituency in the state's Vidhan Sabha. The size of the Vidhan Sabha varies across states, ranging from 32 members in the northeastern mountain state of Sikkim (population 600,000) to 403 in the giant northern state of Uttar Pradesh (population 200 million). The party (or alliance) that wins a majority—50 percent plus one—of the assembly constituencies and therefore of the seats in the Vidhan Sabha gets to form the state government, and the cabinet, headed by the chief minister of the state, is accountable to the Vidhan Sabha.

Vishwa Hindu Parishad (World Hindu Forum; VHP): The organization within the Hindu nationalist *sangh-parivar* (family of organizations) that deals with religious affairs. Played a leading role in the political campaign in the middle to late 1980s and early 1990s to "reclaim" a site in Ayodhya, a small town in eastern Uttar Pradesh, occupied since the early sixteenth century by a mosque and held by Hindu nationalists to be the exact birthplace of the Hindu deity Lord Ram.

Yadav, Akhilesh (born 1973): A son of Mulayam Singh Yadav and a leader of the Samajwadi Party established by his father. Chief minister of Uttar Pradesh, March 2012–.

Yadav, Laloo Prasad (born 1948): Chief minister of Bihar, 1990–1997, and its de facto chief minister, 1997–2005. A politician from the Other Backward Classes Yadav caste who rose to power in his state through the political assertion of the Other Backward Classes in the late 1980s as the Congress party's supremacy in the politics of Bihar (and Uttar Pradesh) crumbled. Founded his own Bihar-based party, the Rashtriya Janata Dal, in 1997. Dogged by charges of corruption and a record of poor governance while in power in Bihar. Was railways minister in the Congress-led coalition government in New Delhi in 2004–2009.

Yadav, Mulayam Singh (born 1939): Uttar Pradesh politician of the Other Backward Classes Yadav caste who rose to prominence in the state in the late 1980s as four decades of the Congress party's supremacy in Uttar Pradesh (and Bihar) crumbled. Founded the Samajwadi Party as a regional party in Uttar Pradesh in late 1992. Chief minister of Uttar Pradesh from December 1989 to January 1991, December 1993 to June 1995, and August 2003 to May 2007.

YSR Congress: A rising regional party in Andhra Pradesh. Formally the Yuvajana Sramika Ryothu (Youth, Workers, and Peasants) Congress Party; the name is based on the initials of Y. S. Rajasekhara Reddy, the Congress chief minister of the state from 2004 until 2009, when he was killed in a helicopter crash. The YSR Congress is led by his son Jagan Mohan Reddy (known as Jagan). Y. S. Rajasekhara Reddy's family became bitterly estranged from Congress after his death.

Acknowledgments

This book has been influenced by many people, events, and experiences.

It has its roots in my being born and raised in the city of Calcutta (now Kolkata) in West Bengal State in eastern India, where I finished high school. The family in which I grew up was keenly interested in India's politics and the public life of the country. This was mostly because of my father, Sisir Kumar Bose. A pediatrician in his professional life in postindependence India, he was a son of Sarat Chandra Bose (1889–1950), a lawyer who was a leader of the independence movement in Bengal and India, and a nephew of Subhas Chandra Bose (1897–1945), a legendary leader of the Indian independence movement who is known as Netaji (The Leader) in the subcontinent. During World War II my father worked closely with his uncle, who escaped from India with my father's help in 1941 and between 1943 and 1945 spearheaded a movement for India's liberation based among the several million people of Indian origin living in the Japanese-occupied countries of Southeast Asia. This "Azad Hind" (Free India) movement had an army over 40,000 strong—the Indian National Army—composed almost equally of Indian officers and soldiers of Britain's imperial army who had been captured during the lightning Japanese advance through Southeast Asia and volunteers from among the population of Indian origin in Southeast Asia. In the latter stages of the war, Indian National Army units fought in what is today India's northeast in areas abutting Myanmar. My father paid a price for his role as a key contact and worker of the underground inside India affiliated to this movement. He was incarcerated repeatedly between 1942 and 1945 and barely survived solitary confinement in a notorious detention center for political prisoners in British-occupied India: the dungeons of the fort in the city of Lahore, in Punjab province, built by India's Mughal dynasty several centuries earlier. Deeply imprinted by this experience of his youth, he stood all his life for an enlightened patriotism and a spirit of public service—values my mother, Krishna Bose, *née* Chaudhuri, a college professor, writer, and broadcaster who was born into a largely apolitical family with origins in eastern Bengal (now Bangladesh), came to share.

My earliest memories of an Indian national election to constitute the Lok Sabha (House of the People), the directly elected 543-member chamber of India's Parliament, are those of an 11-year-old in 1980. My awareness of Indian politics was of course rudimentary. Still, I was somewhat drawn into the excitement of the national election because my parents were very interested. (This was the election that saw Indira Gandhi's return to power in New Delhi, after a polyglot alliance that had won power in 1977 and formed India's first non-Congress national government fell apart amid squabbles halfway through its five-year term.)

Through the 1980s I became more and more interested in India's politics, nationwide and in our home state, West Bengal. This was partly spurred by my father being elected in 1982 as a member of the state legislature of West Bengal from an electoral district in the heart of Calcutta (as a candidate of Indira Gandhi's Congress, which was the ruling party nationwide but the main opposition party in West Bengal). During his term as a legislator, which lasted until 1987, I had my first experiences of democratic politics in practice—of grassroots campaigning, electoral factors, strategies and calculations, partisan divides and factional feuds.

At Amherst College in Massachusetts, where I was an undergraduate from 1988 to 1992, I discovered my interest in studying politics in all its worldwide variants and manifestations. Amherst introduced me to critical thinking and analysis in the best traditions of the American liberal arts, and my teachers there, particularly William Taubman, John Petropulos, and Amrita Basu, helped to shape my intellectual interests and future career. A year spent in 1990–1991 as a "year abroad" student at the London School of Economics and Political Science (LSE) was both great fun and intellectually enriching.

As a graduate student at Columbia University from 1992 to 1998, I trained broadly as a comparative political scientist, supported by the faculty members Lisa Anderson and Mark Kesselman (scholars of the Middle East and France, respectively). During that time I developed my interests in Kashmir and the former Yugoslavia, both of which became subjects of much subsequent work. But I continued to maintain an avid interest in the politics of India's democracy. During my years as a student in the United States, I would go home to India at least twice every year and spend extended periods there. After I moved from New York to London in the autumn of 1999 to work at the LSE, the distance to India halved, and I was able to visit more frequently and spend even more time there. After growing up in India in the 1970s and 1980s, I was able to closely follow a changing country over the next two decades, especially the transformation of India's democracy that developed after 1990.

The opportunity to reconnect with India's politics at a practical level came in 1996, when my mother stood for election to the Lok Sabha from West Bengal. She contested as a Congress candidate from a constituency covering parts of inner-city Calcutta and a vast sprawl of the city's suburbs and adjacent rural areas. This was an electoral district entirely different in scale and composition from the urban Calcutta constituency, a mix of middle-class neighborhoods and shantytowns with a sprinkling of wealthy pockets, that had elected my father to the state legislature of West Bengal in the 1980s. My mother's constituency had nearly 1.4 million voters, of whom about 1.1 million voted in the four national elections she entered from there between 1996 and 2004; my father's constituency had had about 100,000 voters. In 1996 she was not expected to win, as the constituency was a stronghold of the entrenched ruling party of West Bengal, the Communist Party of India-Marxist. She won narrowly, and in subsequent mid-term national elections in the spring of 1998 and the autumn of 1999 she won handsomely as a candidate of the Trinamool ("Grassroots") Congress, a regional party specific to West Bengal formed in late 1997, which gained the allegiance of the bulk of Congress activists and voters in the state. These years of getting to know the people of the Jadavpur parliamentary constituency, and at a time of transformative changes in India's democracy, were an invaluable lesson in the dynamics of mass politics. Observing the political bubble of New Delhi at close range was also instructive.

During my first years at the LSE, I benefited from the support of a senior colleague, Brendan O'Leary, and subsequently from the support of another senior colleague, Dominic (Chai) Lieven. Two junior colleagues at the LSE, Nebojsa Vladisavljevic and Zhand Shakibi, also became close friends over the years. Peter Loizos, an LSE anthropologist who died in 2012, was another valued friend. Between 2000 and 2013 I have had the opportunity to teach and in some cases mentor over 1,000 graduate students from all over the world at the LSE. (The LSE's greatest asset is the global mix of its student body.) It has been a joy to teach them and to build friendships with many of them. I know many of my former students will read this book, and I hope they enjoy it as much as I enjoyed their company.

Sugata Bose, my older brother by 12 years, gently suggested in 2007 after reading a commentary I wrote on the state election that year in Uttar Pradesh, India's most populous state, that perhaps I should consider writing a book on India's democracy. Saugata Mukherjee, who is now head of Pan, Macmillan, and Picador publishing in India, has insisted ever since I met him in 2007 that I must write a book on India's democracy in the early twenty-first century. Amala Singh (Gomma), who joined our family as my teenaged nanny four decades ago, kept me fortified with delicious food and regaled with doses of humor during my long stays in Kolkata and her periodic visits to London.

My work on Kashmir over the past two decades has benefited greatly from conversations with Ved Bhasin, who is now in his eighties and has observed Jammu & Kashmir's politics for over 60 years. Two young friends, Soyeb and Pallab, acted as field research guides in the West Medinipur district of West Bengal during a period of severe violence. I am also grateful to Major General Dipankar Banerjee, formerly of the Indian Army, and to Ambassadors Howard and Teresita Schaffer, formerly of the U.S. Foreign Service, for their warm encouragement.

The initial research for this book was funded in 2009–2010 by the Suntory-Toyota Centers for Economics and Related Disciplines at the LSE. Then the Leverhulme Trust in London awarded me a two-year Research Fellowship (2010–2012) to support the advanced research and writing of this book. Among grantmaking bodies in the United Kingdom, the Leverhulme Trust stands out for living up to its credo of supporting work that matters in a variety of fields, and for the courtesy with which its staff interact with Leverhulme Fellows.

Mina Moshkeri of the LSE's Design Unit produced Maps 1, 2, and 3; it was a pleasure to work with her. Claire Harrison and Liz Trumble of the LSE Design Unit facilitated the process. Map 4 was made by Philip Schwartzberg of Meridian Mapping, in the United States, and appeared in my previous books published by Harvard University Press, *Kashmir: Roots of Conflict, Paths to Peace* (2003), and *Contested Lands: Israel-Palestine, Kashmir, Bosnia, Cyprus, and Sri Lanka* (2007). The staff at the London office of Getty Images researched the photographs that accompany this book. Martha Ramsey copyedited the manuscript, and Melody Negron supervised the production process.

The two scholars who served as anonymous reviewers of the manuscript for Harvard University Press provided both warm endorsement and penetrating comments. And I was honored to receive the support yet again of the Board of Syndics of Harvard University Press for this book. Andrew Kinney, assistant editor at Harvard University Press, helped to prepare the book for publication, and Susan Wallace Boehmer, the Press's editor-in-chief, was very helpful as well. My biggest debt is to Kathleen McDermott, my commissioning editor at Harvard University Press, for our third fruitful collaboration in the space of a decade.

Index